Migration and Mortality

Edited by Jamie Longazel and
Miranda Cady Hallett

Migration and Mortality

*Social Death, Dispossession, and
Survival in the Americas*

TEMPLE UNIVERSITY PRESS
Philadelphia • *Rome* • *Tokyo*

TEMPLE UNIVERSITY PRESS
Philadelphia, Pennsylvania 19122
tupress.temple.edu

Library of Congress Cataloging-in-Publication Data

Names: Longazel, Jamie, editor. | Hallett, Miranda Cady, 1976– editor.
Title: Migration and mortality : social death, dispossession, and survival in the Americas /
edited by Jamie Longazel and Miranda Cady Hallett.
Description: Philadelphia : Temple University Press, 2021. | Includes bibliographical
references and index. | Summary: "This book uses theories of social death and the
construction of lives as disposable across legal, public health, criminal, carceral, media,
labor, and medical arenas to examine the fatal stakes of migration policy and practice
for migrants crossing the U.S. southern border"—Provided by publisher.
Identifiers: LCCN 2020043374 (print) | LCCN 2020043375 (ebook) | ISBN 9781439919774
(cloth) | ISBN 9781439919781 (paperback) | ISBN 9781439919798 (pdf)
Subjects: LCSH: Immigrants—United States—Social conditions. | Immigrants—Health
and hygiene—United States. | Central Americans—United States—Social conditions. |
Marginality, Social—United States. | United States—Emigration and immigration—
Social aspects. | United States—Emigration and immigration—Health aspects. | Central
America—Emigration and immigration—Social aspects. | Central America—
Emigration and immigration—Health aspects.
Classification: LCC JV6475 .M525 2021 (print) | LCC JV6475 (ebook) |
DDC 305.9/069120973—dc23
LC record available at https://lccn.loc.gov/2020043374
LC ebook record available at https://lccn.loc.gov/2020043375

9 8 7 6 5 4 3 2 1

For Filomena
And in loving memory of my brother, Josh
—J.L.

For Luther, a warrior of the people
—M.C.H.

And to Oscar Lopez Acosta, in the name of the many Hondurans
and other Central Americans whose lives have been
cut short by deadly exclusionary policies

Contents

Preface: Why Study Death?   ix

Introduction: Murder It Remains
/ Miranda Cady Hallett and Jamie Longazel   1

I HAUNTED HUMANITARIANISM

1   Death by Enclosure: Human Rights Organizations,
    Migrant Fatalities, and the Delimitation of the Global Commons
    / Joseph Nevins   23

2   Living and Dying in *El Norte*: The Framing of Maya Migration
    / Alicia Ivonne Estrada   41

3   Proprietors of Death: An Ethnography of the 2019 San Antonio
    Border Security Expo
    / Marianne Madoré and Nicholas Rodrigo   60

II DEATH AND DISPOSSESSION

4   Anonymous Brown Bodies: The Productive Power of the
    Deadly U.S.-Mexico Border / Nicholas De Genova   83

5   Detention Economies: Commodifying Migrant Social Death
    / Deirdre Conlon and Nancy Hiemstra   101

6   Heat-Related Illness and Death among Migrant Farmworkers:
    Dispatches from the Girasoles Study
    / Nathan J. Mutic and Linda A. McCauley   123

III EPIDEMIOLOGIES OF LIVING WITH DEATH

7   Morbidity and Mortality in Immigrant Narratives: A Public
    Health Perspective on State Violence, Social Exclusion,
    and Experiences of Harm among Deportable Immigrants
    / DANIEL L. STAGEMAN AND SHIRLEY P. LEYRO   143

8   Death and Disabilities in Divergent Deportation Contexts:
    Revisiting the Hispanic Epidemiological Paradox
    / JUAN M. PEDROZA AND PIL H. CHUNG   165

9   The Dead and Living Dead: Legal Violence and Undocumented
    Kidney Failure Patients in Atlanta, Georgia / NOLAN KLINE   186

IV OUTSOURCED SUFFERING AND SURVIVAL IN THE AMERICAS

10 Expanding Exclusion: Migration, Asylum, and Transnational
    Death in Mexico and the United States
    / JARED P. VAN RAMSHORST   207

11 Better in Jail There than Dead Here: Deportation and
    (Social) Death in Honduras / AMELIA FRANK-VITALE   222

12 Miskitu Labor and Immigrant Struggles: U.S.
    Anti–Central American Policies of Social Death
    / KARINA ALMA   238

13 A Politics of Survival / ABBY C. WHEATLEY   255

    Epilogue: Death in Detention / ANNA M. BABEL,
    WITH MIRANDA CADY HALLETT AND JAMIE LONGAZEL   275

    Contributors   287

    Index   293

Preface

Why Study Death?

I t is, perhaps, not profound to point out that U.S. citizenship and border policy and their discretionary enforcement have violent and even deadly impacts. This is viscerally clear to hundreds of thousands of recent transborder migrants—including the 69,550 children held in Immigration and Customs Enforcement (ICE) custody during the year 2019, along with those who have been supporting or working with migrants and asylum seekers. In light of the hypervisible spectacle of state violence and control against terrestrial migrants at the southern border, alongside the virulently racist and xenophobic rhetoric of prominent political figures and the consistent framing of immigration as a problem by both major political parties (Denvir 2020), the profound harms caused to transborder migrants via immigration policy and enforcement may seem unremarkable and self-evident in the current political moment. Indeed, an abundance of human rights reports and journalistic exposés—with titles like *Fatal Journeys* (International Organization for Migration 2017), *Disappeared* (La Coalición de Derechos Humanos and No More Deaths, n.d.), *Deported to Danger* (Human Rights Watch 2020), and *You Will Never See Your Child Again* (Physicians for Human Rights 2020)—already document in vivid detail the pain and suffering dished out by the contemporary migration enforcement regime.

Why then, a book about migrants' death and suffering? The reports named above have already documented and dissected this pain. The violence has largely been driven by callous disregard and nativist animosity, rather than a lack of information. The main priority for scholars should perhaps be to strategize to *end this violence*, rather than further describe an anatomy of suffering.

As editors, we are sympathetic to this point; and along with these critics, we share a fundamental goal: *the abolition of policies and institutions that underpin and perpetuate these forms of oppression*. Nonetheless, we see a few good reasons for this book at the current moment, and ways that this research can serve transformative ends.

First, if we are to address this systemic violence, there is a need to go beyond the deadly border in examining migration and mortality. The chapters herein build on past research highlighting the border and immigration enforcement as sources of state violence and death through policy (e.g., De León 2015; Hing 2019), but expand on these analyses by mapping out the violent impacts of enforcement regimes far beyond the narrow geographic strip of the borderlands. This allows for a more theoretically and empirically complex understanding of the reach of this system of "legal violence" (Menjívar and Abrego 2012)—an understanding that includes but also transcends the obvious harms of detention and deportation. The ensuing chapters describe how systems of global capitalism, U.S. imperialism, and white supremacy converge to produce social death in Central America; how immigration policy interacts with health-care and labor policy enabling the extraction of resources and the disallowance of life; how migrants who survive deal with the lingering consequences of death and its looming possibility for them; and how the ways institutions *respond to* death—even those that mean well—too often contribute to the reproduction of these deadly regimes.

Second, the work gathered here illustrates the breadth of empirical evidence and conceptual sophistication with which scholars are mapping this broad system of state violence. Rigorous quantitative research that merges the social and health sciences shows how the insights and methods of public health scholarship can make otherwise-invisible violence visible. Ethnography that takes place at sites of power and at sites of struggle similarly lets us in on the day-to-day realities that involved actors encounter. And innovative interpretations challenge frameworks shaped by ideological and methodological nationalism to reveal the ways that immigration enforcement plays a part within a broader system of global inequality built on what we identify as a *parasitic* (Patterson [1982] 2018) relationship between ruling elites and the global working class. In other words, the critical work assembled in this book aims to make visible "how law materializes dispossession, and in far more corporeal ways than its abstract precepts might suggest" (Dayan 2011, 40).

Third, this book is intended to press readers to *crystallize* the fragmented impressions that we receive about the current regime of state violence toward migrants into a dialectical image that will help us grasp and confront the historical and contemporary political realities that shape this violence and the compelling need for action at the present moment. In this, we are inspired by the ideas of critical theorist Walter Benjamin, especially as refracted through the work of sociologist Avery Gordon. Death is productive: spaces of death produce ghosts, confronting us with our social obligations to kin and community. And dwelling on death, especially rescuing the occluded causation and historical significance of death, is important work for restorative and transformative global justice. This is a technique of remembering, to generate "marginal and therefore potentially critical spaces of memory . . . from which contestation of these mutually bound orders of national history and global time can be launched from the sidelines, now or in the future" (Klima 2002, 9).

We are indebted to and inspired by the efforts of social movement and civil society actors to reframe migration from dominant technocratic or security narratives into demands for human and civil rights. Legal scholar Camilo Pérez-Bustillo (2018) captures this well in a piece penned in the wake of the politicization of migrant exodus from Central America. The moment when Central American migrants confronted Mexican agents at the Rodolfo Robles bridge with Guatemala, only to be teargassed and beaten, will be remembered, he writes, as a "Selma moment," equivalent to the repression of Martin Luther King Jr. and others in a peaceful march opposing segregation. In his words:

Years from now . . . [the] confrontation at Mexico's southern border will be commemorated as the beginning of an equivalent kind of juncture. This will be understood as having framed a "kairos" or "messianic" moment reflected in the emergence of a powerful new transnational migrant rights movement, that is undermining long held orthodoxies regarding the imperatives of state sovereignty within the context of migration policy and human rights. ([Pérez-Bustillo] 2018)

His words echo the work of José Luis Rocha (2017), a Nicaraguan scholar who speaks of Central American migration as a contemporary social movement in the Americas, centered on civil disobedience for human and civil rights. Migrants' flouting of regulatory restrictions around migration, argues Rocha, is best understood as a conscious act of collective civil disobedience. Similarly, we aim to emphasize the deeply political questions at the heart of migration and mortality, arguing in the end for a right to the world, and, in the broadest sense of the term, a *right to live.*

———————

This book came to fruition with the help of many others who deserve recognition. We thank our editor, Ryan Mulligan, as well as the rest of the crew at Temple University Press. Anita Hueftle deserves credit for her superb copyediting, as does Susan Thomas for her work on the index. We were also very fortunate to have research assistance from Guadalupe Hernandez, Sara Ortiz, and Fanni Sampson, with support from the International Migration Studies (IMS) program at the Graduate Center of the City University of New York. Funding for a portion of this work was provided by a grant from the Office for the Advancement of Research at John Jay College. Excellent feedback from anonymous reviewers prompted us to clarify and deepen our framework, and we thank them for this valuable contribution. Any remaining errors or omissions are our own. We are also grateful for the commentary we received from students in the spring 2020 Migration Policy seminar, as well as from our colleagues who offered thoughtful suggestions when we presented a portion of the book at the 2019 Law and Society Association and 2020 Eastern Sociological Society meetings. Thanks also go to our comrades in the struggle for liberation who have taught us so much: COMADRES; the Social Anatomy of a Deportation Regime; the Hope Border Institute; Ohio Immigrant Alliance; the Poor People's Campaign: A National Call for Moral Revival; Put People First! Pennsylvania; Anthracite Unite; the Movement for Black Lives; and the Miami Valley Immigration Coalition, among many others. Special thanks go to Lourdes María Mejías and her children for sharing their stories and their memory of Oscar. Every author in this book, in addition to producing excellent scholarship, was a joy to work with; we appreciate each of them for their patience, collegiality, and camaraderie. Finally, we thank our families and friends for the solidarity and support as we finished up this project during a tumultuous time.

REFERENCES

Dayan, Colin. 2011. *The Law Is a White Dog: How Legal Rituals Make and Unmake Persons.* Princeton, NJ: Princeton University Press.
De León, Jason. 2015. *The Land of Open Graves: Living and Dying on the Migrant Trail.* Oakland: University of California Press.
Denvir, Daniel. 2020. *All-American Nativism: How the Bipartisan War on Immigrants Explains Politics as We Know It.* New York: Verso Books.
Hing, Bill Ong. 2019. *American Presidents, Deportations, and Human Rights Violations: From Carter to Trump.* Cambridge: Cambridge University Press.
Klima, Alan. 2002. *The Funeral Casino: Meditation, Massacre, and Exchange with the Dead in Thailand.* Princeton, NJ: Princeton University Press.

Menjívar, Cecilia, and Leisy Abrego. 2012. "Legal Violence: Immigration Law and the Lives of Central American Immigrants." *American Journal of Sociology* 117 (5): 1380–1421.

Patterson, Orlando. (1982) 2018. *Slavery and Social Death: A Comparative Study.* Cambridge, MA: Harvard University Press.

[Pérez-Bustillo, Camilo]. 2018. "From Migrant Caravan to Exodus: Myths, Origins, Implications." *Frontera Facts*, December 17. https://www.hopeborder.org/bo-migrant-caravan-to-exodus.

Rocha, José Luis. 2017. *La desobediencia de las masas: La migración no autorizada de centroamericanos a Estados Unidos como desobediencia civil.* San Salvador: UCA Editores.

Migration and Mortality

Introduction

Murder It Remains

Miranda Cady Hallett

Jamie Longazel

When one individual inflicts bodily injury upon another, such injury
that death results, we call the deed manslaughter; when the assailant
knew in advance that the injury would be fatal, we call his deed murder.
But when society places hundreds of proletarians in such a position that
they inevitably meet a too early and an unnatural death, one which is
quite as much a death by violence as that by the sword or bullet; when it
deprives them thousands of the necessities of life, places them under
conditions in which they cannot live—forces them, through the strong
arm of the law, to remain in such conditions until that death ensues
which is the inevitable consequence—knows that these thousands of
victims must perish, and yet permits these conditions to remain, its deed
is murder just as surely as the deed of a single individual; disguised,
malicious murder, murder against which none can defend himself, which
does not seem what it is, because no man sees the murderer, because the
death of the victim seems a natural one, since the offence is more one of
omission than of commission. But murder it remains.

—Friedrich Engels, *The Condition of the Working Class in England*

The differential exposure to death experienced by global migrants is not
random or unpredictable. Rather, it represents "the translation into
bodies of unequal social relations in which history left its mark" (Fassin 2018, 118). One of our goals in assembling this book is to cut through the
disguises that make the disproportionate death and suffering of people who
cross borders appear natural. As the chapters herein demonstrate, exclusionary policies and practices *deliberately* take aim at racialized, dispossessed people in transit in the Americas, becoming the unseen murderers to
whom Engels refers. A system of parasitic violence (Patterson [1982] 2018)
is responsible not only for increasing exposure to biological death for terrestrial migrants but also for the stripping of people's personhood, for the

denial of resources, and for countless obstacles that deprive dispossessed migrants of their ability to *live*, in the fullest sense of that term. What follows is thus part of a broader, transformative effort to draw attention to and implicate destructive policies of legal exclusion, and the broader systems of exploitation and inequality they perpetuate, in order to imagine and build a better world where everyone's life is fully valued.

Linking exclusionary migration policies to deeper inequalities requires an understanding of the interconnected and systemic nature of oppression. As Dr. Martin Luther King Jr. (1967) put it in his "Beyond Vietnam" speech:

> I am convinced that if we are to get on the right side of the world revolution, we as a nation must undergo a radical revolution of values. We must rapidly begin . . . the shift from a thing-oriented society to a person-oriented society. When machines and computers, profit motives and property rights, are considered more important than people, the giant triplets of racism, extreme materialism, and militarism are incapable of being conquered.

These "giant triplets" converged at the Homestead Temporary Shelter for Unaccompanied Children. Located on the Homestead Air Force Base, just south of Miami, Florida, the facility was, for all intents and purposes, a prison that detained Central American children for profit. Comprehensive Health Services, Inc. (CHS), a subsidiary of Caliburn International Corporation, operated the facility intermittently from 2016 to 2019. Homestead was the largest child detention center in the country, and its status as an "emergency influx facility" allowed it to get around regulations and standards established in the *Flores* Settlement Agreement regarding the wellbeing and protection of children in government custody (Kumpf 2019). Homestead held more than two thousand teenagers (thirteen- to seventeen-year-olds) at a given time and detained individuals for sixty-seven days, on average. Most of the youth were either traveling without other family when they crossed the border or forcibly removed from their kin and taken into custody by the U.S. government.

The historical operation of racialized citizenship in the United States and the long history of exclusionary policies against nonwhite immigrant communities made the incarceration of children in this camp possible (Paik 2020). As a country, the United States was intentionally forged in a crucible of settler colonialism, involving strategies of genocide, displacement, enclosure, forced labor, and forced assimilation against nonwhite Others (Saito 2020). Racism and its accompanying violence became both alibi and mechanism for the process of colonization in the Americas, and immigration and naturalization policies in the United States unabashedly promoted a white nation (Paik 2020; Ngai 2004). Even in the wake of the social movements of the mid-twentieth century that struck down formal racial bans in immigration law, social perceptions and political actions related to the migration of Indigenous-descended peoples in the Americas are indelibly haunted by this history (Gordon 1997; Stoler 2006; Volpp 2015). Consider how the forced separation of families by the U.S. Border Patrol replicates other genocidal acts of seizing children from their parents—the separation of Black families under slavery, and the taking of American Indian children from their families to force their attendance at boarding schools from 1869 to the 1960s. While the forced separation of children from their mothers shocked the conscience of U.S. residents enough to spur protests in the summer of 2018, the reality is that such patterns are far more endemic—indeed, children were imprisoned at Homestead before and after that brief moment of reckoning. Such histories demonstrate consistent links between racialization, settler colonial nationalism, and the normalization of violent techniques of political domination.

Profit-seeking has also played a constitutive role in the emergent system of mass incarceration of migrants and asylum seekers in the twenty-first century. In its first twenty-four months, CHS acquired almost half a billion dollars of public money for running the Homestead camp, on top of nearly a million dollars in tax breaks (AFSC 2019a). In its initial public offering filing with the Securities Exchange Commission, CHS made quite clear its strategy of profiting from racist punishment, assuring investors that the Trump administration's "border enforcement and immigration policy . . . is driving significant growth" (Kennedy 2019). General John Kelly, who served as President Donald Trump's chief of staff from July 2017 to June 2019, has served on the boards of both Caliburn and its parent investment firm, DC Capital Partners. Kelly, it is also worth noting, led the U.S. Southern Command overseeing military operations in Central and South America from 2012 to 2016. The connections between racism, capitalism, and militarism in this case do not end there: the investors who own CHS also own Sallyport Global—a company that "supports U.S. military and strategic objectives under a for-profit model," receiving more than $1.75 billion in public funds to operate the scandal-ridden, mercenary-staffed Balad Air Base in Iraq—as well as Global Operations, which specializes "in determining post-war and conflict zone areas to facilitate oil, gas, and mineral extraction" (AFSC 2019a).

What is most pernicious about the Homestead case is that the facility is, quite literally, toxic. Homestead is a Superfund site, and the Environmental Protection Agency (EPA) thoroughly reported on the existence of toxins at the location as early as 1999 (Environmental Protection Agency 1999). While held captive, youth at Homestead were exposed to more than fifty-three toxic chemicals—arsenic, lead, and mercury, among many others—toxins that "cause a variety of serious chronic health problems, including kidney failure, hemolytic anemia, and developmental damage" (AFSC 2019b, 5–6). The dangerous chemicals exist as "imperial debris" (Stoler 2013)—the remnants of years of airline combustions and munitions testing. The youth detained at the camp also had to endure the unbearable sound of F-16 fighter jets taking off at decibel levels capable of causing lifelong cognitive impairment (AFSC 2019b). Which is all to say that the facility's ruling-class owners and enablers profited both politically and financially *with full knowledge* that they were putting thousands of traumatized youth at potentially fatal risk. To our knowledge, there have not been any deaths *at* Homestead, but by commodifying human beings to turn a profit, CHS, with generous assistance from the state, is unquestionably stripping migrants of their right to life and enhancing their vulnerability to premature death.

The metaphor of "imperial debris" (Stoler 2013) disrupting and threatening migrant lives is worth emphasizing, as it resonates with the historical reasons Central American children end up on the move across international borders. The youth at Homestead—"almost all from Guatemala, El Salvador, and Honduras" (Burnett 2019)—were in many cases fleeing conditions of acute violence in their countries of birth. Contemporary violence in Central America is a direct legacy of over a century of U.S. economic and military interventions within what Cecilia Menjívar and Néstor Rodríguez call "the U.S.-Latin American interstate regime" (2005, 10). Most recently, these took the form of counterinsurgency wars such as those in Guatemala and El Salvador in the late twentieth century. Such imperial adventures and extractive regimes have helped produce a region full of U.S.-made weapons and wracked by multilateral armed conflict, with livelihoods destabilized by the Dominican Republic–Central America Free Trade Agreement (CAFTA-DR) and other neoliberal reforms.

North American market demand for illicit drugs and services has also contributed to such violence. As argued by feminist philosopher Sayak Valencia in *Gore Capitalism*, illicit entrepreneurs such as drug traffickers take capitalism's subordination of human lives for profit to its logical extreme, undoing taboos against murder and fusing shadow economies to the heart of state power and terror in an "episteme of violence" (2018, 36):

> Gore capitalism has been created remotely from a distance to satiate the demands of the U.S. market, which has been able to set up branches and laboratories of illegality in Third World countries. These supply illegal services and dismantle the available spectrum of economic possibilities, relegating these nations to a single type of

economy based on violence, bloodshed, and trading in illegal products and services. (191)

When we consider the particular histories and economic dynamics of the region, layered onto broader environmental and structural challenges, we can see clearly how the dispossession and displacement of people is not an unexpected or spontaneous outcome. Instead, the northward migratory movements of Latin Americans are predictable effects of the hemispheric economy, representing another dimension of what journalist Juan Gonzalez has aptly dubbed a "harvest of empire" (2011). Children in particular are disproportionately affected by the most recent spike in violence in the region, as boys and youth living in marginalized communities are especially vulnerable to this complex interplay of organized criminal and state-sponsored violence (see Chapter 11).

This pattern—the disproportionate vulnerability of children—is reflected in recent demographic shifts among those crossing the U.S.-Mexico border: while in 2013 the vast majority (87 percent) of migrants apprehended by Border Patrol were single adults, as of fiscal year 2019 a majority of migrants arrived either as part of family units fleeing together (55 percent of all apprehended persons) or as unaccompanied children traveling without an adult caregiver (9 percent). Child and family detention sites like Homestead were set up precisely to incarcerate and immobilize this exodus of young and unrecognized refugees, compounding the trauma and suffering of those who seek sanctuary. As one Central American man who had spent months detained before winning his asylum case stated, "They aggravate the suffering with psychological torture" (personal communication, November 3, 2019).

Indicative of the "minimalist humanitarianism" (see Chapter 4) that characterizes contemporary migration policy—the tendency of officials to do *just enough* to avoid blame and moral culpability for human rights abuses—journalists who have visited the facility report being given sanitized tours by facility staff, who showcase "the soccer field, the phone-room, the medical clinic and the school classrooms" and boast to visitors about "holiday parties, talent shows and pizza and ice cream for good behavior" (Burnett 2019). By contrast, lawyers with access to the children say that many are "extremely traumatized." "Some . . . sit across from us [lawyers] and can't stop crying over what they're experiencing," said Leecia Welch of the National Center for Youth Law (Burnett 2019). Indeed, recent reports by medical associations provide evidence of the massive traumas imposed on children through separation and incarceration in migration detention, demonstrating that these harms rise to the level of torture under international human rights law, affirming the claim made by the asylee mentioned above (Habbach, Hampton, and Mishori 2020).

Opening with the grim scene of children trapped in what many have come to call a concentration camp situates us at the site of the most visible element of the weaponization of migration restriction in the twenty-first-century Americas: the spectacular punishment enacted on migrants by enforcement agents and within migration detention. The incarceration and public spectacles of violent deterrence against migrants are, of course, perpetuated by false narratives. So much hardline immigration enforcement, including the assertion of the state's right to indefinitely imprison migrants without a right to a hearing, is justified on the grounds that it will keep "us" safe, replicating the false impression that those punished are a threat to society—if not, so the implicit logic goes, the state would not be making all this effort and spending all this money to address it. But by being attentive to how global capitalism, white supremacy, and U.S. imperialism (or settler colonialism) all benefit from the mass detention of poor Central American children, we reject the mythical narrative—constructed largely through opportunistic political rhetoric—of the so-called border crisis as a threat to national security. Such claims are laughable in the face of these mass casualties and this widespread social suffering—of lives lost, ruined, and plastered under the punitive conditions of the contemporary detention and deportation system. Migration in the Americas today is not a security crisis for the United States but a crisis of imposed and politically produced *in*security for transborder migrants themselves.

At the same time, the chapters that follow collectively expand our conception of state violence directed at dispossessed migrants to include less visible, often-indirect systemic actions—what Engels refers to in our epigraph as crimes of "omission." For instance, since 2010, at least 102 people have died as a result of encounters with Border Patrol, and Immigration and Customs Enforcement (ICE) records—which, of course, should be taken with a grain of salt—suggest twenty people died in its custody between April 10, 2018, and January 27, 2020. As disturbing as these numbers are, what they ignore are the countless others who succumbed to a too early and unnatural death while attempting to make a living under grueling labor and living conditions or while trying to cope with the constant possibility of upheaval through detention or deportation. We know that thousands more have died while attempting to cross the U.S.-Mexico border in recent years, but how many additional migrants suffer and die inside the United States because of stress-related complications, because of inhumane working conditions, and because they cannot access the health care they need?

In short, when we examine the profiteering and the systems of social control that permeate migration exclusion, it is clear that the violence is not the result of mere negligence, and it is not an unfortunate but unavoidable side effect of the need to control some overwhelming influx of migrants (in fact, according to the Department of Homeland Security's own data, apprehensions of people crossing without authorization have declined significantly in the twenty-first century; see U.S. Border Patrol 2020). Nor are these abuses just an example of the wanton cruelty of a few bad apples among law enforcement officers, or a result of thoughtless institutional patterns that can be repaired by electing leaders willing to make minor policy tweaks. They are not accidentally harmful policies that are unintentionally out of step with international norms and laws related to the treatment of asylum seekers. They are not exclusive to right-wing politics, brought on by a temporary wave of reactionary nativism or the last gasp of civil rights backlash. Instead, they are clues to an underlying system of social and political domination and dispossession, a system rooted in the dehumanizing logics of racism and made possible by imperialistic U.S. economic and military interventions. In the next section, we propose a theoretical framework to understand this system, to discern an order and a pattern of persecution in the fragmented accounts of migrant suffering that permeate contemporary public media, and to illuminate strategic points of critique, struggle, and survival.

Reckoning with Parasitic Violence: Migration and Imperial Haunting in the Americas

In the treatment of migrants, we see how the bodies of those deemed unworthy of citizenship or recognition—in other words, those sentenced to *social death* (e.g., Patterson [1982] 2018; Dayan 2011; Cacho 2012)—easily become scapegoats within the ritualized political spectacle of the state's protective gesture toward public security. We see this clearly in the erosion of due process and human rights over the past two decades; in the ways immigration law and criminal law are converging (Stumpf 2006); in the ways migrants lack constitutional protections, including the right to a court-appointed attorney, which has forced some *toddlers* to defend themselves in immigration court; and in the ways the state treats migrants who die—erasing records (e.g., Baume 2019), carelessly constructing mass graves (Frey 2015), and prioritizing cost savings over the construction of meaningful spaces for mourning (Alonso and Nienass 2016).

We see it, too, in the recent Supreme Court case *Hernández v. Mesa* (2020), which considered whether the Mexican family of fifteen-year-old Sergio Adrian Hernández Guereca had standing to sue Border Patrol agent Jesus Mesa, who shot and killed Hernández in 2010. The teenager and his friends—completely unarmed—had been playing on the Mexico side of the border separating El Paso, Texas, from Ciudad Juarez when Mesa fired at least two shots, killing the boy. Although the Border Patrol agent's claim was that he was "responding to a group of suspected undocumented immigrants throwing rocks" (Wolf 2020), cell-phone video shows that Hernández was hiding beneath a train trestle when he was shot. Echoing Justice Roger Taney's infamous *Dred Scott* declaration—that Blacks "had no rights which the white man was bound to respect"—Samuel Alito, writing for the majority, relied on legal fictions that prevented Mesa from being held accountable. One can only imagine how the United States would react if, over the past few decades, dozens of U.S. citizens had been shot across the border by Mexican border agents, especially if the Mexican Corte Suprema said victims' families had no standing to sue.

Yet the Supreme Court's decision is perfectly aligned with settler colonialism's persistent and systemic failure to value the lives of Others, or to hold authorities accountable for such incidents of racialized state violence. The profound dehumanization of migrants through public discourse, especially over the past four decades or so, has built "popular consensus . . . around the idea that the state ought to control certain others . . . by jailing them, depriving them of basic services and civil rights, deporting them, or even killing them," leading to the overt persecution and bald repression of the current era (Nagengast 2002, 338). In other words, "symbolic violence is displayed in the myths that depict certain people as both somewhat less than human beings, and who therefore deserve their subordinate position, and at the same time as superhumans who are capable of subverting the given social order" (339). Judith Butler points to the need to unmask what she calls "phantasmagoric inversions" (2020, 62), fantasies "in which some lives are figured as pure violence or as an imminent threat of violence" (143). Through falsely framing migrants as invaders posing an existential threat to U.S.-born people, they become marked as "ineligible for personhood," leaving subjects in a condition of racialized rightlessness (Cacho 2012, 6).

What we are witnessing, in other words, is virulent racism, exemplified by "the state-sanctioned or extralegal production and exploitation of group differentiated vulnerability to premature death" (Gilmore 2007, 28). As Ruth Wilson Gilmore makes clear, this is best understood in conjunction with a critical analysis of capitalism. That is, while this description of the production of racialized rightlessness and the emotional politics of public violence aptly links migrants' mortality to racism, it is crucial to also recognize the extent to which racism and capitalism are coconspirators (e.g., Du Bois [1935] 2013; Robinson 1983). As Cedric Robinson writes in his classic *Black Marxism*, "The historical development of world capitalism was influenced in a most fundamental way by particularistic forces of racism and nationalism" (1983, 9). Our contention is likewise that capitalism and racism—each of which also drive contemporary militarism—are *deeply* intertwined, working in harmony to produce and reproduce dispossession, with dispossession understood as the opposite of "the right to the world" (Nevins 2017)—a denial of the earth's life-sustaining common resources brought on, in part, by an exclusion from recognition as human.

Putting death through dispossession at the center of our collective analysis, the chapters in this book thus collectively illuminate what James Tyner calls "an emerging *necrocapitalism*," by which, first, (racialized) lives are valued differently based on their ability to generate wealth and, second, those "who are subjected to both direct and structural violence are judged by society to be responsible for their own suffering and demise—a perverted variant of blaming the victim" (2019, xiii; emphasis in original). Necrocapitalism renders racialized bodies disposable, deciding whether one is to be kept alive or left for dead based on how much use value they offer the capitalist class. Meanwhile, the prevailing rhetoric places blame on anyone *but* the system: mothers who had their children ripped from their arms made a bad choice or are frauds trying to game the system; migrants making political and legal claims are accused of taking it too far, demanding special rather than equal rights (e.g., Longazel 2018); exploited, illegalized workers are framed as having failed to go through the proper procedures; and U.S.-stoked social and economic disruptions in Central America are attributed to an irresponsible citizenry.

In *Slavery and Social Death* ([1982] 2018), Orlando Patterson describes the slaveholder-slave relationship as a form of *parasitic domination*. "The slave," he explains, "was natally alienated and condemned as a socially dead person, his existence having no legitimacy whatever." Perversely, this created for the slaveholder an "ideal human tool, an *instrumentum vocal*—perfectly flexible, unattached, and deracinated" (337). Ever-parasitic and with an eerie similarity to those at the reins of contemporary migration-control regimes, the slaveholder "fed on the slave"—for labor, profit, and even the affective pleasures that come with domination (compare this to the "emotional politics of racism" explored by Ioanide 2015)—while "the slave, losing in the process all claim to autonomous power, was degraded and reduced to a state of liminality" (Patterson [1982] 2018, 337).

Despite this, or perhaps because of it, slaveholders craftily inverted reality, disguising their parasitism "by defining it as the opposite of what it really is," as Patterson explains ([1982] 2018, 337). They insisted on the dependency *of the slave*, using stereotypes to project onto the enslaved person their own tendency for violence, domination, and freeloading. Such dynamics of projection, according to Michael Taussig's classic study of cultures of terror, drove the paranoid brutality of colonizers during the rubber boom in the Putumayo region of Colombia (1987). They are also replicated in the sweeping rhetoric and policy criminalizing transborder workers and their movements.

While Patterson's analysis provides a useful analogy that helps us understand the intricacies of racialized capitalistic state violence, it is at the same time important that we recognize the direct historical lineages between former systems of slavery, colonialism, and genocide, and the structural oppressions of contemporary racial capitalism. The chapters in this book speak to both of these patterns. Many rely on the wide-ranging work that has deployed Patterson's concept of social death (e.g., Chapters 5, 11, and 12), while others—such as Chapter 6, on agricultural labor—more directly engage with historical trajectories.

Either way, it is our contention that centering death and illuminating differential exposures to mortality enables us to leverage empirical truths for critical ends. Yet death also pushes us beyond the material; death produces ghosts. One effect of meditating on death is to invite ghosts to disrupt dominant social fantasies and bring a flash of recognition, revealing the settler colonial logics naturalized within systems of migration restriction (Volpp 2015). As sociologist Avery Gordon articulates in her seminal work *Ghostly Matters*, the ghost is "a symptom of what's missing"—in this case, an insistent recognition of the unstated ugly truth of racism, materialism, and militarism at the basis of suffering—and at the same time "a future possibility, a hope" (1997, 64). The ghost is relational; ghosts shock us into a different insight about "what has happened or is happening" (63) and, through their kinship, spur us to a reckoning, "out of a concern for justice" (64). Gordon entreats us to search for lessons in the everyday hauntings we encounter, evoking the need to attend to the unseen and the unknown in the contexts of epistemic murk (Taussig 1987) fostered by violent political regimes:

There are thousands of ghosts; when entire societies become haunted by terrible deeds that are systematically occurring and are simultaneously denied by every public organ of governance and communication . . . when the whole situation cries out for clearly distinguishing between truth and lies, between what is known and what is unknown, between the real and the unthinkable and yet that is what is precisely impossible; when people you love are there one minute and gone the next; when familiar things and words transmute into the most sinister of weapons and meanings; when an ordinary building you pass every day harbors the façade separating the scream of its terroristic activities from the hushed talk of fearful conversations; when the whole of life has become so enmeshed in the traffic of the dead and the living dead . . . the ghosts return, demanding a different kind of knowledge, a different kind of acknowledgment. (Gordon 1997, 64)

Ghosts, in other words, can be restless. And rebellion is always imminent. Patterson (1982, 337) writes, "The slave resisted his desocialization and forced service in countless ways, only one of which, rebellion, was not subtle." This is after all why Patterson employed the analogy of the parasite to complement his rich study of social death. Typical explicators like "exploitation" and "domination," he acknowledged, "focus upon the dominator or exploiter as the active agent in the relationship and place upon the exploited the further burden of passivity" (335).

While the following chapters most certainly recount migrants facing untold horrors, the authors simultaneously remain attentive to migrant agency and resistance. In fact, one of our larger aims is to transform death to generative purposes, falling into a tradition of similar efforts by social movements, advocates, and critical journalists. Funereal space—spaces of public mourning—have often been the spaces of last resort for communities that are heavily repressed (Gordon 1997; Klima 2002, 55–57). In Argentina, El Salvador, and other places, the Mothers of the Disappeared were among the most powerful of social movements during authoritarian regimes (Taussig 1992). Focusing on the dead, in other words, is not inherently an invocation of powerlessness and unabridged victimhood. As the world saw quite clearly after Minneapolis police murdered George Floyd, the dead can also *electrify* the living, mobilizing memory into resistance.

Consider the description Alan Klima gives of "the political work of the abject" in the aftermath of government-sponsored massacres against pro-democracy protesters in Thailand:

> Spontaneous shrines pop up everywhere, especially at the Democracy Monument and around bloodstained trees and articles of clothing, around brains, bone, or fragments of flesh found drying in the intense heat. Jasmine garlands are strung in great numbers from the bloodstained Tree of Democracy. . . . Crowds come to the tree and bring offerings of fruits, food, and water for the spirits of the dead. (2002, 137–138)

By mobilizing the images of the dead, Thai pro-democracy activists constituted a new public sphere, which "refashioned itself out of the stuff and spiritual matter of the charnel ground itself" (Klima 2002, 151–152). This practice of mourning and remembrance mediates and negotiates "both the relations among the living and the relations between the living and the dead, and so generates an economy that connects both people and time from within the very heart of the latest in capitalism" (7).

The dead, that is, have great political efficacy: social death can engender biological death, but biological death can engender what we call *social resurrection*. It is with good reason that the couplet penned by Greek poet Dinos Christianopoulos (1995) has gone viral in modified form: "What didn't you do to bury me / but you forgot I was a seed." Fittingly, the coalition that successfully fought to have Homestead shut down evoked such imagery while protesting. As the names of the seven children who have died in ICE custody were read aloud, one of the protesters poured water into a potted plant for each name. As Lucy Duncan of the American Friends Service Committee said of the ceremony, "We need for justice to break through. We need to remember those names" (CBS News 2019).

Through these two pathways—the conscious mobilization of mourning for the dead, and the unconscious circulation of ghosts that remind us of the unavoidable past and the accounting of debts, we intend for our contemplation of death in these pages to advance the aims of justice. In that regard, this book is also a contribution to calls for a new scholarship of accountability (Schwenkel 2009) and "ethical witnessing" (Ioanide 2015, 23). Through critical research, we share in efforts to *(re)member* (Coutin 2016) marginalized experiences and negotiate more inclusive forms of belonging. In Susan Coutin's formulation, to *(re)member* means to put back together what has been dismembered by racialized systems of exclusion, and to reassemble the missing pieces of collective memory from whitewashed nationalist histories. Such a task is a necessary response to dispossession, or "the *dismemberment* associated with civil war, displacement, emigration, the denial of legal status, and removal" (Coutin 2016, 3; emphasis in original).

While they approach the issue of migration policy regimes and mortality from remarkably diverse angles, the contributions to this book share a unifying set of purposes: First, we aim to illuminate the violence that permeates and reproduces systems of exclusion and exploitation and that is built in large part through migration regulations and citizenship law and their policing and enforcement—thus, to trace the causal contours of this violence through social autopsies of human mortality (e.g., Klinenberg 2002). Second, we intend to deconstruct and denounce the mechanisms by which this violence is normalized, justified, and reproduced. And finally, we call for an invigorated solidarity with dispossessed peoples in movement and an amplification of collective movements for the right to the world by attending to and centering the loss and the survival of transborder migrant communities.

Book Overview

The ensuing chapters are divided into four parts. The first, titled "Haunted Humanitarianism," is intended to deconstruct humanitarian logics and unpack their relationship to systemic lethal violence. It is an attempt, in other words, to draw attention to the ghosts that haunt mainstream humanitarian discourse around migration, and the ways in which even such (mostly) well-intentioned practices reproduce violent parasitism.

Joseph Nevins opens Chapter 1 with a powerful critique of how international human rights organizations (e.g., Amnesty International, Human Rights Watch), by clinging to a nation-statist framing of migration that is exclusionary in nature, fail to "indict the very system that kills individuals trying to reach spaces of security of various sorts." He places this critique in the larger context of global struggles over resources, where bordering also helps reproduce vast global inequalities, providing a global elite with freedom and ability to roam as they please, while dramatically restricting the global poor's right to the world.

In Chapter 2, Alicia Ivonne Estrada uses a case study of Maya-K'iche' migrant Hugo Alfredo Tale Yax, who was killed on a sidewalk in Queens, New York, after rescuing a woman from her violent assailant. The media's liberal humanitarian response to Tale Yax's death, she argues, "illustrates the selective ways in which the experiences of Maya migrants in the United States are made (il)legible and (in)visible." She juxtaposes the media's homogenizing depictions with the very particular Maya experience of state violence, exploitation, and dispossession as a result of the lingering consequences of the Maya genocide. Her careful analysis of media coverage and tribute videos strips off their humanitarian veneer to reveal how Tale Yax was narrowly presented as an "American hero," rendering the genocide, like Maya migrants themselves, effectively invisible.

Marianne Madoré and Nicholas Rodrigo share findings in Chapter 3 from their ethnography of the 2019 Border Security Expo in San Antonio, Texas. They show how ICE has similarly taken up a discourse of humanitarianism, often to justify its pleas for additional funding, and even as vendors showcase high-grade militaristic tools of death in the background. Part of this construction, they reveal, involves border enforcement agents forging an esprit de corps through memorialization of fallen officers and a corresponding glorification of their own sacrifice. The reality of death at the border thus gets ritualistically converted into a tale of agents going above and beyond to both save lives and help halt a seemingly spontaneous invasion.

With the humanitarian veneer disassembled, death and dispossession are the subject of Part II. Parasitism is on full display here, as this set of chapters explores how U.S. migration law and policy create ripe conditions for the further extraction of money, resources, and labor power from the dispossessed. In this regard, death is *productive* from the parasitic perspective; as the chapters show, there is a clear tendency of the state to employ tactics of entrapment (e.g., Núñez and Heyman 2007), which harnesses death and the threat thereof in various ways to maximize capitalists' ability to strip resources from migrants.

Building on his highly regarded theoretical work about border spectacles and the production of deportability and illegality (e.g., De Genova 2002, 2013; De Genova and Peutz 2010), Nicholas De Genova, in Chapter 4, draws attention to the productive power of mass casualties in the U.S.-Mexico border region—namely, by drawing links between the spectacle of border deaths and the exploitation endured by those who survive. Mass death at the border, caused by policies written *with full knowledge* that they would cause many to die, he writes, "prove to be much more reliable for enacting a strategy of *capture* than for functioning as mere technologies of exclusion. Once migrants have successfully navigated their ways across such borders, the onerous risks and costs of departing and later attempting to cross yet again become inordinately prohibitive."

Deirdre Conlon and Nancy Hiemstra collected and analyzed mounds of data obtained via the Freedom of Information Act on detention centers in three New Jersey counties. Their findings, detailed in Chapter 5, convincingly reveal how extraction is at the core of migrant detention in the United States. From excessive commissary fees and unpaid labor to profit-pursuing transportation companies and local government contracts with ICE, they show how private- and public-sector actors work together to create robust "detention economies" made possible only by the commodification of migrant life. The result, they argue, is an amplification of migrant social death, experienced by migrants as a set of losses that correspond directly to the financial gains enjoyed by the state (i.e., cost-cutting) and the corporations with which it contracts.

In Chapter 6, nursing scientists Nathan J. Mutic and Linda A. McCauley share findings from the Girasoles Study, which tracks the health consequences of migrant farmworkers' exposure to excessive heat in Florida. Death is a very real possibility for these workers, who, they show, represent the continuation of a long, racist history—dating back to slavery—of parasitism in the agricultural sector. In this case, farmworkers confront entrapment at multiple levels—body positioning, immobility, a lack of breaks, no access to shade, and H-2A visa restrictions that prohibit them from changing employers. That, coupled with the biometric data they share, makes clear the parasitic extent to which racialized workers are indeed forced to work *beyond* their bodies' physical limitations to satisfy capital's relentless quest for profit.

Part III, "Epidemiologies of Living with Death," features three chapters, which, although written from an array of methodological and disciplinary perspectives, coalesce around the theme of migration and public health. In each case, dispossession, hyperenforcement, and other antimigrant policies create a situation in which death maintains a haunting presence for migrants living in the territorial United States who—with agency, resilience, and creativity—struggle to stay fully alive.

Criminologists Daniel L. Stageman and Shirley P. Leyro begin this part in Chapter 7 with an analysis of data from focus groups and interviews with eighty noncitizens living in New York City. They explore the relationship between postmigration traumas and migrants' experiences of *mortality* and *morbidity*. The voices of research participants vividly express the impacts of nostalgia, stress, and trauma. People excluded from citizenship expressed a state of consciousness that was unfree—"mental slavery," in the words of one interviewee. In the context of extreme state repression, things like suicidal ideation represent "a response to a sense of inescapable entrapment in a life stripped of meaning," Stageman and Leyro point out. Their analysis attends to the intimate relationship between resilience for individuals and collective resistance, born of a consciousness of injustice.

In Chapter 8, sociologists and demographers Juan M. Pedroza and Pil H. Chung take as their jumping-off point the Hispanic epidemiological paradox (HEP), which shows that Hispanics living in the United States, especially Hispanic immigrants, have unexpectedly enjoyed more favorable health outcomes, including a longer life expectancy, compared to other groups. However, the HEP may be beginning to erode, and Pedroza and Chung use statistical modeling to study whether the prevalence of mass deportation is part of the reason why. Merging deportation data from the Department of Homeland Security (DHS) with Centers for Disease Control and Prevention (CDC) data on mortality and American Community Survey data on disability rates, they find "that residents living in metro areas hit particularly hard by the rise of mass deportations were more likely to report health problems." In other words, "part of the price of settling in the United States seems to have risen."

In Chapter 9, anthropologist Nolan Kline explores the implications that the closing of a dialysis center at Grady Memorial Hospital in Atlanta, Georgia, has had for undocumented patients. In particular, this case illustrates how exclusionary migration policy and exclusionary health policy collide. Cut out from public programs, undocumented patients, he shows, are left to rely on the emergency room (ER) as their only viable option for dialysis treatment. The problem is that if they are not close enough to death upon arriving at the ER, they are turned away. Only patients exhibiting "immediate potential for death" receive the treatment. To save their own lives, undocumented patients teeter on the brink of death, in a way that forces the state to meet its obligation of providing minimal care. But even so, this is no way to live; as one provider succinctly described the policy violence at hand, "The dialysis is just enough to keep them living, and that's about it."

The book's final part illuminates the means by which the United States government *outsources* the suffering produced via its exclusionary policies. Borrowing a neoliberal trick, the states' parasitic violence is externalized to spaces and actors beyond the territorial nation. Chapters in this section explore social death, physical mortality, and survival, both in Central America and along an increasingly weaponized migrant trail. Work herein directly engages with the imperial ruination brought by U.S. militarism and economic imperialism—the "colonial and neocolonial alchemy" that has made Latin America "the region of open veins" (Galeano 1973, 2). It also confronts and deconstructs the techniques by which the United States increasingly outsources its harsh exclusion of migrants to deflect obligations to refugees and asylum seekers.

In Chapter 10, Jared P. Van Ramshorst offers a critical analysis of a "metering" policy, initiated by President Barack Obama but embraced by President Donald Trump, that allows enforcement agents to place drastic limits on the number of asylum seekers allowed to enter the United States each day. With resemblance to the ways prevention-through-deterrence strategies reroute migrants through dangerous *natural* terrain, this policy diverts migrants blocked at ports of entry back to Mexican border cities, where they wait in shelters, parks, and other public places. "Stranded in these open spaces for days, weeks, and sometimes months," he writes, "migrants were vulnerable to kidnapping, disappearances, and death." By reconstructing the events leading to the disappearance and death of two different asylum seekers, Van Ramshorst makes a strong case for using a transnational lens, revealing how a diverse set of actors and agencies are implicated in such tragedies, and the ways that accountability for such harms are deflected.

In Chapter 11, Amelia Frank-Vitale draws from the nearly two years of ethnographic data she collected in and around San Pedro Sula, Honduras. She vividly documents how many young Honduran deportees are locked in a cruel dilemma: risk potential death or incarceration by migrating again, or remain "encaved" and socially isolated in Honduras to avoid the rampant violence plaguing their communities. She places her analysis in the context of U.S. imperialist interventions and a global capitalist system that treats such poor, urban, undereducated youth of color as surplus labor. While local elites push a narrative that blames young Hondurans for the country's prevailing social and economic insecurity, many young people, in the spirit of survival, "look externally . . . for the possibility of having a better life or, simply, a life at all."

Karina Alma follows in Chapter 12 by drawing connections between U.S. immigration and foreign policy toward Central America and the Afro-Indigenous Miskitu men who are killed at troubling rates while working in the sweet-lobster industry off the coast of Nicaragua. Consumers in the Global North, she explains, enjoy lobster as a delicacy with little to no regard for the conditions of the fisheries that produce them. Exploring the ways that Miskitu are made socially dead, Alma invites us to recognize how the apparatus of power centered in the United States helps reproduce the exploitation, entrapment, and often death of Indigenous workers who "remain behind" in a postwar and post-CAFTA Central America.

In Chapter 13, Abby C. Wheatley emphasizes the importance of remaining attuned to migrant agency—of recognizing a *politics of survival*. She starts from the important premise that while there is something to be said for publicizing the causal relationship between exclusionary immigration policies and migrant death, "telling postmortem stories of migrants strips them of their agency and limits community-based strategies to respond to policies that kill." Drawing on *testimonios* of migrants in the Arizona Sonora migration corridor, she highlights how Central American and Mexican migrants "*survive* and *resist* a highly militarized border and weaponized migrant trail." Border crossings from this angle become far more than desperate attempts to avoid detection: they are part of a larger "effort to escape the constraints of a highly inequitable global system of labor" and represent a bigger struggle "over the right to life, livelihood, and autonomy."

The book concludes with an Epilogue, which shares testimony authored by anthropologist Anna Babel. Through the story of the life and death of Oscar Lopez Acosta, Babel applies some of the central lessons of this book to the context of the COVID-19 pandemic.

In the opening of this Introduction, we quite intentionally emphasize the structural conditions at Homestead, leaving aside an evocation of the people who were locked up there. But we do intend the absent figure of the child at Homestead to be *presente* in a ghostly fashion, present as a dialectical image.

In his "Theses on the Philosophy of History," Walter Benjamin asks us to look for dialectical images—images like the vision of a displaced child held in a prison on polluted ground—that flare up in a moment of danger. Such images arrest our thoughts, giving us "a revolutionary chance in the fight for an oppressed past," a hidden history of the marginalized (1968, 263). As Gordon elaborates on Benjamin's call, she asserts that "the oppressed past or the ghostly will shock us into recognizing its animating force[, and] . . . to fight for an oppressed past is to make this past come alive as the lever for the work of the present, ending this history and setting in place a different future" (1997, 66).

The long-standing reality that this dialectical image brings into view is that the spectacular state violence visited on migrants is not exceptional, but a logical extension of the exclusionary apparatus of neoliberal capitalism, U.S. imperialism, and racism writ large. The fact that many of the case studies analyzed herein predate the Trump administration, or span multiple eras and multiple sites, demonstrates that the interdependency between migration policy and enforcement and the "giant triplets" has always been there, right under our noses. As we go to press, uprisings against police violence and the differential effects of the COVID-19 pandemic are, for a growing number of people, unmasking the racialized abandonment and dispossession of the global poor. Removing the disguise can enable us "to move from expressing compassion to recognizing injustice," as Didier Fassin observes (2018, 124). In other words, seeing these evils clearly—grasping the significance of this moment and its relationship to the past and to the future—is the only way to build a common future beyond walls and cages.

REFERENCES

AFSC (American Friends Service Committee). 2019a. "The Corporate Interests behind the Homestead Migrant Youth Detention Center." April 24. https://investigate.afsc.org/updates/homestead-detention-center.

———. 2019b. "Health at Risk: Potential Toxic and Noise Exposure Endangering Children at the Homestead Temporary Shelter for Unaccompanied Migrant Children." August. https://www.afsc.org/sites/default/files/documents/AFSC%27s%20Report%20on%20Health%20at%20Risk%20at%20Homestead%20Detention%20Center.pdf.

Alonso, Alexandra Délano, and Benjamin Nienass. 2016. "Death, Visibility, and Responsibility: The Politics of Mourning at the US-Mexico Border." *Social Research* 83 (2): 421–451.

Baume, Matt. 2019. "ICE Destroyed Footage of Trans Woman Who Died in Its Custody." *Out*, October 24. https://www.out.com/crime/2019/10/24/ice-destroyed-footage-trans-woman-who-died-its-custody.

Benjamin, Walter. 1968. "Theses on the Philosophy of History." In *Illuminations*, translated by Harry Zohn, 253–264. New York: Schocken Books

Burnett, John. 2019. "Inside the Largest and Most Controversial Shelter for Migrant Children in the U.S." *NPR*, February 13. https://www.npr.org/2019/02/13/694138106/inside-the-largest-and-most-controversial-shelter-for-migrant-children-in-the-u-.

Butler, Judith. 2020. *The Force of Nonviolence: An Ethico-Political Bind.* New York: Verso.

Cacho, Lisa Marie. 2012. *Social Death: Racialized Rightlessness and the Criminalization of the Unprotected.* New York: New York University Press.

CBS News. 2019. "Protestors Brave Drenching Downpour outside South Florida Detention Center for Kids." *CBS News*, June 16. https://www.cbsnews.com/news/homestead-florida-children-detention-center-protests-today-2019-06-16/.

Christianopoulos, Dinos. 1995. *Poems.* Translated by Nicholas Kostis. Athens: Odysseas.

Coutin, Susan Bibler. 2016. *Exiled Home: Salvadoran Transnational Youth in the Aftermath of Violence.* Durham, NC: Duke University Press.

Dayan, Colin. 2011. *The Law Is a White Dog: How Legal Rituals Make and Unmake Persons.* Princeton, NJ: Princeton University Press.

De Genova, Nicholas. 2002. "Migrant 'Illegality' and Deportability in Everyday Life." *Annual Review of Anthropology* 31 (1): 419–447.

———. 2013. "Spectacles of Migrant 'Illegality': The Scene of Exclusion, the Obscene of Inclusion." *Ethnic and Racial Studies* 36 (7): 1180–1198.

De Genova, Nicholas, and Natalie Peutz, eds. 2010. *The Deportation Regime: Sovereignty, Space, and the Freedom of Movement.* Durham, NC: Duke University Press.

Du Bois, W.E.B. (1935) 2013. *Black Reconstruction in America: Toward a History of the Part of Which Black Folk Played in the Attempt to Reconstruct Democracy in America, 1860–1880.* New Brunswick, NJ: Transaction.

Environmental Protection Agency. 1999. "Superfund Record of Decision: Homestead Air Force Base, OUs 18, 26, 28, and 29." https://bit.ly/3o2VVKD.

Fassin, Didier. 2018. *Life: A Critical User's Manual.* Cambridge, UK: Polity Press.

Frey, John Carlos. 2015. "Graves of Shame: New Evidence Indicates Wrongdoing in the Handling of Migrant Remains in Brooks County." *Texas Observer,* July 6. https://www.texasobserver.org/illegal-mass-graves-of-migrant-remains-found-in-south-texas/.

Galeano, Eduardo. 1973. *Open Veins of Latin America: Five Centuries of the Pillage of a Continent.* Translated by Cedric Belfrage. New York: Monthly Review Press.

Gilmore, Ruth Wilson. 2007. *Golden Gulag: Prisons, Surplus, Crisis, and Opposition in Globalizing California.* Berkeley: University of California Press.

Gonzalez, Juan. 2011. *Harvest of Empire: A History of Latinos in America.* 3rd ed. New York: Penguin Books.

Gordon, Avery. 1997. *Ghostly Matters: Haunting and the Sociological Imagination.* Minneapolis: University of Minnesota Press.

Habbach, Hajar, Kathryn Hampton, and Ranit Mishori. 2020. "'You Will Never See Your Child Again': The Persistent Psychological Effects of Family Separation." Physicians for Human Rights, February 25. https://phr.org/our-work/resources/you-will-never-see-your-child-again-the-persistent-psychological-effects-of-family-separation/.

Ioanide, Paula. 2015. *The Emotional Politics of Racism: How Feelings Trump Facts in the Age of Colorblindness.* Stanford, CA: Stanford University Press.

Kennedy, Thomas. 2019. "A Corrupt System Profits from Immigrant Detention." *South Florida Sun-Sentinel,* March 22. https://www.sun-sentinel.com/opinion/commentary/fl-op-com-migrant-detention-20190316-story.html.

King, Martin Luther, Jr. 1967. "Beyond Vietnam." April 4. https://kinginstitute.stanford.edu/king-papers/documents/beyond-vietnam.

Klima, Alan. 2002. *The Funeral Casino: Meditation, Massacre, and Exchange with the Dead in Thailand.* Princeton, NJ: Princeton University Press.

Klinenberg, Eric. 2002. *Heat Wave: A Social Autopsy of Disaster in Chicago.* Chicago: University of Chicago Press.

Kumpf, Kristin. 2019. "How We Shut Down the Nation's Largest Child Detention Center." *Yes! Magazine,* September 6. https://www.yesmagazine.org/opinion/2019/09/06/trump-detention-center-children-shut-down/.

Longazel, Jamie. 2018. "Racing the Oven Bird: Criminalization, Rightlessness, and the Politics of Immigration." In *Insiders, Outsiders, Injuries, and Law: Revisiting "The*

Oven Bird's Song," edited by Mary Nell Trautner, 161–180. New York: Columbia University Press.

Menjívar, Cecilia, and Néstor Rodriguez. 2005. *When States Kill: Latin America, the U.S., and Technologies of Terror.* Austin: University of Texas Press.

Nagengast, Carole. 2002. "Inoculations of Evil in the U.S.-Mexico Borderlands: Reflections on the Genocidal Potential of Symbolic Violence." In *Annihilating Difference: The Anthropology of Genocide*, edited by Alexander Laban Hinton, 325–346. Berkeley: University of California Press.

Nevins, Joseph. 2017. "The Right to the World." *Antipode* 49 (5): 1349–1367.

Ngai, Mae. 2004. *Impossible Subjects: Illegal Aliens and the Making of Modern America.* Princeton, NJ: Princeton University Press.

Núñez, Guillermina Gina, and Josiah McC. Heyman. 2007. "Entrapment Processes and Immigrant Communities in a Time of Heightened Border Vigilance." *Human Organization* 66 (4): 354–365.

Paik, A. Naomi. 2020. *Bans, Walls, Raids, Sanctuary: Understanding Immigration for the Twenty-First Century.* Oakland: University of California Press.

Patterson, Orlando. (1982) 2018. *Slavery and Social Death: A Comparative Study.* Cambridge, MA: Harvard University Press.

Robinson, Cedric J. 1983. *Black Marxism: The Making of the Black Radical Tradition.* Chapel Hill: University of North Carolina Press.

Saito, Natsu Taylor. 2020. *Settler Colonialism, Race, and the Law: Why Structural Racism Persists.* New York: New York University Press.

Schwenkel, Christina. 2009. "From John McCain to Abu Ghraib: Tortured Bodies and Historical Unaccountability of US Empire." *American Anthropologist* 111 (1): 30–42.

Stoler, Ann. 2006. *Haunted by Empire: Geographies of Intimacy in North American History.* Durham, NC: Duke University Press.

———. 2013. "Introduction: 'The Rot Remains'; From Ruins to Ruination." In *Imperial Debris: On Ruins and Ruination*, edited by Ann Stoler, 1–36. Durham, NC: Duke University Press.

Stumpf, Juliet. 2006. "The Crimmigration Crisis: Immigrants, Crime, and Sovereign Power." *American University Law Review* 56 (2): 367–419.

Taussig, Michael. 1987. *Shamanism, Colonialism, and the Wild Man: A Study in Terror and Healing.* Chicago: University of Chicago Press.

———. 1992. *The Nervous System.* New York: Routledge.

Tyner, James. 2019. *Dead Labor: Toward a Political Economy of Premature Death.* Minneapolis: University of Minnesota Press.

U.S. Border Patrol. 2020. "U.S. Border Patrol Nationwide Apprehensions by Citizenship and Sector." https://www.cbp.gov/sites/default/files/assets/documents/2020-Jan/U.S. %20Border%20Patrol%20Nationwide%20Apprehensions%20by%20Citizenship %20and%20Sector%20%28FY2007%20-%20FY%202019%29_1.pdf.

Valencia, Sayak. 2018. *Gore Capitalism.* Translated by John Pluecker. Cambridge, MA: MIT Press.

Volpp, Leti. 2015. "The Indigenous as Alien." *University of California Irvine Law Review* 5:289–396.

Wolf, Richard. 2020. "Supreme Court Denies Mexican Family's Damages Claim for Cross-Border Shooting," *USA Today*, February 25. https://www.usatoday.com/story/ news/politics/2020/02/25/cross-border-shooting-supreme-court-clears-border -patrol/4860246002/.

I

Haunted Humanitarianism

1

Death by Enclosure

Human Rights Organizations, Migrant Fatalities,
and the Delimitation of the Global Commons

Joseph Nevins

Sunday, April 19, 2015, saw what is likely the single deadliest incident involving unauthorized migrants or refugees in recorded history. On that day, an estimated 850 people seeking refuge in Europe—from a variety of countries, including Eritrea, Syria, Sierra Leone, and Bangladesh—perished when their vessel capsized in the waters between Libya and the Italian island of Lampedusa; only 28 people survived (Faiola 2015; Yardley and Bilefesky 2015). According to one report, "Authorities described a grisly scene of bodies floating and sinking in the warm waters, with the majority of the dead apparently trapped in the ship at the bottom of the sea" (Yardley 2015).

In response, Italy's prime minister, Matteo Renzi, effectively reproduced the talking points of U.S. authorities when decrying fatalities of individuals clandestinely traversing the U.S.-Mexico borderlands (see Nevins 2008). He did so by pointing the finger at those who assist the passage (i.e., smugglers) of individuals seeking to escape, among other factors, extraordinary violence, poverty, or far-reaching ecological degradation. Using words that obscure how the European Union's border-policing apparatus—the figurative wall of what many call Fortress Europe (e.g., Carr 2016)—essentially requires such individuals to rely on professional guides and take ever-riskier routes to reach their hoped-for destinations, Renzi called smugglers "the slave drivers of the 21st century" (Yardley 2015).

It is unsurprising that officials charged with policing national territorial boundaries do not indict the very system that kills individuals trying to reach spaces of security of various sorts—the nation-state and its associated apparatus of exclusion for those deemed undesirable or unworthy—and instead reproduce it. In the case of international human rights organizations, however, one can and should expect much better. As stated in the preamble of the Universal Declaration of Human Rights (UDHR), "recognition of the inherent dignity and of the equal and inalienable rights of all members of the human family is the foundation of freedom, justice and peace in the world" (United Nations 1948). The deaths of those negotiating the borderlands between rich and poor, secure and insecure, privileged and disadvantaged manifest a world in which such "inherent dignity" and equal, inalienable rights of all human beings are sorely lacking. That which effectively compels them to take great risks to circumvent the controls that deny them entry to the national spaces to which they seek access is also what results in their avoidable, premature deaths, the ultimate human rights violation.

Nonetheless, what establishment human rights bodies[1] offer in response to such deaths is (at best) handwringing and calls for national and supranational governments to increase the number of noncitizens authorized to enter the territories over which they exercise control and to make greater efforts to rescue endangered migrants. Meanwhile, these entities, while criticizing specific governmental policies and practices, generally uphold and legitimize the larger regime of noncitizen exclusion that makes inevitable the fatalities of illegalized and unwanted people on the move. In other words, many human rights organizations help construct the nation-state-based apparatus of control and exclusion and their associated "violent borders" (see Jones 2016), divides that function to facilitate the mobility of a privileged global minority while stymieing the movement of a heavily disadvantaged and impoverished global majority (see Miller 2019). By refusing to call into question this globalized political geography that gives primacy to nation-states and their associated territorial practices, establishment human rights organizations deny the existence of a "right to the world" (see Nevins 2017), reproducing a worldwide system of national enclosures. In doing so, they undermine human rights as whole, given that the achievement of rights often requires access to nationalized spaces outside of the one in which an individual or group of individuals find themselves.

Here I explore the work of entities such as Amnesty International, Human Rights Watch, and United Nations bodies that monitor and advocate for human rights. In doing so, I demonstrate how they help reproduce the spatial logic that harms, and often kills, those seeking refuge outside their countries of birth or ancestry. These entities thus effectively uphold the enclosure of the global commons—by way of national territorial boundaries—and bolster the appropriation by an ecologically privileged minority of an unsustainable and socially unjust share of the biosphere's resources and, relatedly, the grossly unequal distribution of life and death circumstances across the planet.[2]

This manifests how "nature" is organized in terms of how it is allocated and controlled, in addition to how the benefits and detriments associated with its consumption are divided up. The organization of nature and its production over time and space helps illuminate how it is possible that a small slice of the world's population consumes a grossly disproportionate share of the planet's resources. Nature's making and organization also help us understand who dies, where they are from, and why, as they flee their homelands made unviable—say, because of climate change—and try to access nationalized spaces of privilege across the globe, access that is often denied them. In many cases, these nationalized spaces of privilege have played an outsized role in producing the conditions—again, climate change is an example—that have given rise to their flight in the first place (see, for example, Nevins 2017, 2019).

In what follows, I consider enclosure as it relates to nation-states and supranational entities (in the form of the European Union) and the work that such enclosure does. I then offer a critical examination of the discourse of prominent global human rights bodies in recent years in regard to migrant deaths. Following that, I reflect briefly on violence while making the argument that a human rights regime that champions freedom of mobility, residence, and work along with a right to nature—to the global commons—is necessary to put an end to the deaths of illegalized people on the move.

Enclosing the Commons, Enclosing the World

The making of nation-states and their policed boundaries is a form of enclosure. Enclosure, as typically understood, involves the consolidation and bounding of a component of nature managed and accessed in some sort of collective or communal fashion—say, a forest or agricultural lands—and turning it into a private or state holding (see Fields 2017; Peluso and Lund 2011). In other words, it entails various forms of dispossession and exclusion (and inclusion). The result is a landscape that has evolved from one in which something of nature was a shared bundle of rights into increasingly a bounded "thing" that individuals possess as their private property, and thus a commodity, or that states control in the name of the citizenry (say, a national park). Thus, land—and, relatedly, wealth—has become increasingly concentrated in the hands of the few, and many former commoners became displaced (Jones 2016). Maps, surveys, and the law—and, with law, the threat of violence—have been key technologies in bringing about this new regime of ownership (see Blomley 2003; Fields 2017).

Tied to the transition from feudalism to capitalism, enclosure as a form of dispossession (an ongoing process) is temporally tied to the rise of the nation-state system. The making of nation-states and their territories (and thus borders) is also an ongoing process with its origins in the seventeenth century (see Jones 2016). Changing perceptions of time and space associated with the Enlightenment and its antecedents helped lay the foundations of thinking favoring new relations between people and territory as well as rulers and the governed. Innovations in mathematics, as well as the increasingly rational ordering of space in the form of cartographic innovations such as Renaissance maps, led to the increasingly accurate definition of a variety of spatial entities such as privatized landholdings, territorial boundaries, and administrative areas (Harvey 1990, 240–249). Associated mapping innovations led to the depiction, for the first time, of the entire earth's surface within a single spatial frame, facilitating the rise and growth of socio-spatial "otherness" (258–259).

A key manifestation of this shift in perception is what Nandita Sharma refers to as "the territorialization of people's consciousness" (2020, 114). As a result, spatialized notions of what constitutes "ours" and "theirs" and "us" and "them" in relation to nationalized peoples and places is dramatically stronger than it was just a century ago. Also stronger are the associated efforts by states aimed at stymieing unauthorized entries into the territories they claim. This undertaking involves denying access to those dispossessed of previously held rights—whether those of passage through the now-bounded lands or access to resources within—and, relatedly, emptying national space of those officially deemed as having no right to stay (see, e.g., Provenzano and Nevins 2019).

Such restriction of human movement and residence is tied to the rise of territorial states. While territorial states have existed for thousands of years, their capacity to define territory with precision, and to make legible who belongs and who does not, is only a few hundred years old. Prior to that, overtly violent mechanisms such as slavery and serfdom, in addition to vagrancy laws (laws concerned with controlling the movement of those deemed poor or undesirable), served to limit people's mobility. With the rise of nation-states and their bureaucracies, new systems of citizenship and technologies of identification—and with them, enhanced mechanisms of spatial control—emerged (see Jones 2016). Still, movement across national boundaries was relatively unregulated through most of the nineteenth century (see, for example, Jones 2016; McKeown 2008; Torpey 2000). The U.S. Border Patrol, for instance, was not established until 1924, with only four hundred agents, charged with policing several thousand miles along the U.S.-Mexico and U.S.-Canada divides. The number of agents did not reach two thousand until the early 1970s (Nevins 2010). Over the last few decades, however, there has been a dramatic growth in the size of the U.S. policing apparatus concerned with the control of national territorial boundaries and noncitizens (see Miller 2014). This is also true in many countries throughout the world (Jones 2016). Key to the proliferation of these borders have been the efforts of the European Union and the United States to effectively enroll other countries into their boundary policy regime. This manifests what Todd Miller calls an emerging "global border system," involving the Global North's "sorting, classifying, and repelling or incarcerating people from the Global South, while employing and deploying countries of the Global South as enforcers" (Miller 2019, 157–158). This is part and parcel of a "global caste system" (Miller 2019, 162), one that allows a globalized elite to cross national boundaries with ease while stymieing the movement of the world's poor majority (see Nevins 2008, 2012, 2017).

This apartheid-like world is one that is increasingly interlinked via transportation infrastructure and technologies and one that is markedly unequal in a socioeconomic sense. In such a context, states—particularly privileged ones in terms of wealth and power—perceive and construct unwanted people on the move as threats, facilitating the rise of what anthropologist Ruben Andersson (2014) calls the "illegality industry." It is an industry with the goal of repelling and expelling people deemed by the state to be present in (or aiming to enter), without authorization, the territory it claims. A key technology of this industry are border walls, the number of which has exploded in recent decades. According to geographer Elizabeth Vallet, there were seven border walls at the end of World War II. By 1989, when the Berlin Wall came down, the number was fifteen. As of 2018, there were at least seventy-seven such walls (Hjelmgaard 2018). Typically, it is relatively wealthy and powerful territorial states that build and maintain these walls to "protect" themselves from less powerful neighbors or people from disadvantaged places and populations or both (see Hassner and Wittenberg 2015; Miller 2019).

This wall-building and, more broadly, the "hardening" and "thickening" of so many national territorial boundaries, go a long way in explaining why tens of thousands of individuals have perished, over the last decade or so alone, in trying to reach nationalized spaces of refuge—to say nothing of other manifestations of violence that have harmed even greater numbers of would-be border crossers. In the case of the U.S.-Mexico divide over the last two decades, the death toll is in the several thousands (Slack et al. 2016). Worldwide, the situation is markedly more dire: according to a 2016 report from the International Organization of Migration (Brian and Laczko 2016), over sixty thousand migrants had perished over the preceding two decades while trying to reach their destinations, with more than ten thousand of the deaths occurring in 2014 and 2015. These estimates, based only on fatalities for which there exist evidentiary records, are conservative.

In the face of such a death toll, one might reasonably expect human rights organizations to strongly criticize and challenge the underlying policies and structures that produce the deaths of illegalized and rejected people on the move. Instead, what we get, more often than not, are expressions of concern that do little to challenge these policies and structures, the political geography of nation-states and their exclusionary boundaries, and the associated legal categories that produce people of privilege ("citizens") as well as nonpersons, people of disadvantage (see Dayan 2011).[3] Indeed, the human rights establishment more often than not helps normalize them—both through its silence and what it says—and thus contributes to the killing of (officially unwelcome) people on the move attempting to cross national boundaries.

Human Rights Talk

Human rights as a globalized discourse and an associated set of practices and institutions (in the form of international covenants, official bodies, or international nongovernmental organizations) are a recent creation, one born in World War II's aftermath. This is what Stephen Hopgood (2013) refers to as Human Rights (capital "H," capital "R"). Human Rights focuses on the extraordinary—torture, crimes of the state, and mass atrocities. Everyday violence and oppression, "that which constitutes 99 percent of the oppression people suffer, and where the need is greatest, comes a distant second," writes Hopgood (2013, 173).[4] In terms of matters of international mobility and its regulation, Human Rights accepts international norms—as defined by nation-states and their collective expressions (such as the United Nations)—as unproblematic. It does so largely through silence, by way of an effective refusal to call into question national border-policing regimes. This "violence of silence" (see Wolkin and Nevins 2018, 56), by not problematizing borders and their apparatuses of exclusion, serves to normalize that which causes harm.

In April 2015, for example, Amnesty International criticized European governments following an incident involving the deaths of about four hundred migrants in the Mediterranean. Their "ongoing negligence towards the humanitarian crisis in the Mediterranean," the organization wrote, "has contributed to a more than 50-fold increase in migrant and refugee deaths since the beginning of 2015." To help rectify this tragedy, Amnesty called on leaders of European Union countries to "throw their full weight behind a robust and concerted humanitarian operation in the Mediterranean"

(Amnesty International 2015). What Amnesty did *not* do was question the principle of nation-state exclusion or defend migrants' freedom of movement. In other words, the problem for the world's preeminent, nongovernmental human rights organization is not how state efforts to repel desperate migrants inevitably put them in harm's way, but that those responsible to a large degree for creating the dangerous conditions of passage do not do enough to save those whom they have imperiled.

In taking the stance that it did, Amnesty was building on a report it issued in 2012. Titled *In Hostile Terrain: Human Rights Violations in Immigration Enforcement in the US Southwest*, the report, most notably its title, reflects Amnesty's analytical and political geographical stance: the human rights organization dedicates itself to scrutinizing what takes place *within* immigration enforcement carried out by nation-states. What is *not* scrutinized is the very existence of the policing apparatus itself and its picking and choosing of who is allowed to safely enter nationalized territory—bounded space to which the country in question lays effective claim—and who is not. Amnesty implicitly justified this stance by pointing out that "while it is generally accepted that countries have the right to regulate the entry and stay of non-nationals in their territory, they can only do so within the limits of their human rights obligations" (Amnesty International 2012, 11). In other words, Amnesty International accepts "that countries have the right to regulate the entry and stay of non-nationals in their territory." Of course, this is not an unlimited right in that there are restrictions (in terms of international norms) as to what nation-states can do in carrying out the regulation of entry and stay. At the same time, nation-states have responsibilities to "irregular" people on the move or in residence.[5] As the Amnesty report goes on to say in regard to the U.S. government (the report's focus), it "has an obligation under international human rights law to ensure that its laws, policies and practices do not place immigrants at an increased risk of human rights abuses" (Amnesty International 2012, 11). Thus, once noncitizens are present, for instance, in U.S. territory, the U.S. government cannot allow discriminatory practices such as racial profiling and must respect the rights of those detained or jailed by immigration authorities. In the report, Amnesty also defends the right of day laborers—regardless of migratory or citizenship status—to solicit employment in public space.

These positions are quite remarkable for various reasons. One is that Amnesty does not question detention or deportation in and of themselves. So, while day laborers—even "illegal" ones—deserve a right to solicit work on a street corner, they do not have a right to access the bounded space (the United States) in which that street corner exists. And if somehow they are able to enter that space—via "irregular" means—or enter it with state permission but overstay their visa, they are rightfully subject to deportation or imprisonment. Amnesty International never explicitly states this—indeed, the organization asserts in the report that "detention or deportation of individuals can have devastating consequences for families" (Amnesty International 2012, 51). However, a reading of the report in full makes clear that Amnesty's criticism of these practices is limited to particular cases and incidents—how and where one is deported, for instance, or what takes places while one is detained—not the practices per se. Also clear is that the organization does not consider how nation-state exclusion can contribute to diminished life chances for those denied access to spaces of privilege.

A Human Rights Watch report published in 2020 does so, but in a narrow fashion. Focusing on deportations to El Salvador between 2013 and 2019, it explores the killings of individuals after their exile from the United States as well as other forms of physical violence against deportees. For Human Rights Watch, the primary responsibility for such persecution lies with individuals and entities in El Salvador. But the organization also blames U.S. authorities for putting "Salvadorans in harm's way in circumstances where [they know] or should know that harm is likely" (Human Rights Watch 2020a, 1). It thus demonstrates that the U.S. government is in violation of international law, which prohibits returning or deporting people to countries where they risk persecution, torture, or related forms of violence. On this basis, the report makes numerous recommendations aimed at enhancing the U.S. asylum process, as stated in a press release, by "providing broad protection to anyone . . . who would face a real risk of serious harm upon return" to El Salvador (Human Rights Watch 2020b).

Among the problems with such recommendations is the assumption that U.S. authorities are able to assess who faces "real risk" and who does not (and have an actual desire to do so independent of political considerations); the wording thus obscures the inherently subjective nature of the process. Furthermore, by championing the asylum process, Human Rights Watch upholds a system that excludes, by design, most of the world's people who need to be able to migrate to access the resources required for a dignified life. A "risk of serious harm," given its basis in international refugee law, is only concerned with brutality of the direct, physical variety. The very real threat of violence by poverty, for instance, and the resulting diminished life chances, is not grounds for asylum or for stopping deportation (see Nevins 2017). As an Amnesty report from 2010 makes clear, the very manners in which illegalized people exercise international mobility are tied to these diminished life chances. The document explores the harm often visited on Central Americans (particularly individuals from El Salvador, Guatemala, and Honduras) as they travel—in an "irregular" manner—to and through Mexico. As the report explains in reference to one of the more dangerous forms of travel undertaken by these individuals, "Riding precariously on the tops of freight trains, many are met with discrimination and xenophobia, targeted by people smugglers and prey to kidnapping by criminal gangs. Every year thousands of migrants are ill-treated, abducted or raped. Arbitrary detention and extortion by public officials are common." The report goes on to say that "some disappear without trace, kidnapped and killed, or robbed, assaulted and thrown off speeding trains by one of the many criminal gangs that prey on irregular migrants," while highlighting that women and children are particularly vulnerable to such brutality (Amnesty International 2010, 5).

In the report, Amnesty importantly highlights the fact that both state and nonstate actors enact violence on noncitizens—sometimes because of criminal opportunism (in light of the heightened vulnerability of illegalized individuals, thus making them relatively "easy prey"), sometimes because of xenophobia (Amnesty International 2010, 5). What is missing from the analysis is how the state's very categorization of the victimized as people who do not belong—in this case, in Mexico—helps produce and exacerbate their vulnerability. During anti-immigrant pogroms in South Africa in 2008, Paul Verryn, a Johannesburg-based Methodist bishop critical of South Africa's leadership for not being more welcoming of migrants, spoke to this matter directly. "The locals believe they are doing what the government is doing anyway," he asserted, "getting rid of the 'illegals'" (Karimakwenda 2008). In other words, rule-based exclusion can and often does contribute to a broader (and sometimes more overtly or directly violent) exclusion, and to the production of what various scholars have referred to as social death (see, e.g., Cacho 2012).

It is an exclusion that is nationalized—and thus spatialized. It is also based on class, gender, sexual orientation, and race. Thus, different bodies are marked as mobile (and welcome), while others are constructed as threatening and in need of policing. As Bridget Anderson, Nandita Sharma, and Cynthia Wright point out, for example, lots of people move, but they are classified in various ways: "US financiers, Australian backpackers, and British 'expats' are, generally, not categorized as migrants," for instance (2009, 10). As such, their mobile bodies are typically not subject to the forms of violence that are the focus of human rights reports.

The United Nations (UN) Human Rights Council, via its special rapporteur, takes a position similar to that of Amnesty International. In a report issued in 2018, the UN body focused, in part, on the criminalization of humanitarian aid to those engaged in "irregular migration" (Callamard 2018, 14). In highlighting the centuries-old, worldwide tradition of humanitarian action, the report references historical examples of individuals providing aid to those in distress (e.g., abolitionists in the United States assisting those defying enslavement; lawmakers living under Nazi occupation who helped Jews escape arrest)—and doing so in defiance of the law. The report then speaks of the obligation of member states "to take all appropriate measures to preserve and protect the rights of migrants, including, in particular, the right to life," an obligation that requires that states *not* criminalize the provision of humanitarian aid to migrants in distress (Callamard 2018, 15).[6]

In referring to "the rights of migrants" and "the right to life," the UN report is referencing the right of "irregular migrants" to be free of mistreatment by those who smuggle them and by state authorities. It also involves the obligation of states "to provide basic assistance to migrants and illegal residents in cases where their lives or safety have been endangered" (Callamard 2018, 15). A reading of the entire report makes clear that this "right to life" is one narrowly construed. It applies to those whose lives are under extraordinary and imminent threat. Examples would seem to include those in immediate need of rescue at land or sea, medical assistance, food, or water because of the arduous nature of their passage. In other words, it is, in the words of Miriam Ticktin, "the most disenfranchised, the most wretched of the earth," who are worthy of humanitarianism; it is only they who are allowed to occupy this "paradoxically privileged" position (2011, 11–12). Those who face threats that are less pressing—what we might consider a "violence of everyday life" (Scheper-Hughes 1993) or a "silent violence" (Watts 2013), such as crushing poverty, or a lack of economic opportunity and inadequate means to provide for the basic needs of themselves and their dependents—are not eligible for humanitarian action. Instead, they are subject to the regime-of-exclusion-related rules of the territorial states they are trying to enter in an "irregular" manner or in which they find themselves "illegally."

This helps explain the position of Benjamin Ward, the deputy director of the Europe and Central Asia Division of Human Rights Watch. In an article from 2015, one in which he decried the "estimated 20,000 people" who had died over the previous decade while crossing the Mediterranean to reach Europe, he took European governments to task for not doing enough to rescue migrants imperiled at sea. In doing so, he called for the provision of "mechanisms to identify political refugees and other vulnerable people . . . to enable them to come to Europe in a safe and orderly manner" so that such individuals would not have to take life-threatening journeys to reach spaces of safety. Yet Ward also insisted that "there is nothing wrong with border control or enforcement efforts" (Ward 2015).

There is something fundamentally wrong with such efforts, however, if the goal is to end the deaths of illegalized and rejected people on the move across the borderlands dividing and connecting spaces of privilege and security and those of disadvantage and insecurity. There is also something wrong if one embraces human rights of an expansive sort, one that appreciates that such rights, as declared by the Office of the High Commissioner of the United Nations Human Rights Commission, are "universal," "inalienable," and "indivisible and interdependent" (OHCHR, n.d.). After all, given high levels of physical, direct violence; environmental deprivation; and profound socioeconomic insecurity that plague many countries (violence, deprivation, and instability in which the world's most powerful nation-states are often implicated), the realization of human rights often requires the ability to go to spaces where the necessary resources are located. These sorts of inequalities and restrictions likely compelled Hannah Arendt (1973, 298) to speak of the "right to have rights." If having human rights is part of being human, denying people freedom of movement and residence—and thus the effective ability to access a host of other rights—is to essentially deny their humanity. The obverse of this is a radical human solidarity that reaches across national territorial boundaries and rejects the logic of nation-state exclusion (see, e.g., "Relaxe pour Martine Landry," 2018; Grossman 2015; Aguilera and Perrigo 2019). It is one that embraces a right to the world, which includes first and foremost freedom of mobility across global space and a just, sustainable share of the planet's resources for all (Nevins 2017).

Conclusion

In the context of the coronavirus pandemic, seven human rights and humanitarian groups issued a statement in March 2020 calling on the Trump administration to abandon its reported plan to close U.S. borders to asylum seekers. The statement reminded the administration of its domestic and international legal obligations toward refugees, obligations that do not allow for a "blanket ban on asylum" (Amnesty International et al. 2020). What is allowed (implicitly) are rejections of individual asylum requests.

In the front matter of its reports, Amnesty proclaims the organization's goals: "OUR VISION IS FOR EVERY PERSON to enjoy all the rights enshrined in the Universal Declaration of Human Rights and other international human rights standards." This statement manifests how human rights (in their best sense) are predicated on one's humanity, not on national citizenship. Hence, they transcend, or at least they are supposed to, the constraints of nation-statism and national citizenship. The language of the Universal Declaration of Human Rights, which describes itself as "a common standard of achievement for all peoples and all nations" and which the United Nations characterizes as "a milestone document in the history of human rights," speaks to aspirations that go above and beyond the nation-state (United Nations 1948).

In practice, however, human rights are tightly tied to national citizen-ship and nation-statism. Thus, the ability to realize human rights is often linked to the space where one resides (see Benhabib and Resnick 2009). The (im)mobility across national boundaries of refugees and unwanted, illegal-ized migrants—categories of people who by their very existence embody the contradiction between human rights and nation-statism (see Agamben 2000)—is perhaps the starkest reflection of this linkage.

This tension between the global and the national is manifest within the very articles of the UDHR that pertain to spatial mobility (see Benhabib and Resnick 2009). Article 13(2) says, "Everyone has the right to leave any coun-try, including his own, and to return to his country" (United Nations 1948). This is noteworthy because it is the UDHR's only article that speaks to free-dom of mobility between countries. Meanwhile, the declaration says noth-ing about a right to enter a country (except "his own"—meaning a country in which one is a national citizen). Although a right to leave any country implies the freedom to enter somewhere else—as the former is meaningless without the latter—this is clearly not what the architects of the declaration intended. Such status-quo-ism demonstrates the argument of Samuel Moyn (2010a, 2010b) that human rights, despite their transformational pretense, are in many ways conservative (see also Brown 2004). In their twentieth-century version, they arose, Moyn contends, as a minimalist alternative to demands for a radical reworking of the world order. If, as Moyn asserts, "human rights have become prisoners of the contemporary age of inequal-ity" (2018, 6), they also help maintain that inequality, particularly to the extent that the current, nation-state-centric practice of human rights both arises from and helps reproduce inequities in global mobility (see Jones 2016; Miller 2019; Nevins 2008, 2012, 2014, 2018).

For those who are stateless, or for those whose homelands are insuffi-ciently secure to provide what is needed to achieve basic human rights, the UDHR offers little—except "the right to seek and to enjoy in other countries asylum from persecution" (United Nations 1948, Article 14, 1). Among other reasons, it offers little because, in practice, the international refugee regime defines persecution and thus the right to seek asylum in narrow terms. Drawing on the definition of the United Nations High Commis-sioner for Refugees, Amnesty International (2019, 5) describes refugees as "individuals who fled their countries-of-origin due to a well-founded fear of persecution, from which their governments cannot or will not protect them." National governments, the ones that rule over the territories in which asylum seekers hope to find refuge, are charged with determining the legitimacy of claims to refugee-hood. Per this logic, those fleeing depriva-tion, insecurity, and poverty of the everyday, normal sort—normal in terms of reigning political-economic conditions within their home country—are mere migrants, whereas refugees are compelled to leave their homelands because of sociopolitical persecution. Even on these terms, however, the international refugee regime falls woefully short in ensuring that places of asylum are accessible to those in need (see, e.g., Harding 2000; Johnson 2014)—and this is increasingly so (see United Nations 2020). For those fleeing environmental disasters and degradation (e.g., earthquakes, droughts), the international refugee regime simply does not apply.

The human rights establishment's failure to perceive, protest, and advocate for remedying the contradiction inherent in mainstream notions of human rights and nation-statism speaks to an inadequate appreciation of the political nature of human rights. As Wendy Brown (2004) points out, many acknowledge that human rights are necessarily political, but often their notion of what political means (and of what the political does) is narrow. Thus, to say that human rights are political is insufficient. What we need to also do is ask: What other political projects do human rights (of the conventional sort discussed above) displace, compete with, undermine, challenge, and reject? What is clear is that human rights—as a set of dominant practices and discourses—is nation-state-centric and, as such, works to discipline human bodies in ways that contain them within national territories while effectively relegating a large swath of humanity to the realm of the disposable or expendable (Tyner 2019, 83). This speaks to how human rights have become "bound up with the power of the powerful" (Moyn 2010b, 227); they also have become "a worldwide slogan in a time of downsized ambition" (Moyn 2018, 6). It is a downsized ambition that seems to accept not only gross socioeconomic inequalities and market triumphalism, as Moyn (2018) asserts, but also the nation-state system's regime of "violent borders" (Jones 2016) and global apartheid (Nevins 2008, 2010, 2012; Sharma 2020).

Countering this downsized ambition and striving to realize a more expansive conceptualization of human rights necessarily entails making claims on "'organized power relationships' in order to advance the dignity of (or, more concretely, equal respect and concern for) human beings" (Sjoberg, Gill, and Williams 2001, 25; see also Sinden 2007). A key manifestation of this power is the parceling up and enclosure of the planet's bounty—whether through private property or nation-state-based forms of territoriality and its associated restrictions on mobility—and the legal regimes that underlie these enclosures. Hence, the struggle against these restrictions necessitates efforts to make visible and contest the violence embodied by the law—violence of the structural sort, institutionalized injustice (see Galtung 1969; Nevins 2012), as well as the discursive violence (see Galtung 1990; Nevins 2005; Wolkin and Nevins 2018) put forth by human rights bodies that justifies and obscures it.

To accept restrictions on mobility in a world in which the earth's bounty is not distributed in any sort of proportionate or egalitarian manner, a world that is marked by dramatic socioeconomic differences, is to enshrine those inequities and to reproduce them (see Anderson, Sharma, and Wright 2009). It is to deny, in the words of Tim Hayward, the "fundamental right of each individual to an equitable share of the planet's aggregate natural resources and environmental services that are available on a sustainable basis for human use"—what Hayward refers to as "ecological space" (2007, 445; see also Nevins 2017).

Even if establishment human rights organizations begin to directly challenge the machinery of nation-state border policing that emerges out of and reproduces great inequities in relation to access to nature (land being a key component) and that gives rise to untold numbers of premature deaths each year, the injustices and associated manifestations of human suffering will endure. However, by calling the principle of exclusion into question, the organizations would help delegitimize the very practices and structures that make highly predictable the premature deaths of those born on the "wrong side" of the boundaries that divide rich and poor, privileged and disadvantaged. This is a small but necessary first step in the struggle to dismantle the institutionalized injustice of nation-state boundaries predicated on an ongoing process of violent exclusion.

NOTES

Acknowledgment: I thank Jasmin Walters for assistance with research and editorial matters.

1. By establishment human rights bodies, I mean international and supranational organizations—both nongovernmental and official ones—that dominate mainstream discourse of what constitutes human rights. Such bodies include Amnesty International, Human Rights Watch, the International Committee of the Red Cross, and various United Nations agencies.

2. Elsewhere, I refer to this as dys-ecologism (see Nevins 2014).

3. If, as James Tyner asserts, "one's exposure to death is more and more conditioned by one's position in capitalism" (2019, x), it is also the case that one's exposure to death is conditioned by one's position in relation to a world of nation-states.

4. For Hopgood, this is distinct from "human rights" (lowercase "h" and "r"), which involve "local and transnational networks of activists who bring publicity to abuses they and their communities face and who try to exert pressure on governments and the United Nations, for action, often at tremendous personal cost." More broadly, he sees "human rights" (which he embraces) as a language (among other languages) useful for "combating violence and deprivation," as a set of "ethical and political claims . . . rooted in our shared interest in fair and equal treatment" (Hopgood 2013, viii).

5. "Irregular" migration involves "movement . . . that takes place outside the laws, regulations, or international agreements governing the entry into or exit from the State

of origin, transit or destination," according to the UN's International Organization for Migration (n.d.).

6. This is an obligation many nation-states—from Italy to the United States—often fail to respect. See, for example, Aguilera and Perrigo 2019.

REFERENCES

Agamben, Giorgio. 2000. *Means without End: Notes on Politics.* Minneapolis: University of Minnesota Press.

Aguilera, Jasmine, and Billy Perrigo. 2019. "They Tried to Save the Lives of Immigrants Fleeing Danger; Now They're Facing Prosecution." *Time,* November 11. https://time.com/5713732/scott-warren-retrial/.

Amnesty International. 2010. "Invisible Victims: Migrants on the Move in Mexico." https://www.amnesty.org/download/Documents/36000/amr410142010eng.pdf.

———. 2012. *In Hostile Terrain: Human Rights Violations in Immigration Enforcement in the US Southwest.* New York: Amnesty International USA. https://www.amnestyusa.org/files/ai_inhostileterrain_final031412.pdf.

———. 2015. "Mediterranean Crisis: UN Points to 50-Fold Increase in Deaths amid European Government Inaction." April 15. https://www.amnesty.org/en/latest/news/2015/04/mediterranean-crisis-50-fold-increase-in-deats-amid-european-inaction/.

———. 2019. "'Saving Lives Is Not a Crime': Politically Motivated Legal Harassment against Migrant Human Rights Defenders by the USA." https://www.amnestyusa.org/wp-content/uploads/2019/06/Amnesty-Report_SLINAC_FINAL005.pdf.

Amnesty International, Refugees International, Human Rights First, Physicians for Human Rights, Women's Refugee Commission, and Doctors without Borders. 2020. "Responding to the COVID-19 Crisis while Protecting Asylum Seekers." March 19. https://reliefweb.int/sites/reliefweb.int/files/resources/COVID-19%20Asylum%20Statement.pdf.

Anderson, Bridget, Nandita Sharma, and Cynthia Wright. 2009. "Editorial: Why No Borders?" *Refuge* 26 (2): 5–18.

Andersson, Ruben. 2014. *Illegality, Inc.: Clandestine Migration and the Business of Bordering Europe.* Berkeley: University of California Press

Arendt, Hannah. 1973. *The Origins of Totalitarianism.* New York: Harcourt Brace.

Benhabib, Seyla, and Judith Resnik. 2009. "Introduction: Citizenship and Migration Theory Engendered." In *Migrations and Mobilities: Citizenship, Borders, and Gender,* edited by Seyla Benhabib and Judith Resnik, 1–44. New York: New York University Press.

Blomley, Nicholas. 2003. "Law, Property, and the Geography of Violence: The Frontier, the Survey, and the Grid." *Annals of the Association of American Geographers* 93 (1): 121–141.

Brian, Tara, and Frank Laczko, eds. 2016. *Fatal Journeys.* Vol. 2, *Identification and Tracing of Dead and Missing Migrants.* Geneva: International Organization for Migration. https://publications.iom.int/system/files/fataljourneys_vol2.pdf.

Brown, Wendy. 2004. "'The Most We Can Hope For . . .': Human Rights and the Politics of Fatalism." *South Atlantic Quarterly* 103 (2–3): 451–464.

Cacho, Lisa Marie. 2012. *Social Death: Racialized Rightlessness and the Criminalization of the Unprotected.* New York: New York University Press.

Callamard, Agnes. 2018. "Report of the Special Rapporteur of the Human Rights Council on Extrajudicial, Summary or Arbitrary Executions: Saving Lives Is Not a Crime." United Nations Office of the High Commissioner for Human Rights. https://undocs.org/A/73/314.

Carr, Matthew. 2016. *Fortress Europe: Dispatches from a Gated Continent*. New York City: New Press.

Dayan, Colin. 2011. *The Law Is a White Dog: How Legal Rituals Make and Unmake Persons*. Princeton, NJ: Princeton University Press.

Faiola, Anthony. 2015. "U.N. Estimates up to 850 Migrants Perished in Capsized Boat off Libya." *Washington Post*, April 21. https://www.washingtonpost.com/world/un-says-between-800-and-850-migrants-died-in-boat-capsizing-off-libya/2015/04/21/a8383770-e803-11e4-9767-6276fc9b0ada_story.html?.

Fields, Gary. 2017. *Enclosure: Palestinian Landscapes in a Historical Mirror*. Berkeley: University of California Press.

Galtung, Johan. 1969. "Violence, Peace, and Peace Research." *Journal of Peace Research* 6 (3): 167–191.

———. 1990. "Cultural Violence." *Journal of Peace Research* 27 (3): 291–305.

Grossman, Zoltan. 2015. "The Kindness of Strangers: Today's Refugees in Hungary and My Family during WWII." *Common Dreams*, September 21. http://www.commondreams.org/views/2015/09/21/kindness-strangers-todays-refugees-hungary-and-my-family-during-wwii.

Harding, Jeremy. 2000. "The Uninvited." *London Review of Books* 22 (3): 3–25.

Harvey, David. 1990. *The Condition of Postmodernity*. Cambridge, MA: Blackwell.

Hassner, Ron E., and Jason Wittenberg. 2015. "Barriers to Entry: Who Builds Fortified Boundaries and Why?" *International Security* 40 (1): 157–190.

Hayward, Tim. 2007. "Human Rights versus Emissions Rights: Climate Justice and the Equitable Distribution of Ecological Space." *Ethics and International Affairs* 21 (4): 431–450.

Hjelmgaard, Kim. 2018. "From 7 to 77: There's Been an Explosion in Building Border Walls since World War II." *USA Today*, May 24. https://www.usatoday.com/story/news/world/2018/05/24/border-walls-berlin-wall-donald-trump-wall/553250002/.

Hopgood, Stephen. 2013. *The End Time of Human Rights*. Ithaca, NY: Cornell University Press.

Human Rights Watch. 2020a. *Deported to Danger: United States Deportation Policies Expose Salvadorans to Death and Abuse*. New York: Human Rights Watch. https://www.hrw.org/sites/default/files/report_pdf/elsalvador0220_web_0.pdf.

———. 2020b. "US: Deported Salvadorians Abused, Killed." February 5. https://www.hrw.org/news/2020/02/05/us-deported-salvadorans-abused-killed.

International Organization for Migration. n.d. "Key Migration Terms." Accessed November 24, 2020. https://www.iom.int/key-migration-terms.

Johnson, Heather L. 2014. *Borders, Asylum and Global Non-citizenship: The Other Side of the Fence*. Cambridge: Cambridge University Press.

Jones, Reece. 2016. *Violent Borders: Refugees and the Right to Move*. New York: Verso Books.

Karimakwenda, Tererai. 2008. "South Africa: Mbeki Blamed after 20 More Die in Xenophobic Attacks." *SW Radio Africa*, May 19. https://allafrica.com/stories/200805191523.html.

McKeown, Adam M. 2008. *Melancholy Order: Asian Migration and the Globalization of Borders*. New York: Columbia University Press.

Miller, Todd. 2014. *Border Patrol Nation: Dispatches from the Frontlines of Homeland Security*. San Francisco: Open Media/City Lights Books.

———. 2019. *Empire of Borders: The Expansion of the U.S. Border around the World*. New York: Verso.

Moyn, Samuel. 2010a. "Human Rights in History." *The Nation*, August 11. https://www.thenation.com/article/human-rights-history/.

———. 2010b. *The Last Utopia: Human Rights in History*. Cambridge, MA: Harvard University Press.

———. 2018. *Not Enough: Human Rights in an Unequal World*. Cambridge, MA: Harvard University Press.

Nevins, Joseph. 2005. *A Not-So-Distant Horror: Mass Violence in East Timor*. Ithaca, NY: Cornell University Press.

———. 2008. *Dying to Live: A Story of U.S. Immigration in an Age of Global Apartheid*. San Francisco: Open Media/City Lights Books.

———. 2010. *Operation Gatekeeper and Beyond: The War on "Illegals" and the Remaking of the U.S.-Mexico Boundary*. New York: Routledge.

———. 2012. "Policing Mobility, Maintaining Global Apartheid—from South Africa to the United States." In *Beyond Walls and Cages: Bridging Immigrant Justice and Anti-Prison Organizing in the United States*, edited by Jenna M. Loyd, Matt Mitchelson, and Andrew Burridge, 19–26. Athens: University of Georgia Press.

———. 2014. "Academic Jet-Setting in a Time of Climate Destabilization: Ecological Privilege and Professional Geographic Travel." *Professional Geographer* 66 (2): 298–310.

———. 2017. "The Right to the World." *Antipode* 49 (5): 1349–1367.

———. 2018. "The Speed of Life and Death: Migrant Fatalities, Territorial Boundaries, and Energy Consumption." *Mobilities* 13 (1): 29–44.

———. 2019. "Nature, Energy, and Violence on the U.S.-Mexico Border." *NACLA Report on the Americas* 51 (1): 95–100.

OHCHR (Office of the High Commissioner for Human Rights). n.d. "What Are Human Rights?" Accessed November 24, 2020. https://www.ohchr.org/en/issues/pages/whatarehumanrights.aspx.

Peluso, Nancy Lee, and Christian Lund. 2011. "New Frontiers of Land Control: Introduction." *Journal of Peasant Studies* 38 (4): 667–681.

Provenzano, Adriana, and Joseph Nevins. 2019. "Arming the Environment, and Colonizing Nature, Territory, and Mobility in Organ Pipe Cactus National Monument." *ACME: An International Journal for Critical Geographies* 18 (2): 456–485.

"Relaxe pour Martine Landry, la bénévole d'Amnesty poursuivie pour 'délit de solidarité.'" 2018. *Le Monde*, July 14. https://www.lemonde.fr/police-justice/article/2018/07/14/relaxe-pour-martine-landry-la-benevole-d-amnesty-poursuivie-pour-delit-de-solidarite_5331246_1653578.html.

Scheper-Hughes, Nancy. 1993. *Death without Weeping: The Violence of Everyday Life in Brazil*. Berkeley: University of California Press.

Sharma, Nandita. 2020. *Home Rule: National Sovereignty and the Separation of Natives and Migrants*, Durham, NC: Duke University Press.

Sinden, Amy. 2007. "Climate Change and Human Rights." *Journal of Land, Resources and Environmental Law* 27 (2): 255–271.

Sjoberg, Gideon, Elizabeth Gill, and Norma Williams. 2001. "A Sociology of Human Rights." *Social Problems* 48 (1): 11–47.

Slack, Jeremy, Daniel E. Martínez, Alison Elizabeth Lee, and Scott Whiteford. 2016. "The Geography of Border Militarization: Violence, Death and Health in Mexico and the United States." *Journal of Latin American Geography* 15 (1): 7–32.

Ticktin, Miriam. 2011. *Casualties of Care: Immigration and the Politics of Humanitarianism in France*. Berkeley: University of California Press.

Torpey, John. 2000. *The Invention of the Passport: Surveillance, Citizenship and the State*. Cambridge: Cambridge University Press.

Tyner, James. 2019. *Dead Labor: Toward a Political Economy of Premature Death*, Minneapolis: University of Minnesota Press.

United Nations. 1948. "Universal Declaration of Human Rights." https://www.un.org/en/universal-declaration-human-rights/.

———. 2020. "UN Refugee Chief Laments Nearly 80 Million People Forcibly Displaced." *UN News*, June 18. https://news.un.org/en/story/2020/06/1066492.

Ward, Benjamin. 2015. "The EU Stands By as Thousands of Migrants Drown in the Mediterranean." *Quartz*, February 25. https://qz.com/350181/the-eu-stands-by-as-thousands-of-migrants-drown-in-the-mediterranean/.

Watts, Michael J. 2013. *Silent Violence: Food, Famine and Peasantry in Northern Nigeria*. Athens: University of Georgia Press.

Wolkin, Kenneth and Joseph Nevins. 2018. "'No Sovereign Nation, No Reservation': Producing the 'New Colonialism' in Cayuga Count(r)y." *Territory, Politics, Governance* 6 (1): 42–60.

Yardley, Jim. 2015. "Hundreds of Migrants Are Feared Dead as Ship Capsizes off Libyan Coast." *New York Times*, April 19. https://www.nytimes.com/2015/04/20/world/europe/italy-migrants-capsized-boat-off-libya.html?.

Yardley, Jim, and Dan Bilefsky. 2015. "Migrant Boat Captain Steered toward Tragedy in Mediterranean, Authorities Say." *New York Times*, April 21. https://www.nytimes.com/2015/04/22/world/europe/italy-libya-migrant-boat-capsize.html?.

2

Living and Dying in *El Norte*

The Framing of Maya Migration

ALICIA IVONNE ESTRADA

On April 18, 2010, Hugo Alfredo Tale Yax was killed on a busy sidewalk in Jamaica, Queens, New York. Surveillance video from a nearby shop shows Tale Yax stabbed several times as he saves a woman from her assailant. The black-and-white footage reveals over twenty people walking by the Maya-K'iche' migrant as he bleeds to death. *New York Times* journalists A. G. Sulzberger and Mick Meenan (2010) reported that one man bent down to shake the dying Tale Yax. He proceeds to lift his body and, in the process, exposes "a pool of blood before walking away." Later, "two men appeared to have a conversation about the situation, one pausing to take a photo of the body before departing." The *New York Times* article, like much of the news coverage, focuses on reproducing in great detail the horrific scenes captured on the one-hour video.

Additionally, the vast majority of these news reports center on the ethical issues the murder raises for New Yorkers. Several of the articles draw parallels with the 1964 killing of Kitty Genovese and employ the bystander effect, or Genovese syndrome, to explain the multiple layers of violence experienced by Tale Yax. By evoking this popular concept based in social psychology, the actions of those who failed to render lifesaving assistance to the dying migrant are redeemed, and the historically grounded violence that continues to shape the lives of Indigenous peoples is erased. And while psychology plays a role in understanding the ways individuals in society relate, the discursive frames employed by the media through the images and stories circulated require that we consider other points of departure to better understand how Indigenous migrants are constituted as socially dead and disposable. In many of these news accounts Tale Yax's Maya identity is eclipsed to privilege his Guatemalan origin, migration to the United States, and houselessness at the time of the murder. This public omission erases not only his Indigenous identity but also the ongoing material and discursive effects of settler colonialism. Additionally, it conceals the enduring legacies of the genocide in Guatemala that continue to shape the lives of survivors and their descendants. Hence, I argue that the media's framing of Tale Yax's murder illustrates the selective ways in which the experiences of Maya migrants in the United States are made (il)legible and (in)visible. For instance, they often employ homogenous national (Guatemalan) and U.S.-based ethnic (Latina/o) identities to inscribe Indigenous migrants from the Global South in familiar American narratives. In doing so, they maintain violent settler practices that eradicate Indigenous peoples through metaphorical and literal erasures. It is in this context that I analyze the news articles on Tale Yax's life and murder as well as two tribute YouTube music videos published by local artists.[1]

I begin by arguing that the continuous migration of thousands of Mayas to *el norte* is not the result of falling coffee prices, or the search for the American Dream, as much of the media has suggested,[2] but rather the enduring impact of the genocide that continues to create precarious conditions for Indigenous peoples in Guatemala (Nelson 2015; O'Neill and Thomas 2011; Martínez Salazar 2012; McAllister and Nelson 2013; Weld 2014). Departing from an understanding that the recent Maya genocide is rooted in a historical and systemic denial of Indigenous peoples' humanity, I further situate the perpetual forced displacement of Mayas from their territories as a consequence of U.S. settler colonialism. The unceasing violence waged against Mayas is evident in the assassination of activists by state forces; the overexploitation of their labor, which leads to hunger and subhuman living conditions; and dispossession from their lands; as well as the complete immunity maintained by most perpetrators of the genocide. In an effort to survive these precarious conditions, thousands are forced to migrate to the United States. Moreover, I argue that the media, like the state, homogenize immigrant experiences to reinforce prevailing notions that construct the United States as inclusive, democratic, and prosperous. These frames eclipse the structural and discursive racism that contributes to the multiple deaths that Maya migrants, like Tale Yax, experience. At the same time, they inform social perceptions and relations, as well as immigration laws and policies (Volpp 2015; McKinnon 2016). It is within this context that I also consider the ways Tale Yax's death is mourned by New Yorkers, particularly by analyzing two YouTube music videos published within four years (2010–2014) of the murder. While well intentioned, the videos reframe

Tale Yax as a tragic, homeless hero, and in this way, they reinforce dominant U.S. national myths (American Dream) and tropes (American hero) that further erase his existence. By reproducing these familiar tropes, the songs and videos absolve the United States of the historical and perpetual violence waged against Indigenous peoples that produced Tale Yax's multiple deaths. I conclude by suggesting that the erasures of these material and historical contexts reinforce global mechanisms that disavow "the status of living" for Mayas (Holland 2000, 15). In other words, this public erasure of their Indigenous identity, as well as the denial of the genocide, must be understood as rooted in settler colonialism and its aim to eradicate Mayas both in Guatemala and the United States.

Enduring Legacies of Genocide: (Re)Framing Maya Migration

The violence of colonialism including genocidal processes has persisted in various forms in Guatemala since the colonial period and continued during the creation of the republic; the thirty-six years of a U.S.-sponsored civil war (1960–1996), which was marked by genocide causing over two hundred thousand deaths and forty-five thousand forcefully disappeared; and the neoliberal era.[3] Guatemalan sociologist Egla Martínez Salazar explains genocide as "a process that does not necessarily begin with mass murder, but with the teaching of a mentality that denies humanity to groups whose humanity has been questioned for centuries" (2012, 137). If we understand the genocide as rooted in the historical dehumanization of Maya communities, this process does not cease to exist with the deaths of the subjects the state eradicated but remains after those deaths. In this context of ongoing structural violence, Maya survivors and their descendants continue to be forcefully displaced from their territories.

Consequently, it is not a coincidence that Maya migration to the United States arose in the 1980s during the height of the genocidal policies directed by Generals Romeo Lucas García (1978–1982) and Efraín Ríos Montt[4] (1982–1983). Throughout their dictatorships they created death squads, civilian self-defense patrols (PACs), and policies such as *tierra arrasada* (scorched earth), and they directed massacres like those in Panzós (1978) and the Spanish Embassy (1980), among more than six hundred others. For Maya activists in the United States, these genocidal policies and practices cannot simply be rendered as an aspect of their past, since they continue to shape their present (Estrada 2021). In the diaspora, as has been the case in Guatemala, Maya survivors and activists often make these lived experiences visible under the shadows of national as well as public social denials and erasures.

Dominant media outlets actively contribute to these erasures as they unceasingly frame Maya migration as the result of extreme poverty, a consequence of regionally based violence including drug trafficking, epidemics, and natural disasters (earthquakes, hurricanes, droughts). In these discursive configurations, the genocide continues to be eclipsed from the public to protect the United States' presumed neutrality from seemingly locally created conflicts. By using these framings, the media not only erase the material effects of settler colonialism but also often attribute responsibility to victims and survivors. Hence, these constructions must be understood as an integral part of the social, political, and economic transnational structures that produce Maya peoples' social death in Guatemala and the diaspora. For instance, historian Greg Grandin notes that even large-scale killings like the 1978 Panzós massacre received minimal attention in U.S. news.[5] He adds that at the request of the Central Intelligence Agency (CIA), the *New York Times*'s limited reporting on Guatemala started in 1954 during the U.S.-orchestrated coup d'état against the democratically elected president Jacobo Arbenz Guzmán (Grandin 2004, 67). Reflecting on the coverage of the Panzós massacre, twenty-nine years later, journalist Marlise Simons echoes Grandin's account as she recalls that her short report in the *Washington Post* "was one of the only comments to appear in the U.S. press" (Simons 2007). This absence not only worked to conceal the role of the United States in the genocidal strategies employed by the Guatemalan military but also served as an important weapon in the eradication of Maya peoples.[6]

The disposability of Maya lives is visually captured in one of the photos taken soon after the Panzós massacre on May 29, 1978. The grainy black-and-white photograph depicts the back of a construction truck filled with the massacred bodies of Maya activists. The piles of faceless bodies become yet another substance hauled by the Guatemalan government-owned truck in which they are deposited. The photo shows the ways the state renders the massacre as both unproblematic and necessary to the nation's development, since the bodies become disposable materials that are moved and dumped into a collective grave. The dreadful photo, which continues to circulate in Guatemala and on the internet, visually demonstrates the literal and metaphorical disposability of Maya bodies. Similarly, the virtual silence on the massacre by U.S. media outlets,[7] as noted by journalist Simons, reproduces the epistemological frames that render Maya lives as not fully lives and thus not deemed "lose-able" (Butler 2016, 2).

Consequently, U.S. immigration judges, like the media and government, continue to frame Maya migration in familiar tropes (economic migrants) dismissing their legitimate "well-founded fear of persecution," as stipulated by the U.S. Refugee Act of 1980 and the Geneva Conventions. Given this minimal coverage, requests for asylum are repeatedly rejected. Once in the United States, Maya migrants are incorporated into U.S. settler frameworks that have historically constructed Indigenous peoples as foreign aliens in their own territories. As legal scholar Leti Volpp notes, "Immigration law, as it is taught, studied and researched in the United States, imagines away the fact of preexisting indigenous peoples" (2015, 289). Within these settler paradigms, Indigenous peoples continue to be marked as racially inferior, anachronistic, and extinct. Consequently, Mayas in the United States are more likely to live in the shadows of society and "illegality," which, as Nicholas De Genova (2005) suggests, is not merely the result of the migrants' unauthorized border crossing but a status created to keep them as exploitable workers.

According to the Pew Research Center's "Hispanic Trends," in 2017 approximately 1.4 million Guatemalans were living in the United States (Noe-Bustamante, Flores, and Shah 2019). Guatemalan studies scholars and activists suggest that half of that projected population is Maya.[8] The Migrant Policy Institute (MPI) estimates that between 2012 and 2016, 525,000 Guatemalans were undocumented (O'Connor, Batalova, and Bolter 2019). These statistics, as well as a lack of immigration reform, suggest that Maya Guatemalan migrants tend to be undocumented and thus legally exploitable and disposable. Hence, it is not a coincidence that the largest immigration workplace raids in U.S. history—at New Bedford, Massachusetts (March 2007); Chattanooga, Tennessee (April 2008); Postville, Iowa (May 2008); and Mississippi (2019)—have disproportionately affected Maya-K'iche', Kaqchikel, Q'anjob'al, and Mam migrants (see, e.g., Rios 2017; WBUR 2018; Associated Press 2019). Additionally, from December 2018 to August 2019 the highest number of apprehensions at the U.S.-Mexican border were Guatemalans (Gramlich and Noe-Bustamante 2019). During the same period, the majority of children who died in U.S. Immigration and Customs Enforcement (ICE) detention centers were Mayas: Jakelin Caal Maquin (Q'eqchi', December 8, 2018), Felipe Gómez Alonzo (Chuj, December 24, 2018), Juan de León Gutiérrez (Ch'orti', April 30, 2019), Wilmer Josúe Ramírez Vásquez (Ch'orti', May 14, 2019), and Carlos Gregorio Hernández Vásquez (Achi, May 20, 2019).[9] While these statistics minimally show who has been lost (disposed of, deported, murdered), they continue to hide why these losses mainly affect Maya lives. Recognizing the enduring legacies of the genocide in Guatemala allows us to reframe our understanding of Maya migration, as well as their reception and lives in the United States.

Reporting the American Dream: Hugo Alfredo Tale Yax's Life and Death

Michel Foucault employs the term "discourse" in much of his work to depict how knowledge and meaning are organized in Western social systems. He notes in particular that discourse aids in the production of a certain truth and stresses that the truth status ascribed to these meaning systems serves to legitimize unequal power relations (Foucault 1981). For Judith Butler, visual and discursive "frames are means through which social norms are relayed and made effective" (2016, xix). Foucault's and Butler's analyses on the function of discourse provide a useful framework from which to examine widely circulated U.S. media articles as well as online Guatemalan news accounts on Tale Yax's murder. Rooted in abstract liberal humanistic inquiries on individual responsibility, sacrifice, and heroic actions, many of these articles serve to reinforce the U.S. national ethos. In doing so, these public visual and discursive (settler) frames further exploit, dispose of, and vanish Indigenous migrants.

Several of the articles that circulated during the weeks that followed Tale Yax's murder were detailed depictions of the one-hour surveillance video obtained and disseminated by the *New York Post*. A week after the murder, the *New York Times* and *Los Angeles Times* elaborated some of the reporting through two feature stories that framed Tale Yax as a "tragic hero," who in life aspired, like so many others, to achieve the American Dream. Spanish-language community newspapers in New York simply provided general information about the murder and funeral services that followed. Most newspapers, with a single *New York Times* article as an exception, did not mention Tale Yax's Indigenous identity. For instance, one of the *Huffington Post*'s online articles provides English-language readers the phonetic pronunciation of Tale Yax's last name, but also erases his indigeneity.[10] These news reports limit identifying markers to basic official state data like name, age, national origin, and occupation. By not presenting other information about the Maya-K'iche' migrant, the media encase Tale Yax's life within standardized narratives that effectively strip his indigeneity and subjectivity. Additionally, they restrict the public's understanding of the structural conditions that forced Tale Yax to migrate, experience houselessness, and, ultimately, bleed to death on a busy street in Queens, New York. This control of public knowledge and opinion, as Noam Chomsky explains, "is designed to induce conformity to established doctrine" (2013, 10). And while Chomsky does not root the "established doctrine" within settler colonialism, I argue that the perpetual erasure of Indigenous subjectivities from these public spaces is central to its mode of operation. This is further illustrated in the media's "choice of topics and highlighting of issues, the range of opinion permitted expression, and the general framework imposed for the presentation of a certain view of the world" (12). The global broadcasting of these established settler doctrines is made evident in the transnational coverage of the Maya-K'iche' migrant's agonizing death.

In Guatemala, Tale Yax's murder was scarcely covered. *Diario La Hora* reprinted a translated version of the Associated Press's five-line paragraph, which provides general information about the incident. The newspaper's reproduction of the Associated Press article is not isolated; often reports printed by the Guatemalan press on migrants in the United States are exported stories from U.S. media outlets. These articles disseminate U.S. (settler) frameworks, perceptions, terminologies ("illegal" immigrants), ideals (individualism), and myths (American Dream) to Guatemalans and others across the globe. *Diario La Hora* also published an op-ed titled "Indiferencia en Queens, Nueva York" by longtime journalist Roberto Arias (2010). While the column mainly offers a translated summary of Fernanda Santos's *New York Times* article, Arias does recognize that as a result of the global attention the murder prompted, "the corpse of a Guatemalan . . . will now not be buried as XX in any mass grave."[11] His statement alludes to the thousands of migrants whose remains are never identified. The XX employed by Arias references the ways Guatemalan morticians record unidentified bodies. It is that country's version of Jane/John Doe and it has shaped the national imaginary, since the remains of the more than forty-five thousand forcefully disappeared by the armed forces were often marked XX. Similarly, common graves were part of the military strategies used during the war and genocide. These tactics allowed the military to erase material evidence, maintain fear in the population, and strip the victims of their humanity. Though Arias's final comments broadly allude to these forms of structural violence, they do not overtly condemn the specific violence Mayas experience in Guatemala and the United States.

Aside from the two newspaper articles, the widely circulated newspaper *Prensa Libre* produced and uploaded to its YouTube channel a two-minute report about the murder.[12] With a title similar to those of stories published in the United States, "Familia de héroe guatemalteco llora su muerte" (Family of Guatemalan hero mourns his death), the video is the only news source that names the region, La Esperanza, Totonicapán, where Tale Yax originated (*Prensa Libre* 2010). The interview with the family patriarch, Juan Pablo Tale, mainly focuses on broadcasting identifying markers often used by Guatemalan state entities. For instance, the migrant's occupation in the United States, how often he called the family, and frequency of the remittances sent home are mentioned. Journalist Antonio Ordoñez's final comments emphasize that "la familia necesita los $200 que enviaba al mes Hugo para mantener a cinco personas" (the family needs the $200 Hugo sent monthly to support five family members). His statement, along with the questions that frame the interview, reduces Tale Yax's life to an economic value, as he primarily highlights the needed monthly remittances the migrant will no longer be able to send. The inclusion of a short clip from the surveillance footage and Ordoñez's explanation that "el hecho habría pasado desapercibido de no ser por la indiferencia de varias personas que pasaron junto al cuerpo del guatemalteco durante la hora que duró su agonía" (the incident would have gone unnoticed had it not been for the indifference of several people who walked by the body of the Guatemalan during the hour that his agony lasted) further strip the migrant and his family of their humanity. Ordoñez's reporting, like that of other journalists, reproduces a colonial gaze that transmits a sense of entitlement to Indigenous bodies, labor, suffering, and agony. In other words, the emphasis on the remittances that Tale Yax's labor allowed him to send and the continuous use of the surveillance video illustrate the spectacular character of Indigenous suffering and the ways in which both U.S. and Guatemalan mainstream media encourage the public to participate in its consumption.

In the United States, the surveillance video was accompanied by news reports that focused on Tale Yax's heroic action, his search for the American Dream, and houselessness. Though his murder occurred on the same month that Arizona, and the nation, debated the passage of the Support Our Law Enforcement and Safe Neighborhoods Act (Arizona Senate Bill 1070), which had devastating material consequences for Mexican and Central American immigrants, none of the news articles provided this sociopolitical context. With abysmal possibilities to regulate their immigration status, migrants like Tale Yax found themselves experiencing underpaid and unpaid work, which often leads to houselessness. The articles instead emphasized Tale Yax's desire to achieve the American Dream, resonating with national myths that position the United States, and New York in particular, as the land of opportunities.

While the feature articles published in the *New York Times* and *Los Angeles Times* turn the gaze back to Tale Yax's life, they employ a liberal humanitarian discourse that reflects the foundational perspectives and interests of the nation. In "Questions after Homeless Man's Lonely Death," by Tina Susman (2010), and "Here to Aid His Family, Left to Die on the Street," by Fernanda Santos (2010), as in the YouTube music videos that are examined in the following section, Tale Yax's life is reduced to familiar national tropes that are entangled within the politics of domination. This is particularly so in the ways that immigrants are portrayed as desiring to live in the United States to reinforce prevailing notions that construct the nation as inclusive and democratic. After speaking to one of Tale Yax's brothers at his funeral, Susman (2010) notes that the five brothers, two sisters, and several cousins "made their way to the United States separately over the years, all for the same reason[:] 'to get a better life.'" Santos's (2010) article begins by noting the migrant's reassurance to the family patriarch that "he would go to New York, work hard and save enough money to buy his family a bigger piece of land." The repetition of these familiar tropes serves to reinforce narratives that construct the United States as a nation of immigrants. These narratives, as Volpp explains, obscure "the nonconsensual bases of American society—if America is a product of free choice, there is no slavery, colonial possession, conquest and genocide," and, of course, there are no forced displacements (2015, 321). These familiar discourses not only tell and retell national myths but also reinforce the global structures that produce precarious lives, disposability, and death.

The titles of other news reports superficially engage readers in ethical questions about humanitarian aid and individual responsibility: "Good Samaritan Left for Dead on City Sidewalk" (ABC News), "Hugo Alfredo Tale-Yax: Good Samaritan Ignored while Bleeding to Death" (*Huffington Post*), and "Tribute to Hugo, a Man Who Had Nothing, Gave Everything and Was Left to Die" (Associated Press). In these articles, Tale Yax's murder merely operates as a side reference for the presumed social reflection the articles propose. As reporters A. G. Sulzberger and Mick Meenan note, in "Questions Surround a Delay in Help for a Dying Man," published in the *New York Times* on April 25, 2010:

> Regardless of the explanation, the death has become another unfortunate case study in bystander behavior in emergencies, a psychological field that developed after the notorious 1964 killing of Kitty Genovese. She was stabbed to death at an apartment building in Kew Gardens, Queens, where a large number of neighbors heard her screams but did not call the police.

More than a search for answers, these newspaper accounts provide readers a familiar frame and context to ease the discomfort produced by the recognition of Tale Yax's multiple assailants (perpetrators of the genocide, the unknown man who stabbed him, bystanders, and settler structures and practices). Yet none of these assailants seem to command attention from the media, since doing so would expose what Chomsky calls the "manufacture of consent" and "necessary illusions" used to deceive the masses (2013, 19). The universality these media sources employ as they root the conversations within popular psychology and superficial ethical inquiries on human nature and responsibility limit any possibility for debate and discussion and instead reinforce stereotypes and social inequalities.

In one of its reports ABC News notes that the bystanders' apathy is "a symptom of [New York] city living," which it explains as a common trait of large urban centers (Hutchison 2010). Additionally, these news accounts situate Tale Yax's murder as a contemporary textbook example of the bystander effect or syndrome, often citing parallels with the Catherine Susan "Kitty" Genovese (1964) and Sandra Zahler (1974) cases that set this precedent. In fact, Tale Yax's murder appears as another such case in several psychology syllabi online, in textbooks, and in encyclopedia references. These public reflections erase the historically grounded violence that shapes Indigenous people's lives, and they continue to displace the gaze from the power relations that produce violent murders to moralistic, and often times individualistic, responsibility.

The social authority attributed to Western academics is often employed in many of these articles through direct citations that serve to legitimize dominant discourses. ABC News reporter Courtney Hutchison (2010) cites Paul Wolpe, director of Emory University's Center for Ethics, as stating, "When you see homeless people sleeping on the streets all the time, another body on the street becomes unremarkable." Such statements serve to protect public understanding of the structural conditions that produce houselessness and displacement for migrants like Tale Yax. Though Wolpe's declaration points to the social death of unhoused peoples in the United States, its broadness serves to deracialize such violence and normalize the precarity of Indigenous peoples—particularly those who are unhoused. This is reinforced by Hutchison (2010), who notes, "[Wolpe] hesitates to criticize those who passed by Tale-Yax 'because though we imagine that we would have stopped, studies show that in these situations, most people don't.' Though we view ourselves as altruistic, when it's time to act, other motivations often get in the way." Her liberal humanistic explanation naturalizes the structural inequalities that produce social deaths. Within these structures, the lives of Indigenous people are justifiably disposable, since they cannot be rendered as fully grievable or lost. This is evident in Art Caplan's recognition that "people see the homeless as a blight, like spilled garbage. They wouldn't even think to pay attention to whether they were in trouble. . . . It's dehumanization and it's terrible" (quoted in Hutchison 2010). The emphasis on these decontextualized scientific studies, which allegedly prove that most people would not render aid in similar circumstances, normalizes not only the disposability of unhoused peoples but also our collective complicity as it maintains a seemingly public consensus of these violent social structures that render certain lives as "spilled garbage." Just as Tale Yax is inserted within this narrative, Maya migrants like him are forcefully assimilated into familiar social categories, since their particular experiences and struggles continue to be incomprehensible and untranslatable for the U.S. public. In this way, Tale Yax's life and murder operate as another resource extracted for U.S. public consumption.

YouTubing the Tragic (Maya) American Hero

YouTube is considered the largest video-sharing site in the world. Since its launch in 2005 it has made video sharing accessible through the use of various formats that include "nearly every device with an internet connection—from desktops to phones, tablets to TVs, game consoles, and even VR headsets" (Mohan 2017). In his work on video activism, William Merrin notes that "as [YouTube is] the leading site and center of online video production and sharing," much of the material produced and uploaded to it continues to be nonprofessional (2012, 98). This aspect is championed by YouTube, which proposes that the "video [format] is universal." While YouTube videos are produced in many different languages, nearly half of Latin Americans are not regularly participating in these online platforms (Galperin 2017). Communication studies scholar Hernan Galperin (2017) explains that a central barrier to internet adoption is the deep-rooted development inequalities in the region, which informs service availability and high costs. His research allows us to highlight the limited accessibility of YouTube videos for non-English-speaking communities and Indigenous populations, which often do not have the material resources needed to connect. Cultural studies scholar Freya Schiwy reminds us that audiovisual productions, along with other discourses, are "an integral part of the coloniality of power" (2009, 91). It is in this context that I situate the YouTube videos examined in this section as also projecting a colonial gaze that continues to reinforce racial hierarchies and unequal power relations.

The two most-viewed YouTube videos on Hugo Alfredo Tale Yax's life and murder were produced in the United States. "The Patron Saint of Jamaica Queens," by Luke Austin Daugherty, is available only in English. Marcos Perla's video, which includes an untitled song and concludes with brief reflections by Rabbi Dennis Schulman and psychologists Henry Solomon and Linda Solomon, includes Spanish subtitles. Though the music videos differ in their visual narrative, both songs are tragic ballads in the style popularized by American folk icons like Bob Dylan, Woody Guthrie, and Pete Seeger. The English lyrics transform the Maya migrant from a tragically average (unhoused) man, as depicted by many of the news stories that circulated, to a messianic American hero. Borrowing from popular culture, what are presumed to be Tale Yax's flaws are redeemed by his bravery against the unknown assailant in Queens.

U.S.-based musician Luke Austin Daugherty's YouTube video and song, "The Patron Saint of Jamaica Queens" from the album *Half Life*, was published on April 27, 2014, four years after the murder. Of the three music videos published on YouTube and dedicated to Tale Yax, this is the most watched, with 1,163 views as of December 2020. From the very title the migrant's life is framed within Christian values that privilege docility, self-sacrifice, and hard work. The song's use of Christian and neoliberal ideologies that emphasize universal human experiences normalizes the precarity of Indigenous migrant lives. In a romanticized rendition of the night that Tale Yax is stabbed, the lyrics suggests that the Maya migrant decided his fate: "I saw her in danger and frozen in fright—thought I'd be her angel tonight" (Daugherty 2014).[13] These "angelic" heroic actions enshrine him as a humble servant willing to sacrifice his life in the name of love. The last moments of the migrant's life are (re)constructed in the third verse:

> Sometimes a knife to the heart is not just a metaphor—
> some things are fair in New York that are not in love and war—
> and standing there they just watched me here—
> like I'm Jesus with no cross and no beard

The acceptance—"some things are fair"—by the Jesus Christ figure that Tale Yax presumably embodies cements his (saintly) innocence, submissiveness, and purity. Hence, in becoming the "Patron Saint of Jamaica Queens," he loses his own subjectivity, Indigenous identity, and histories. In this way, his sainthood works to delegitimize the daily struggles, as an undocumented Indigenous migrant in New York, that forced him to live in such precarity. In fact, his death can no longer be rendered as a loss, since sainthood grants him a holy life.[14] Ultimately, though well intentioned, the song's reproduction of these humanistic narratives deny any political and social responsibility for Tale Yax's precarious life and death. It also successfully extinguishes his Maya identity and presence.

The video that accompanies the song uses the widely circulated images and settler discourses employed by U.S. media outlets, reproducing a color photo of a smiling Tale Yax wearing blue jeans and a white sweatshirt, the black-and-white surveillance video, newspaper headlines, and footage at his funeral. The incorporation of these news clips frames the music video as exhibiting a social reality, in which the injustice, inequality, and oppression that Maya migrants experience is not challenged. The song ends with the dedication "For Hugo." The omission of his last name produces a false familiarity and closeness. Moreover, it further erases the unassimilable traces of his indigeneity and uproots him from his ancestors and community. Hence, the song assures an anxious U.S. nativist population that Tale Yax's life and the graphic depiction of his murder do not disrupt American ideals and self-image; rather, the song is used, like the news articles, to reinforce them.

Marcos Perla's video, simply titled "Hugo Alfredo Talé Yax," is almost five minutes long (Perla 2012). It was published on May 8, 2012 and, with

124 views as of December 2020, is the second most viewed. In the description, Perla notes that the music video is about a "Guatemalteco valiente" (brave Guatemalan). The names of the singer and writer of the song are not provided. The video begins with a black background and yellow lettering that references the date Tale Yax was murdered, April 18, 2010, as well as the location, Jamaica, Queens, New York. The Spanish subtitles note that the song and video tell "una historia basada en hechos reales," a story based on real events. Many of the subtitles either do not adequately translate the lyrics or omit them, creating a different narrative for the video's Spanish-speaking audience. For instance, the first line that introduces the song, "Hugo Alfredo Tale-Yax earns his community nickname, 'The Homeless Hero,'" is not translated to Spanish, which erases the hero trope sustained in the English version.

Presented as the social reality faced by many, presumably Latina/o, immigrants, the reenactments focus not only on Tale Yax's murder but also on his departure from Guatemala to the United States. The visual frames that begin the video are shots of a tranquil rocky river, which supposedly represents the Maya highlands. Like the news reports and Daugherty's song, Perla also erases Tale Yax's Indigenous identity as he is represented wearing emblematic western clothing: dark brown Stetson hat, a white, long-sleeved dress shirt, and blue jeans. The performer's solitary presence in the pristine natural landscape conjures popular images of westward migration for U.S. viewers. This westernization of Tale Yax's life reproduces settler practices that vanish Indigenous peoples' presence and histories.

While in Perla's music video Tale Yax is not personified as a saint, he continues to be a tragic (American) hero. The song's first verse depicts him as a good person with a strong work ethic and who, like so many others, aspires to achieve the American Dream. The emphasis on his goodness is defined by an unyielding commitment to working and providing for others. Additionally, the ability to fulfill his role as provider is only possible "here," which is understood as the United States, since the lines that follow suggest he migrates for the opportunity to start a new, prosperous life. The lyrics are accompanied by a luminous image of New York City's Times Square to visually project the American ethos. This emphasis on the American Dream constructs the United States as a pastoral nation-state that provides protection and hope for poor migrants. In doing so, the lyrics and images employed in the video obscure the United States' violent history, particularly against Indigenous peoples and the racialized poor of the Global South.

Tale Yax's ability to work hard is cemented throughout the first half of the song. The lyrics bolster the migrant's manual work as a carpenter and day laborer. Thus, they evoke not only familiar tropes of the American Dream but also popular images that depict poor racialized migrants as mere extensions of the gears of production, who "do the work Americans don't want" to do but need done. The verse that follows normalizes the structural violence that produced Tale Yax's social death, casting his multiple losses as the universal hard times many people face. Hence, the recognition of the migrant's precarious conditions takes place only within standardized national narratives that generalize these struggles to deracialize and depoliticize them. The hero status attributed to the Maya migrant is only possible because his last sacrifice serves to reinforce familiar American narratives. The song's depiction of the migrant as a "broken man," whose "last act" was to save someone he did not know, cements Tale Yax's role as the humble and victimized immigrant whose place in the United States is to serve others (family, employers, and nation). In this way, his subjectivity is erased as he is reduced to servitude and satisfying the needs of others. The historical transgenerational violence he and his people have endured since colonialism is normalized.

Though these tribute music videos intend to honor and remember Tale Yax's life, they continue to reproduce U.S. dominant narratives that mask the settler violence that produced the Maya migrant's precarious life and murder. The hero status that the music videos ascribe to Tale Yax comes at a high cost since it is contingent on his physical death and victimization, as well as the erasure of his Indigenous ancestry. Additionally, in the videos his body continues to be regarded as dominated. They represent his life as solely bound to servitude, and in death, he becomes the material from which the U.S. public can reaffirm normative ideals, values, and myths. Ultimately, the artists' good intentions are limited by the varied ways in which their music videos replicate standard liberal narratives employed by the media. In other words, the reproduction of these representations, including the video depicting Tale Yax's agonizing final hour, project a colonial gaze that frames unequal regimes of power as existing naturally.

Broadcasting Maya Deaths on the Borderlands

On May 23, 2018, a resident of Laredo, Texas, Marta Martínez, made a video recording on her cell phone of the fatal shooting of twenty-year-old Claudia Patricia Gómez González (Mam) by a Border Patrol agent in Rio Bravo, Texas. The video aimed to document the violence faced by migrants attempting to cross the U.S.-Mexican border. Its extensive circulation on social media made the border crossings of Indigenous women migrants more visible to a global public. Likewise, on December 5, 2019, the independent news source *ProPublica* released surveillance footage of sixteen-year-old Carlos Gregorio Hernández Vásquez (Achi). The footage was taken while the teen was in U.S. Immigration and Customs Enforcement (ICE) custody. It shows

Hernández Vásquez in agony in his cell before succumbing to the flu and complications from other infections. Similar to the cases of Tale Yax and Gómez González, authorization from the teen's parents was never solicited by *ProPublica* and other media outlets that circulated the excruciating video. His family in the small town of San José El Rodeo, Cubulco, Baja Verapaz, witnessed his dreadful final moments online as did thousands of people who never met the teen. Like the surveillance video that recorded Tale Yax's murder and the footage of Gómez González's fatal shooting, the video released by *ProPublica* of the teen's final moments in ICE custody also produced global public shock. Yet the outcry after witnessing the loss of a human life in "real" time only created an ephemeral affective response of outrage and confusion that has not been transformed into effective political engagement.

This lack of political action is intrinsically linked to the colonial gaze that often frames the precarious lives and deaths of Maya migrants. As my analysis of the news reports and tribute YouTube music videos on Tale Yax's murder illustrates, the erasure of these material and historical contexts reinforces violent global mechanisms that disavow Mayas "the status of living" (Holland 2000, 15). For instance, three months after Gómez González's murder, the *Washington Post* reported that state and international institutions, including the U.S. Agency for International Development (USAID) and the United Nations, suggested that Mayas, like Claudia Patricia Gómez González, Hugo Alfredo Tale Yax, Carlos Gregorio Hernández Vásquez, and the countless unnamed Mayas who have died in ICE custody, or attempting to cross the U.S.-Mexican border, migrate in high numbers to the United States because of "hunger and not violence" (Miroff and Sieff 2018). The erasure of the enduring legacies of the genocide, which produce hunger and forced displacements, continues to situate Maya Guatemalan refugees as economic immigrants. In doing so, these discursive framings simultaneously eradicate Indigenous histories and presence. At the same time, they reinforce settler colonialism as evidenced by the media and the public taking an interest only when the agonizing deaths of Maya migrants become globally viewed. The lives of Maya migrants and the multifaceted contributions they make to U.S. and Guatemalan societies never go viral; nor are they considered newsworthy. Ultimately, these framings and erasures illustrate the ways in which the humanity of Indigenous peoples continues to be denied, thus disavowing their right to life.

NOTES

1. Scholarship on the Maya diaspora has concentrated on the economic reasons for migration and the creation of hometown associations, patron saint festivities, and religious organizations (Hamilton and Stoltz Chinchilla 2001; LeBaron 2012; Loucky and Moors 2000; Popkin 1999, 2005).

2. On coffee prices and migration, see Sieff 2019; Arroyo and Contreras 2018; and Leutert 2018. Articles that emphasize the American Dream include Córdoba 2019; La Jeunesse 2018; and Reuters 2018.

3. According to the Archdiocese of Guatemala's human rights report *Guatemala: Never Again!* (1999), the United States backed the Guatemalan Armed Forces with financial assistance, weapons, and training of officers in counterinsurgency techniques.

4. General Ríos Montt maintained close ties to the United States throughout his military career and dictatorship. In 1951, he attended the School of the Americas in Fort Benning, Georgia. He also had very close connections with U.S. evangelical Christians and former president Ronald Reagan (Nolan 2018).

5. About a thousand Maya peasant activists gathered at the central plaza in Panzós to meet with the mayor, Walter Overdick, and discuss enduring land disputes. Overdick, who was known for (il)legally taking property that belonged to Maya families, did not meet with the peasants. A dispute arose and a military unit arrived in the area. Soldiers surrounded the crowd, eventually opening fire. The number of Mayas killed is unknown. Many wounded people died running to the mountains; others were shot as they fled. Official estimates suggest that about fifty-three people including women, children, and the well-known Maya activist Mamá Maquín, or Adelina Caal Maquín, were among the dead. For Maya studies scholars, the Panzós massacre initiated the genocidal process that reached its height in the 1980s.

6. In *Turning the Tide: U.S. Intervention in Central America and the Struggle for Peace* (1985) and *Necessary Illusions: Thought Control in Democratic Societies* (2013), Noam Chomsky illustrates the complicity of the media in covering violent U.S. policies and military actions that have killed thousands of peoples in the region and ultimately forced thousands more to continue fleeing their countries of origin. Similarly, Leigh Binford provides a parallel analysis on El Salvador in *The El Mozote Massacre: Human Rights and Global Implications* (2016).

7. A search on Nexis Uni, formerly LexisNexis, for "Guatemalan Genocide" and "Guatemala Genocide," showed that between 1982 and 1996 only thirty-four articles appeared in English, with several published by the BBC. A search for "Mayan Genocide" produced only four articles between 1994 and 1996.

8. The systemic erasure of their Indigenous identity is evident in official statistics that fail to record the number of Maya migrants from Guatemala who live in the United States, as well as those who have been deported, detained, or murdered at the U.S.-Mexico border.

9. Though twenty-year-old Claudia Patricia Gómez González (Mam, May 23, 2018) did not die in ICE custody like the children, she was fatally shot by a Customs and Border Protection (CBP) agent at the Rio Bravo, near Laredo, Texas.

10. The newspaper articles about Tale Yax's death that I examine in this chapter were published between April 24 and June 24, 2010.

11. Unless otherwise noted, all translations are mine.

12. As of June 15, 2020, the video had 5,657 views, illustrating its limited accessibility.

13. "The Patron Saint of Jamaica Queens" words and music by Luke Austin Daugherty. Copyright 2010 Luke Austin Daugherty. All rights reserved. Lyrics used with permission from Luke Austin Daugherty.

14. A parallel example can be drawn with Archbishop Óscar Arnulfo Romero. While many Salvadorans celebrated his canonization on October 14, 2018, others said

that the official proclamation of Romero's sainthood involved a co-option and sanitation of his radical denunciations of the violent inequalities produced by capitalism. In the United States, similar claims have been made about Dr. Martin Luther King, who many argue has also been sanctified as a way of reducing his revolutionary ideas to universal humanistic beliefs that reinforce neoliberal multiculturalism.

REFERENCES

Archdiocese of Guatemala. 1999. *Guatemala, Never Again!* Maryknoll, NY: Orbis Books; CIIR; Latin America Bureau.

Arias, Roberto. 2010. "Indiferencia en Queens, Nueva York." *La Hora*, May 8. https://lahora.gt/hemeroteca-lh/indiferencia-en-queens-nueva-york.

Arroyo, Lorena, and Andrea Patiño Contreras. 2018. "The Great Guatemalan Migration Industry." *Univision*. https://www.univision.com/especiales/noticias/2018/the-great -guatemalan-migration-industry/.

Associated Press. 2019. "680 People Arrested as Part of Largest US Immigration Raids in a Decade." *Chattanooga Times Free Press*, August 7. https://www.timesfreepress .com/news/breakingnews/story/2019/aug/07/immigration-raids-under-way -mississippi-food-plants/500669/.

Binford, Leigh. 2016. *The El Mozote Massacre: Human Rights and Global Implications.* Rev. ed. Tucson: University of Arizona Press.

Butler, Judith. 2016. *Frames of War: When Is Life Grievable?* London: Verso.

Chomsky, Noam. 2013. *Necessary Illusions: Thought Control in Democratic Societies.* Toronto: House of Anansi Books.

———. 2015. *Turning the Tide: U.S. Intervention in Central America and the Struggle for Peace.* Chicago: Haymarket Books.

Córdoba, José de. 2019. "The Guatemalan City Fueling the Migrant Exodus to America." *Wall Street Journal*, July 21. https://www.wsj.com/articles/the-guatemalan-city -fueling-the-migrant-exodus-to-america-11563738141.

Daugherty, Luke Austin. 2014. "'The Patron Saint of Jamaica Queens' Music Video—a Tribute to Hugo Alfredo Tale-Yax." *YouTube*, April 27. https://www.youtube.com/ watch?v=HRrXVMCyG7s&t=88s.

De Genova, Nicholas. 2005. *Working the Boundaries: Race, Space, and "Illegality" in Mexican Chicago.* Durham, NC: Duke University Press.

Estrada, Alicia Ivonne. 2021. "Weaving Strategies of Survival: Maya Women's Activism in the Diaspora." In *Violence and Indigenous Communities: Confronting the Past and Engaging the Present*, edited by Susan Sleeper-Smith, Jeffrey Ostler, and Joshua L. Reid, 297–312. Evanston, IL: Northwestern University Press.

Foucault, Michel. 1981. "The Order of Discourse." In *Untying the Text: A Post-structuralist Reader*, edited by Robert Young, 51–78. London: Routledge and Kegan Paul.

Galperin, Hernan. 2017. "Why Are Half of Latin Americans Not Online? A Four-Country Study of Reasons for Internet Nonadoption." *International Journal of Communication* 11 (2017): 3332–3354.

Gramlich, John, and Luis Noe-Bustamante. 2019. "What's Happening at the U.S.-Mexico Border in 5 Charts." Pew Research Center, November 1. https://www.pew research.org/fact-tank/2019/11/01/whats-happening-at-the-u-s-mexico-border-in -5-charts/.

Grandin, Greg. 2004. *The Last Colonial Massacre: Latin America in the Cold War*. Chicago: University of Chicago Press.

Hamilton, Nora, and Norma Stoltz Chinchilla. 2001. *Seeking Community in a Global City: Guatemalans and Salvadorans in Los Angeles*. Philadelphia: Temple University Press.

Holland, Sharon Patricia. 2000. *Raising the Dead: Readings of Death and (Black) Subjectivity*. Durham, NC: Duke University Press.

Hutchison, Courtney. 2010. "Why Homeless Hero Hugo Alfredo Tale-Yax Died on NYC Street." *ABC News*, April 28. https://abcnews.go.com/Health/Wellness/dying-good-samaritan-hugo-alfredo-tale-yax-symptom/story?id=10488434.

La Jeunesse, William. 2018. "Migrant Caravan Grabs for American Dream, as Immigrants Forge Unique Challenge for US, Mexico." *Fox News*, October 21. https://www.foxnews.com/world/migrant-caravan-grabs-for-american-dream-as-immigrants-forge-unique-challenge-for-us-mexico.

LeBaron, Alan. 2012. "When Latinos Are Not Latinos: The Case of Guatemalan Maya in the United States, the Southeast and Georgia." *Latino Studies Journal* 10 (1–2): 179–195.

Leutert, Stephanie. 2018. "Why Are So Many Migrants Leaving Guatemala? A Crisis in the Coffee Industry Is One Reason." *Time*, July 27. https://time.com/5346110/guatemala-coffee-escape-migration/.

Loucky, James, and Marilyn M. Moors, eds. 2000. *Maya Diaspora: Guatemalan Roots, New American Lives*. Philadelphia: Temple University Press.

Martínez Salazar, Egla. 2012. *Global Coloniality of Power in Guatemala: Racism, Genocide, Citizenship*. Lanham, MD: Lexington Books.

McAllister, Carlota, and Diane M. Nelson. 2013. *War by Other Means: Aftermath in Post-genocide Guatemala*. Durham, NC: Duke University Press.

McKinnon, Sara L. 2016. *Gendered Asylum: Race and Violence in U.S. Law and Politics*. Urbana: University of Illinois Press.

Merrin, William. 2012. "Still Fighting 'the Beast': Guerrilla Television and the Limits of YouTube." *Cultural Politics* 8 (1): 97–119.

Miroff, Nick, and Kevin Sieff. 2018. "Hunger, Not Violence, Fuels Guatemalan Migration Surge, U.S. Says." *Washington Post*, September 22. https://www.washingtonpost.com/world/national-security/hunger-not-violence-fuels-guatemalan-migration-surge-us-says/2018/09/21/65c6a546-bdb3-11e8-be70-52bd11fe18af_story.html.

Mohan, Neal. 2017. "A New YouTube Look That Works for You." *YouTube Official Blog*, August 29. https://blog.youtube/news-and-events/a-new-youtube-look-that-works-for-you.

Nelson, Diane M. 2015. *Who Counts? The Mathematics of Death and Life after Genocide*. Durham, NC: Duke University Press.

Noe-Bustamante, Luis, Antonio Flores, and Sono Shah. 2019. "Facts on Hispanics of Guatemalan Origin in the United States, 2017." Pew Research Center, September 16. https://www.pewresearch.org/hispanic/fact-sheet/u-s-hispanics-facts-on-guatemalan-origin-latinos/.

Nolan, Rachel. 2018. "Ríos Montt, the Evangelist." North American Congress on Latin America, April 24. https://nacla.org/news/2018/04/24/r%C3%ADos-montt-evangelist.

O'Connor, Allison, Jeanne Batalova, and Jessica Bolter. 2019. "Central American Immigrants in the United States." Migration Policy Institute, August 15. https://www

.migrationpolicy.org/article/central-american-immigrants-united-states
-2017.

O'Neill, Kevin Lewis, and Kedron Thomas. 2011. *Securing the City: Neoliberalism, Space, and Insecurity in Postwar Guatemala.* Durham, NC: Duke University Press.

Perla, Marcos. 2012. "Hugo Alfredo Talé Yax." *YouTube,* May 8. https://www.youtube.com/watch?v=tTUVfYWcNWY.

Popkin, Eric. 1999. "Guatemalan Mayan Migration to Los Angeles: Constructing Transnational Linkages in the Context of the Settlement Process." *Ethnic and Racial Studies* 22 (2): 267–289.

———. 2005. "The Emergence of Pan-Mayan Ethnicity in the Guatemalan Transnational Community Linking Santa Eulalia and Los Angeles." *Current Sociology* 53 (4): 675–706.

Prensa Libre. 2010. "Familia de héroe guatemalteco llora su muerte." *YouTube,* April 28. https://www.youtube.com/watch?v=EgECt1x80Ho.

Reuters. 2018. "Deadly Crossing Ends American Dream for Guatemalan Migrant." *ABC News,* November 17. https://abcnews.go.com/International/deadly-crossing-ends-american-dream-guatemalan-migrant/story?id=59243100.

Rios, Simón. 2017. "'A Day of Anguish': Workers, Agents Recall State's Biggest Immigration Raid." *WBUR News,* March 6. https://www.wbur.org/news/2017/03/06/new-bedford-immigration-raid.

Santos, Fernanda. 2010. "Here to Aid His Family, Left to Die on the Street." *New York Times,* April 27. https://www.nytimes.com/2010/04/28/nyregion/28laborer.html.

Schiwy, Freya. 2009. *Indianizing Film: Decolonization, the Andes, and the Question of Technology.* New Brunswick, NJ: Rutgers University Press.

Sieff, Kevin. 2019. "The Migration Problem Is a Coffee Problem." *Washington Post,* June 11. https://www.washingtonpost.com/world/2019/06/11/falling-coffee-prices-drive-guatemalan-migration-united-states/.

Simons, Marlise. 2007. "Guatemala: Peasant Massacre." North American Congress on Latin America, September 25. https://nacla.org/article/guatemala-peasant-massacre.

Sulzberger, A. G., and Mick Meenan. 2010. "Questions Surround a Delay in Help for a Dying Man." *New York Times,* April 25. https://www.nytimes.com/2010/04/26/nyregion/26homeless.html.

Susman, Tina. 2010. "Questions after Homeless Man's Lonely Death." *Los Angeles Times,* May 11. https://www.latimes.com/archives/la-xpm-2010-may-11-la-na-stabbing-20100511-story.html.

Volpp, Leti. 2015. "The Indigenous as Alien." *UC Irvine Law Review* 5 (289): 289–325.

WBUR. 2018. "'What Did It Achieve?' Documentary Examines Largest Immigration Raid in U.S. History." *Here and Now,* July 30. https://www.wbur.org/hereandnow/2018/07/30/postville-iowa-immigration-raid-documentary.

Weld, Kristen. 2014. *Paper Cadavers: The Archive of Dictatorship in Guatemala.* Durham, NC: Duke University Press.

3

Proprietors of Death

An Ethnography of the 2019 San Antonio Border Security Expo

Marianne Madoré
Nicholas Rodrigo

I n March 2019, San Antonio, Texas, hosted its Thirteenth Border Security Expo, an annual gathering of experts and practitioners in border enforcement, surveillance, and policing. Over the years, the Border Security Expo has become an important meeting for government officials and contractors who come to attend keynotes, participate in networking events, and learn about the latest weapons and equipment. As researchers concerned with the execution of state power against noncitizens, we took the opportunity at the San Antonio Border Security Expo to gain a rare insight into the current debates agitating the complex nexus of state and nonstate actors tasked with inflicting structural violence on undocumented migrants. In a video posted online, Tom Winkowski, the Border Security Expo chair and a former Immigration and Customs Enforcement (ICE) deputy assistant secretary and Customs and Border Protection (CBP) acting commissioner, had announced, "This year's event is shaping up to be the best yet" (Border Security Expo 2019a). So, in March 2019 we entered the Henry B. Gonzalez Convention Center in San Antonio to document what we saw. Over the course of three days, we found ourselves in the company of high-ranking officials from the Department of Homeland Security, private security contractors, and Border Patrol agents.

From the Strategic Roundtables to the Night-Vision Goggles: Three Days at the Border Security Expo

The Border Security Expo occupied the two exhibit halls of the convention center. One had been turned into a conference room with approximately two hundred chairs in front of the speaker stage. These chairs were stocked with numerous uniformed men, mostly white and with crew cuts, from the Department of Homeland Security (DHS). The website announced that representatives of the Nigeria Police Force, the Kuwait Ministry of Defense, and Public Safety Canada would be in attendance as well. Flanking either side of the stage was the star-spangled banner. Keynotes were conducted by senior officials from CBP, ICE, and the U.S. Border Patrol, with other bureaucrats speaking on panels with frighteningly innocuous titles like "Mass Migration and Unaccompanied Children: Financial and National Security Impacts," "Model Ports: How Technology, Public Private Partnerships, and Innovation Will Continue to Change the Way Ports-of-Entry Operate," and "Procurement: Keeping Industry Current in the Complex Area of Government Procurement and the Mission Needs of Border Operators." The catering company had installed a coffee station in the back, and its staff—mostly Black and Latina women—refilled the sugar and pastries.

In the second exhibit hall, vendors set up their booths to form a strip of parallel alleys labeled A to G, creating a marketplace-like aesthetic. The heavyweight companies such as Lockheed Martin, the British BAE Systems, the Israeli Elbit Systems, and the French Airbus Helicopters imposed their presence through intimidating stands with observation balloons and terrain-piercing cameras on full show. However, the majority of the vendors were smaller companies: cutting-edge start-ups like OWL (Observation without Limits) and Innovative Algorithms LLC, many of them staffed by skinny-jean-clad nerds with expensively framed specs and stylish desert boots. Other independent businesses were staffed by retired military personnel selling military-grade equipment for border enforcement. "Does this detect uranium?" we overheard a man wearing a suit ask at a stall selling advanced port-of-entry X-ray equipment. Between the vendors, we also found the stand of the Border Patrol Foundation, where a hostess sold tickets for the golf tournament, the Annual Night of Commemoration at the Alamo, and the Annual Sharpshooter Contest at the Bandera Gun Club. A few meters away, the University of Houston, Texas, presented its Center of Excellence, whose mission is to "secure the borders" and "facilitate legitimate trade and travel." We were struck by the collegial atmosphere, the smiles and nods, which after a few hours seemed rhythmic in their consistency.

Notes on Methods: How to Conduct an Ethnography in Haunted Terrain?

Studying the policies and practices of law enforcement agencies poses a question of access. The possibilities for embedded participant observation among Border Patrol agents have been limited to scholars whose objective was to praise their patriotism and their practices (see, for instance, Maril 2004, 14). Many scholars have creatively gotten around this initial deterrent by diving into the archival records of the Border Patrol (Barrera 2003; Hernandez 2010). In search of a point of entry, we came across the site of the Border Security Expo in San Antonio, which provided a space to study the dispositions and perspectives of those tasked with enforcing the border. Theodore Baird's ethnographic study of border security fairs in Europe has established the importance of these events as sites where commercial and governmental agents share information, experiences, and practices, but also where new practical norms are set (Baird 2017, 195–197).

At the Border Security Expo, we alternated between moments of strategic observation (one of us observed a well-attended keynote while the other took advantage of the deserted alleys to speak with vendors) and moments of wandering. Our ethnographic approach took inspiration from sociologist Avery Gordon's theorization of the unseen that haunts us. In *Ghostly Matters*, haunting is defined as a mediation:

> the process that links an institution and an individual, a social structure and a subject, and history and a biography. In haunting, organized forces and systemic structures that appeared removed from us make their impact felt in everyday life in a way that confounds our analytic separations and confounds the social separations themselves. (Gordon 2008, 19)

Following Gordon, we designed our inquiry into the Border Security Expo to be attentive to the unseen. Gordon argues that in contemporary culture, "seemingly ruled by technologies of hypervisibility, we are led to believe . . . that everything can be seen" (2008, 16). This observation adequately captures the atmosphere of the Border Security Expo, saturated with visibility technology: long-distance radars, surveillance cameras, night-vision goggles, and thermal sensors. We took detailed field notes and several photographs and reported our observations to each other on a regular basis, but along with Gordon, we acknowledge that our careful note-taking of the visible interactions between the Border Security Expo protagonists accounts for only part of the story. Gordon's insistence that attention must be paid to the "ghostly matters" allows us to formulate questions about what we did not see but nonetheless was present: "the persistent and troubling ghosts in the house" (2008, 8). This framework allows us to consider the desires and political forces beyond the actual physical space of the Border Security Expo. It invites us to draw connections between the keynotes and the history of San Antonio as a site of colonial conquest, or between the humanitarian policies of the DHS and the demographic management of colonial subjects.

Under Scrutiny: The Border Security Expo and Its Two-Fold Strategy for (Re)Gaining Legitimacy

The distance between the corporate settings of the Border Security Expo and the everyday hardships of migrants who attempt to cross the U.S.-Mexico border undetected was stark. Only a few months earlier, in December 2018, an Indigenous child from Guatemala, Jakelin Caal Maquin, had died from a bacterial infection while in Border Patrol custody in west Texas (Merchant 2019). Later on, in the spring of 2019, the Border Patrol station of Clint saw mass outbreaks of scabies, shingles, and smallpox (Romero et al. 2019). This violence has not been limited to anecdotal occurrences. Since the introduction of the policy of Prevention through Deterrence (PTD) under the Clinton administration, the U.S. Border Patrol has reported the death of 7,505 people in the Southwest border sectors.[1]

The specter of death at the U.S.-Mexico border has received heightened attention over the course of Donald Trump's presidency, particularly from liberal commentators eager to depict this administration as exceptionally evil in its treatment of undocumented migrants. Critics also emanated from within the ranks of the Border Patrol when a few agents resigned from their position and published fierce accusations of border enforcement practices.[2] In this chapter, we endeavor to understand how border enforcement strategists and agents have reacted to these partisan critiques and the risk of demobilization. In the context of heightened criticism, what have been the strategies that uphold the state-sanctioned violent practices of border enforcement? The central thesis of this chapter is that U.S. border enforcement has adopted a humanitarian strategy to reinforce the legitimacy of its military mandate, and has manufactured an esprit de corps among Border Patrol Agents to keep them driven and dedicated.

The next section of this chapter examines the discourse and practices of humanitarian governance, embedded within contemporary racial typologies of undocumented migrants, which legitimate militarized border practices in the context of mounting criticism from liberal news outlets and elected representatives. This ad hoc discourse promotes the idea that CBP is saving the migrants from death and rescuing them from heartless smugglers, which also helps the agencies plead for resources. However, this public-facing humanitarian turn does not suffice to address the Border Patrol agents' own doubts or hesitations about the rightness of their mission. Then we turn our attention to backstage practices of collective mourning and memorialization. Particularly, we explore the role of the U.S. pioneer imaginary in fostering mobilization within the Border Patrol and crafting a culture of sacrifice. The last section considers the implications of this twofold strategy we observed at the Border Security Expo.

Humanitarianism: Saving from Death

The social sciences literature on the U.S.-Mexico border has paid close attention to the topic of death, notably through the concept of the "state of exception" (Agamben 2005), and depicts the U.S.-Mexico border as a space where modalities of power suspend legal rights and create a state of carcelment (Dorsey and Díaz-Barriga 2015; Salter 2008; Sundberg 2015). Following Giorgio Agamben, Roxanne Doty (2011) argues that PTD has reduced migrants to "bare life," rendering their deaths of little consequence, framing the spatial context of their deaths as a moral alibi, and absolving policy makers and enforcement practitioners of complicity. The effects of border management have also been criticized within the framework of Michel Foucault's theory of governmentality and biopolitics (Nail 2013; Brendese 2014) and Achille Mbembe's addendum to Foucault's theory, necropolitics (Mbembe 2003; De León 2015). For Jason De León, PTD is necropower operationalized as it homes in on "the political afterlives of bodies," with the desert consuming the corpses of dead migrants (De León 2015, 68). De León frames the border as a battleground in the war on migrants, and PTD as a major weapon in the state's arsenal. Although the Border Security Expo's necrophile atmosphere was palpable, there was also a constant performative reference to the humanitarian actions of DHS agencies. In the the keynote speeches and individual conversations we had with border enforcement personnel, the mission of border enforcement was presented as not only defending the nation but also saving migrants from the mortal ravages of the border and their own ignorant decisions. To see the logic of the seemingly contradictory placement of killing technology alongside speeches extolling the humanitarianism of border enforcement, we look into the abundant critical literature on the borders of the European Union (EU) and the role of nongovernmental organizations.

Frontex, the EU agency tasked with enforcing the EU's borders, uses human rights and humanitarian language to both position itself as humanitarian intervener and build techniques to render the migrant more vulnerable. This creates a conduit between territorial security and humanitarism, reinforcing a mandate to militarize border enforcement (Léonard 2010; Perkowski 2018). Despite Frontex's public image as complicit in the migration crisis in the Mediterranean, humanitarian ideals feature prominently in the agency's internal discourse. Migrants at the border are "pathologized as victims needing humanitarian assistance" (Aas and Gundhus 2015, 12). This "humanitarian reasoning" shapes the bandwidth of biopolitical intervention, creating a "humanitarian governmentality" (Lippert 1999, 295; Fassin 2012, 145). This governmentality has allowed for demographic "figures of migration" to contribute to obscuring enforcement through pushing out the European borders to states outside of EU jurisdiction like Morocco and Turkey (Scheel and Ratfisch 2014, 924). The victimization of the refugee through the authoritarian character of humanitarian protection is a corollary of the delegitimization of the movement of the majority of the world's migrants, which is in turn built on their negative, the nation-state citizen and the sovereign order of nations. This perceived natural order of things allows refugees to become pathologized as targets requiring therapeutic interventions (Malkki 1996; see also Chapter 2). At the Border Security Expo, carefully curated statistics and pathologizing narratives were being deployed to shape a humanitarian mandate that needed moral and fiscal support from the state.

Demographic Threats and Opportunities: Building the Numbers for Humanitarian Governmentality

The social science of demography is not refined, perfected, or deployed within political vacuums (Hansen and Jonsson 2011). The use of seemingly innocuous numbers to document changes in migration patterns allows strategic opportunities for the presentation of the border as a liminal space in flux, with new humanitarian demands emerging in need of time-specific interventions. Take, for example, statements made as part of a keynote address during the conference by John P. Sanders, chief operating officer of Border Patrol, regarding the changing composition of border crossers at the Rio Grande:

> I just came from the RGB [Rio Grande Border]. . . . The change is hard to imagine if you just haven't been to some of the facilities. . . . In 2008, roughly 90 percent of the individuals who came across the border were from Mexico; up until 2011, 90 percent of the people who came across the border were single adults.

Single male adults from Mexico conjures up the historically held racialized image of the threatening illegal "wetback" coming to threaten the jobs and economic stability of U.S. citizenry, making securitized frameworks necessary (De Genova and Ramos-Zayas 2003; Kang 2017). In terms of apprehensions in 2019, Sanders noted that the numbers for February stood at the usual rate of 76,000, before projecting that apprehensions for March would increase to 100,000 (the actual number ended up being 103,731; see U.S. Customs and Border Protection 2019). Sanders went on to state:

> Of those 100,000 people, roughly 58,000—58 percent—are family units, so families with children. Of those 100,000, around 9,000 are unaccompanied minors. Of that 100,000, roughly, we are on track for roughly 35,000 of those individuals being children, and so when I get to the border, . . . not only are we overwhelmed by the sheer number of people, but it is the sheer number of children.

Border Patrol Deputy Chief Scott Luck additionally made comments on the increasing number of apprehensions: "Traffic is increasing; in just twenty-eight days in February we apprehended more than . . . 66,000 illegal aliens. So far this year we apprehended more than 337,000. That is 105 percent over what we were last year, and the numbers projected keep growing." Luck further hammered home Sanders's comment on the evolving developments regarding the types of groups arriving at the border, making reference to the so-called caravan phenomenon:[3]

> Another troubling trend is the emerging prevalence of groups of a hundred people or more; some groups, dubbed "caravans" by the media, number in the thousands. Ninety-nine percent of those are citizens of the Northern Triangle countries and fear to be returned home. So far, this fiscal year we have seen an unprecedented rise of these large groups—92 as of yesterday [late March], compared to just 13 in all fiscal year of 2018.

Situating these increasing numbers alongside demographic shifts provides nourishment to a narrative of humanitarian governmental practices that decontextualizes more macro forces, such as the U.S. imperial policy in the Global South and a U.S. labor market increasingly dependent on hyperexploitable labor. Most fundamentally, the positivism of statistics is used to prime the claims of legitimacy for resource requests and elides the link between the border management apparatus and heightened mortality risks faced by migrants.

A Plea for Resources

The opening keynote, delivered by then-acting director of ICE Ron Vitiello, touched on the separation of children at the border but omitted discussion of the children's conditions and DHS's complicity. Vitiello said that DHS sees,

> each and every day in that space, large numbers of unaccompanied children and families bringing their children to the border, in dire conditions as it relates to their health and well-being, and sacrifices and the risks they take on this journey. They come to the border [with] all manner of difficulties, both physically and emotionally . . . and CBP is forced to deal with those scenarios inside of resources that they don't have. The stations that I worked in in my entire career are not built to house children, even for that short amount of time that they need to be booked in and transferred out. In hindsight it is a terrible scenario in . . . the way it is operationalized, and [as a result of] subsequent court cases that have been lost . . . [by] the government, we cannot keep families in detention. There is not enough space.

Vitiello's statement not only elides PTD's role in forcing migrants into deadly border terrains; it also associates the traumatic experiences of encaged children with the financial drain on DHS from lost lawsuits. Undergirding this argument is a plea for resources so that DHS can adequately conduct the pastoral elements of its work.

In a panel concerning procurement and the need for the industry to engage in the "mission needs of border operators," the technical requirements of CBP were laid out. Diane Sahakian from the office of acquisition at CBP stated:

> We buy diapers. We buy formula. We buy medicines, snacks. We buy tacos. We buy everything. Clothes, flip-flops. It's basically taking care of people. We have to hire people to change diapers and things like that—because if we don't do that, the agents have to do it, and that's not what they signed up for.

Here, Sahakian is making a direct appeal for more staff and an expanded recruitment pool to administer the care elements of border enforcement; she is making overtures for on-the-ground resources and extra personnel for this task of meeting material needs. The agents have not "signed up for" humanitarianism, and thus their actions to meet humanitarian needs further reinforce the heroic image they are trying to construct. Key here is a colonial patriarchy perspective that is shaped by the need to intervene to protect the migrants from themselves, completely erasing the context of their conditions rooted in precarious militarized borders (Miller 2019). This grants border enforcement validity in the eyes of liberal lawmakers and policy wonks. This is further reinforced when these humanitarian needs are placed alongside more deviant behavior. During his speech at the expo, Scott Luck commented:

> Border Patrol budget analysts estimate that 13 percent of our operational budget is directed into transportation, medical expenses, diapers, food, and other necessities to care for illegal aliens. Now, you heard yesterday from the chief operating officer that Congress [has passed] the [20]19 [spending] bill . . . [that includes funds for] humanitarian efforts that help us in this fight, and we are certainly grateful for that. Four hundred forty-five million dollars will help us with medical support, transportation, consumables, and the creation of centralized processing centers.

Scott seamlessly links budgetary statistics to operational demands of humanitarianism while referring to legislation as key to facilitating the expansion and development of this process. One would expect these demands to be separate from those of defending the nation from criminal enterprises, but immediately after his comment on humanitarianism, Scott stated:

> Cartels and other transnational criminal organizations, or TCOs, are aggressive, ruthless, and opportunistic. They also watch TV. Our intel efforts advise us that they know where and when these groups arrive in Mexico. They also know that every agent tasked with taking care of a child or family can't remain as the only impediment to their efforts in human trafficking, kidnapping, narcotics and weapons smuggling, and extortion, [so they are] occupying agents by convincing people to cross in remote areas with limited resources and infrastructure, making an easier path and profit for them.

This image of the Border Patrol saving migrants from death has multiple iterations, from the pastoral care provided to migrants picked up at the border after running the gauntlet of the barren border zone to the interdiction of nonstate actors exploiting the situation for nefarious ends. The need for resources in pursuit of the enforcement of the border is also predicated on the maintenance of the emotional well-being of the country's citizens.

Vitiello made this quite clear in response to a question concerning congressional budgets for bed space:

> The funding levels for where we're at are just not adequate, and without making any statements that are political, the American public has for a very long time asked for the border to be secured. I don't think there is any doubt . . . that we are in a situation where there is a lot of enthusiasm for that, and the public dialogue certainly in this administration requires resource levels that just aren't there yet.

In these few sentences, Vitiello triangulates DHS's need for resources with a perceived preexisting public support for border enforcement—and the Trump administration's appeasing of that support. Far from making a statement that is not political, Vitiello is placing DHS as a key facilitator of American democracy. The plea for resources is about not only preventing deaths but also allowing the full realization of the American democratic process. The humanitarian governmentality of the Border Patrol is sold as a performer of saviorism not only for undocumented migrants but also for American democracy and the biopolitical well-being of U.S. citizens in the American political project.

Memories and Sacrifice: The Fabrication of an Esprit de Corps

In addition to the liberal outcry against their practices, border enforcement agencies must also confront the risk of distrust and demobilization within their ranks. In June 2019, ex–Border Patrol agent Jenn Budd wrote an open letter to her former colleagues to encourage them to question some of their methods:

> I mean, you didn't really sign up to put babies in cages and babysit them . . . am I right? . . . When your Field Operations Supervisor (FOS) demands you throw away all the belongings and medicine of those in your custody, you are aware that some men, women and children may die because of your actions. . . . How do you think your family will see you? How do you think your community will view your actions? What do you imagine your relationship with your children to be like after you develop post-traumatic stress disorder from the things you are currently doing and seeing? (Budd 2019)

This letter expresses her resentment against the leadership for tainting the Border Patrol's motto, "Honor First." This bitterness seems widespread. In September 2019, a *New York Times* article titled "'People Actively Hate Us':

Inside the Border Patrol's Morale Crisis" gathered testimonies of frustrated Border Patrol agents. The assistant chief patrol agent for El Centro Sector confided, "The agents feel very demoralized by politicians and the media. . . . I would be lying if I said that those perceptions do not have an impact . . . on us" (Fernandez et al. 2019).

In San Antonio, the Border Security Expo took these concerns seriously. Whereas some of the panels attracted mostly high-ranking officers and security contractors, many aspects of the Border Security Expo were geared toward the entry-level border enforcement agents. The program of the Border Security Expo featured a range of events to address their concerns.

The Ghosts of the Alamo

On the first day of the Border Security Expo, two women representing the Border Patrol Foundation (BPF) were selling tickets for the evening fundraiser event at Fort Alamo: the Fourth Annual Night at the Alamo. Founded in 2009 by a DHS executive and a senior Border Patrol officer, the BPF regularly organizes events to "honor the memory of U.S. Border Patrol agents," "who risk their lives daily protecting our Nation's borders" (Border Patrol Foundation, n.d.c, n.d.b). As of December 2019, the BPF had raised over $1.5 million from its donors. The Alamo Mission—only a short walking distance from the convention center—was built for the Spanish Roman Catholic colonizers during the early eighteenth century. Its complex history is often subsumed into the iconic Battle of the Alamo.[4] The episode has appeared in songs, books, and films that popularized the idea that the cruelty of General Santa Anna during the Battle of the Alamo compelled many Texans to join the Texan Army and seek revenge, which ultimately led to the Battle of San Jacinto and the retreat of the Mexican troops from Texas. Today Fort Alamo welcomes visitors year-round. Through a curated display of military artifacts, the site narrates the patriotism of the Texan soldiers. The BPF had chosen this highly evocative historical site to celebrate its agents. As anthropologist Michel-Rolph Trouillot remarked, the story of the Alamo has been disputed locally. In San Antonio, activists and residents have asked:

> Is that battle a moment of glory during which freedom-loving Anglos, outnumbered but undaunted, spontaneously chose to fight until death rather than surrender to a corrupt Mexican dictator? Or is it a brutal example of U.S. expansionism, the story of a few white predators taking over what was sacred territory and half-willingly providing, with their death, the alibi for a well-planned annexation? (Trouillot 2001, 9)

The Border Security Expo presented the Alamo as the birthplace of U.S. patriotism and effectively silenced counternarratives. As guests trickled in past the fortification walls and to the gardens, the employees of the catering company offered appetizers and cold drinks. A DJ was playing folk and country music. Guests began introducing their spouses and children to each other. They had changed their clothes to more casual outfits. A stage had been set up, and the evening began with an eight-year-old girl, the daughter of a "great fallen Border Patrol agent," singing the U.S. anthem a cappella to a captivated audience. A long round of applause followed the performance. The host, standing on the stage next to the child with the pink dress, encouraged the audience's fervor and requested more applause. The appeal of this patriotic performance was remarkably strong. Throughout the evening, the speakers seemed to belong to a tight-knit family of patriots whose mission is to continue to hold the line as the early Texan pioneers did.

Following Greg Grandin's analysis of the emergence and demise of the myth of the frontier in *The End of the Myth* (2019), we acknowledge that the myth of the frontier has lost its value as political currency, as a framework to guide and explain U.S. policies. Grandin makes the convincing argument that U.S. imperialism is no longer sustained by a nationwide belief in U.S. destiny and exceptionalism (2019, 269–270). Paradoxically, whereas U.S. policies at the border are no longer dictated by the promise of boundless expansion, the appeal to the esthetics and moral currency of the frontier remained strong throughout the Fourth Annual Night at the Alamo. Within the walls of the Alamo Mission, plaques honoring this colonial heritage surrounded border enforcement officials and Border Patrol agents.

Ex-agent Francisco Cantú has written extensively on his years with the Border Patrol and how the myth of the good old days infused current practices:

> I often heard romanticized stories of "the old patrol," a lament for the days when agents had free rein across the borderlands, lighting abandoned cars on fire and "tuning up" smugglers and migrants at will. As young trainees, my colleagues and I were taken to storied places in the desert—a remote pass where earlier generations of agents were rumored to have pushed migrants from clifftops and hidden their corpses. (Cantú 2019b)

Cantú's testimony illustrates how the racialized and romanticized violence of the frontier is mobilized to normalize the current border management practices. At the Border Security Expo, the *ghosts* of the Texas pioneers—in Avery Gordon's sense of the term—made their impact felt. They had died "for the Alamo" more than a hundred years ago, yet their sacrifice resonated with the ethos of today's Border Patrol. One keynote speaker explicitly referred to the "long tradition of sacrifice" of the agents. Several times, Border Patrol agents were congratulated for "holding the line." One vendor had chosen a slogan for its banner that echoed the motto of the first settlers: "Ever Vigilant." By the entrance gate, the information stand advertised the Old Settler's Music Festival, the Country Antiques shop (with its slogan "Made in America/Still in America"), and a local authentic American Indian jewelry shop. Tom Winkowski, the Border Security Expo chair, wore a cowboy hat, which only emphasized how the Border Security Expo tapped into the imaginary of the frontier, the spirit of Fort Alamo, and the prestige of its pioneer families.

Despite its scale, the Border Security Expo soon felt like a familial and intimate event. In the exhibit hall, each booth was immediately adjacent to the next, leaving little room for anonymity. Attendants addressed each other by first name. The Tuesday afternoon keynote speaker was one of the rare newcomers to the world of border enforcement. By the end of his remarks, he explained that he had been deeply moved by the warm welcome of his new colleagues. At that moment, the moderator, a senior CBP officer, hugged him: "Welcome to the family!" he said. This familial spirit and the colonial camaraderie culminated on the third day. The attendees were invited for a day of festivities at the Bandera Shooting Club, an hour drive away from San Antonio. The town of Bandera is known for its Frontier Museum and its two-story antique shop where one can buy cowboy outfits and old postcards. A friendly shooting tournament had been organized. We witnessed a succession of scenes of joyful shooting, and meat-grilling. A few vendors from the Border Security Expo had brought their products and offered the live spectacle of border technology. Clearly, it was not a gathering of unconcerned and heartless bureaucrats. Contrary to our expectations, attendees repeatedly demonstrated unrestrained feelings of devotion and pride. The history of San Antonio and its colonial past served as fertile grounds for the development of an esprit de corps among the agents.

The Celebration of Sacrifice and Death

An additional cement to this subculture in the making came from the official tributes and award ceremonies. The first award ceremony organized by the BPF was dedicated to the courage of the Border Patrol agents: "the men and women in green who have gone above and beyond the call of duty" (Border Security Expo 2019b, 18). The head of the jury that decided the award winner was called onstage to announce the name of the winner. This year, "in particular, was a struggle," he said, because "we had two agents that did some things that are just absolutely amazing." Eventually the jury settled on their hero:

> A group of approximately eleven individuals entering the U.S. illegally had entered the creek which feeds into the Rio Grande River in order to avoid apprehension. The agent entered the creek. . . . He removed his rough-duty belt, handed it to another agent, and entered the creek, *putting his own life in danger*, and swam through the waters. *Without regard for the safety of his own life*, he displayed decisiveness, determination, compassion, and courage while saving the life of three people. (Emphasis added)

When his name was pronounced, the agent walked up to the stage with his wife and two children to have their photograph taken. The audience was applauding the two parents, who were in their early twenties. Some people were crying and holding hands.

Remarkable parallels exist between the BPF and police departments' charity and memorial organizations. Sociologists and criminal justice scholars have highlighted how police officers are socialized into a subculture that revolves around the fear of dying and the consecration of their survival. Given the relatively average mortal risks associated with being a police officer, the fear must be fabricated to instill loyalty and solidarity among the officers. In "Don't Let Them Kill You on Some Dirty Roadway," criminologist Caitlin Lynch traces the elaboration of a police survivability discourse: "From the beginning, police recruits are socialized in the academy to be perpetually cognizant of their own mortality" (Lynch 2018, 34). The police precincts hang "Survival Creed" posters on their walls that recode brutality as survival. Earlier studies of police subculture have insisted on the symbolic dimensions of police funerals that ironically reassert "the significance of life within that moral unit and, in the police case, the respect and dependence of the society upon the police" (Manning 1997, 24). When the death of a fellow police officer is memorialized, it becomes a source of "death guilt" for the "surviving officer" (Henry 1995, 100). Following this argument, membership in the police subculture "does not simply derive from employment" but, rather, is gained once the officer has been exposed to "death" and subsequently adheres to the "surviving" belief (Henry 1995, 96). Constantly, police officers are reminded of the potential threats to their life and shape their actions accordingly (Herbert 1998). Back to the San Antonio Border Security Expo, assessing the authenticity of the rescue episode in the creek was not necessary to think about its impact on the audience. The master of ceremony was recounting to Border Patrol agents and veterans the value of self-sacrifice. The scripted performance (the award speech, the tears, the group picture) reinforced our intuition that the Border Security Expo was not only developing an outward-facing discourse of humanitarianism (as highlighted in the previous section) but also fabricating a system of values, codes, and rewards. The event encouraged the Border Patrol agents, who confront relatively average risks of mortality,[5] to feel acutely the proximity of their own mortality. It served the purpose of reinforcing the legitimacy of their mission and also of facilitating violence against border crossers.

The reception at the Alamo was formally dedicated to the memory of Augustin De La Pena, a Border Patrol agent who died in 1925. The BPF had framed his picture at the entrance gate. Throughout the evening, the host of the ceremony referenced his merits and legacy. Officer De La Pena had died "to protect the nation." According to the BPF's website:

> [Augustin de la Pena] and another inspector were at dinner when a mentally ill man entered and began to argue with the owner. As the man attempted to leave he was confronted by Inspector De La Pena and a struggle ensued in which Inspector De La Pena was shot in the stomach. He continued to struggle with the suspect, and as he grew weak from blood loss, he shot and killed the suspect. (Border Patrol Foundation, n.d.a)

Here the message was clear: regardless of the circumstances, if Border Patrol agents die, the BPF will have their back. Using an episode from the 1920s offered guarantees that the BPF would not go away.

During the evening reception, we heard long tributes to those who had made the "ultimate sacrifice" and had left "a family behind." The names of the Border Patrol agents who died in the years 2018 and 2019 were mentioned several times. As part of its mission to "provide support and resources to families of the fallen and agents seriously injured in the line of duty" (Border Patrol Foundation, n.d.c), the BPF granted "Silent Partner Scholarships" to the children of the "fallen" (also called "the surviving children"), as well as competitive scholarships to the children of active agents. The family service director of the BPF, herself the spouse of a "fallen agent," explained the guidelines of the scholarship system to the audience. As part of the application, children must write an essay on the topic of their choice. For instance, the children can answer the question "What [does] 'Honor First' mean to me?" One after the other, the children who had received the awards walked up to the stage, and their families took photographs. One of the children stated his intent to enroll with the Border Patrol upon graduation, and the audience greeted this announcement with more applause. These commemorations, despite their highly personal and intimate character, must be understood within the context of the Border Security Expo. On that night, the arms manufacturers present at the convention center—Grant Thornton, General Dynamics, ASRC Federal, Sentrillon, Peraton, and Elbit Systems—pledged to donate $33,000 to the BPF to fund its scholarship program (Border Patrol Foundation 2019).

The literature in anthropology on funerals and death-related rituals has warned us against the conception of death as an end. Instead, studies have identified death as a passage and a central element in people's cultures. The tributes to the "fallen" presented striking resemblance to the descriptions of police departments' commemorations. Michael Sierra-Arévalo explains that "the commemoration of dead officers that are temporally and geographically distant ties departments and their officers to the wider occupation of policing, connecting local departments and officers to the broader occupational culture of police and its long-standing emphasis on danger and death" (Sierra-Arévalo 2019, 19). The death of a Border Patrol agent is a relatively rare occurrence, and commemorations of these agents likely have similar functions to those of police officers: the crafting of a subculture, the bonding of the agents to their institution, and the development of a discourse of survivability. With this in mind, it becomes possible to see the Border Security Expo's commemorations as performances producing a palpable effect on their audiences. The Salute to Fallen Heroes Memorial Ceremonies carried a powerful narrative: as a Border Patrol agent, be sure that your memory will be honored. Your picture will be framed, your name will be evoked, and your children will receive scholarships.

Implications

The footage of migrant families at the U.S.-Mexico border during the summer of 2018 alerted the general U.S. public to the plight of undocumented migrants. Elected politicians and the liberal media placed the detention of children and the firing of teargas at the migrant caravans as the inhumane practices of a border enforcement agency let loose by a commander in chief appeasing his voter base. The brutality of border enforcement, particularly its role in the deaths of children in its custody, has served to ignite a debate on the U.S.-Mexico border. However, much of this discussion has had a partisan coloring to it, with progressive commentators placing these horrific stories as the basis for Trump's moral bankruptcy. These theatrics detract from the fact that the question of border enforcement is rooted in the sovereign prerogative of reinforcing the territorial integrity of the nation-state. This prerogative—a kind of originary violence (Delgado 2019)—converts death into a variegated tool for enforcement practices.

In this chapter, we argue that the Border Security Expo deployed a two-fold strategy, in which death is central, to justify and sustain the mandate of border enforcement. First, a humanitarian framework enables DHS to elide responsibility in directly pushing migrants to their death by arguing its need to intervene to save migrants from their own ill-informed decision to cross the border. This humanitarianism also provides ample justification for increased funding and serves to embed border enforcement practices within the broader accountability to human rights standards that liberal democracies purport to adhere to. Second, the Border Security Expo addressed internal criticisms and risks of demobilization through meticulous memorial celebrations of its "fallen heroes." This memorialization helps the DHS foster a work ethic for its lower-ranking agents and strengthens the feeling of duty and devotion. Death as a modus operandi creates and sustains an esprit de corps, converting the death of the "defenders of the nation" into a sacrifice. The narrative around the current task to be done reaches back to the hallowed days of the apogee of manifest destiny and masquerades their work as lifesaving.

Death as a policy tool and a framework for mobilization is intimately tied to the U.S. project of capital accumulation and settler colonialism. The humanitarian governmentality serves to further reify undocumented migrants' separation from the U.S. working class, increasing their hyperexploitability and stationing them at the lower rungs of the economy. Pathologizing them as either the criminal other *or* the helpless border crosser in need of aid is two sides of the same conceptual coin, molded by hundreds of years of racial formation and settler colonial othering, agency stripped to typologies that can be easily processed through a sprawling bureaucratic maze of locks, wares, and entrance points. By situating the practice of death at the border this way, we have located its purpose within the broader design of U.S. statecraft, with the intention of tracing possible lines of solidarity. Methods and systems of social control can be complex and obfuscating. In this chapter we attempt to lay bare the state's use of the technologies of death that allow for the expansion of its existence. Like the border enforcement agencies, other institutions designed to police and surveil communities, such as the National Security Agency (NSA), the Federal Bureau of Investigation (FBI), and local police departments, use liberal discourses and instrumental cultures to sustain their mandate (Puar 2017) and justify, especially in marginalized Black communities, Indigenous communities, and communities of color, their projects of social control and criminalization. At the same time, they employ racialized and classist tropes to extend their enforcement procedures and functions. This chapter, then, is a discussion of the Janus-faced way in which state power is deployed at the border to enforce a regime of dehumanization and control.

We acknowledge the complex entanglements of social and economic forces that lead people to join border enforcement agencies and obey direct orders, while at the same time not absolving them of their role in a process that strips the most marginalized of their humanity and personhood. This chapter leaves unresolved the question of the modalities of participation of the Border Patrol agents themselves in the everyday practices of border enforcement. From the citizens to the documented and undocumented migrants, state power is applied to varying degrees of intensity on the individual, compounded by their race, class, gender, sexuality, and access to some form of legal recourse. To champion the defense of migrants against the most egregious forms of state violence opens the possibility for us all to be free. This chapter represents our attempt to disentangle the complexities of the liberal democratic project and unearth the ghosts of its colonial foundation as they echo into the present and set the tempo for exclusion, alienation, and death.

NOTES

Both authors equally contributed to this paper. We are grateful to Dr. Marcia Esparza for her support and insights. Funding for the fieldwork was generously provided by the Office for the Advancement of Research at the John Jay College of Criminal Justice.

1. This is a total of the number of deaths reported in the years 1998 to 2018; see U.S. Border Patrol 2019.

2. They published testimonies, open letters, or interviews on blogs and in popular media outlets. In addition to Budd 2019 and Fernandez et al. 2019, cited later in the chapter, see Cantú 2018, 2019a; Lenihan 2019; and Washington 2018.

3. The Central American caravans, also known as the *Viacrucis del Migrante*, are migrant caravans that departed from the Guatemala-Mexico border to the Mexico-U.S. border. Caravans arrived throughout 2017 and 2018, resulting in a heightened sense of moral panic from the Trump administration and a threat to deploy military force at the border.

4. In *Line in the Sand*, published in 2017, the historian Rachel St. John replaces the Alamo Mission in a longer history of the development of racial capitalism and the plantation system. The Alamo Mission became a Mexican possession after the Mexican War of Independence of 1810–1821. As part of the Mexican strategy to secure its frontier and fight the resistance of the native indigenous populations, the Mexican government encouraged white settlers from the East Coast of what had been named the United States to settle in Texas, tame its land, kill and displace its people. Soon after, the newly settled white Texans wished to transform their farms into larger plantations and to own slaves. They saw the series of Mexican antislavery laws as an impediment to their economic prosperity and declared their independence from Mexico. In the thirteen-day Battle of the Alamo in 1883, Mexican troops under the leadership of the General Santa Ana regained control of the Alamo Mission.

5. The Officer Down Memorial Page (2020) lists 133 agents who died since 1919. An analysis of the numbers shows that a major cause of death (about 45 percent of the deaths listed) is traffic-related accidents, such as an automobile crash, aircraft crash, motorcycle

crash, or a bodily collision with a train or vehicle. The list includes agents regardless of whether they were on duty when they died. Each one of them is also listed on the Border Patrol Foundation website under the "Memorials" tab.

REFERENCES

Aas, Katja Franko, and Helene O. I. Gundhus. 2015. "Policing Humanitarian Border-lands: Frontex, Human Rights and the Precariousness of Life." *British Journal of Criminology* 55 (1): 1–18.

Agamben, Giorgio. 2005. *State of Exception.* Chicago: University of Chicago Press.

Baird, Theodore. 2017. "Knowledge of Practice: A Multi-Sited Event Ethnography of Border Security Fairs in Europe and North America." *Security Dialogue* 48 (3): 187–205.

Barrera, Eduardo. 2003. "Aliens in Heterotopia: An Intertextual Reading of the Border Patrol Museum." In *Ethnography at the Border,* edited by Pablo Vila, 166–181. Minneapolis: University of Minnesota Press.

Border Patrol Foundation. n.d.a. "Augustin De La Pena." Accessed December 10, 2020. https://www.borderpatrolfoundation.org/de-la-pena.

———. n.d.b. "Our History." Accessed December 10, 2020. https://www.borderpatrol foundation.org/our-history.

———. n.d.c. "Who We Are." Accessed September 22, 2019. https://www.borderpatrol foundation.org.

———. 2019. "Night at the Alamo, 2019." Facebook post, April 17. https://tinyurl .com/u2op2m5.

Border Security Expo. 2019a. "Join Us at Border Security Expo, March 26–27." *YouTube,* February 10. https://www.youtube.com/watch?time_continue=1&v=jY7Z5u18sSM.

———. 2019b. "Official Show Guide." In the author's possession.

Brendese, P. J. 2014. "Borderline Epidemics: Latino Immigration and Racial Biopolitics." *Politics, Groups, and Identities* 2 (2): 168–187.

Budd, Jenn. 2019. "Open Letter from an Ex-Border Patrol Agent." *Southern Border Communities Coalition* (blog). June 18. https://www.southernborder.org/open_letter _from_an_ex_border_patrol_agent.

Cantú, Francisco. 2018. "Confessions of a Former Border Patrol Agent." *GQ,* January 30. https://www.gq.com/story/confessions-of-a-border-patrol-agent.

———. 2019a. "Has Any One of Us Wept?" *New York Review of Books,* January 17. https://www.nybooks.com/articles/2019/01/17/has-any-one-of-us-wept.

———. 2019b. "When the Frontier Becomes the Wall." *New Yorker,* March 4. https://www.newyorker.com/magazine/2019/03/11/when-the-frontier-becomes -the-wall.

De Genova, Nicholas, and Ana Y. Ramos-Zayas. 2003. *Latino Crossings: Mexicans, Puerto Ricans, and the Politics of Race and Citizenship.* New York: Routledge.

De León, Jason. 2015. *The Land of Open Graves: Living and Dying on the Migrant Trail.* Oakland: University of California Press.

Delgado, Richard. 2019. "Rodrigo's Rebuke: Originary Violence and U.S. Border Policy." *UC Davis Law Review Online* 53 (September): 33–52.

Dorsey, Margaret E., and Miguel Díaz-Barriga. 2015. "The Constitution Free Zone in the United States: Law and Life in a State of Carcelment." *PoLAR: Political and Legal Anthropology Review* 38 (2): 204–225.

Doty, Roxanne Lynn. 2011. "Bare Life: Border-Crossing Deaths and Spaces of Moral Alibi." *Environment and Planning D: Society and Space* 29 (4): 599–612.

Fassin, Didier. 2012. *Humanitarian Reason: A Moral History of the Present Times*. Berkeley: University of California Press.

Fernandez, Manny, Caitlin Dickerson, Miriam Jordan, Zolan Kanno-Youngs, and Kendrick Brinson. 2019. "'People Actively Hate Us': Inside the Border Patrol's Morale Crisis." *New York Times*, September 15. https://www.nytimes.com/2019/09/15/us/border-patrol-culture.html.

Gordon, Avery F. 2008. *Ghostly Matters: Haunting and the Sociological Imagination*. New University of Minnesota Press ed. Minneapolis: University of Minnesota Press.

Grandin, Greg. 2019. *The End of the Myth: From the Frontier to the Border Wall in the Mind of America*. New York: Metropolitan Books, Henry Holt.

Hansen, Peo, and Stefan Jonsson. 2011. "Demographic Colonialism: EU–African Migration Management and the Legacy of Eurafrica." *Globalizations* 8 (3): 261–276.

Henry, Vincent E. 1995. "The Police Officer as Survivor: Death Confrontations and the Police Subculture." *Behavioral Sciences and the Law* 13 (1): 93–112.

Herbert, Steve. 1998. "Police Subculture Reconsidered." *Criminology* 36 (2): 343–370.

Hernandez, Kelly Lytle. 2010. *Migra! A History of the U.S. Border Patrol*. Berkeley: University of California Press.

Kang, S. Deborah. 2017. *The INS on the Line: Making Immigration Law on the US-Mexico Border, 1917–1954*. New York: Oxford University Press.

Lenihan, Brendan. 2019. "Rape Trees and Rosary Beads." *American Scholar*, June 3. https://theamericanscholar.org/rape-trees-and-rosary-beads.

Léonard, Sarah. 2010. "EU Border Security and Migration into the European Union: FRONTEX and Securitisation through Practices." *European Security* 19 (2): 231–254.

Lippert, Randy. 1999. "Governing Refugees: The Relevance of Governmentality to Understanding the International Refugee Regime." *Alternatives: Global, Local, Political* 24 (3): 295–328.

Lynch, Caitlin G. 2018. "Don't Let Them Kill You on Some Dirty Roadway: Survival, Entitled Violence, and the Culture of Modern American Policing." *Contemporary Justice Review* 21 (1): 33–43.

Malkki, Liisa H. 1996. "Speechless Emissaries: Refugees, Humanitarianism, and Dehistoricization." *Cultural Anthropology* 11 (3): 377–404.

Manning, Peter K. 1997. *Police Work: The Social Organization of Policing*. 2nd ed. Prospect Heights, IL: Waveland Press.

Maril, Robert Lee. 2004. *Patrolling Chaos: The U.S. Border Patrol in Deep South Texas*. Lubbock: Texas Tech University Press.

Mbembe, Achille. 2003. "Necropolitics." Translated by Libby Meintjes. *Public Culture* 15 (1): 11–40.

Merchant, Nomaan. 2019. "Autopsy: Migrant Child Who Died in US Custody Had Infection." *Associated Press*, March 29. https://apnews.com/d16ac6d3f4d546ac8246a9548c989053.

Miller, Todd. 2019. *Empire of Borders: The Expansion of the US Border around the World*. London: Verso.

Nail, Thomas. 2013. "The Crossroads of Power: Michel Foucault and the US/Mexico Border Wall." *Foucault Studies*, January, pp. 110–128.

Officer Down Memorial Page. 2020. "United States Department of Homeland Security—Customs and Border Protection—United States Border Patrol." https://www

.odmp.org/agency/4830-united-states-department-of-homeland-security-customs
-and-border-protection-united-states-border-patrol-us-government.

Perkowski, Nina. 2018. "Frontex and the Convergence of Humanitarianism, Human Rights and Security." *Security Dialogue* 49 (6): 457–475.

Puar, Jasbir K. 2017. *The Right to Maim: Debility, Capacity, Disability.* Durham, NC: Duke University Press.

Romero, Simon, Zolan Kanno-Youngs, Manny Fernandez, Daniel Borunda, Aaron Montes, and Caitlin Dickerson. 2019. "Hungry, Scared and Sick: Inside the Migrant Detention Center in Clint, Tex." *New York Times,* July 9. https://www.nytimes.com/interactive/2019/07/06/us/migrants-border-patrol-clint.html.

Salter, Mark B. 2008. "When the Exception Becomes the Rule: Borders, Sovereignty, and Citizenship." *Citizenship Studies* 12 (4): 365–380.

Scheel, Stephan, and Philipp Ratfisch. 2014. "Refugee Protection Meets Migration Management: UNHCR as a Global Police of Populations." *Journal of Ethnic and Migration Studies* 40 (6): 924–941.

Sierra-Arévalo, Michael. 2019. "The Commemoration of Death, Organizational Memory, and Police Culture." *Criminology*, August. https://doi.org/10.1111/1745-9125.12224.

St. John, Rachel. 2017. *Line in the Sand: A History of the Western U.S.-Mexico Border.* Princeton, NJ: Princeton University Press.

Sundberg, Juanita. 2015. "The State of Exception and the Imperial Way of Life in the United States—Mexico Borderlands." *Environment and Planning D: Society and Space* 33 (2): 209–228.

Trouillot, Michel-Rolph. 2001. *Silencing the Past: Power and the Production of History.* Boston: Beacon Press.

U.S. Border Patrol. 2019. "Southwest Border Sectors: Southwest Border Deaths by Fiscal Year." https://www.cbp.gov/sites/default/files/assets/documents/2019-Mar/bp-southwest-border-sector-deaths-fy1998-fy2018.pdf.

U.S. Customs and Border Protection. 2019. "Southwest Border Migration FY 2019." November 14. https://www.cbp.gov/newsroom/stats/sw-border-migration/fy-2019.

Washington, John. 2018. "'Kick Ass, Ask Questions Later': A Border Patrol Whistleblower Speaks Out about Culture of Abuse against Migrants." *The Intercept*, September 20. https://theintercept.com/2018/09/20/border-patrol-agent-immigrant-abuse.

II

Death and Dispossession

Anonymous Brown Bodies

The Productive Power of the Deadly U.S.-Mexico Border

Nicholas De Genova

O ver the last two decades, we have witnessed a remarkable escalation in migrant deaths within the U.S.-Mexico border zone (Annerino 1999; Binational Migration Institute 2013; Cornelius 2001; De León 2015; Doty 2011; Dunn 2009; Eschbach et al. 1999; Feldmann and Durand 2008; La Coalición de Derechos Humanos and No More Deaths 2016; Martínez et al. 2014; Nevins 2010, 2008; Regan 2010; Reineke and Martínez 2014; Rosas 2006; Stephen 2008; Sundberg 2011; Urrea 2004; USGAO 2006). From October 2000 through September 2016, the Border Patrol documented 6,023 deaths in Arizona, California, New Mexico, and Texas (Fernandez 2017). In other words, on average, at least one person has died crossing the U.S.-Mexico border every day, year after year. Rising numbers of border deaths are no mere coincidence or accident of geography, but rather a predictable result of U.S. immigration lawmaking, as well as a systemic feature of the routine functioning of the increasing physical fortification of the border and the increasing militarization of border enforcement tactics and technologies. Indeed, for several years now, the U.S. border regime has actively converted the most rugged terrain of the border zone, particularly the Sonoran Desert, into a veritable mass grave.

Remarkably, U.S. border enforcement authorities were quite deliberate and explicit about this strategy. In a notorious 1994 "Strategic Plan," Border Patrol tacticians wrote, "The prediction is that with traditional entry and smuggling routes disrupted, illegal traffic will be deterred, or forced over more hostile terrain, less suited for crossing" (U.S. Border Patrol 1994, 7).

This strategy of prevention through deterrence—the purportedly deterrent effect of which has predictably been negligible—was subsequently litigated in the Inter-American Commission on Human Rights on the grounds that the Border Patrol had organized and implemented its policies in a way that "knowingly and ineluctably led to deaths of an increasing number of immigrants seeking to enter the United States" (IACHR 2005, para. 30; see also Binational Migration Institute 2013; Feldmann and Durand 2008; Martínez et al. 2014). The U.S. authorities replied that the escalation in deaths was simply the "result of people being ill-prepared to cross harsh terrain," for which the United States could not reasonably be held responsible (para. 40). Indeed, the ample evidence of the abject failure of such measures to deter unauthorized migration exposes the sadistic fantasy that always links such logics of deterrence to gratuitous cruelty (Fan 2008; see also Ioanide 2015).[1]

Hence, we must recognize an insidious kind of killing at a distance (Pezzani 2015), in which the desert landscape itself has been converted into a geography that is made to kill (Heller and Pezzani 2017)—a "killing desert" (Rosas 2006, 410). Above all, the U.S. Border Patrol deploys apprehension methods in remote areas, which commonly result in the disorientation and dispersal of migrants into life-threatening terrain. In addition, Border Patrol agents actively interfere with and destroy humanitarian aid through acts of outright vandalism or the removal of life-preserving humanitarian supplies left for migrants, or routinely harass or otherwise interfere with humanitarian aid work. Moreover, various local and federal government actors engage in discriminatory practices of emergency nonresponse for undocumented people in the border zone (La Coalición de Derechos Humanos and No More Deaths 2016; see also De León 2015; Martin 2012; Stephen 2008). These forms of killing at a distance have arisen in addition to migrants being compelled to navigate the sometimes deadly outright violence of the U.S. Border Patrol, as well as the less systematic but no less systemic extra-state paramilitary hunting of migrants and physical attacks by anti-immigrant racists organized into border vigilante militias (Bauer 2016; Belew 2018; Romero 2019; Shapira 2013). The perfectly predictable lethal effects of border fortification thus consign migrants to disappearance and death by turning border crossing itself into a death-defying obstacle course.

In light of the evident systematicity of this (infra-)structural violence (Pezzani 2015; see also Martínez et al. 2014), which actively converts the desert itself into a landscape that kills, we are challenged to critically comprehend the spectacle of border policing in relation to its brute material effects, above all, a ghastly accumulation of dead Brown and Black bodies. This is a racial fact of profound social consequence, not only because of who is killed (or made to die) but also because of the way that these migrant deaths have deep ramifications for those who prevail in their migratory projects and live in the wake of such border brutalities. Following Max Horkheimer and Theodore Adorno's injunction that "only the conscious horror of destruction creates the correct relationship with the dead: unity with them because we, like them, are the victims of the same condition" ([1944] 1972, 215), Avery Gordon (1997) invites us to comprehend that social life is haunted by the ghosts of such dead and missing persons—above all, for those who have witnessed these tragedies, and for all who have in any event endured and survived the same lethal perils.

On a global scale, intensified and increasingly militarized enforcement at border crossings of easiest passage relegates illegalized migrant and refugee mobilities into zones of more severe hardship and potentially lethal passage, and also blocks, diverts, or deports migrants into spaces of abandonment (see also Andersson 2014, 2017; Bredeloup 2012; De Genova 2015, 2017b; Dunn 1996, 2009; Fekete 2004; Lecadet 2013; Nevins 2010; Stephen 2008; Weber and Pickering 2011). The escalation of migrant deaths along the U.S.-Mexico border therefore bears a striking resemblance to the parallel (but still more extreme) proliferation of migrant and refugee deaths instigated by the severities of the European border regime—particularly in crossing the Mediterranean Sea (Heller and Pezzani 2017; Brian and Laczko 2014; Jansen, Celikates, and de Bloois 2015; Pezzani 2015; Rygiel 2014; Stierl 2016). In the Mediterranean, untold tens of thousands of refugees, migrants, and their children have been consigned to horrific, unnatural, premature deaths by shipwreck and drowning, often following protracted ordeals of hunger, thirst, exposure, and abandonment on the high seas, supplying graphic spectacles of a seemingly unrelenting succession of human catastrophes.[2]

Of course, as the U.S.-Mexico border makes abundantly clear, these lethal risks are not the exclusive travails of illegalized maritime journeys on unseaworthy and overcrowded boats and rafts. Illegalized travel by land routes is also increasingly treacherous: exposure and abandonment on perilous terrain similarly multiply the conditions of possibility for deaths in transit. Indeed, the borders of Europe have also been effectively externalized across the entire expanse of the Sahara desert, creating an escalation in border zone deaths across a vast geography that precedes the perilous maritime journeys. Notably, a significant difference is that the extended externalized borders of Europe ensure that migrants and refugees commonly die before they ever set foot on European soil, whereas the U.S.-Mexico border also extends itself *inward* and has ensured that migrant deaths have occurred disproportionately only after having actually crossed the territorial border line. Over the last two decades, the enforcement of the U.S. border has likewise been externalized in significant ways (Andreas and Snyder

2000; Miller 2019). Nonetheless, over more than two decades, the repeated fortification of various forms of U.S.-Mexico border barricades has inevitably served to channel illegalized human mobility into ever-more perilous pathways, and has commonly ensured that even despite having succeeded in crossing the border into U.S. territory, many migrants never, in fact, arrive. In the aftermath of the Donald Trump administration's policies of blocking asylum seekers (overwhelmingly Central American families and unaccompanied minors) from lawfully petitioning for asylum at the border and instituting the so-called Remain in Mexico policy, the externalization of the enforcement of the U.S-Mexico border has become even more crude and blunt, and may also mean that migrant deaths likely begin to escalate at times and in places that precede the actual event of border crossing. Furthermore, with the advent of the COVID-19 coronavirus pandemic, migrant detention in the United States, as well as in Mexico and elsewhere, has viciously escalated the possibility—indeed, the inevitable certainty for ever-increasing numbers—that inhumane conditions of overcrowded containment have converted migrant detention camps into veritable death camps.

Whether in Europe or the United States, the brute racial fact of these increasingly deadly border regimes is seldom acknowledged, because recognizing that the targets of these diverse tactics of bordering are overwhelmingly Black and Brown people immediately confronts us with a cruel fact of (post)coloniality (De Genova 2016, 2018). Simply put, in the face of the inevitable and ever more bountiful harvest of empire, past and present, the mobility of the vast majority of people from formerly colonized countries—indeed, the vast majority of humanity—has been preemptively illegalized. Given that the horrendous risk of border-crossing death systematically generated by these border regimes is disproportionately inflicted on migrants and refugees from the formerly colonized countries, that vast geography formerly known as the Third World and now more commonly rebranded as the Global South, we should be reminded of Ruth Gilmore's poignant proposition that this sort of unequal distribution of the prospect of violence, mutilation, and death may indeed be taken as the very definition of racism: "Racism," she contends, "is the state-sanctioned or extralegal production and exploitation of group-differentiated vulnerability to premature death" (2007, 28). Therefore, in the face of the escalation in border deaths, we find ourselves, in Michael Omi and Howard Winant's words, "compelled to think racially"—because "opposing racism requires that we notice race . . . that we afford it the recognition it deserves and the subtlety it embodies" (1994, 159). The fervent fortification of the borders of the world's richest countries may thus be understood to be nothing less than another redrawing of the global color line (De Genova 2016, 2017b; see also Balibar 2001;

2004, 43–45; Besteman 2019; Doty 2011; Nevins 2008; Sharma 2005; van Houtum 2010).

The border spectacle of mass death in the Mediterranean, in particular, has intensified the contradictions of an increasingly militarized border that has had to also paradoxically shoulder the burden of a kind of minimalist humanitarianism, whereby border patrols become implicated in rescue operations, even as every rescue remains haunted, all the same, by the horizon of arrest, detention, and deportation (Agier 2011; Andersson 2017; Garelli and Tazzioli 2017, 2018; Heller and Pezzani 2017; Pallister-Wilkins 2015; Pezzani 2015; Tazzioli 2014, 2015a; 2015b; Tazzioli and De Genova, 2020; Vaughan-Williams 2015; Walters 2011; Williams 2015, 2016). In Europe, there is nonetheless a dominant discourse that widely acknowledges the border deaths as horrific tragedies, even as it seeks to disingenuously place the blame onto predatory "criminals"—"smugglers" and "human traffickers" (De Genova 2013, 2017b). Comparatively, there is a stunning silence around the accumulating border deaths in the U.S.-Mexico border zone, and an ever more shrill and bellicose outcry for more border enforcement. It is as if the hegemonic common sense in the United States is that daring to defy U.S. borders, inasmuch as this is ubiquitously framed as an illegal act, a violation of the law, pure and simple, could only be understood in terms of migrants taking their lives into their own hands, and deserving—or at least bearing the responsibility for—whatever consequences (see Ioanide 2015). This, after all, was essentially the position of the U.S. Border Patrol when challenged in the Inter-American Commission on Human Rights, arguing that the United States

> cannot be held responsible for the natural landscape or for the illegal activity that its law enforcement personnel are acting to prevent. The State argues that it cannot reasonably be argued that the United States has a duty to make the illegal acts easier for individuals nor to indiscriminately forgo its sovereign right and duty to control the entry of foreign nationals within its territory. The State claims that in the present instance, the right to life is a decision that rests in the hands of an individual of whether or not to take the risk of crossing the harsh terrain of the US southern border. (IACHR 2005, para. 42)

It is as if, in the United States, the callous common sense about border deaths is that "they were asking for it."

Whether in the United States or Europe, through measures that intensify the policing of physical (territorial) borders we all become largely unwitting witnesses to a grand spectacle where "the border" is staged, and where we may be led to believe in the elusive specter of its violation by the seemingly devious and cunning migrants who transgress it. This is what I have called the Border Spectacle, a spectacle of *enforcement* at "the" border, whereby migrant "illegality" is rendered spectacularly visible (De Genova 2002, 2005, 2013). The material practices of immigration and border policing thereby become enmeshed in a dense weave of discourse and representation, and generate a constant redundancy of still more of these languages and images. Thus, the Border Spectacle sets a *scene* of ostensible exclusion, where allegedly unwanted or undesirable—and in any case, "unqualified" or "ineligible"—migrants must be stopped, kept out, and turned around. As a scene of exclusion, the border appears to demonstrate, verify, and legitimate the purported naturalness and putative necessity of such exclusion, repeatedly, redundantly. Through these emphatic and grandiose gestures of exclusion, border enforcement performatively activates the image of migrant illegality as a seemingly real thing, as an apparently objective truth. The spectacle of enforcement ensures that "the border" can be represented as "out of control," beleaguered by "invasions" or "floods" of "illegal" migrants or refugees. A more or less constant Border Spectacle of policing and physical fortification thus appears to verify both the illegality and disorder of seemingly uncontrollable migrant movements as well as to lend credibility and reality to the otherwise elusive border itself.

Migrants can only become "illegal," however, if there have been legislative or enforcement-based measures to render particular migrations or types of migration "illegal"—to *illegalize* them. From this standpoint, there are not really illegal migrants or migrations so much as illegalized migrants. The origins of such illegalizations are usually located where very few of us can ever see them plainly, because they are the product of lawmaking and arise from the deliberations, debates, and decisions of lawmakers. This is what I have called *the legal production of migrant "illegality"* or, more specifically, the legal production of *Mexican*/migrant "illegality" (De Genova 2002; 2004; 2005, 213–249). Consequently, the migrants who have died crossing the U.S.-Mexico border are overwhelmingly Latina/o and disproportionately Mexican or (more recently) Central American. Assessing the real effects of this deadly border, therefore, we are left to ask: Do Brown lives matter within the U.S. border and immigration regime?

Analogous to the police beating of Rodney King and the Los Angeles rebellion in 1992 following the acquittal of the brutalizers, which Omi and Winant astutely identified as a watershed moment for racial politics in the United States (1994, 145; see also Omi and Winant 1993), and likewise analogous to the contemporary Black Lives Matter movement's politicization of racist police killings inordinately perpetrated against African American males across the United States—above all in the monumental aftermath of the racist police murder of George Floyd in Minneapolis on May 25, 2020—is the deadly border regime, and we are challenged to discern its comparably momentous *racial* significance (see Doty 2011; Márquez 2012; Provine and Doty 2011). Thus, we must recognize the contemporary controversy around immigration and asylum in the United States as inseparable from our wider, multifaceted, watershed historical moment of *racial crisis.*

Indeed, the contemporary racial crisis in the United States was crystallized and amplified through the presidency of Donald Trump in a way that situated the U.S.-Mexico border as its centerpiece (De Genova 2017a, 2020). It is well known, and a resounding and well-deserved source of Trump's infamy, that he invoked a luridly criminalized and racialized specter of "illegal" migration, particularly from Mexico, as one of the defining centerpieces of his campaign for the U.S. presidency, when he delivered the speech on June 16, 2015, that officially announced his candidacy and launched his campaign by rallying his supporters with his infamous proposal for the construction of a border wall along the full extent of the nearly two-thousand-mile U.S.-Mexico land border (*Washington Post* 2015). In a dissimulation of the toxicity of his racist appeal, figuring the Mexican menace as a multifarious threat of criminality, violence, sexual predation, and contagion, notably, Trump was careful to reinstate the divisive figure of migrant illegality as the real object of his animus. From the very outset of his bid for the presidency, then, Trump's political strategy depended on castigating Mexican/migrant "illegality" and excoriating the phantasm of a purportedly open U.S.-Mexico border as pivotal elements in his rather crass mobilization of anti-Mexican racism, in particular, and anti-immigrant nativism, more generally. Anti-Mexican racism, in particular, and anti-Latino racism more generally, have been a potent and viral fermenting agent in the long saga of anti-immigration politics in the United States for the greater part of the last century, especially since the landmark reconfiguration of the legal infrastructure of immigration in 1965, which I have depicted in terms of the unprecedented legal production of migrant "illegality" in ways that have been disproportionately deleterious for Mexicans in particular, and for Latin Americans more generally (De Genova 2004; 2005, 213–249; see also Nevins 2010; Ngai 2004). Indeed, what is particularly noteworthy in Trump's discourse is that the racialized figures of Mexican "rapists," drug smugglers, disease, and criminality, in general, were explicitly amplified to encompass all of Latin America (De Genova 2017a).

Subsequently, on April 6, 2018, U.S. Border Patrol agents and prosecutors along the U.S.-Mexico border were effectively directed to enforce family separations when then attorney general Jeff Sessions issued a "zero-tolerance" memorandum requiring that all "improper entry" offenses be referred for criminal prosecution (Sessions 2018).[3] Thousands of predominantly Central American migrant and refugee families, a large proportion of whom were seeking to petition for asylum but who increasingly were systematically blocked from crossing the border at official ports of entry where they could lawfully present themselves to Border Patrol agents and apply for asylum, found themselves the targets of state-sponsored kidnapping and child abuse perpetrated by the border authorities (Tazzioli and De Genova 2020). The atrocities were perpetuated across the country by the U.S. Department of Health and Human Services' Office of Refugee Resettlement charged with superintending the children's secretive internment following their abduction from their parents.[4] Furthermore, these family separations were implemented with no substantive plans or any effective systems in place for maintaining reliable records of the children's familial ties, such that once children were abducted, it frequently became pragmatically impossible to reunite them with their parents or any other family members (whether already resident in the United States, or in their countries of origin). The Trump administration could not even account for the precise number of children abducted. Thousands of migrant and refugee parents were eventually deported without being reunited with their children, who either remained abandoned in indefinite detention or were discharged into the foster care system. Trump administration officials and mass media apologists commonly blamed the parents for knowingly endangering their own children. Recalcitrant about this tactic, in the weeks following the memorandum, Trump remarked with his characteristic disdain for the truth and thinly veiled racist contempt, "You wouldn't believe how bad these people are. These aren't people, these are animals" (Davis 2018). Indeed, by perpetrating the perverse mass-mediated spectacle of the caging, encampment, and veritable torture of Latin American infants, toddlers, and other children through their protracted, indefinite abduction from their likewise traumatized migrant and refugee parents—which very predictably culminated in several of the children's deaths in custody—the Trump regime deliberately and cynically instigated an unprecedented humanitarian crisis and secured for itself an infamy of historic proportions, haunted by analogies with African American slavery, Native American coercive assimilation, Japanese American internment, and the Nazi Holocaust.

Notably, the zero-tolerance dictate mandating this notorious campaign of outlandish border cruelty was issued following Trump's furious reaction to news media reports of a caravan of migrants and refugees (mainly Honduran and other Central American women, children, unaccompanied minors, and lesbian, gay, bisexual, transgender, and queer [LGBTQ] persons), organized as a model of collective migrant and refugee self-protection against the predations of the migrant journey as well as an affirmative protest mobilization against unjust border and immigration policies. Indeed, the arrival of the caravan at the U.S.-Mexico border between Tijuana and San Ysidro on April 23, 2018, culminated in the migrants and refugees triumphantly scaling and perching atop the border fence in a joyous celebration of what, at least at that moment, appeared to be the success of their journey and their defiance and subversion of the barricaded border. Thus, what provoked Trump's vitriolic reaction was precisely the sort of diminutive but nonetheless audacious refugee self-assertion and self-organization that Glenda Garelli, Martina Tazzioli, and I have designated as the "autonomy of asylum" (De Genova, Garelli, and Tazzioli 2018). Indeed, over recent years, the autonomous subjective force of human mobilities from Central America has introduced radical alterations in the U.S. context into the very meaning of asylum and thereby, of asylum-seeking (Coutin 1993, 2000, 2007, 2011; Mountz et al. 2002). Hence, Trump's bombastic project to "make America great again" has been inextricable from the injunction to "build a wall" that promises, however delusionally, to insulate the United States from Latin America and keep the racial contagion of Latino migrants out.

Like the man himself, there was woefully little in Trump's political rhetoric that was original or creative in any way, however. The U.S.-Mexico border has long been a premier site for the deployment of increasingly militarized tactics and technologies of enforcement, including of course more than 640 miles of existing physical barricades that already partition the most densely populated and easily crossed portions of the border (Dunn 1996, 2009; Nevins 2010; see also Loyd, Mitchelson, and Burridge 2012). The unrelenting reinforcement of the U.S.-Mexico border—as a presumptively legitimate response to the putative problem of "illegal" migration—has long been a standard fallback position for all U.S. immigration politics: when in doubt, further militarize, securitize, or simply barricade the intractable border with Mexico. Hence, when Trump incited his supporters with the utterly implausible fantasy of building a wall, it was little more than a hyperbolic expression of what has otherwise been a rather routine fixture of U.S. immigration policy.

The ceaseless fortification of the U.S.-Mexico border—that infamous partition between the United States and Latin America—presents the epitome of what I have depicted as a spectacle of exclusion that mystifies its own *obscene* secret: the permanent subordinate inclusion of illegalized (predominantly Latin American) migration (De Genova 2013). Such spectacles of border enforcement conceal the fact that even those migratory movements that are officially prohibited, branded as illegal, and supposed to be absolutely unwanted and rejected are in fact, objectively speaking, actively encouraged and enthusiastically facilitated. So-called illegal and officially unauthorized migrations are, to various extents, actively and deliberately imported, and welcomed by prospective employers as a highly prized variety of labor-power. Thus, the increasing fortification of the U.S.-Mexico border, in its grand and increasingly deadly performance of exclusion, is permanently accompanied nonetheless by the fact of illegalized migration.

Consequently, the brute fact is that some border crossers die while many others survive and prevail in their illegalized migratory projects. Thus, the outright disposability of migrant lives so routinely verified by the deadly border cannot be seen as a purely "necropolitical" phenomenon (Mbembe 2003; see also De Genova 2015). Border policing has plainly become cruel, indeed murderous, but it is not about cruelty, pure and simple, and not exclusively about mass murder. The blunt truth is that some migrants must die—which is to say, some are killed and many more are *made to die*—yet most survive as illegalized migrants who may proceed from this deadly endurance test to commence their lifelong careers as precarious, ever-deportable workers. Hence, we must see the production of literal deaths for border crossers as part of the larger dynamics for illegalized migrants of cultivating the sociopolitical conditions of what Orlando Patterson (1982) famously depicted as *social death*. Elaborating on Patterson's insights, Lisa Marie Cacho identifies racism's systemic production of "spaces of living death and populations 'dead-to-others,'" characterized by an outright "ineligibility to personhood" (2012, 7). "The act of ascribing legible, intelligible, and normative value," Cacho notes incisively, "is inherently violent and relationally devaluing" (149). Thus, the largely anonymous Brown bodies that populate the U.S.-Mexico border zone as often unidentified and unidentifiable corpses must be apprehensible as specifically Latina/o/x migrant *lives*. We are confronted, therefore, with not only a lethal border but one that contributes systematically to the production of Mexican, Central American, and other Latina/o/x lives as *disposable*. The deadly border not only kills but also plays a productive role: its power is *productive*, crucial for the continuous (re)production of Latina/o/x lives as disposable (deportable) labor-power (De Genova 2002; 2005, 213–249; Golash-Boza 2012, 2015). Hence, we begin to see not only the cruel extremities of U.S. border control as a regulatory regime but also the regularities that it truly produces, foremost among them the very "irregularity"—the "illegality"—of "illegal" migration. In a de facto process of artificial selection, these deadly obstacle courses serve to sort out the most able-bodied, disproportionately favoring the younger, stronger, and healthier among prospective (labor) migrants, and likewise inordinately favoring men over women (see also Pickering and Cochrane 2013).

Thus, there is a profound continuity of ever-rising border body counts and the disposability of life at the borders of the United States and Europe with the deportability of illegalized migrant labor. The vicious severities of these extended and expansive border zones present a fierce endurance test, a preliminary apprenticeship in what promises to be a more or less protracted career of migrant "illegality," precarious labor, arduous exploitation, and deportability. Susan Coutin (2010) incisively notes that these tactics of bordering effectively convert the full interior of the nation-state into a zone of confinement—a veritable "border police state," in the words of Todd Miller (2014, 243; see also Talavera, Nuñez, and Heyman 2010). The militarization and ostensible fortification of borders, as a result, prove to be much more reliable for enacting a strategy of *capture* than for functioning as mere technologies of exclusion. Once migrants have successfully navigated their ways across such borders, the onerous risks and costs of departing and later attempting to cross yet again become inordinately prohibitive (Cornelius 2001; Durand and Massey 2004, 12; Massey 2005, 1, 9). Rather than keeping illegalized Latina/o/x (and other) migrants out, therefore, the militarization of the border simply tends to *trap* the great majority of those who succeed in getting across, now caught—indefinitely—*inside* the space of the U.S. nation-state as a very prized kind of highly vulnerable migrant labor. Thus, in spite of the dominant discourse that the U.S. immigration system and border enforcement regime are "broken"—and in spite of the perennial appearance of the U.S.-Mexico border's inadequacy or dysfunction—the border has long served quite reliably and predictably as a *filter* for the subordinate (illegalized) inclusion of migrant labor from Latin America (and above all, from Mexico). Again, the multiplication of anonymous migrant and refugee corpses that is the direct effect of border militarization and fortification and other enforcement tactics must be recognized as inseparable from the systemic relegation of the lives of those who survive the border's lethal perils to a racialized condition of permanent disposability.

The logic of capture through migrant illegalization and border fortification was only more perniciously and extravagantly amplified in the Trump administration's state-mandated kidnapping of migrants' and refugees' children. The atrocity of "family separations" entailed the cruel infliction of permanent trauma, and indisputably qualifies as a particularly devious form of torture for both the children and their parents. Nonetheless, it also instituted in a new and particularly vicious way the overall racialized degradation that upholds and exacerbates the disposability of illegalized migrants' lives—a sociopolitical condition that has an impact far beyond the actual fact of some migrants being literally disposed of and excluded outright. Hence, the heterogeneous forms of the overall disposability of migrants' lives generated by border violence again underscores that this violence serves the ends of a power that is repressive and indeed deadly but also, and above all, productive.

Migrant "illegality," much like the illegalization of asylum-seeking, always has a history within each particular juridical and border enforcement

context. Similarly, present-day border policing and immigration enforcement practices confirm that such histories are never finished; rather than
faits accomplis, established once and for all time, these diverse and historically specific productions of migrant "illegality" must continue to be reproduced through ongoing practices of bordering and re-bordering. This is
so because they are sites of ongoing and unresolved struggle. Notably, these
border-making and border-enforcing activities have been increasingly and
pervasively relocated to sites within the interior of migrant-receiving states,
such that illegalized migrants and refugees are made, in effect, to carry borders on their very bodies as border enforcement becomes a deportation regime (De Genova and Peutz 2010), and the border comes to permeate the
full spectrum of the spaces and activities of everyday life. Nonetheless, the
border formations of state power and sovereignty, and immigration law and
politics, more generally, must be understood to be *reaction* formations:
through diverse tactics and techniques of bordering, state power *reacts* to
the primary exercise of an elementary freedom of movement, whereby, in
practice, migrants and refugees make a priority of their human needs, over
and against any border, law, or state power. Furthermore, migrants' needs,
desires, and aspirations always supersede these border regimes' death-
defying obstacle courses—albeit, at times, at the cost of their lives. It is, after
all, the sheer vitality of migrant life that these border and immigration regimes serve to subordinate as labor, and it is the subjectivity and autonomy
of migration that precedes these regimes that is finally the incorrigible productive power that they seek to domesticate through their tactics of illegalization. Thus, these processes of illegalization remain the open-ended sites
for unforeseen political disputes over migrant and refugee life, with the full
extent and scope of the spaces of state sovereignty saturated and encom-
passed by border struggles.

NOTES

1. There is perhaps no more flagrant example of this perverse pretense of deterrence
than the state-sponsored kidnapping and child abuse perpetrated by the U.S. border
authorities enforcing the Trump administration's draconian zero-tolerance policy of
family separations, which was defended as a "deterrent" that would "send a message" to
would-be migrants and refugees (Bump 2018).

2. The Mediterranean has incontestably earned the disgraceful distinction of being
the veritable epicenter of such lethal border crossings. The most comprehensive database documenting migrant and refugee deaths during attempts to traverse the borders
of Europe estimates the total number of European border deaths at more than thirty
thousand (see www.themigrantsfiles.com).

3. Because minor children cannot be held in criminal custody with an adult, adult
migrants and refugees who were deemed to have entered the United States "illegally"
would have to be separated from any accompanying minor children when the adults

were referred for criminal prosecution and no longer available to provide for the children's care. The children were thereby reclassified as "unaccompanied minors."

4. It was later revealed that the family separation policy had been implemented at least several months prior to the official zero-tolerance proclamation and that thousands more had been subjected to the abject cruelty of kidnapping migrant and refugee children.

REFERENCES

Agier, Michel. 2011. *Managing the Undesirables: Refugee Camps and Humanitarian Government*. Cambridge, UK: Polity.

Andersson, Ruben. 2014. *Illegality, Inc.: Clandestine Migration and the Business of Bordering Europe*. Berkeley: University of California Press.

———. 2017. "Rescued and Caught: The Humanitarian-Security Nexus at Europe's Borders." In *The Borders of "Europe": Autonomy of Migration, Tactics of Bordering*, edited by Nicholas De Genova, 64–94. Durham, NC: Duke University Press.

Andreas, Peter, and Timothy Snyder, eds. 2000. *The Wall around the West: State Borders and Immigration Controls in North America and Europe*. Lanham, MD: Rowan and Littlefield.

Annerino, John. 1999. *Dead in Their Tracks: Crossing America's Borderlands*. New York: Four Walls Eight Windows.

Balibar, Étienne. 2001. "Outlines of a Topography of Cruelty: Citizenship and Civility in the Era of Global Violence." *Constellations* 8 (1): 15–29.

———. 2004. "*Droit de Cité* or Apartheid?" In *We, the People of Europe? Reflections on Transnational Citizenship*, edited by Étienne Balibar, 31–50. Princeton, NJ: Princeton University Press.

Bauer, Shane. 2016. "I Went Undercover with a Border Militia: Here's What I Saw." *Mother Jones*, November–December. https://www.motherjones.com/politics/2016/10/undercover-border-militia-immigration-bauer/.

Belew, Kathleen. 2018. *Bring the War Home: The White Power Movement and Paramilitary America*. Cambridge, MA: Harvard University Press.

Besteman, Catherine. 2019. "Militarized Global Apartheid." *Current Anthropology* 60 (suppl. 19): S26–S38.

Binational Migration Institute. 2013. "A Continued Humanitarian Crisis at the Border: Undocumented Border Crosser Deaths Recorded by the Pima County Office of the Medical Examiner, 1990–2012." https://papers.ssrn.com/sol3/papers.cfm?abstract_id=2633209.

Bredeloup, Sylvie. 2012. "Sahara Transit: Times, Spaces, People." *Population, Space and Place* 18 (4): 457–467.

Brian, Tara, and Frank Laczko, eds. 2014. *Fatal Journeys: Tracking Lives Lost during Migration*. Geneva: International Organization for Migration. https://publications.iom.int/system/files/pdf/fataljourneys_countingtheuncounted.pdf.

Bump, Phillip. 2018. "Here Are the Administration Officials Who Have Said That Family Separation Is Meant as a Deterrent." *Washington Post*, June 19. https://www.washingtonpost.com/news/politics/wp/2018/06/19/here-are-the-administration-officials-who-have-said-that-family-separation-is-meant-as-a-deterrent.

Cacho, Lisa Marie. 2012. *Social Death: Racialized Rightlessness and the Criminalization of the Unprotected*. New York: New York University Press.

Cornelius, Wayne A. 2001. "Death at the Border: The Efficacy and 'Unintended' Consequences of U.S. Immigration Control Policy, 1993–2000." *Population and Development Review* 27 (4): 661–685.

Coutin, Susan Bibler. 1993. *The Culture of Protest: Religious Activism and the U.S. Sanctuary Movement.* Boulder, CO: Westview Press.

———. 2000. *Legalizing Moves: Salvadoran Immigrants' Struggle for U.S. Residency.* Ann Arbor: University of Michigan Press.

———. 2007. *Nations of Emigrants: Shifting Boundaries of Citizenship in El Salvador and the United States.* Ithaca, NY: Cornell University Press.

———. 2010. "Confined Within: National Territories as Zones of Confinement." *Political Geography* 29 (4): 200–208.

———. 2011. "Falling Outside: Excavating the History of Central American Asylum Seekers." *Law and Social Inquiry* 36 (3): 569–596.

Davis, Julie Hirschfeld. 2018. "Trump Calls Some Unauthorized Immigrants 'Animals' in Rant." *New York Times*, May 16. https://www.nytimes.com/2018/05/16/us/politics/trump-undocumented-immigrants-animals.html.

De Genova, Nicholas. 2002. "Migrant 'Illegality' and Deportability in Everyday Life." *Annual Review of Anthropology* 31:419–447.

———. 2004. "The Legal Production of Mexican/Migrant 'Illegality.'" *Latino Studies* 2 (1): 160–185.

———. 2005. *Working the Boundaries: Race, Space, and "Illegality" in Mexican Chicago.* Durham, NC: Duke University Press.

———. 2013. "Spectacles of Migrant 'Illegality': The Scene of Exclusion, the Obscene of Inclusion." *Ethnic and Racial Studies* 36 (7): 1180–1198.

———. 2015. "Extremities and Regularities: Regulatory Regimes and the Spectacle of Immigration Enforcement." In *The Irregularisation of Migration in Contemporary Europe: Detention, Deportation, Drowning*, edited by Yolande Jansen, Robin Celikates, and Joost de Bloois, 3–14. London: Rowman and Littlefield.

———. 2016. "The European Question: Migration, Race, and Postcoloniality in Europe." *Social Text* 34 (3): 75–102.

———. 2017a. "The Incorrigible Subject: Mobilizing a Critical Geography of (Latin) America through the Autonomy of Migration." *Journal of Latin American Geography* 16 (1): 17–42.

———. 2017b. "Introduction: The Borders of 'Europe' . . . and the 'European' Question." In *The Borders of "Europe": Autonomy of Migration, Tactics of Bordering*, edited by Nicholas De Genova, 1–35. Durham, NC: Duke University Press.

———. 2018. "The 'Migrant Crisis' as Racial Crisis: Do *Black Lives Matter* in Europe?" *Ethnic and Racial Studies* 41 (10): 1765–1782.

———. 2020. "'Everything Is Permitted': Trump, White Supremacy, Fascism." *American Anthropologist*, March 23. http://www.americananthropologist.org/2020/03/23/everything-is-permitted-trump-white-supremacy-fascism.

De Genova, Nicholas, Glenda Garelli, and Martina Tazzioli. 2018. "Autonomy of Asylum? The Autonomy of Migration Undoing the Refugee Crisis Script." *South Atlantic Quarterly* 117 (2): 239–265.

De Genova, Nicholas, and Nathalie Peutz, eds. 2010. *The Deportation Regime: Sovereignty, Space, and the Freedom of Movement.* Durham, NC: Duke University Press.

De León, Jason. 2015. *The Land of Open Graves: Living and Dying on the Migrant Trail.* Oakland: University of California Press.

Doty, Roxanne. 2011. "Bare Life: Border-Crossing Deaths and Spaces of Moral Alibi." *Environment and Planning D: Society and Space* 29 (4): 599–612.

Dunn, Timothy J. 1996. *The Militarization of the U.S.-Mexico Border, 1978–1992: Low-Intensity Conflict Doctrine Comes Home.* Austin: Center for Mexican American Studies Books/University of Texas Press.

———. 2009. *Blockading the Border and Human Rights: The El Paso Operation That Remade Immigration Enforcement.* Austin: University of Texas Press.

Durand, Jorge, and Douglas S. Massey. 2004. *Crossing the Border: Research from the Mexican Migration Project.* New York: Russell Sage Foundation.

Eschbach, Karl, Jacqueline Hagan, Nestor Rodriguez, Ruben Hernandez-Leon, and Stanley Bailey. 1999. "Death at the Border." *International Migration Review* 33 (2): 430–454.

Fan, Mary D. 2008. "When Deterrence and Death Mitigation Fall Short: Fantasy and Fetishes as Gap-Fillers in Border Regulation." *Law and Society Review* 42 (4): 701–733.

Fekete, Liz. 2004. "Death at Europe's Borders." *Race and Class* 45 (4): 75–83.

Feldmann, Andreas and Jorge Durand. 2008. "Die Offs at the Border." *Migración y Desarrollo* 10 (1): 11–34.

Fernandez, Manny. 2017. "A Path to America, Marked by More and More Bodies." *New York Times*, May 4. https://www.nytimes.com/interactive/2017/05/04/us/texas-border-migrants-dead-bodies.html.

Garelli, Glenda, and Martina Tazzioli. 2017. "Choucha beyond the Camp: Challenging the Border of Migration Studies." In *The Borders of "Europe": Autonomy of Migration, Tactics of Bordering*, edited by Nicholas De Genova, 165–184. Durham, NC: Duke University Press.

———. 2018. "The EU Humanitarian War against Migrant Smugglers at Sea." *Antipode* 50 (3): 685–703.

Gilmore, Ruth Wilson. 2007. *Golden Gulag: Prisons, Surplus, Crisis, and Opposition in Globalizing California.* Berkeley: University of California Press.

Golash-Boza, Tanya. 2012. *Immigration Nation: Raids, Detentions, and Deportations in Post-9/11 America.* New York: Paradigm.

———. 2015. *Deported: Immigrant Policing, Disposable Labor, and Global Capitalism.* New York: New York University Press.

Gordon, Avery F. 1997. *Ghostly Matters: Haunting and the Sociological Imagination.* Minneapolis: University of Minnesota Press.

Heller, Charles, and Lorenzo Pezzani. 2017. "Liquid Traces: Investigating the Deaths of Migrants at the EU's Maritime Frontier." In *The Borders of "Europe": Autonomy of Migration, Tactics of Bordering*, edited by Nicholas De Genova, 95–119. Durham, NC: Duke University Press.

Horkheimer, Max, and Theodore W. Adorno. (1944) 1972. *Dialectic of Enlightenment.* New York: Seabury Press.

IACHR (Inter-American Commission on Human Rights). 2005. "Victor Nicolas Sanchez et al. ('Operation Gatekeeper') v. United States." Inadmissibility Report No. 104/05, Petition 65/99, October 27. http://www.cidh.oas.org/annualrep/2005eng/USA.65.99eng.htm.

Ioanide, Paula. 2015. *The Emotional Politics of Racism: How Feelings Trump Facts in an Era of Colorblindness*. Stanford, CA: Stanford University Press.

Jansen, Yolande, Robin Celikates, and Joost de Bloois, eds. 2015. *The Irregularization of Migration in Contemporary Europe: Detention, Deportation, Drowning*. London: Rowman and Littlefield.

La Coalición de Derechos Humanos and No More Deaths. 2016. "Disappeared: How the US Border Enforcement Agencies Are Fueling a Missing Persons Crisis." http://www.thedisappearedreport.org.

Lecadet, Clara. 2013. "From Migrant Destitution to Self-Organization into Transitory National Communities: The Revival of Citizenship in Post-deportation Experience in Mali." In *The Social, Political and Historical Contours of Deportation*, edited by Bridget Anderson, Matthew Gibney, and Emanuela Paoletti, 143–158. New York: Springer.

Loyd, Jenna, Matthew Mitchelson, and Andrew Burridge, eds. 2012. *Beyond Walls and Cages: Prisons, Borders, and Global Crisis*. Athens: University of Georgia Press.

Márquez, John D. 2012. "Latinos as the 'Living Dead': Raciality, Expendability, and Border Militarization." *Latino Studies* 10 (4): 473–498.

Martin, Lauren L. 2012. "'Catch and Remove': Detention, Deterrence, and Discipline in US Noncitizen Family Detention Practice." *Geopolitics* 17 (2): 312–334.

Martínez, Daniel E., Robin C. Reineke, Raquel Rubio-Goldsmith, and Bruce O. Parks. 2014. "Structural Violence and Migrant Deaths in Southern Arizona: Data from the Pima County Office of the Medical Examiner, 1990–2013." *Journal on Migration and Human Security* 2 (4): 257–286.

Massey, Douglas S. 2005. "Backfire at the Border: Why Enforcement without Legalization Cannot Stop Illegal Immigration." *Trade Policy Analysis*, June 13. https://www.cato.org/sites/cato.org/files/pubs/pdf/tpa-029.pdf.

Mbembe, Achille. 2003. "Necropolitics." *Public Culture* 15 (1): 11–40.

Miller, Todd. 2014. *Border Patrol Nation: Dispatches from the Front Lines of Homeland Security*. San Francisco: City Lights Books.

———. 2019. *Empire of Borders: The Expansion of the US Border around the World*. New York: Verso.

Mountz, Alison, Richard Wright, Ines Miyares, and Adrian J. Bailey. 2002. "Lives in Limbo: Temporary Protected Status and Immigrant Identities." *Global Networks* 2 (4): 335–356.

Nevins, Joseph. 2008. *Dying to Live: A Story of U.S. Immigration in an Age of Global Apartheid*. San Francisco: Open Media/City Lights Books.

———. 2010. *Operation Gatekeeper and Beyond: The War on "Illegals" and the Remaking of the U.S.-Mexico Boundary*. 2nd ed. New York: Routledge.

Ngai, Mai M. 2004. *Impossible Subjects: Illegal Aliens and the Making of Modern America*. Princeton, NJ: Princeton University Press.

Omi, Michael, and Howard Winant. 1993. "The Los Angeles 'Race Riot' and Contemporary U.S. Politics." In *Reading Rodney King, Reading Urban Uprising*, edited by Robert Gooding-Williams, 97–114. New York: Routledge.

———. 1994. *Racial Formation in the United States: From the 1960s to the 1990s*. 2nd ed. New York: Routledge.

Pallister-Wilkins, Polly. 2015. "The Humanitarian Politics of European Border Policing: Frontex and Border Police in Evros." *International Political Sociology* 9:53–69.

Patterson, Orlando. 1982. *Slavery and Social Death: A Comparative Study*. Cambridge, MA: Harvard University Press.

Pezzani, Lorenzo. 2015. "Liquid Traces: Spatial Practices, Aesthetics and Humanitarian Dilemmas at the Maritime Borders of the EU." Ph.D. diss., University of London.

Pickering, Sharon, and Brandy Cochrane. 2013. "Irregular Border-Crossing Deaths and Gender: Where, How and Why Women Die Crossing Borders." *Theoretical Criminology* 17 (1): 27–48.

Provine, Doris Marie, and Roxanne Lynn Doty. 2011. "The Criminalization of Immigrants as a Racial Project." *Journal of Contemporary Criminal Justice* 27 (3): 261–277.

Regan, Margaret. 2010. *The Death of Josseline: Immigration Stories from the Arizona Borderlands*. Boston: Beacon Press.

Reineke, Robin, and Daniel Martínez. 2014. "Migrant Deaths in the Americas (United States and Mexico)." In *Fatal Journeys: Tracking Lives Lost During Migration*, edited by Tara Brian and Frank Laczko, 45–84. Geneva: International Organization for Migration. https://publications.iom.int/system/files/pdf/fataljourneys_countingthe uncounted.pdf.

Romero, Simon. 2019. "Militia in New Mexico Detains Asylum Seekers at Gunpoint." *New York Times*, April 18. https://www.nytimes.com/2019/04/18/us/new-mexico -militia.html.

Rosas, Gilberto. 2006. "The Managed Violences of the Borderlands: Treacherous Geographies, Policeability, and the Politics of Race." *Latino Studies* 4 (4): 401–418.

Rygiel, Kim. 2014. "In Life through Death: Transgressive Citizenship at the Border." In *Routledge Handbook of Global Citizenship Studies*, edited by Engin F. Isin and Peter Nyers, 62–72. New York: Routledge.

Sessions, Jeff. 2018. "Memorandum for Federal Prosecutors along the Southwest Border: Zero-Tolerance for Offenses under 8 U.S.C. § 1325(a)." April 6. https://www .justice.gov/opa/press-release/file/1049751/download.

Shapira, Harel. 2013. *Waiting for José: The Minutemen's Pursuit of America*. Princeton, NJ: Princeton University Press.

Sharma, Nandita. 2005. "Anti-Trafficking Rhetoric and the Making of a Global Apartheid." *NWSA Journal* 17 (3): 88–111.

Stephen, Lynn. 2008. "*Los nuevos desaparecidos*: Immigration, Militarization, Death, and Disappearance on Mexico's Borders." In *Security Disarmed: Critical Perspectives on Gender, Race, and Militarization*, edited by Barbara Sutton, Sandra Morgen, and Julie Novkov, 122–158. New Brunswick, NJ: Rutgers University Press.

Stierl, Maurice. 2016. "Contestations in Death: The Role of Grief in Migration Struggles." *Citizenship Studies* 20 (2): 173–191.

Sundberg, Juanita. 2011. "Diabolic Caminos in the Desert and Cat Fights on the Río: A Posthumanist Political Ecology of Boundary Enforcement in the United States–Mexico Borderlands." *Annals of the Association of American Geographers* 101 (2): 318–336.

Talavera, Victor; Guillermina Gina Nuñez; and Josiah Heyman. 2010. "Deportation in the U.S.-Mexico Borderlands: Anticipation, Experience, and Memory." In *The Deportation Regime: Sovereignty, Space, and the Freedom of Movement*, edited by Nicholas De Genova and Nathalie Peutz, 166–195. Durham, NC: Duke University Press.

Tazzioli, Martina. 2014. *Spaces of Governmentality: Autonomous Migration and the Arab Uprisings*. New York: Rowman and Littlefield.

———. 2015a. "The Desultory Politics of Mobility and the Humanitarian-Military Border in the Mediterranean: Mare Nostrum beyond the Sea." *REMHU: Revista Interdisciplinar da Mobilidade Humana* 23 (44). http://www.scielo.br/scielo.php?pid=S1980-85852015000100061&script=sci_arttext&tlng=es.

———. 2015b. "The Politics of Counting and the Scene of Rescue: Border Deaths in the Mediterranean." *Radical Philosophy* 192. https://www.radicalphilosophy.com/commentary/the-politics-of-counting-and-the-scene-of-rescue.

Tazzioli, Martina, and Nicholas De Genova. 2020. "Kidnapping Migrants as a Tactic of Border Enforcement." *Environment and Planning D: Society and Space*, May 22. https://journals.sagepub.com/doi/abs/10.1177/0263775820925492.

Urrea, Luis Alberto. 2004. *The Devils Highway: A True Story*. New York: Little, Brown.

U.S. Border Patrol. 1994. "Border Patrol Strategic Plan: 1994 and Beyond." https://assets.documentcloud.org/documents/355856/border-patrol-strategic-plan-1994-and-beyond.pdf.

USGAO (U.S. Government Accountability Office). 2006. "Illegal Immigration: Border-Crossing Deaths Have Doubled since 1995; Border Patrol's Efforts to Prevent Deaths Have Not Been Fully Evaluated." GAO-06-770, August 15. http://www.gao.gov/assets/260/251173.pdf.

van Houtum, Henk. 2010. "Human Blacklisting: The Global Apartheid of the EU's External Border Regime." *Environment and Planning D: Society and Space* 28 (6): 957–976.

Vaughan-Williams, Nick. 2015. *Europe's Border Crisis: Biopolitical Security and Beyond*. Oxford: Oxford University Press.

Walters, William. 2011. "Foucault and Frontiers: Notes on the Birth of the Humanitarian Border." In *Governmentality: Current Issues and Future Challenges*, edited by Ulrich Bröckling, Susanne Krasmann, and Thomas Lemke, 138–164. New York: Routledge.

Washington Post. 2015. "Full Text: Donald Trump Announces a Presidential Bid." *Washington Post*, June 16. https://www.washingtonpost.com/news/post-politics/wp/2015/06/16/full-text-donald-trump-announces-a-presidential-bid.

Weber, Leanne, and Sharon Pickering. 2011. *Globalization and Borders: Death at the Global Frontier*. London: Palgrave.

Williams, Jill M. 2015. "From Humanitarian Exceptionalism to Contingent Care: Care and Enforcement at the Humanitarian Border." *Political Geography* 47:11–20.

———. 2016. "The Safety/Security Nexus and the Humanitarianisation of Border Enforcement." *Geographical Journal* 182 (1): 27–37.

5

Detention Economies

Commodifying Migrant Social Death

DEIRDRE CONLON
NANCY HIEMSTRA

The 2020 U.S. Department of Homeland Security (DHS) budget plan proposed "the creation of a Border Security and Immigration Enforcement Fund . . . to meet the President's border security and immigration enforcement goals, [which] include the expansion of immigration detention capacity to 60,000" (U.S. Government 2019, 51). This was on top of a request for $2.7 billion to fund 54,000 immigration detention beds.[1] These figures represent a 130 percent increase in the number of individuals detained by immigration authorities in the United States on any given day in 2019 (45,000 according to Human Rights First [2019]) and a massive increase in the use of detention as a tool of the U.S. immigration enforcement regime in the space of a decade.

In this chapter we identify immigration detention as a key institutional mechanism that contributes to migrants' social death in the United States and elsewhere. Continued growth and expansion of immigration detention is driven by detention economies, a term that encapsulates the extensive array of infrastructure—including operations and management, transport, communications, food, and medical care systems—that makes up the detention system and the range of private- *and* public-sector actors involved in these systems. We argue that detention economies generate losses that produce and amplify migrant social death while they also ensure gains for both private and public sectors. Central to this process is the commodification of migrant life in detention. Here, we identify key examples of losses for individual detainees and their families as well as for wider networks and institutions. We trace these losses to gains in the form of profits and claims of revenue savings and other efficiencies that are linked to the commodification of migrants' lives and their social death in immigration detention.

Our investigation draws on social death as a conceptual framework. From Jana Králová (2015) and Erica Borgstrom (2017), we understand social death as a series of losses—loss of identity, loss of social connectedness, loss associated with the body's disintegration—that are produced when an individual's social sphere becomes diminished through segregation and exclusion. The persons or group for whom social death is meted out are designated as having limited utility: unable or unwilling to conform to the neoliberal norms of market competitiveness and profit seeking and associated mechanisms of neoliberal governmentality (Larner 2000; Mitchell 2016). Importantly, however, this does not equate with outright expulsion from society; instead, those who experience social death are excluded from daily social life while being included in circuits of economic value. In the case of immigration detention, social death becomes a source of revenue for a host of actors that are bound up with immigrants' lives through detention economies. Continued growth of the immigration detention industry is promoted and supported by a range of private- and public-sector actors. In this chapter we highlight how detention conditions exacerbate exclusions that migrants experience in society at large. We argue that in detention, social death's perniciousness lies in its value in terms of revenue gains, profit, and market expansion for all those involved in detention economies. In short, immigration detention rests on a paradoxical relation: losses that produce and accelerate migrants' social death and gains linked to the commodification of migrants' lives.

The chapter develops as follows: First, we situate our approach to social death as it relates to our research on immigrant detention and detention economies. By triangulating a range of information sources including public records, local and national media, and advocacy-sector reports, we examine the myriad ways in which detention in these facilities effects the social death of detained immigrants. Then we turn to the gains made through and in the meting out of detainees' social death, highlighting who, beyond private prison companies, makes these gains. We conclude by briefly considering some of the implications of our social autopsy of losses, gains, and commodification of migrant detainees as it might inform analyses of the erosion of society's moral compass vis-à-vis migrants' rights and (im)mobility in these times.

Framing Our Research: Social Death, Commodification, and Detention

Social death is deployed across a range of interdisciplinary social science contexts and interpreted in a number of interrelated ways. Of particular note are Erving Goffman's concepts of "disculturation," by which people are extracted from their habitual social setting and community, resulting in the loss of social roles, and mortification of the self, which refers to repeated humiliations that undermine self and social identity and is experienced by people who are placed in degrading institutional settings (1961, 13, 24). In his global historical account of slavery, Orlando Patterson (1982) calls attention to how social death is linked to conditions of authoritarian control and alienation. Lisa Marie Cacho (2012) examines contemporary social life for racialized minorities in the United States and details how racialization, criminalization, and rightlessness pivot around legal status. Importantly for our discussion in this chapter, Cacho links these structures of exploitation to capitalist measures of worth that produce social groups deemed "ineligible for personhood" (Baker 2014, 1889). Others have examined social death and allied concepts in the context of social marginality, ill health, or housing insecurity. For example, João Biehl's ethnography of social abandonment among individuals who have been cast out of Brazilian society in connection with medical or psychological conditions is a richly disturbing account of stigma, economic vulnerability, and diminished legal protections that, together, render people "ex-human" (2005, 85). In refugee studies, social death is used in investigations of "displacement, social exclusion, loss of citizenship, of economic capital and of access to resources" (Králová 2015, 236).

In her review article, Králová (2015) considers these varied renderings and identifies three kinds of loss that recur in discussions of social death: loss of identity, losses linked to bodily disintegration, and loss of social connectedness. This useful syncretic framework is central to our analysis in this chapter. In addition, we are guided by scholars' attention to inclusive exclusions that undergird social death. In this respect, Giorgio Agamben's (1998) concept of "bare life," in which stigmatized groups are included as targets for segregation, is resonant. Sweeping changes to U.S. immigration laws since the 1980s have cast migrants as de facto criminals (see Hiemstra 2019; Conlon 2017; Loyd and Mountz 2018) and thus as a targeted, stigmatized group, while massive growth of immigration detention, as outlined below, ensures their segregation from community life. Equally important is attention to the weakening of legal protections, and, indeed, of legal status, for migrants as it relates to social death. Our research (Conlon and Hiemstra

2014, Hiemstra and Conlon 2016) has demonstrated how conditions linked to social death are exacerbated for detained migrants—whose legal status is already precarious—through their exclusion from labor rights and minimum wage laws in the United States. With this, migrants not only experience losses; they also become a more readily exploitable workforce for the actors and agents who operate detention facilities. This highlights another facet of scholarship on social death that we draw into our investigation in this chapter—namely, the relation to and significance of capital. Some scholars emphasize how social death is linked to loss of cultural capital, which is amplified across generations (Patterson 1982). In our discussion, we call attention to economic capital. Like Cacho (2012), we identify questions of worth and value as central to understanding social death. As detained migrants are rendered worthless and losses linked to social death accumulate, their value as an excluded, exploitable population accrues.

Detention, Privatization, and Commodification

Mirroring prison expansion from the 1970s onward, immigration detention has escalated rapidly, particularly in the last decade. Critical scholars highlight processes of racialized social control that operate in, and increasingly overlap in, these systems (Sudbury 2005; Gilmore 2007; Rodríguez 2008; Golash-Boza 2009; Silverman 2010; Fleury-Steiner and Longazel 2013). In immigration detention, as with incarceration, attention has also turned to the central role of privatization: involvement of private companies in what previously had been considered the purview and responsibility of government entities (e.g., Doty and Wheatley 2013). It is no secret that anti-immigration policies emphasizing detention directly result in increased profits for companies that own and operate detention facilities. Indeed, this clear link was evident in the outright celebrations among companies like GEO Group and CoreCivic (formerly CCA) when Donald Trump was elected president and the subsequent dramatic rises in the companies' stocks (Fang 2017; Pauly 2018). But it is important to recognize that this relationship is not just incidental, coincidental, or a happy (for the private companies) consequence of changing policies. Instead, the relationship is causal and iterative. That is, increased use of detention in U.S. immigration enforcement is directly linked to the involvement of private companies, in numerous ways.

First, the involvement of private companies has enabled the U.S. government's increased use of detention; when existing capacity has fallen short, private companies are quick and eager to step in and provide more. For example, in 1981, when Ronald Reagan declared that all asylum seekers would be mandatorily detained, the policy could not have been carried out with the sole use of the government's existing detention capacity. However, the willingness of private prison corporations to detain immigrants on the government's behalf made it possible to realize Reagan's new policy (Welch 2002). Recent examples of private companies' enabling role include the DHS's reliance on private companies to set up massive child- and family-detention facilities (Torbati and Cooke 2019). Second, private entities in the business of detention have themselves contributed to continued detention expansion, through involvement in the development of enforcement policies that result in greater need for detention capacity. Private companies have funded extensive lobbying of policy makers, with wildly successful results for their investors. An early example of this was a sudden shift in federal government enforcement practices that resulted in large-scale raids and detentions in 2006 (Cervantes-Gautschi 2010). After the election of Donald Trump, private prison companies intensified aggressive lobbying to further tighten restrictions on immigration and increase enforcement efforts, in order to increase the detainable population (Kim 2019). Companies also participate in organizations like the American Legislative Exchange Council (ALEC), formed by lobbyists, interest groups, and elected legislators, to craft new bills to bring to state governments. ALEC task forces on immigration have been responsible for writing numerous pieces of anti-immigrant legislation, such as Arizona's controversial Senate Bill 1070 in 2010 (Sullivan 2010). Third, many individuals move back and forth between work in the federal government contributing to policies around detention and border enforcement, and work or investment in detention and security industries that profit from the policies made (Cervantes-Gautschi 2010). Recent examples include Trump's former chief of staff and secretary of the Department of Homeland Security John Kelly and former defense secretary James Mattis, both of whom after leaving the Trump administration joined the boards of private companies that profit from policies they helped put in place (Rizzo 2019; Honl-Stuenkel and White 2019). These golden conveyor belts for personnel between government and private corporations offer lucrative incentives for policy makers to push policies that ensure detention remains a lucrative investment.

While private-sector involvement in the ownership and operation of detention facilities clearly remains a key driver in continued detention expansion, recent scholarly work and investigative reports have begun to look *beyond* private prison companies, to recognize additional actors and entities that profit from immigration detention. In our own work (Conlon and Hiemstra 2014; Hiemstra and Conlon 2016, 2017), as discussed below, we focus on the range of private companies and individuals that provide services vital to the interior operation of detention facilities, such as food, commissaries, security, medical care, cleaning, communication, and transportation. We also identify public entities that have become major players in immigration detention—namely, county governments that contract with Immigration and Customs Enforcement (ICE, part of the Department of Homeland Security) to provide space for detention. Our recognition of the importance of this mix of a wide range of public and private entities has led us to argue that a consideration of processes of *commodification* of detainees—beyond only privatization of detention—offers a broader, more accurate framework for understanding the relentless expansion of detention in the United States, as well as the relationship of policy making with detention capacity and operation (Hiemstra and Conlon 2016). In this sense, our analysis concurs with other analyses examining how various stages of migration become opportunities for profiting in some way, such as the account by Wendy Vogt of how transit migration exposes the ways "migrant bodies, labor and lives are transformed into useful objects of exchange and exploitation" (2013, 765). In this chapter we extend this discussion to scrutinize how processes of commodification work to exact the social death of detained migrants.

Researching Detention Economies in New Jersey County Jails

This chapter draws on our ongoing research project on detention economies in the greater New York City area. Here, we focus on immigration detention in the New Jersey counties of Bergen, Essex, and Hudson for two principal reasons. First, these counties serve as major providers of detention not just on the East Coast but within the U.S. detention apparatus in general, together holding around two thousand immigrants (Katz 2018b). As reported by Matt Katz (2018c) based on an analysis by CityLab (Misra 2018), Essex and Hudson Counties detain the second- and third-highest numbers of detainees of the more than one hundred county jails housing immigrants for ICE. Second, the participation of these three counties in immigration detention is interesting because of the liberal, Democratic leanings of the counties. In current political discourse, detention is often pegged as part of a politically conservative approach to immigration enforcement. While this belief is in many ways false—given that the existing infrastructure of the U.S. immigration detention system was built over decades in processes that spanned both Republican and Democratic administrations—it is a common perception considering former Republican president Donald Trump's aggressive and open attacks on racialized immigrants. In the midst of this heated political climate, these counties, all under Democratic leadership, were generally perceived as anti-Trump bastions. Many would presume, therefore, that these counties would act in opposition to Trump immigration enforcement policies. To the contrary, these counties were leading facilitators of Trump's immigration policy by providing detention capacity. Essex County even detains immigrants for ICE in Newark, which declared itself a sanctuary city for immigrants (O'Dea 2019).

All three counties are located in northeast New Jersey. Their detention facilities primarily hold immigrants apprehended in or near New York City and Long Island, which currently do not have long-term immigrant detention facilities. Recently, the facilities have received more detainees sent from the U.S.-Mexico border region, including asylum seekers (Davis 2019). The Bergen County Jail (BCJ), located in Hackensack, New Jersey, currently detains around 450 immigrant men and women per their contract for ICE detainees, accounting for the bulk of the total jail daily population of around 700 (Janoski 2018).[2] The Essex County Correctional Facility (ECCF) in Newark, New Jersey, holds 800–900 immigrants per day for ICE, and has the largest detention contract in New Jersey (Guha 2019). The Hudson County Jail (HCJ), located in Kearney, New Jersey, holds approximately 600 men and 30 women detainees for ICE (Katz 2018b), out of the resident total of around 2,300.

We have been gathering data about immigration detention in these facilities since 2013, primarily employing public records requests (Freedom of Information Act [FOIA] and Open Public Records Act [OPRA] requests) for government documents (see Conlon and Hiemstra 2014; Hiemstra and Conlon 2016, 2017). To date we have received over three thousand pages of documents that shed light on the day-to-day operation of facilities; entities involved in the provision of detention; and guidelines for an array of procedures, spaces, and activities. In addition, we have collated media coverage and reports from migrant and human rights advocacy organizations on U.S. immigration detention at the national level and pertaining to the facilities in our study. In this chapter we analyze the public records we have gathered alongside media and investigative reports. In the next section we triangulate these sources to present a social autopsy of migrant life, which articulates as social death, in detention. We then investigate how migrant social death becomes a vehicle for gains for some actors and entities.

Detention Conditions and Migrants' Losses

Here we draw on the data sources outlined above and adopt Králová's framework for understanding social death to examine how detention conditions produce deindividuation, dehumanization, and losses to personal networks that contribute to migrant social death.

Orientation as Deindividuation

As we have noted, significant numbers of migrants who are detained in the United States are held in jails and prisons, and the New Jersey facilities in our study are used to detain almost two thousand migrants. While immigrants are detained separately from those incarcerated by the criminal justice system, migrants experience a process of deindividuation analogous to the experience of prisoners (Longazel, Berman, and Fleury-Steiner 2016; Morin and Moran 2015; Crewe et al. 2014; Moran, Gill, and Conlon 2013). In the facilities we study, immigrants are thrust into a space where the differentiation between prison and detention is not apparent. They are immediately confronted with a loss of individual identity when their clothes, identity documents—including passport or birth certificate—and other personal effects are taken away (see Conlon and Hiemstra 2017). Journalist Matt Katz (2018b), reporting on a tour of the Hudson County jail, noted, "Immigrant detainees were housed separately from regular county inmates, but they lived under the same restrictions. They wore a mix of gray sweatpants and t-shirts, and orange jumpsuits." This process conflates migrants— whose detention is for civil, administrative reasons—with prisoners in the penal system and reproduces problematic representations and perceptions that link migration with criminality.

The process of deindividuation continues during detainees' orientation to a facility. Every migrant is provided with a detainee handbook, which lays out rights and responsibilities, conditions, and the daily schedule in detention. Handbooks are brimming with information that works to dehumanize migrants. This includes details about the initial "classification interview," which assumes criminality while determining "appropriate custody level" (Essex County Correctional Facility 2018, 9), housing unit allocation, and participation or exclusion from facility programs. Handbooks also detail routines for "headcounts"; these are conducted six times a day, at minimum. Talking and movement are among the actions that can be deemed noncompliance and grounds for disciplinary action. In addition, there are strict rules for and limitations on interactions and communication between migrant detainees and facility staff (Essex County Correctional Facility 2018, 4). Notably, in our research we have compared Spanish translations of handbooks with the original English edition for Bergen and Essex County detention facilities, and we found that translations into Spanish are poor quality with numerous errors and sometimes missing critical pieces of information. Not only does this illustrate a disregard for ethnic identity; in addition, translation errors could lead to detainees being unaware of rules and regulations and potentially subjected to the loss of rights or privileges as punishment.

Neglect of Detained Bodies

In August of 2019, a lawyer defending the Trump administration's treatment of detained migrant children argued that the definition of "safe and sanitary" conditions does not necessarily include provision of basic hygiene items including soap and a toothbrush (see Dickerson 2019). While federal judges ruled against the government in this widely publicized court case, the adult detention facilities in our study are riven with conditions that effectively disparage the bodily needs of detained bodies and contribute to their disintegration. Adult detention facilities are supposedly expected to adhere to the national ICE-established Performance-Based National Detention Standards (PBNDS), which outline minimum detention standards for admission, security, health and safety, sanitation, and discipline, among other areas. In reality, however, little is done to ensure adherence to these guidelines, and consequently, there are frequent violations.

Access to toiletry items for basic self-care is required by the PBNDS, as explained in facility handbooks: "You will be provided with personal hygiene items (e.g., toothbrush, comb). If you need to replace any of your personal hygiene items at a later time, you must request replacements from your housing unit officer(s) or purchase them from the commissary" (Essex County Correctional Facility 2018, 8). Elsewhere (Conlon and Hiemstra 2014) and later in the chapter, we describe how dependence on commissaries plays into the commodification of migrants. Migrants are also reminded that "poor personal hygiene or unsanitary habits can also have a negative impact on the health and safety of yourself and others" (Essex County Correctional Facility 2018, 40). Such admonishment adds insult to neglect, since our research as well as national reporting on detention centers repeatedly finds that the toiletry items provided to detainees for hygiene are insufficient and inadequate (Human Rights First 2018).[3] A DHS Office of the Inspector General inspection of five detention facilities, including Hudson County Jail, corroborates these findings. In interviews detainees complained that some of the basic hygienic supplies, such as toilet paper, shampoo, soap, lotion, and toothpaste, were not provided promptly or at all when detainees ran out of them. For example, women "reported receiving an insufficient number of sanitary pads, leaving them no choice but to purchase them at the commissary for high prices" (Human Rights First 2018, 4).

Losses linked to the body's disintegration in association with inadequate medical care and abuse in detention are also well documented in media, advocacy, and scholarly accounts (e.g., Cho and Shah 2016; Freed Wessler 2016). Reports of the facilities in our study repeatedly highlight "substandard or denials of medical care, long waits to be seen by medical professionals, and a lack of proper medication" (Human Rights First 2018, 1). One report on Hudson County Jail, which, on account of poor conditions, is monitored by national immigrant rights organizations, noted that of the grievances filed by detainees, "medical issues" are the number one complaint, making up 50 percent of grievances filed (Bernstein 2016).

Substandard medical care combines with practices of neglect and abuse in New Jersey jails, as Katz (2018b, 2019a) details, while another report notes "verbal abuse based on religious identity by facility staff" in Essex County Jail (Freedom for Immigrants, n.d.). As detailed in Hiemstra's (2013, 2019) research with deportees in Ecuador, detained migrants feel dehumanized and demoralized in the routine neglect of their bodily needs.

Finally, the poor quality of food is another way in which detention conditions result in bodily disintegration and losses linked to social death. Inspection reports on the Essex County detention facility detail poor-quality food, nausea-inducing practices around food preparation, and health consequences as a result. For example, the DHS Office of Inspector General reviewed grievances filed by detainees over a seven-month period (from January to July 2018) and found approximately two hundred (12 percent of the total) were kitchen-related grievances, with comments including "It's becoming impossible to eat [the food]. It gets worse every day. It literally looks like it came from the garbage dumpster" (Office of Inspector General 2019, 6). Inspectors also observed issues with food handling and food safety: "We observed open packages of raw chicken leaking blood all over refrigeration units and identified slimy foul-smelling lunch meat, which appeared to be spoiled, held in the refrigeration unit. Although this mishandling of meats can spread . . . serious foodborne illness, we observed facility staff serving this potentially spoiled meat to detainees" (4). Such findings echo our earlier research (see Conlon and Hiemstra 2014; Hiemstra and Conlon 2016) on New Jersey's detention facilities and resound others' findings as well (e.g., Katz 2019b). The impacts of such poor food provisions for detainees' physical health are clear; equally, detainees are dehumanized as they are presented with substandard food on a regular basis. Significantly, in an effort to find some sustenance or merely to stave off hunger, detainees report having to rely on buying food from the commissary. With this we see that the losses detainees must endure are linked to gains for commissary providers. Further on, we examine in more depth how migrant losses and their commodification entwine with revenue generation for subcontractors as well as other actors that make and sustain the detention system.

Social Isolation

We have established that migrants experience significant losses related to identity as well as physical and mental health in connection with detention conditions. They also experience the loss of social roles in relation to their friends and family. Detention facilities are often located in remote or hard-to-access sites. This results in both detention centers and detainees being made invisible (see Mountz 2011). Importantly, and much like decisions that drove growth of U.S. prisons in the late twentieth century (see Bonds 2009; Gilmore 2007), purported economic savings are a key factor in the siting of detention facilities, and, as noted earlier, jails and prisons now routinely double as detention facilities. Such sites are located where fixed capital costs—land or rent, for instance—are relatively inexpensive. Often these sites are poorly served by public transportation, which means that for a family member or friend to visit necessitates access to a car or lengthy, convoluted, and costly journeys on public transport. Moreover, several facilities in our study are located in districts that are zoned for heavy industry, where exposure to air pollution and other environmental hazards are severely elevated (see Freeman and Major 2012; Mitchell 2016). In their report on Hudson County Jail, for instance, Lindsay Curcio and colleagues note that the siting of the facility in an industrial area near trains "poses health concerns as well as access and safety issues for attorneys, family, and friends using public transportation to visit people in detention" (Curcio et al. 2012, 2). Consequences for detained immigrants are clear: deleterious health effects of detention are compounded by the isolated location of facilities in what are effectively toxic environments that amplify losses to social networks and connections.

The high cost of communications exerts losses for migrants and their family and support networks. Elsewhere we have detailed how profits are generated for telecommunications providers and local governments through contracts (see Conlon and Hiemstra 2014). Migrants and support networks also bear additional costs through fees charged for depositing money into a detainee's account. Our review of documents indicates that, for example, Hudson County's contract with Keefe Commissary Network (KCN) includes fees between $3.95 and $11.95, depending on amount deposited and form of transfer (web, phone, credit, cash). Migrants rely on money in their account not only to supplement, and sometimes even replace, food provided by the facility but also to communicate with family and other networks. Email communication is also costly for detained migrants. The contract between KCN and Hudson County Jail shows that detainees can use email by purchasing email packages. However, costs range from $0.44 for a single message to $9.99 for a forty-message package (in effect, a rate of $0.20 per email message), with options to send and receive photos for $0.25 to $0.40 per photo. As we elaborate below, these charges guarantee gains for contracted service providers and government entities. Meanwhile, for detained migrants, their families, and extended networks, communication is possible only with significant economic and emotional costs. On top of fees for accounts and for email, all email communications are monitored, with the provider, KCN, ensuring that every message sent or received is automatically scanned with their cutting-edge Word Watch software to monitor for contraband or illegal activity. This frustrates possibilities for maintaining contact with family and friends who are literally and figuratively further and further removed from the migrant detainee.

Reports are emerging on the impacts of family separation and detention of migrant children under the Trump administration (Stange and Stark 2019; Human Rights Watch 2019). These reports highlight a harrowing and morally bereft practice where lasting traumas are being meted out to immigrant children. They also accentuate the impact of long-standing policies that materialize loss of social connectedness, and that are experienced across the current immigration detention regime, as shown here. Isolation and loss of social connections in the facilities in our study are corroborated by investigative reports. In his accounts of immigration detention in New Jersey, Katz has found that in some detention centers physical contact, such as hugging loved ones, is allowed, but in others it is not (Katz 2018a). As one immigration attorney observed, speaking about the emotional toll of being cut off from family: "It's similar to being in isolation—not seeing the sun, not seeing other people. People are not meant to be in that situation," she said. "Immigration detention is supposed to be civil detention. We hear that it's not supposed to be a punishment, but when things like this happen people are suffering in real time, and will probably suffer long-term with the ramifications of being held" (Katz 2019b).

Gains for an Array of Actors and Institutions

All aspects of immigration detention—the loss of personal freedom; the places, spaces, and conditions of detention—bring about gains for various actors and institutions. As in the prison industry (Mitchelson 2014), the incarceration of migrant bodies immediately translates to profits through the rates per bed paid by the federal government to detention facility operators. Then, webs of gain are woven out to additional players involved in the operation of facilities. Moreover, faced with the series of losses we have described, detained migrants' agentic efforts add to these webs of profit-making and dependence as they try to maintain their health, recoup some dignity, and respond to the repeated humiliations and loss of social connectedness.

County Coffers and Private Profits

Detaining immigrants for ICE brings in serious money for the governments of Bergen, Essex, and Hudson Counties, amounts that have increased dramatically since Donald Trump took office. As calculated by Katz (2018c), the revenue paid by ICE to the three counties went up 46 percent from 2015 to

2018, in 2018 totaling roughly $6 million per month. Bergen County receives $110 per detainee per day. In 2018, the county took in over $17 million through its ICE contract (Janoski 2019), or $1.1 million per month (Katz 2018b). Essex County's contract brings it $117 daily per detainee, for $3 million per month (Katz 2018b), or over $45 million per year (Guha 2019). Hudson County receives $120 per day per detained immigrant, taking in around $35 million annually through its contract with ICE (Katz 2018b).

For all three counties, this money constitutes an important component of county government budgets. Bergen's ICE contract provides over 15 percent of the sheriff's office budget (Janoski 2018). Approximately half of the $45 million per year that Essex takes in from ICE goes to the running of ICE detention; the rest is profit for the county (O'Dea 2019). Estimates show that the ICE revenue means that Hudson County has to collect about $11 million less in taxes than it otherwise would have to from residents; the city of Hoboken would have to raise an additional $2.3 million in taxes, Jersey City $4.5 million, and Kearny $3.09 million (Katz 2018b). The upsurge in immigration detainees in these counties has occurred precisely as a 2017 bail reform law in New Jersey led to a quick drop in inmate populations. For example, Katz (2018b) reported that the 37 percent drop in Bergen's inmates after bail reform has been made up in immigrant detainees. So detention is viewed as using available space as well as bringing in critical revenues.

Maintaining humans captive for any amount of time requires enormous resources. As the prison and detention populations in the United States have skyrocketed since the 1980s, so too have the industries involved in providing for the daily and long-term needs of those forcefully held inside. While Bergen, Essex, and Hudson Counties own and administer the jails they contract with ICE, the facilities contract out multiple aspects of their operation, including food, medical care, communication, and security. These contracts are lucrative, meaning that many more players come to rely on immigration detention—and the social death of detainees—for their financial survival. Many of the companies involved build all or parts of their business around carceral facilities, aiming to service multiple facilities at regional, national, and even international scales. These contracting relationships also offer additional ways through which Bergen, Essex, and Hudson Counties make money off of detainees.

The provision of food and medical care to immigrant detainees in these counties involves multimillion-dollar agreements. Bergen County's food contract with Aramark Correctional Services to the Bergen County Jail is $9 million over five years (based on 825 total inmates). Both Essex and Hudson Counties contract with GD Correctional Services to provide meals for their carceral facilities. Essex's contract is worth $5.4 million per year, and Hudson's is for $15 million over three years (for 2,300 inmates). Medical contracts are also lucrative. Bergen County contracts with Morse Correctional Health, plus a number of individual medical providers for various services.[4] The Essex contract with CFG Health Systems for medical care at ECCF is for $37 million over three years. Hudson's contract, also with CFG Health Systems, is worth $29 million over five years.[5]

As detailed above, the food and medical care provided to detainees are frequent sources of complaints. The amount per meal calculated by winning bidders alongside complaints around insufficient quality and quantity of food suggests that keeping costs as low as possible, not nutrition or edibility, is the primary goal. For example, GD Correctional Services' contract with Essex County states its cost per meal as $1.547; even considering the economy of scale of serving hundreds of inmates, it is difficult to imagine a satisfying meal for a mere $1.50. All three county facilities have received a plethora of complaints from immigrant detainees regarding the (in)frequency of medical attention as well as the appropriateness of medical treatments (Cho and Shah 2016; Freed Wessler 2016). In the deprivation of bodily care, then, private companies and counties make money, as do all the companies who supply food and medical services in detention facilities.

Profits from Detainees' Purchases

In addition, the conditions of detention create consumer demand on the part of detainees to buy things to make life in detention more bearable (Conlon and Hiemstra 2014; Hiemstra and Conlon 2016, 2017). Every facility has a commissary that sells hundreds of items, including food (from snacks to instant meals); over-the-counter medicines; personal hygiene products; clothing (underwear, changes of clothing, sweatpants, and sweatshirts); and entertainment (playing cards, portable music devices). Bergen, Essex, and Hudson Counties all contract with KCN. Commissaries are a nodal point of profit in multiple ways. Contract documents state that all three counties determine the commissary operator to whom they award their facilities' commissary contract based on the commission (of commissary sales) that the county will receive. Bergen County's commission rate is 38 percent. Essex's rate is currently 20 percent, though prior to 2019 it was 48.5 percent. Hudson's commission is 33 percent. Counties receive revenue *on top of* their ICE contract per-bed amount when processes of social death drive detainees to buy from the commissaries to ameliorate the conditions of deprivation in which they are forced to live.

The commissary companies have developed multiple ways to profit from detainees. Obviously, they profit from their sales to detainees. Their prices are often higher than typical retail stores. For example, at the Essex commissary, one Hostess cupcake was marked up by 54 percent in comparison to Target store prices.[6] At the Bergen County Jail, one AA battery costs $1.10, while a Target brand AA battery costs $0.84, which means that the jail battery has a 31 percent markup (if purchased in a package of ten; $0.65 if purchased in a package of twenty, or a 69 percent markup). While these markups may be only cents per item, they add up across purchases, translating to real profits for the commissary companies. Even prices that are comparable to retail prices (such as $0.75 for a toothbrush at the Hudson facility commissary) likely bring in profits to commissary operators. For example, KCN is a subsidiary of Keefe Group, and the largest supplier of commissary services to carceral facilities in the United States. Because KCN is so big, it can be expected to negotiate low per-item prices with suppliers. KCN's bulk buying power, however, is not passed on to detained consumers. Additionally, apparent shortages or misallocations force detainees into some purchases. For example, ECCF was found to issue inappropriately large underwear (size 3x and 4x), as well as failing entirely to issue toiletries, so that if detainees wanted underwear that stayed on or the ability to brush their teeth or use soap they had to purchase these items from the commissary (Keifer 2019). What is more, as described earlier, Hudson's contract with KCN shows that inmates have to pay for any monies deposited into their account. So, in addition to making money on marked-up goods sold in the commissary, Keefe and the counties are making money on the initial depositing of the money to be spent.

Conclusion

In this chapter we describe ways in which immigration detention produces and reinforces migrant social death, understood as a series of losses: loss of identity, losses linked to bodily disintegration, and loss of social connectedness. Drawing on our research on immigration detention in New Jersey, we show how immigrants are confined in facilities that parallel—indeed many detention centers also function as—penal institutions. Performatively this renders immigrants as criminals and produces deindividuation. Provisions, including toiletries for self-care, food, and medical care, give the lie to notions of safe and sanitary detention conditions and highlight that detention standards are nominal only or enforced minimally at best.[7]

As a consequence, detained immigrants suffer the deterioration of physical and mental health. Significantly, they are frequently driven to rely on commissaries in an effort to meet basic needs. Finally, we demonstrate how loss of social connectedness is produced in association with the spatiality of immigration detention: maintaining contact with family and networks is time consuming, logistically challenging, and at times hazardous because detention facilities are frequently located in hard-to-reach, environmentally degraded, industrial areas. Communication is costly for both detainees and their networks because of commission charges and fees that are applied, seemingly, to almost every transaction.

Our analysis demonstrates that each one of these losses and the cumulative consequence—migrant social death—can be traced to political-economic decisions that result in gains for a range of actors including private prison companies, subcontracted service providers, and local and state government entities. Thus, it is clear that migrant social death is imbricated with capitalist accumulation and dispossession, or the accrual of benefits as a direct consequence of migrants' personal losses (see also Hiemstra and Conlon 2016). Importantly, however, this is not a straightforward relation of exclusion or excision from capitalism's circuits in association with limited utility or noncompliance with neoliberal social norms, as some accounts of social death suggest. Deindividualized and criminalized, detained migrants are a source of revenue for county jails, and thus for local and state governments. Being made unable to meet or sustain their basic needs renders detained migrants valuable to private subcontractors as consumers of commissary provisions. Further, because subcontracts are linked to commission rates, state and local governments reap some of the revenue generated from migrant deprivations as well. Similarly, migrants' efforts to maintain social networks become a source of revenue, and thus loss of social connectedness has value for telecommunications providers and for government entities. Following all these revenue streams, the wide array of actors and agencies that gain from migrant social death becomes clear. In short, this chapter, and our work more broadly, shows that detained migrants become valuable in and through losses that produce and exacerbate social death.

Finally, this paradoxical relation of migrants' losses as a source of value from which others gain also helps shed light on concerns about the current loss of a moral compass in U.S. society, and elsewhere, when it comes to migrants. The escalation in punitive immigration enforcement in the United States in recent years is both shocking and familiar, particularly under the Trump administration. From January 2017 to early 2021, there were repeated extensions of a Muslim ban; the everywhere and everyday threat of immigration raids; zero tolerance and incarceration for unauthorized border crossing; family separation and detention of children as normalized practice; regular reports of the mistreatment and abuse of migrants at border crossings and in detention; rejection of international protocols and agreements for those seeking sanctuary and protection; and slashing of numbers admitted to the United States via refugee resettlement (see Wadhia 2019). There was a seemingly daily barrage and assault on migrants, whether they lived in or were attempting to reach the United States. In short, the United States has seemingly lost whatever semblance of moral compass it may have had. As of this writing in January 2021, the extent to which the administration of President Joe Biden is able to change course remains to be seen.

In response to these recent punitive and cruel measures, a number of sectors of society—including activists, legal advocates, religious communities, professional bodies, and ordinary people—have voiced outrage and significant legal action has been undertaken in an effort to mitigate, stymie, or undo these policies. Our analysis suggests that questioning the commodification of migrants and identifying how various peoples and entities benefit from such commodification is key to understanding this current (a)social norm. As routine processes of detention deindividuate migrants, we can find ways to counter these forces of erasure by extracting concrete, relatable examples of how detainees are stripped of personhood. While the neglect of detained migrants' bodies is seemingly sanctioned by and ingrained in the operation of detention, we can lay bare the cruelty of denying common human needs. We can trace tactics for isolating detainees in a way that produces counter-maps for maintaining migrants' support networks. All efforts to expose how detained migrants experience social death are critical to unraveling the economic value of social death across a wide swath of society, from the private sector to local government, and thus critical to reestablishing the moral and social value of migration and migrants' lives.

NOTES

1. Annual appropriations for DHS were enacted December 20, 2019, in a bill that included a net discretionary budget of $50.47 billion ($1.06 billion or 2.1 percent higher than in fiscal year [FY] 2019). The final approved budget for Immigration and Customs Enforcement for FY 2020 was $8.08 billion (up from $7.58 billion in FY 2019) (Painter 2020).

2. Different from Essex and Hudson, Bergen's contract is with the U.S. Marshals Service (part of the Department of Justice). This is likely due to the existence of an established relationship between Bergen and the U.S. Marshals Service prior to 2002, when the Department of Homeland Security (which houses ICE) was created.

3. Our efforts to gain access to the facilities and to detainees in our study have routinely been stymied (see Conlon and Hiemstra 2014), and available information about who is detained in these facilities is limited; consequently, we refer to reports from advocacy groups such as Human Rights Watch and journalistic reporting to offer some insight into migrants' experiences of conditions in the detention centers we study.

4. Because Bergen contracts with various individual providers for varying amounts of time, it is difficult to calculate the total the county pays for medical services at BCJ.

5. It is beyond the scope of this chapter to trace the manifold profit-seeking ventures, revenue, and wealth generated by these companies. Our long-term project aims to follow the money in this way. Each of these companies has contracts with immigrant detention and other custodial care facilities around the United States.

6. An October 2019 Target store price for an eight-count box of Hostess chocolate cupcakes was $2.99 ($0.37 each), and the January 2019 commissary price for a package of two cupcakes was $1.15 ($0.57 each).

7. At final editing of this chapter in January 2021, this point is clearly, violently illustrated in the blatant failure to protect detainees from exposure to COVID-19 amid its rampant spread in detention facilities (Freed Wessler 2020).

REFERENCES

Agamben, Giorgio. 1998. *Homo Sacer: Sovereign Power and Bare Life*. Stanford, CA: Stanford University Press.

Baker, James. 2014. "Social Death: Racialized Rightlessness and the Criminalization of the Unprotected." *Ethnic and Racial Studies* 37 (10): 1889–1891.

Bernstein, Nina. 2016. "Health Care in New Jersey Immigrant Jail is Substandard, Watchdog Groups Say." *New York Times*, May 11. https://www.nytimes.com/2016/05/12/nyregion/health-care-at-new-jersey-immigrant-jail-prompts-claim.html.

Biehl, João. 2005. *Vita: Life in a Zone of Social Abandonment*. Oakland: University of California Press.

Bonds, Anne. 2009. "Discipline and Devolution: Constructions of Poverty, Race, and Criminality in the Politics of Rural Prison Development." *Antipode: A Radical Journal of Geography* 41 (3): 416–438.

Borgstrom, Erica. 2017. "Social Death." *QJM: An International Journal of Medicine* 110 (1): 5–7.

Cacho, Lisa Marie. 2012. *Social Death: Racialized Rightlessness and the Criminalization of the Unprotected*. New York: New York University Press.

Cervantes-Gautschi, Peter. 2010. "Wall Street and the Criminalization of Immigrants." *Counterpunch*, October 15. https://www.counterpunch.org/2010/10/15/wall-street-and-the-criminalization-of-immigrants/.

Cho, Eunice, and Paromita Shah. 2016. "Shadow Prisons: Immigrant Detention in the South." Southern Poverty Law Center, National Lawyers Guild, and Adelante Alabama Worker Center, November. https://www.splcenter.org/sites/default/files/ijp_shadow_prisons_immigrant_detention_report.pdf.

Conlon, Deirdre. 2017. "Immigration Policy and Migrant Support Organizations in an Era of Austerity and Hope." In *Immigration Policy in the Age of Punishment: Detention, Deportation and Border Control*, edited by David Brotherton and Philip Kretsedemas, 57–74. New York: Columbia University Press.

Conlon, Deirdre, and Nancy Hiemstra. 2014. "Examining the Everyday Microeconomies of Migrant Detention in the United States." *Geographica Helvetica* 69:335–344.

———. 2017. "Mobility and Materialization of the Carceral: Examining Immigration and Immigration Detention." In *Carceral Mobilities: Interrogating Movement in Incarceration*, edited by Jennifer Turner and Kimberley Peters, 100–114. Abingdon, UK: Routledge.

Crewe, Ben, Jason Warr, Peter Bennett, and Alan Smith. 2014. "The Emotional Geography of Prison Life." *Theoretical Criminology* 18 (1): 56–74.

Curcio, Lindsay, Anu Joshi, Camille Mackler, and Michael Mandel. 2012. "Expose and Close: Hudson County Jail, New Jersey." *Detention Watch Network*, November.

https://www.detentionwatchnetwork.org/sites/default/files/reports/DWN%20
Expose%20and%20Close%20Hudson%20County.pdf.

Davis, Tom. 2019. "235 Undocumented Immigrants at Mexico Border Sent to NJ, NY."
NJ Patch, May 31. https://patch.com/new-jersey/manasquan/235-undocumented
-immigrants-mexico-border-sent-nj-ny.

Dickerson, Caitlin. 2019. "Migrant Children are Entitled to Toothbrushes and Soap,
Federal Court Rules." *New York Times*, August 15. https://www.nytimes.com/
2019/08/15/us/migrant-children-toothbrushes-court.html.

Doty, Roxanne Lynn, and Elizabeth S. Wheatley. 2013. "Private Detention and the Immigration Industrial Complex." *International Political Sociology* 7:426–443.

Essex County Correctional Facility. 2018. "ICE Detainee Handbook." In the authors'
possession.

Fang, Lee. 2017. "Trump's New Immigration Crackdown Has Private Prison Investors
Salivating." *The Intercept*, February 22. https://theintercept.com/2017/02/22/geo
-group-trump/.

Fleury-Steiner, Benjamin, and Jamie Longazel. 2013. *The Pains of Mass Imprisonment*.
New York: Routledge.

Freedom for Immigrants. n.d. "Persecuted in U.S. Immigration Detention: A National
Report on Abuse Motivated by Hate." Accessed December 10, 2020. https://static1
.squarespace.com/static/5a33042eb078691c386e7bce/t/5b3174e46d2a73f2d1f56aab/
1529967847644/FFI_NatReportAbuse_062518.pdf.

Freed Wessler, Seth. 2016. "ICE Plans to Reopen the Very Same Private Prison the Feds
Just Closed." *The Nation*, October 27. https://www.thenation.com/article/ice-plans
-to-reopen-the-very-same-private-prison-the-feds-just-closed/.

———. 2020. "Fear, Illness and Death in ICE Detention: How a Protest Grew on the
Inside." *New York Times*, July 10. https://www.nytimes.com/2020/06/04/magazine/
covid-ice.html.

Freeman, Semuteh, and Lauren Major. 2012. "Immigration Incarceration: The Expansion and Failed Reform of Immigration Detention in Essex County, NJ." New
York University School of Law Immigrant Rights Clinic, March. https://www
.law.nyu.edu/sites/default/files/upload_documents/Immigration%20Incarceration
.pdf.

Gilmore, Ruth Wilson. 2007. *Golden Gulag: Prisons, Surplus, Crisis, and Opposition in
Globalizing California*. Los Angeles: University of California Press.

Goffman, Erving. 1961. *Asylums: Essays on the Social Situation of Mental Patients and
Other Inmates*. London: Penguin.

Golash-Boza, Tanya. 2009. "The Immigration Industrial Complex: Why We Enforce
Immigration Policies Destined to Fail." *Sociology Compass* 3 (2): 295–309.

Guha, Auditi. 2019. "'Complicit' New Jersey Democrats Face Pressure to End ICE Contracts." *Rewire*, July 12. https://rewire.news/article/2019/07/12/complicit-new-jersey
-democrats-face-pressure-to-end-ice-contracts/.

Hiemstra, Nancy. 2013. "'You Don't Even Know Where You Are': Chaotic Geographies
of US Migrant Detention and Deportation." In *Carceral Spaces: Mobility and Agency
in Imprisonment and Migrant Detention*, edited by Dominique Moran, Nick Gill,
and Deirdre Conlon, 57–75. Burlington, VT: Ashgate.

———. 2019. *Detain and Deport: The Chaotic U.S. Immigration Enforcement Regime*.
Athens: University of Georgia Press.

Hiemstra, Nancy, and Deirdre Conlon. 2016. "Captive Consumers and Coerced Labourers: Intimate Economies and the Expanding US Detention Regime." In *Intimate Economies of Immigration Detention: Critical Perspectives*, edited by Deirdre Conlon and Nancy Hiemstra, 123–139. London: Routledge.

———. 2017. "Beyond Privatization: Bureaucratization and the Spatialities of Immigration Detention Expansion." *Territory, Politics, Governance* 5 (3): 252–268.

Honl-Stuenkel, Linnaea, and Lauren White. 2019. "Mattis Joins Board of Contractor Profiting from Zero Tolerance Policy." Citizens for Responsibility and Ethics in Washington, August 8. https://www.citizensforethics.org/mattis-zero-tolerance -policy-general-dyanmics/.

Human Rights First. 2018. "Ailing Justice: New Jersey; Inadequate Healthcare, Indifference, and Indefinite Confinement in Immigration Detention." February. https:// www.humanrightsfirst.org/sites/default/files/Ailing-Justice-NJ.pdf.

Human Rights Watch. 2019. "US: Family Separation Harming Children, Families." *HRW News*, July 11. https://www.hrw.org/news/2019/07/11/us-family-separation -harming-children-families.

Janoski, Steve. 2018. "Bergen County Will Collect $12M for Housing Immigrant Detainees." *NorthJersey*, July 2. https://www.northjersey.com/story/news/bergen/ 2018/07/02/bergen-county-collect-housing-immigrant-detainees/585842002/.

———. 2019. "ICE Detainees at Bergen County Jail Draw Activists' Attention." *NorthJersey*, April 9. https://www.northjersey.com/story/news/bergen/2019/04/09/ice -detainees-bergen-county-jail-draw-activist-attention/3416728002/.

Katz, Matt. 2018a. "No Family Contact Visits Allowed: Life for Immigrants at Bergen County Jail." *WNYC*, September 20. https://www.wnyc.org/story/no-family -contact-visits-allowed-life-immigrants-bergen-county-jail/.

———. 2018b. "Should New Jersey Democratic Officials Keep Jailing Immigrants for ICE?" *WNYC*, August 16. https://www.wnyc.org/story/should-new-jersey-demo cratic-officials-keep-jailing-immigrants-ice.

———. 2018c. "Under Trump, Democratic New Jersey Counties Cash in on Detaining Immigrants." *WNYC*, July 11. https://www.wnyc.org/story/under-trump-liberal -new-jersey-counties-cash-in-detaining-immigrants.

———. 2019a. "Abandoned Gun, Moldy Bread Pudding and 'Unrecognizable' Hamburgers Found in New Jersey Immigrant Lock-Up." *WNYC*, February 15. https://www.wnyc.org/story/abandoned-gun-moldy-bread-and-unrecognizable -hamburgers-found-new-jersey-immigrant-lock-/.

———. 2019b. "Immigrant Detainees Held in Cells for Days during Lockdown at NJ Jail." *WNYC*, February 21. https://www.wnyc.org/story/immigrant-detainees-held -cells-days-during-security-lockdown-new-jersey-jail/.

Kiefer, Eric. 2019. "Essex County Jail Stuck ICE Detainees with Giant Underwear: Feds." *New Jersey Patch*, June 12. https://patch.com/new-jersey/newarknj/essex-county -jail-stuck-ice-detainees-giant-underwear-feds.

Kim, Sunny. 2019. "Private Prison Firm Quietly Ramps Up GOP Lobbying Efforts as Trump Expands Immigrant Detention Centers." *CNBC*, October 4. https:// www.cnbc.com/2019/10/04/private-prison-firm-ramps-up-lobbying-amid-trump -immigration-crackdown.html.

Králová, Jana. 2015. "What Is Social Death?" *Contemporary Social Science* 10 (3): 235–248.

Larner, Wendy. 2000. "Neoliberalism, Policy, Ideology, Governmentality." *Studies in Political Economy* 63 (1): 5–25.

Longazel, Jamie, Jake Berman, and Benjamin Fleury-Steiner. 2016. "The Pains of Immigrant Imprisonment." *Sociology Compass* 10:989–998.

Loyd, Jenna, and Alison Mountz. 2018. *Boats, Borders, and Bases: Race, the Cold War and the Rise of Migration Detention in the United States.* Oakland: University of California Press.

Misra, Tanvi. 2018. "Where Cities Help Detain Immigrants." *CityLab*, July 10. https://www.bloomberg.com/news/articles/2018-07-10/where-u-s-counties-are -detaining-immigrants.

Mitchell, Katharyne. 2016. "Neoliberalism and Citizenship." In *Handbook of Neoliberalism*, edited by Simon Springer, 104–115. New York: Routledge.

Mitchelson, Matthew. 2014. "The Production of Bedspace: Prison Privatization and Abstract Space." *Geographica Helvetica* 69:325–333.

Moran, Dominique, Nick Gill, and Deirdre Conlon, eds. 2013. *Carceral Spaces: Mobility and Agency in Imprisonment and Migrant Detention.* Farnham, UK: Ashgate.

Morin, Karen M., and Dominique Moran, eds. 2015. *Historical Geographies of Prisons: Unlocking the Usable Carceral Past.* Abingdon, UK: Routledge.

Mountz, Alison. 2011. "Specters at the Port of Entry: Understanding State Mobilities through an Ontology of Exclusion." *Mobilities* 6 (3): 317–334.

O'Dea, Colleen. 2019. "Protestors Demand Essex County End Contract to House ICE Detainees." *NJ Spotlight News*, April 25. https://www.njspotlight.com/2019/04/19 -04-24-protestors-demand-essex-county-end-lucrative-contract-to-house-ice -detainees/.

Office of Inspector General. 2019. "Issues Requiring Action at the Essex County Correctional Facility in Newark, New Jersey." OIG-19-20, February 13. https://www .oig.dhs.gov/sites/default/files/assets/2019-02/OIG-19-20-Feb19.pdf.

Painter, William L. 2020. "Department of Homeland Security Appropriations: FY2020." *Congressional Research Service*, January 21. https://crsreports.congress.gov/product/ pdf/R/R46113.

Patterson, Orlando. 1982. *Slavery and Social Death: A Comparative Study.* London: Harvard University Press.

Pauly, Madison. 2018. "Trump's Immigration Crackdown Is a Boom Time for Private Prisons." *Mother Jones*, May–June. https://www.motherjones.com/politics/2018/05/ trumps-immigration-crackdown-is-a-boom-time-for-private-prisons/.

Rizzo, Salvador. 2019. "John F. Kelly Joins Board of Contractor Running Shelters for Migrants." *Washington Post*, May 4. https://www.washingtonpost.com/politics/ john-kelly-joins-board-joins-board-of-contractor-running-shelter-for-migrant -teens/2019/05/04/e28000fc-6e87-11e9-a66d-a82d3f3d96d5_story.html.

Rodríguez, Dylan. 2008. "'I Would Wish Death on You...': Race, Gender and Immigration in the Globality of the U.S. Prison Regime." *Scholar and Feminist Online* 6 (3). http://sfonline.barnard.edu/immigration/drodriguez_01.htm.

Silverman, Stephanie J. 2010. "Immigration Detention in America: A History of Its Expansion and a Study of Its Significance." COMPAS Working Paper No. 80. https://papers.ssrn.com/sol3/papers.cfm?abstract_id=1867366.

Stange, Mia, and Brett Stark. 2019. "The Ethical and Public Health Implications of Family Separation." *Journal of Law, Medicine and Ethics* 47 (S2): 91–94.

Sudbury, Julia. 2005. *Global Lockdown: Race, Gender, and the Prison-Industrial Complex*. New York: Routledge.

Sullivan, Laura. 2010. "Prison Economics Help Drive Arizona Immigration Law." *NPR*, October 28. https://www.npr.org/2010/10/28/130833741/prison-economics-help-drive-ariz-immigration-law.

Torbati, Yeganah, and Kristina Cooke. 2019. "First Stop for Migrant Kids: For-Profit Detention Center." *Reuters*, February 14. https://www.reuters.com/article/us-usa-immigration-children/first-stop-for-migrant-kids-for-profit-detention-center-id USKCN1Q3261.

U.S. Government. 2019. *A Budget for a Better America*. Washington, DC: U.S. Government Publishing Office. https://www.govinfo.gov/content/pkg/BUDGET-2020-BUD/pdf/BUDGET-2020-BUD.pdf.

Vogt, Wendy A. 2013. "Crossing Mexico: Structural Violence and the Commodification of Undocumented Central American Migrants." *American Ethnologist* 40 (4): 764–780.

Wadhia, Shoba S. 2019. *Banned: Immigration Enforcement in the Time of Trump*. New York: New York University Press.

Welch, Michael. 2002. *Detained: Immigration Laws and the Expanding I.N.S. Jail Complex*. Philadelphia: Temple University Press.

6

Heat-Related Illness and Death among Migrant Farmworkers

Dispatches from the Girasoles Study

Nathan J. Mutic
Linda A. McCauley

When Carlos signed up to participate in our research study, which was designed to elucidate the effects of occupational exposure to heat stress on immigrant agricultural workers, his creatinine level was 14.6 mg/dL (normal range is 0.7–1.3 mg/dL), and his blood urea nitrogen (BUN) was 123 mg/dL (normal range is 6–20 mg/dL). His blood pressure was 175/96, and his hemoglobin level was 7.8 g/dL (normal range is 13.8–17.2 g/dL). Carlos, like many of his coworkers, was not under care for any health problem and lacked the time and money for preventive screenings. He reported feeling healthy and able to complete his normal daily activities. However, when he returned the next morning for a second screening, researchers again observed abnormal levels and responded by scheduling a follow-up appointment at the local clinic. Health-care workers at the clinic quickly referred Carlos to the nearest emergency care facility, where he was admitted with acute renal failure and anemia, secondary to obstructed uropathy.

As a result of his kidney failure, Carlos spent seventy-nine consecutive days in the hospital and underwent eight independent surgeries. In the ensuing months, he continued to receive dialysis three times a week. Because he is uninsured and undocumented, hospital administrators urged him to voluntarily repatriate to Mexico, even though he had not lived there in more than a decade and was estranged from any remaining family there. Repatriation would have included cost of transportation, three months of dialysis, and enrollment in the Seguro Popular, a current initiative of the Mexican government to cover uninsured workers, retirees, and their families. Yet the insurance would not cover dialysis services indefinitely and he had no financial means to pay for continued treatment out of pocket. Thus, he refused repatriation and the hospital remained legally responsible for his well-being until he could be stabilized. As a result of his extended hospitalization and health condition, he was unable to work and was subsequently evicted from his employer-owned housing. With no remaining family connections, no transportation, and no housing, he must now rely on the farmworker community for basic necessities like food, shelter, and health care (Flocks et al. 2018).

Carlos is lucky to be alive; others in similar circumstances did not survive. Maria Vasquez Jimenez, who migrated to California's Central Valley to seek employment with her fiancé, was seventeen years old and pregnant when she collapsed from heat stroke while pruning grape vines in 95-degree-Fahrenheit heat and direct sun. She was denied access to shade and water by her supervisor. After becoming aware of her condition, her boss recommended she rest in a hot van and suggested she be revived with rubbing alcohol. Maria was comatose by the time she was treated at a hospital and had a fever of 108 degrees Fahrenheit. She died days after being admitted (Guidi 2018).[1] Two years earlier in Immokalee, Florida, one of the communities in which we conducted our study, a Haitian immigrant farmworker lost his life to occupational exposure to heat while harvesting tomatoes. Jean Francais Alcime, fifty years old, had complained of heat exhaustion and was observed stumbling while working in the field. On the bus trip back to Immokalee, Jean said he needed help, but his supervisor said he should rest on the bus and call the paramedics once he arrived if he was not feeling better. When the bus arrived back at Immokalee, Jean was not breathing and could not be revived (Perez 2016).

In this chapter, we present an overview of the findings from our Girasoles Study, which examines the physiological effects of occupational heat exposure on agricultural workers in Florida. We present these findings in the social context of *entrapment*, whereby immigrants "are not just enclosed inside the country as a whole but are also impeded from moving around locally to access vital resources" (Núñez and Heyman 2007, 354). Migrant agricultural workers often cannot change employers, lax labor protections keep them from accessing much-needed shade and water under the sweltering sun, their pay structure incentivizes them to push the physiological limits of their bodies, and their access to health care is severely limited. Carlos, Maria, and Jean all experienced forms of entrapment. This chapter details the historical and current legal landscape and occupational hazards facing agricultural workers in light of the idea of entrapment.

The Dangers of Occupational Heat Exposure

Agricultural work has long been recognized as one of the most hazardous types of employment in the United States, with an industry death rate "seven times greater than all occupations combined" (Gasperini 2017, 309). Not even children are protected from many of the risks: fifteen- to seventeen-year-olds who work in agriculture have a death rate of approximately 28 per 100,000, compared to less than 1 per 100,000 in all other occupations combined (NCCRAHS 2018). While this high death rate can be attributed in part to accidents and ergonomic strain involving repetitive tasks, these risks are primarily associated with occupational pesticide and heat exposure (Arcury et al. 2014; Fleischer et al. 2013; Tonelli, Culp, and Donham 2014).

In the decade starting in 1999, an average of 618 people died annually from exposure to excessive heat (CDC 2012). According to the Centers for Disease Control and Prevention (CDC), U.S. agricultural workers, of which 78 percent are Hispanic, are twenty times more likely than the general workforce to die from heat exposure. Approximately 7 heat exposure deaths per year occurred in the agriculture, forestry, fishing, and hunting (AFFH) industries between 2003 and 2008 (U.S. Bureau of Labor Statistics, n.d.)— the highest rate of any sector during that period. In a fourteen-year stretch starting in 1992, 68 deaths among agricultural workers were reported as due to heat exposure in the United States (Jackson and Rosenberg 2010). Unfortunately, these estimates are likely low, in part because of clinicians' inability to recognize and identify heat-related deaths (Ostro et al. 2009; Wolfe et al. 2001).

As the Intergovernmental Panel on Climate Change has warned, these problems are only going to worsen as temperatures continue to rise (Roelofs and Wegman 2014). The 2016 Climate and Health Assessment report highlights that people who work outdoors, people who are socially isolated, the poor, those suffering from chronic illnesses, and communities of color are at disproportionately high risk of heat-related illness or death (USGCRP 2016). Immigrant and migrant workers fall into one or several of these categories and are the largest group regularly exposed to the elements at work. Indeed, an estimated 71 percent of today's U.S. agricultural workforce are from Mexico or Central or South America (CDC 2008). Agricultural workers are often required to work long workdays in direct sun and high temperatures (Stoecklin-Marois et al. 2013). In some instances, such as in fern production and harvesting, work is conducted under black shade tarps that trap heat and humidity and limit airflow in the work environment (Mac et al. 2017).

Regulatory Context and History

The agriculture, forestry, fishing, and hunting industry is historically one of the least regulated yet most hazardous (Liebman et al. 2013). Employers often do not provide agricultural laborers with workday breaks, a minimum wage, insurance coverage, or overtime pay (Luna 2014; Flocks et al. 2018). This dichotomy is in many ways attributable to a history of "agricultural exceptionalism," the historical exclusion of agricultural workers from federal and state regulations designed to protect workers in other sectors (Rodman et al. 2016). In this way, the unfair treatment of agricultural workers is not unique to the current agricultural workforce, which is primarily composed of immigrant workers from Mexico and Central America. Rather, it is a continuation of a systemic racialized approach to maintaining a cheap and controllable labor force to maximize profits in the agricultural industry.

The National Labor Relations Act (NLRA) of 1935 specifically leaves agricultural workers outside of its protections, putting them at increased risk for occupational injury and death. The original version of the NLRA, which was established to protect employees' right to organize and engage in collective bargaining (National Labor and Safety Act of 1935), included farmworkers or domestic laborers. Unfortunately, the final version of the NLRA excluded farmworkers and domestic laborers. In part, this was fostered by the belief that small family-run farms would be burdened by collective bargaining (LeRoy 1999). It has also been documented that the NLRA's author, Senator Robert Wagner of New York, did not want to risk a fight in the U.S. Senate, which was largely controlled by rural white southerners with an interest in preserving racial inequities (Perea 2010). The exclusion of agricultural workers afforded southern elites more control over the majority African American workforce (Farhang and Katznelson 2005). Without legal protections from employer retaliation, agricultural workers were and still are limited in their ability to organize and advocate for appropriate safety standards. They are also denied the ability to strike, a tactic that would provide them with significant leverage given the time-sensitive nature of farm work during planting and harvesting periods.

Similarly, the Fair Labor Standards Act (FLSA), which was created following the Great Depression and provided specific worker protections including a minimum wage, maximum work hours, and overtime provisions, did not include farmworkers from the time of its creation in 1938 until it was amended in 1966 (Rodman et al. 2016). Again, these exclusions were primarily made in the interest of large southern agricultural employers who historically depended on cheap or slave labor (Linder 1986). Their positions were clearly racially discriminatory as evident in the hearings on the FLSA.

For example, during the debate over the FLSA, James Wilcox, a representative from Florida, asserted, "You cannot put the Negro and the white man on the same basis and get away with it," referring to the notion of establishing a uniform equal minimum wage (Perea 2010). Some recognized the political interests at play and vocalized their opposition. Representative Fred Hartley from New Jersey called out this unequal treatment of agricultural workers and pointed out southern political influence (Canny 2005). Even though in 1966 agricultural workers on large farms were included under the FLSA protections, workers on extremely small farms remain exempt to this day. In the more recent version of the law, worker protections are still not granted to those who did not work in agriculture for thirteen or more weeks in the previous year, those who are paid by piece rate, and those under seventeen years of age working on the same farm as their parents (Rodman et al. 2016).

We also see the denial of worker protections in programs designed to bring vulnerable populations into the United States for work. The Bracero Program was a bilateral agreement between the United States and Mexico in 1942 that lasted six years and resulted in 4.6 million contracts to bring single, male Mexicans into the United States for agricultural work (Calavita 2010; Sifuentez 2016). While certain worker rights were to be protected under the program and many workers benefited from it (Cohen 2011), the program was by and large exploitative and subjected workers to dehumanizing conditions. Bracero workers were to be provided employment for at least three-quarters of their contract, transportation to and from Mexico, housing, and prevailing industry wages. However, many workers in the program had to sell family heirlooms and take loans to travel to worksites. Workers endured invasive medical exams, were routinely sprayed with the pesticide DDT, were not fairly compensated for their work, received inadequate medical care, and often lived in overcrowded barracks (Loza 2016). Here again we see the process of entrapment at play as millions of workers were by and large trapped without their own transportation at their worksite, trapped in substandard housing, and trapped by their inability to access quality health-care services.

From the 1970s until the turn of the century, farm labor became primarily sustained by immigrants from Latin America, and approximately 75 percent were undocumented. Migrant routes became prevalent across the United States with a dependable agricultural workforce, many of whom crossed back and forth over the U.S. border with minimal to no consequences. As workers moved from one part of the country to another, they often experienced poor housing conditions and economic insecurity. Many did not speak English and had little access to health care or other social support services in communities.

Since the 2007–2009 recession, the makeup of the immigrant population in the United States has changed drastically. As the number of Mexican and undocumented immigrants dropped, increasing numbers of farmworkers entered the country on legal H-2A work visas. H-2A is a federal program that permits employers to apply for guest workers to perform seasonal or temporary farmwork for a maximum of ten months. Most of these workers are not accompanied by family. An H-2A worker's spouse and children are prohibited from working in the United States, though they may seek admission in another visa category. Thirty-six percent of H-2A jobs certified in 2016 were in just three southeastern states: Florida, North Carolina, and Georgia (Martin 2017). In no circumstances is the H-2A visa allowed to serve as a stepping-stone to a green card or citizenship, though it can be extended multiple times.

Farmworker Justice (2011) published an often-cited report on how employers abuse the H-2A visa program. It details how wages are kept low, how workers have no access to economic bargaining, high instances of wage theft, abuses in the worker recruitment program including fees from workers, poor and crowded housing, and migrant workers' lack of access to health care. In the past five years as the U.S. government has tightened its borders, there has been a rapid increase in H-2A visas. In 2014, approximately 90,000 H-2A visas were issued (U.S. Department of State 2014). The number grew to 196,409 in 2018 (U.S. Department of State 2018), and H-2A guest workers now constitute about 7 percent of the U.S. agricultural workforce, increasing the potential for abuse. A visa program in which the guest workers can be shipped home at any time if they complain about working conditions is unjust. There is no systematic oversight or a mechanism to ensure protection if a worker complains, and employers know that the visa prohibits the workers from seeking other employment if they are unhappy. All of these factors set the stage for ignoring labor infractions or abuse, and the entrapment experienced by current H2-A workers bears striking parallels to what Bracero workers faced decades ago.

According to the Occupational Safety and Health (OSH) Act of 1970, federal law requires that employers provide a workplace that is "free from recognized hazards that are causing or are likely to cause death or serious physical harm to his employees."[2] The OSH Act also established the National Institute for Occupational Safety and Health (NIOSH), which conducts occupational health and safety research that can be used to make recommendations for the prevention of injury and illness. In 1986 NIOSH published an evaluation of the scientific data on heat stress and comprehensive recommendations for employers to protect their workers. This 192-page document was updated in 2016 and provides clear guidance for employers on how to protect their employees, as well as the data to support the recommendations (NIOSH 2016). Yet presently, *only* three states have legal protections in place specifically designed to address occupational exposure to heat (Occupational Safety and Health Administration, n.d.). While some of the protections are helpful, they are still insufficient and lack enforcement and accountability. California has the most comprehensive standards, which require employers to focus on four key areas to protect their workers from occupational heat exposure. The four areas are (1) heat illness prevention training, (2) providing water, (3) providing shade and rest breaks, and (4) maintaining and implementing a heat illness prevention plan.[3] Minnesota's regulations on heat exposure focus on the indoor work environment only and set limits on the maximum indoor environmental heat that workers can be exposed to based on how vigorous their work is. Minnesota law also requires that employees exposed to occupational heat are provided special safety training.[4] Interestingly, the Minnesota administrative rules that specify what the safety training must require do not include the word "heat." They generally describe how and when trainings must be delivered and do specifically address hazardous substances, physical agents, and infectious agents but do not address heat-related illness specifically.[5] Washington State has developed specific requirements that clearly outline the responsibilities of the employer and employee in preventing heat-related illness. The Washington rules focus on drinking water, responding to signs and symptoms of heat-related illness, and training requirements for employees and employers.[6]

The Girasoles Study

Our research team studies the effects of occupational heat exposure on agricultural workers in the context of the Farmworker Vulnerability to Heat Hazards Framework (Mac and McCauley 2017). This framework consists of an input, environmental heat stress, which can lead to varying degrees of heat stress response depending on vulnerability factors including workplace exposures, individual sensitivities, and adaptive capacity. The American Conference of Government and Industrial Hygienists has established heat exposure guidelines that are designed to prevent workers from exceeding a core temperature of 100.4 degrees Fahrenheit to avoid the progression of heat-related illness and heat stroke (ACGHI 2007). Importantly, even this threshold has been criticized by some as an inadequate limit because it has not been validated in a wide enough array of populations (Lamarche et al. 2017) and settings (Meade et al. 2016).

Our study, known as the Girasoles Study, tracked 257 farmworkers in five different communities in the state of Florida to characterize and understand the effects of occupational heat exposure on their health. Participants in the Girasoles Study were recruited by our partners at the Farmworkers Association of Florida. The majority of study participants were female,[7] were originally from Mexico or Guatemala, and worked in either nurseries, ferneries, or crops. Each participant followed the standard study protocol described previously (Mix et al. 2018). Briefly, biometric data collection began on a baseline pre-work day; then we tracked workers' data over the course of three consecutive workdays. Participants wore activity, heart rate, and external temperature sensors. Additionally, they swallowed a pill that measured their internal body temperature every thirty seconds throughout the workday (Hertzberg et al. 2017). We also administered questionnaires and other biological samples to capture workplace characteristics, symptoms experience, dehydration status, and kidney function. Following three days of data collection, participants were given copies of all their individual data, which a study team nurse reviewed with the workers in their native language.

The first and perhaps most alarming finding was the number of heat-related illness (HRI) symptoms reported. In order of frequency, workers reported excessive sweating, headache, dizziness, nausea and vomiting, muscle cramps, confusion, and fainting. Eighty-four percent of workers reported experiencing at least one symptom, 42 percent reported experiencing two or more symptoms, and 18 percent reported experiencing three or more symptoms (Figure 6.1) (Mutic, Mix, et al. 2018). Our initial real-time measurements of the internal body temperatures of a subset of participants revealed that they frequently exceeded the 100.4-degree Fahrenheit cutoff (Hertzberg et al. 2017). We later found that 49 percent of our total study population exceeded the 100.4-degree Fahrenheit threshold, and the median time spent above this threshold was over an hour (Mac et al. 2021). Almost a quarter of the study population reached 38.5 degrees Celsius during the workday. This is the equivalent of running a 101.3-degree Fahrenheit fever. These data clearly demonstrate that agricultural workers are pushing the physiological limits of their bodies and are in dire need of adequate breaks, at a minimum. This is supported by reports from individuals surveyed in this community who describe how the heat affects their bodies. An individual working in the same community reported, "It is because of the heat that you can't see clearly. Sometimes I see a person walking, but I can't see his/her face. I can't distinguish them (when I have a headache)" (Flocks et al. 2013).

We also investigated the relationships between physical activity, work type, and environmental heat exposure. Workers were stratified by the type of work they conducted (fernery, field crop, or nursery work). We observed significant differences in the activity levels among work types. Fernery workers spent the majority of their workday in the moderate to vigorous category

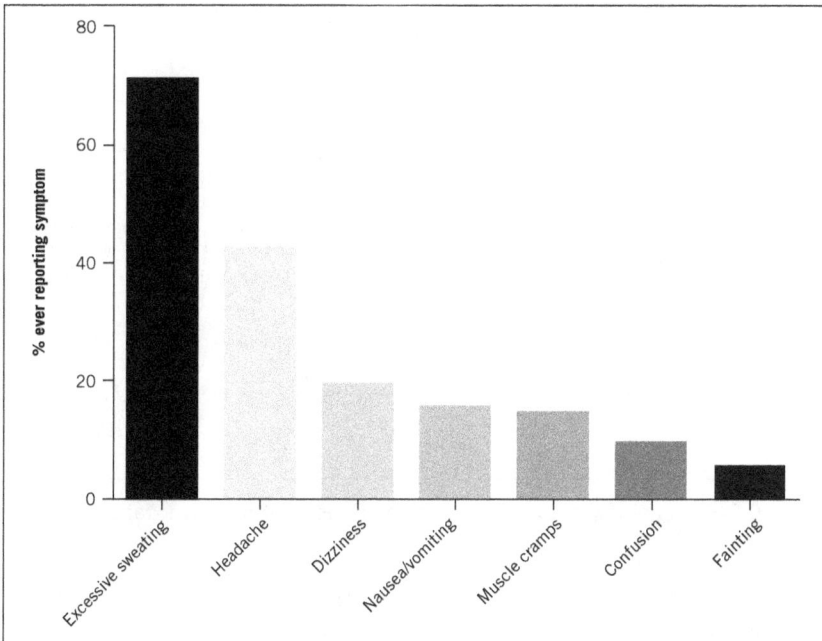

Figure 6.1 Percentage of workers who reported symptoms anytime during the observation period.

for work intensity. Ferneries are unique work environments where black shade cloths are often draped over fields of ferns, limiting airflow and trapping additional heat (Flocks et al. 2013). Fernery workers spend long hours bending over to cut and bundle ferns and quickly transport them to trailers.

Participants in our study working in Pierson, Florida, primarily worked in ferneries, and the intensity of their work was higher compared to other locations with different primary work types (Figure 6.2). We also observed that some workers did not reduce their physical activity when exposed to dangerously hot environmental conditions (Mix et al. 2019). Fernery workers are paid by piece rate, or by the volume of their harvest. This pay structure is infamous for encouraging workers to overexert themselves and is associated with HRI (Spector, Krenz, and Blank 2015). Fernery workers spend a substantial portion of their day either bent over or moving quickly from the field to the trailer where the fern bundles are deposited. In essence the pressure to harvest quickly leads to physical entrapment of their bodies in a particular position, and forces them to move at a rigorous pace. Dehydration results from the intense physical exertion in a hot work environment and excessive sweating. Analysis of blood and urine samples collected over 555 workdays from participants in the Girasoles Study revealed that

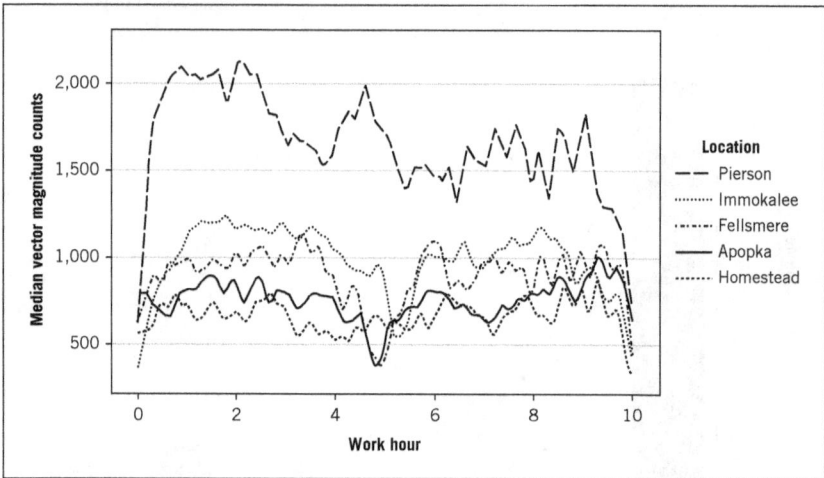

Figure 6.2 Work activity of participants in the Girasoles Study by location.

81 percent of workers were dehydrated at the end of a shift. Thirty-three percent of participants had acute kidney injury on at least one workday (Mix et al. 2018). The piece-rate pay structure discourages hydration because of the increased need to take restroom breaks, which reduce earning potential. For female workers, using restrooms not located in close proximity to the rest of the work crew puts them at additional risk of being sexually harassed or assaulted (Murphy et al. 2014; Kim et al. 2016). Both the concern of lost wages and fear of assault are clear examples of occupational entrapment. Additionally, water may not be available, and crew leaders frequently lack training in recognizing the signs and symptoms of HRI. Crew leaders also often face pressure to overlook signs and symptoms of their laborers' health problems in an effort to maximize production. Our observations of kidney injury in agricultural workers are consistent with reports in the United States of acute kidney injury (AKI) and a larger global trend of kidney injury in other agricultural settings.

AKI is characterized by sudden kidney failure occurring over a few hours or days. It is triggered by an increase in serum creatinine and ultimately leads to an inability of the kidneys to maintain a normal fluid balance in the body (Rahman, Shad, and Smith 2012). AKI can affect brain, heart, and lung function and can put individuals at elevated risk of kidney disease, stroke, or heart disease (National Kidney Foundation 2020). Agricultural workers may be at increased risk for developing AKI as a result of their unique occupational and environmental exposures (Moyce et al. 2016). In a study in California of three hundred agricultural workers, primarily of Mexican origin, 11.8 percent of participants developed AKI during the workday. Disturbingly, those working under a piece-rate payment structure were over four times more likely to develop AKI than individuals paid hourly. We posit that this increased risk may be due to the combined effect of factors including the increased physical intensity of piece-rate workers, as previously reported in our data, and a system that discourages employees from using the restroom, or taking breaks and hydrating. None of the standard risk factors for AKI were associated with development of AKI in this study, which supports the hypothesis that intense physical labor under hot environmental conditions is putting agricultural workers at increased risk of kidney injury (Moyce et al. 2016). Further investigation of the same cohort revealed that heat strain was statistically associated with AKI in male agricultural workers (Moyce et al. 2017). Agricultural workers' increased susceptibility to AKI related to heat and physically demanding work is compounded by additional occupational risk factors such as insect stings (Dhanapriya et al. 2016) and snake bites (Li, Chen, and Wu 2016).

Taking a global perspective, these observations of AKI among U.S. farmworkers are worrying in light of international concerns about chronic kidney disease of unknown etiology (CKDu) in agricultural workers especially. CKDu has emerged as a global epidemic that has particularly affected poor Mesoamerican agricultural workers and has taken the lives of over twenty thousand people globally (Pan American Health Organization 2013). CKDu lacks any of the traditional risk factors for chronic kidney disease (CKD) including diabetes, hypertension, and cardiovascular disease, yet it presents similarly to CKD (Crowe et al. 2013). In a recent review, Roxana Chicas and colleagues (2019) make the case that while CDKu has not been observed to date in the United States, many U.S. agricultural workers emigrate from Mesoamerican countries and they face the same hot work environments and physically demanding labor. Therefore, we can anticipate things will only get worse over time for U.S. workers without interventions, as ambient temperatures in the United States steadily rise to those observed in Central America and more workers emigrate to the United States. Our team is currently engaged in a continuation of the Girasoles Study to better understand how heat is affecting kidney function among agricultural workers in Florida.

Lack of Access to Health Care

Our studies and others have documented the significant health risks among this population including core body temperature elevations above Occupational Safety and Health Administration (OSHA) recommendations, kidney injury, and symptoms such as headache, nausea, muscle cramps, and fainting (Chicas et al. 2019; Flocks et al. 2018; Mix et al. 2018; Mutic, Mix, et al. 2018). The story of Carlos in the opening of the chapter exemplifies the impossible position many farmworkers are in when occupational exposures lead to health concerns they are not able to overcome with available resources, particularly a lack of access to health care (Flocks 2018).

A disproportionately high risk of occupational hazards, lack of access to health services, and underutilized health care among immigrant farmworkers have been well documented in over a decade of research (Arcury and Quandt 2007; Colt et al. 2001; Mobed, Gold, and Schenker 1992; Villarejo and Baron 1999). Agricultural workers face unique policy, linguistic, and cultural barriers to mitigating the effects of their occupational hazards and accessing care. For example, many agricultural employers are exempt from provisions of the Fair Labor Standards Act: they can permit children as young as twelve years old to work, and they are exempt from OSHA regulations if employing fewer than eleven employees (Villarejo and Baron 1999). Most work and live in rural areas where health care facilities are sparse. Many of the clinics that may be in close proximity to the farmworker population are subsidized only for eligible residents, thereby preventing access to many who need it the most. Additionally, communication barriers may also prevent workers from accessing care or impede follow-through if patients do not fully understand the medical advice. Current H-2A and permanent resident workers have real concerns about employer retaliation if they report injuries.

The National Agricultural Workers Survey (NAWS) collects data from a random sample of 1,500–3,600 U.S. workers annually. The survey is designed to monitor the status of agricultural employment and characterize the conditions of farmworkers. In a secondary analysis of a subset of NAWS data, we performed a bivariate analysis of characteristics to elucidate factors that were associated with increased likelihood of accessing care in the last two years. We found education, insurance status, and transportation were associated with increased utilization of care (Mutic, Mutic, and McCauley 2018). These three areas represent practical opportunities for legal or public health interventions that could give agricultural workers a better chance of getting lifesaving health-care services.

Conclusion

The United States has a dark history of exploiting agricultural workers that began with slavery. The current agricultural workforce experiences the negative impact of laws that were designed to protect the health and safety of our workforce but deliberately exclude agricultural workers from those protections. Migrant agricultural workers are paid unfair wages, are apparently forced to push themselves beyond normal physiological limits at their workplaces, and are not supported with adequate health care. Intense occupational heat exposure, coupled with physically demanding work conditions, leads to alarming numbers of adverse symptoms and preventable deaths of farmworkers every year. Agricultural workers face entrapment and immobilization, which are permitted by a lack of legal protection and enhanced by their occupational environment. While individuals in some occupations such as first responders are inherently prone to specific workplace hazards, there is no acceptable rationale for the degree of physiological strain and symptoms we observed among our study participants. Additional research, advocacy, and policies are needed to protect the health of immigrant farmworkers.

NOTES

1. This California death represents a flagrant violation of California labor laws requiring access to rest, water, and shade for agricultural workers working in hot environments. See California Code of Regulations, Title 8, §3395, Heat Illness Prevention in Outdoor Places of Employment, available at https://www.dir.ca.gov/title8/3395.html.

2. See the text of the OSH Act of 1970, available at https://www.osha.gov/laws-regs/oshact/completeoshact.

3. See California Code of Regulations, Title 8, §3395, Heat Illness Prevention in Outdoor Places of Employment, available at https://www.dir.ca.gov/title8/3395.html.

4. See Minnesota Administrative Rules, Part 5205.0110, available at https://www.revisor.mn.gov/rules/5205.0110.

5. See Minnesota Administrative Rules, Part 5206.0700, available at https://www.revisor.mn.gov/rules/5206.0700.

6. See Washington Industrial Safety and Health Act of 1973, Chapter 296-307 WAC, Safety Standards for Agriculture, available at https://www.lni.wa.gov/safety health/safety-rules/chapter-pdfs/WAC296-307.pdf#WAC_296_307_097.

7. While we cannot be certain, we believe the larger proportion of females may be due to either (1) the male workforce seeking employment in construction or landscaping, in which wages are higher, or (2) female workers being more receptive to participating in a study that will give them information on their health.

REFERENCES

ACGIH (American Conference of Governmental Industrial Hygienists). 2007. *Heat Stress and Strain: TLV Physical Agents.* 8th ed. Cincinnati, OH: ACGIH.

Arcury, Thomas A., Ha T. Nguyen, Phillip Summers, Jennifer W. Talton, Lourdes Carrillo Holbrook, Francis O. Walker, Haiying Chen, Timothy D. Howard, Leonardo Galván, and Sara A. Quandt. 2014. "Lifetime and Current Pesticide Exposure among Latino Farmworkers in Comparison to Other Latino Immigrants." *American Journal of Industrial Medicine* 57 (7): 776–787.

Arcury, Thomas A., and Sara A. Quandt. 2007. "Delivery of Health Services to Migrant and Seasonal Farmworkers." *Annual Review of Public Health* 28 (1): 345–363.

Calavita, Kitty. 2010. *Inside the State: The Bracero Program, Immigration, and the I.N.S.* New Orleans: Quid Pro Books.

Canny, Autumn L. 2005. "Lost in a Loophole: The Fair Labor Standards Act's Exemption of Agricultural Workers from Overtime Compensation Protection." *Drake Journal of Agricultural Law* 10:355–386.

CDC (Centers for Disease Control and Prevention). 2008. "Heat-Related Deaths among Crop Workers—United States, 1992–2006." *Morbidity and Mortality Weekly Report* 57 (24): 649–653.

———. 2012. "QuickStats: Number of Heat-Related Deaths, by Sex—National Vital Statistics System, United States, 1999–2010." https://www.cdc.gov/mmwr/preview/mmwrhtml/mm6136a6.htm.

Chicas, Roxana, Jacqueline Mix, Valerie Mac, Joan Flocks, Nathan Eric Dickman, Vicki Hertzberg, and Linda McCauley. 2019. "Chronic Kidney Disease among Workers: A Review of the Literature." *Workplace Health and Safety* 67 (9): 481–490.

Cohen, Deborah. 2011. *Braceros: Migrant Citizens and Transnational Subjects in the Postwar United States and Mexico.* Chapel Hill: University of North Carolina Press.

Colt, Joanne S., Lorann Stallones, Lorraine L. Cameron, Mustafa Dosemeci, and Shelia Hoar Zahm. 2001. "Proportionate Mortality among US Migrant and Seasonal Farmworkers in Twenty-Four States." *American Journal of Industrial Medicine* 40 (5): 604–611.

Crowe, Jennifer, Catharina Wesseling, Bryan Román Solano, Manfred Pinto Umaña, Andrés Robles Ramírez, Tord Kjellstrom, David Morales, and Maria Nilsson. 2013. "Heat Exposure in Sugarcane Harvesters in Costa Rica." *American Journal of Industrial Medicine* 56 (10): 1157–1164.

Dhanapriya, Jeyachandran, Thanigachalam Dineshkumar, Ramanathan Sakthirajan, Palaniselvam Shankar, Natarajan Gopalakrishnan, and Thoppalan Balasubramaniyan. 2016. "Wasp Sting-Induced Acute Kidney Injury." *Clinical Kidney Journal* 9 (2): 201–204.

Farhang, Sean, and Ira Katznelson. 2005. "The Southern Imposition: Congress and Labor in the New Deal and Fair Deal." *Studies in American Political Development* 19 (1): 1–30.

Farmworker Justice. 2011. "No Way to Treat a Guest: Why the H-2A Agricultural Visa Program Fails U.S. and Foreign Workers." http://s3.amazonaws.com/migrants_heroku_production/datas/1803/No_Way_To_Treat_A_Guest_H-2A_Report_original.pdf?1417533357.

Fleischer, Nancy L., Hope M. Tiesman, Jeri Sumitani, Terry Mize, Kumar Kartik Amarnath, A. Rana Bayakly, and Matthew W. Murphy. 2013. "Public Health Impact of Heat-Related Illness among Migrant Farmworkers." *American Journal of Preventive Medicine* 44 (3): 199–206.

Flocks, Joan, Valerie Vi Thien Mac, Jennifer Runkle, Jose Antonio Tovar-Aguilar, Jeannie Economos, and Linda A. McCauley. 2013. "Female Farmworkers' Perceptions of Heat-Related Illness and Pregnancy Health." *Journal of Agromedicine* 18 (4). https://www.ncbi.nlm.nih.gov/pmc/articles/PMC5682625/.

Flocks, Joan, J. Antonio Tovar, Eugenia Economos, Valerie Vi Thien Mac, Abby Mutic, Katherine Peterman, and Linda McCauley. 2018. "Lessons Learned from Data Collection as Health Screening in Underserved Farmworker Communities." *Progress in Community Health Partnerships: Research, Education, and Action* 12 (1S): 93–100.

Gasperini, Frank A. 2017. "Agricultural Leaders' Influence on the Safety Culture of Workers." *Journal of Agromedicine* 22 (4): 309–311.

Guidi, Ruxandra. 2018. "Farmworkers Face Illness and Death in the Fields." *High Country News*, August 20. https://www.hcn.org/issues/50.14/agriculture-califor nias-farmworkers-face-illness-and-death-in-the-fields.

Hertzberg, Vicki, Valerie Mac, Lisa Elon, Nathan Mutic, Abby Mutic, Katherine Peter- man, J. Antonio Tovar-Aguilar, Eugenia Economos, Joan Flocks, and Linda Mc- Cauley. 2017. "Novel Analytic Methods Needed for Real-Time Continuous Core Body Temperature Data." *Western Journal of Nursing Research* 39 (1): 95–111.

Jackson, Larry L., and Howard R. Rosenberg. 2010. "Preventing Heat-Related Illness among Agricultural Workers." *Journal of Agromedicine* 15 (3): 200–215.

Kim, Nicole Jung-Eun, Victoria Breckwich Vásquez, Elizabeth Torres, R. M. Bud Nicola, and Catherine Karr. 2016. "Breaking the Silence: Sexual Harassment of Mexican Women Farmworkers." *Journal of Agromedicine* 21 (2): 154–162.

Lamarche, Dallon T., Robert D. Meade, Andrew W. D'Souza, Andreas D. Flouris, Ste- phen G. Hardcastle, Ronald J. Sigal, Pierre Boulay, and Glen P. Kenny. 2017. "The Recommended Threshold Limit Values for Heat Exposure Fail to Maintain Body Core Temperature within Safe Limits in Older Working Adults." *Journal of Occu- pational and Environmental Hygiene* 14 (9): 703–711.

LeRoy, Michael H. 1999. "Should 'Agricultural Laborers' Continue to Be Excluded from the National Labor Relations Act?" *Emory Law Journal* 48 (3). https://ssrn.com/ abstract=992923.

Li, Wei, Fang Chen, and Shukun Wu. 2016. "The Related Risk Factors Analysis of Snake- Bite Induced Acute Kidney Injury." *Medical Science Monitor* 22 (July): 2335–2339.

Liebman, Amy K., Melinda F. Wiggins, Clermont Fraser, Jeffrey Levin, Jill Sidebottom, and Thomas A. Arcury. 2013. "Occupational Health Policy and Immigrant Workers in the Agriculture, Forestry, and Fishing Sector." *American Journal of Industrial Medicine* 56 (8): 975–984.

Linder, Marc. 1986. "Farm Workers and the Fair Labor Standards Act: Racial Dis- crimination in the New Deal." *Texas Law Review* 65 (1986–1987): 1335–1393.

Loza, Mireya. 2016. *Defiant Braceros: How Migrant Workers Fought for Racial, Sexual, and Political Freedom.* Chapel Hill: University of North Carolina Press.

Luna, Guadalupe T. 2014. "The Dominion of Agricultural Sustainability: Invisible Farm Laborers." *Wisconsin Law Review* 2014 (2): 265–288.

Mac, Valerie, Lisa Elon, Jacqueline Mix, Antonio Tovar-Aguilar, Joan Flocks, Eugenia Economos, Vicki Hertzberg, Linda McCauley. 2021. "Risk Factors for Reaching Core Body Temperature Thresholds in Florida Agricultural Workers." *Journal of Occu- pational and Environmental Medicine*, January 29. https://journals.lww.com/ joem/Abstract/9000/Risk_Factors_for_Reaching_Core_Body_Temperature .97962.aspx.

Mac, Valerie Vi Thien, and Linda A. McCauley. 2017. "Farmworker Vulnerability to Heat Hazards: A Conceptual Framework." *Journal of Nursing Scholarship* 49 (6): 617–624.

Mac, Valerie Vi Thien, Jose Antonio Tovar-Aguilar, Joan Flocks, Eugenia Economos, Vicki S. Hertzberg, and Linda A. McCauley. 2017. "Heat Exposure in Central Florida Fernery Workers: Results of a Feasibility Study." *Journal of Agromedicine* 22 (2): 89–99.

Martin, Philip. 2017. "The H-2A Farm Guestworker Program Is Expanding Rapidly: Here Are the Numbers You Need to Know." *Economic Policy Institute*, April 13. https://www.epi.org/blog/h-2a-farm-guestworker-program-expanding-rapidly/.

Meade, Robert D., Martin P. Poirier, Andreas D. Flouris, Stephen G. Hardcastle, and Glen P. Kenny. 2016. "Do the Threshold Limit Values for Work in Hot Conditions Adequately Protect Workers?" *Medicine and Science in Sports and Exercise* 48 (6): 1187–1196.

Mix, Jacqueline, Lisa Elon, Valerie Vi Thien Mac, Joan Flocks, Eugenia Economos, Antonio J. Tovar-Aguilar, Vicki Stover Hertzberg, and Linda A. McCauley. 2018. "Hydration Status, Kidney Function, and Kidney Injury in Florida Agricultural Workers." *Journal of Occupational and Environmental Medicine* 60 (5): e253–260. https://doi.org/10.1097/JOM.0000000000001261.

———. 2019. "Physical Activity and Work Activities in Florida Agricultural Workers." *American Journal of Industrial Medicine* 62 (12): 1058–1067.

Mobed, K., Ellen B. Gold, and Marc B. Schenker. 1992. "Occupational Health Problems among Migrant and Seasonal Farm Workers." *Western Journal of Medicine* 157 (3): 367–373.

Moyce, Sally, Jill Joseph, Daniel Tancredi, Diane Mitchell, and Marc Schenker. 2016. "Cumulative Incidence of Acute Kidney Injury in California's Agricultural Workers." *Journal of Occupational and Environmental Medicine* 58 (4): 391–397.

Moyce, Sally, Diane Mitchell, Tracey Armitage, Daniel Tancredi, Jill Joseph, and Marc Schenker. 2017. "Heat Strain, Volume Depletion and Kidney Function in California Agricultural Workers." *Occupational and Environmental Medicine* 74 (6): 402–409.

Murphy, Jeanne, Julie Samples, Mavel Morales, and Nargess Shadbeh. 2014. "'They Talk Like That, but We Keep Working': Sexual Harassment and Sexual Assault Experiences among Mexican Indigenous Farmworker Women in Oregon." *Journal of Immigrant and Minority Health* 17 (6): 1834–1839.

Mutic, Abby D., Jacqueline M. Mix, Lisa Elon, Nathan J. Mutic, Jeannie Economos, Joan Flocks, Antonio J. Tovar-Aguilar, and Linda A. McCauley. 2018. "Classification of Heat-Related Illness Symptoms among Florida Farmworkers." *Journal of Nursing Scholarship: An Official Publication of Sigma Theta Tau International Honor Society of Nursing* 50 (1): 74–82.

Mutic, Abby D., Nathan Mutic, and Linda McCauley. 2018. "Secondary Analysis of National Agricultural Workers Survey." Unpublished manuscript.

National Kidney Foundation. 2020. "Acute Kidney Injury (AKI)." https://www.kidney.org/atoz/content/AcuteKidneyInjury.

NCCRAHS (National Children's Center for Rural and Agricultural Health and Safety). 2018. "2018 Fact Sheet: Childhood Agricultural Injuries in the U.S." https://www.marshfieldresearch.org/Media/Default/NFMC/PDFs/2018%20Child%20Ag%20Injury%20Factsheetpdf.pdf.

NIOSH (National Institute for Occupational Safety and Health). 2016. "Criteria for a Recommended Standard: Occupational Exposure to Heat and Hot Environments." https://www.cdc.gov/niosh/docs/2016-106/pdfs/2016-106.pdf?id=10.26616/NIOSHPUB2016106.

Núñez, Guillermina Gina, and Josiah M. Heyman. 2007. "Entrapment Processes and Immigrant Communities in a Time of Heightened Border Vigilance." *Human Organization* 66 (4): 354–365.

Occupational Safety and Health Administration. n.d. "Standards." Accessed February 21, 2021. https://www.osha.gov/heat-exposure/standards.

Ostro, Bart D., Lindsey A. Roth, Rochelle S. Green, and Rupa Basu. 2009. "Estimating the Mortality Effect of the July 2006 California Heat Wave." *Environmental Research* 109 (5): 614–619.

Pan American Health Organization. 2013. "Chronic Kidney Disease in Agricultural Communities in Central America." https://www.paho.org/hq/dmdocuments/2013/CD52-8-e.pdf.

Perea, Juan F. 2010. "The Echoes of Slavery: Recognizing the Racist Origins of the Agricultural and Domestic Worker Exclusion from the National Labor Relations Act." *Social Science Research Network*, July 24. https://ssrn.com/abstract=1646496.

Perez, Maria. 2016. "Farmworker Dies after Complaining of Heat Exhaustion on Bus Ride Back to Immokalee." *Naples Daily News*, May 19. https://www.naplesnews.com/story/news/local/2016/05/19/farmworker-dies-after-complaining-of-heat-exhaustion-on-bus-ride-back-to-immokalee/85968364/.

Rahman, Mahboob, Fariha Shad, and Michael C. Smith. 2012. "Acute Kidney Injury: A Guide to Diagnosis and Management." *American Family Physician* 86 (7): 631–639.

Rodman, Sarah, Colleen Barry, Megan Clayton, Shannon Frattaroli, Roni Neff, and Lainie Rutkow. 2016. "Agricultural Exceptionalism at the State Level: Characterization of Wage and Hour Laws for U.S. Farmworkers." *Journal of Agriculture, Food Systems, and Community Development* 6 (2): 1–22.

Roelofs, Cora, and David Wegman. 2014. "Workers: The Climate Canaries." *American Journal of Public Health* 104 (10): 1799–1801.

Sabarwal, Akash, Kunal Kumar, and Rana P. Singh. 2018. "Hazardous Effects of Chemical Pesticides on Human Health—Cancer and Other Associated Disorders." *Environmental Toxicology and Pharmacology* 63:103–114.

Sifuentez, Mario Jimenez. 2016. *Of Forests and Fields: Mexican Labor in the Pacific Northwest*. Rutgers, NJ: Rutgers University Press.

Spector, June T., Jennifer Krenz, and Kristina N. Blank. 2015. "Risk Factors for Heat-Related Illness in Washington Crop Workers." *Journal of Agromedicine* 20 (3): 349–359.

Stoecklin-Marois, Maria, Tamara Hennessy-Burt, Diane Mitchell, and Marc Schenker. 2013. "Heat Related Illness Knowledge and Practices among California Hired Farm Workers in the MICASA Study." *Industrial Health* 51 (1): 47–55.

Tonelli, Shalome, Kennith Culp, and Kelley Donham. 2014. "Work-Related Musculoskeletal Disorders in Senior Farmers." *Workplace Health and Safety* 62 (8): 333–341.

U.S. Bureau of Labor Statistics. n.d. "Injuries, Illnesses, and Fatalities." Accessed December 14, 2020. http://www.bls.gov/iif/.

U.S. Department of State. 2014. "Worldwide NIV Workload by Visa Category, FY 2014." https://travel.state.gov/content/dam/visas/Statistics/Non-Immigrant-Statistics/NIVWorkload/FY2014NIVWorkloadbyVisaCategory.pdf.

———. 2018. "Nonimmigrant Visas Statistics: Fiscal Year 2018." https://travel.state.gov/content/dam/visas/Statistics/Non-Immigrant-Statistics/NIVDetailTables/FY18NIVDetailTable.pdf.

USGCRP (U.S. Global Change Research Program). 2016: *The Impacts of Climate Change on Human Health in the United States: A Scientific Assessment*. Washington, DC: USGCRP.

Villarejo, Don, and Sherry L. Baron. 1999. "The Occupational Health Status of Hired Farm Workers." *Occupational Medicine: State of the Art Reviews* 14 (3): 613–635.

Wolfe, Mitchell I., Reinhard Kaiser, Mary P. Naughton, Maria C. Mirabelli, Steven S. Yoon, Randy Hanzlick, and Alden K. Henderson. 2001. "Heat-Related Mortality in Selected United States Cities, Summer 1999." *American Journal of Forensic Medicine and Pathology* 22 (4): 352–357.

III

Epidemiologies of Living with Death

Morbidity and Mortality in Immigrant Narratives

A Public Health Perspective on State Violence, Social Exclusion, and Experiences of Harm among Deportable Immigrants

Daniel L. Stageman
Shirley P. Leyro

> Physical symptoms felt by separated children are manifestations of their psychological pain. You get a lot of "my chest hurts," even though everything is fine [medically]. Children describe symptoms, "Every heartbeat hurts," "I can't feel my heart," of emotional pain.
>
> —Medical director, U.S. Office of Refugee Resettlement child detention facility (Chiedi 2019, 11)

In September 2019, the acting inspector general of the U.S. Department of Health and Human Services (HHS) released a report titled "Care Provider Facilities Described Challenges Addressing Mental Health Needs of Children in HHS Custody" (Chiedi 2019). As the department housing the Office of Refugee Resettlement, HHS had been charged with detaining unaccompanied minors and children removed from their parents as part of the Donald Trump administration's family separation policy.[1] Perhaps unsurprisingly, the effects of these experiences of trauma manifested as mental health issues, the severity of which was further exacerbated by extended detention in the "care facilities" under review. A common reaction among imprisoned children to this negation of their humanity—first through violence in their countries of origin, and later, upon fleeing from these circumstances, through state violence in the land to which they hoped to escape—was self-erasure: "longer stays resulted in higher levels of defiance, hopelessness, and frustration among children, along with more instances of self-harm and suicidal ideation" (Chiedi 2019, 12). The findings report children steeped in trauma, which was often rooted in their experiences bearing witness to death, being subjected to physical injury, or otherwise having their bodily autonomy invalidated or violated. These findings undermine the nativist framing of immigrants as perpetrators of violent crime and are in keeping with the scholarly consensus that they are in fact more likely to be the victims of violence, both in their home countries and upon their arrival in the United States (McDonald and Erez 2007; Zatz and Smith 2012).

Traumatizing vulnerable immigrants through enforcement policy has not been unique to the Trump administration. Large-scale detention and deportation resulting in family separation is a hallmark of post–September 11 immigration enforcement policy throughout the preceding presidential administrations, and has been adopted throughout (and beyond) the Anglophone world (Welch 2014; Welch and Schuster 2005). Hopelessness, mental illness, and internalized constraints on life choices are predictable results of the trauma that characterizes contemporary patterns of immigration and stems from immigration policy (Chu, Keller, and Rasmussen 2013; Levers and Hyatt-Burkhart 2012). The processes that drive migration include both *push factors* that motivate immigrants to leave their home countries, and *pull factors* that influence the choice of a particular destination country (Parkins 2010). The history of immigration policy in receiving countries is closely tied to those nations' prior colonial activities, wherein the deadly application of state violence negated native peoples' humanity in service of unfettered exploitation. Upon their arrival in destination countries, immigrants face the socially bulimic[2] dynamic of a political-economic structure designed to absorb their labor power and other economic contributions while simultaneously denying their personhood through state violence in the form of arrest, detention, and banishment (Brotherton and Naegler 2014; Young 1999). The frequently failed, chaotic, and authoritarian governments left behind in the aftermath of nineteenth- and twentieth-century colonialism have abetted Western nations' evolving approaches to exploitation, perpetuating the intolerable living conditions that provide an important push factor in the decision to undertake arduous, expensive, and dangerous migration journeys (Rosenblum and Ball 2016). These dehumanizing circuits of global exploitation are best described by the individuals trapped within them; immigrant narratives are, however, undervalued in policy and academic discourse surrounding their well-being (De Fina 2000; De Fina and King 2011).

In this chapter, we draw on concepts from public health literature to describe the physical and mental health effects of the late-modern migration experience. These concepts—*mortality,* or death, and *morbidity,* or disease—speak to the limits of the human life course[3] and meaning-making: mortality for obvious reasons, and morbidity because of the constraints that it places on actions and decisions, self-care, and pro-social behaviors. In the medical literature, these concepts are discussed as a continuum of the human body's physical responses to *trauma* (Hernandez and Kim 2020). In the mental health field, exposure to trauma is a widely accepted causal factor in psychological morbidity and mortality (Gadeberg et al. 2017; Soegaard et al. 2020). While physical trauma is closely associated with many kinds of contemporary immigration journeys (Baker 2017; Duzkoylu, Basceken, and Kesilmez 2017; Koleski, Aldulaimi, and Moran 2019), our interest is in the postmigration traumas defined by Bonnie Burstow as "a reaction to a kind of wound . . . a reaction to profoundly injurious events and situations in the real world and, indeed, to a world in which people are routinely wounded" (2003, 1302).

We posit morbidity stemming from trauma as an expansive conceptual category that includes any physical or mental condition of disease, defect, or disability likely to constrain an individual's ability to act in the world. Crucially, it does not refer to externally imposed constraints, but it may refer to individual responses to those constraints that—much like the responses of the children in HHS custody—manifest in mental illness and self-destructive actions that reinforce them. As trauma is often discussed (particularly in psychology and mental health literature) in tandem with *resilience* (Tummala-Narra 2007), we want to stress that morbidity does not imply the absence of resilience; rather, resilience can be considered a generative or redemptive response to morbidity (McAdams and McLean 2013; Ong et al. 2014; Silva Ribeiro et al. 2017). Mortality in this conceptual framework is defined by suicide: the reaction of an individual overwhelmed by trauma and seeking an irreversible escape from the experience. To expand the sociological utility of the term "mortality," we also consider its social significance: the effects of death on the living.

Both of these concepts provide unique insights into commonalities among the experiences of migrants in a late-modern, neoliberal context. If mortality represents an unintended consequence of instrumental exploitation targeting immigrants—implying as it does the loss of labor power resulting from death[4]—morbidity represents state violence and exclusion in equilibrium with economic exploitation. While physical injury and disease are real risks for the immigrants caught up in this tension, other injuries are psychological and existential: post-traumatic stress disorder (PTSD) and other stress responses to unendurable trauma, the circumscription of life chances and choices, the narrowing of identity and self-concept to a body at labor (Brotherton and Barrios 2011; Lonegan 2007; Mendoza and Olivas 2009; Patler and Pirtle 2018; Zayas 2015). The internalization by vulnerable immigrants of this constrained status—a narrow focus on labor to the exclusion of other life domains such as education, child care, and organizing to build cultural, social, and political capital—represents a system of instrumentalization and exploitation working exactly as intended (Leyro and Stageman 2018). Immigrants, constantly threatened by an immigration enforcement system that nevertheless cannot practically operate at a scale necessary to accomplish their wholesale physical removal, become an instrument of their own punitive inclusion. In the face of this looming threat, immigrants have little choice other than to continue providing flexible, low-cost labor power to a hostile society that denies them meaningful inclusion, recognition, reciprocal obligation, or even fair compensation.

Here we examine data from Shirley Leyro's (2017) New York City–based study of the impact that vulnerability to deportation has on noncitizen immigrants. Eighty immigrants participated in six focus groups and thirty-three in-depth interviews, which taken together provide clear evidence that immigrant residents' lives were directly affected by fear arising from harsh immigration enforcement policies. Importantly, as interviewees' fears intensified, so did the likelihood that they expressed these fears as a sort of internalized social death: in the avoidance of everyday social activities and political participation, and in hopelessness, major depression, and suicidal ideation (Leyro 2017; Leyro and Stageman 2018). We seek to expand on our previous work examining the criminalization and social exclusion of immigrants, by using the public health concepts of morbidity and mortality to explore the ways that immigrants make meaning from the physical and mental health consequences of their vulnerability to state violence and neoliberal exploitation.

Scope and Context

Immigrants and Mental Health

The existence of a mental health crisis among immigrants is widely agreed on by scholars in public health and the social sciences (Dozier 1993; Hacker et al. 2011; Menjivar and Abrego 2012; Potochnick and Perreira 2010). Moreover, this crisis appears to be cross-national and cross-cultural. Writing about the refugee crisis in Europe, Alison Abbott (2016) concludes that higher rates of experiencing trauma were the likely explanation for the higher frequency of severe mental disorders among the European refugee population, though she also found that reception in destination countries was a statistically significant mediating factor. Among the most salient of the mental disorders occurring at higher frequency among immigrants is suicidal ideation and behavior: a study of immigrants to Sweden found that immigrants were at 30 percent greater risk of suicide than the native-born (Johansson et al. 1997).

Significant recent scholarly and media attention has focused on the increase in postrecession suicide rates among white men in the United States, with a particular emphasis on the role of gun culture and the widespread availability of firearms making suicide *attempts* more likely to be lethal among this demographic (Metzl 2019). Data on successful suicides, however, are by definition significantly more reliable and accessible than data on suicide attempts and suicidal ideation. While research has shown that immigrant status and Latino ethnicity appear in most contexts to be protective factors for suicide risk, there is some evidence that these groups experience higher rates of suicide attempts and suicidal ideation (Forte et al. 2018; Fortuna et al. 2016). The most important risk factors facing immigrants are racial discrimination and roadblocks to integration in destination countries—as well as experiences of trauma in home countries and in the course of migration journeys (Goodman et al. 2017; Lane and Miranda 2017).

Trauma

The concept of trauma is essential to understanding the causes of morbidity and mortality, and it provides a crucial link between the public health and sociological meanings of these terms. Critical and radical definitions of trauma, such as those proposed by Burstow (2003) and Miriam George (2010), further lead us to collective, postcolonial, and political-economic understandings of these terms. Individual immigrant experiences of trauma must be understood in the context of colonial histories in which the nations of the Global North—contemporary destination countries—visited collective traumas on the lands and peoples of source countries as a matter of imperial political-economic policy. While morbidity and mortality provide a powerful metaphor for colonial approaches to exploitation, specific colonial practices exemplify this dynamic in a manner that is entirely literal. Enforced morbidity was an essential aspect of colonial labor exploitation, through the mutilation of slaves and other forced laborers. Belgian Congo is a notorious example, where rubber plantation overseers "made use of dehumanizing and painful methods, including the severing of a worker's hand or foot as an example to other workers" (Verstraete, Verhaegen, and Depaepe 2017, 232). Amputation has a long history as punishment for slaves: French and English colonial slave codes declare it "an appropriate punishment for disobedience and rebellion" (Allewaert 2013, 90), mandating severing of ears for short-term escapes, and severing of leg tendons for longer ones. Mutilation as punishment rightly shocks the conscience, but colonial regimes saw these horrific practices as utilitarian: a powerful deterrent short of execution, leaving much of the subject's labor value intact. Michael Taussig refers to these practices of terror as "the mediator *par excellence* of colonial hegemony" (1986, 5), while resisting a narrowly instrumental interpretation of their historical use. Nevertheless, in instances such as the codification of physical mutilation as punishment in laws governing slave labor, their instrumental *intent* is clear.

Echoes of these practices have become a staple in the postcolonial realities facing residents of source countries, as strategies employed by both criminal organizations[5] and government actors to instill fear among civilian populations (Cruz 2011; Farah and Meacham 2015). Violence is an important push factor motivating out-migration (Sawyer and Marquez 2017). Driving residents to destination countries in the Global North is not an unintended consequence of these strategies, since remittances are another source of wealth for local elites and criminal organizations.[6]

Resilience

Resilience presumes the presence of adverse circumstances, and it is particularly salient to understanding responses to trauma. Michael Ungar and colleagues (2007) propose a definition integrating "individual, or individually mediated factors, that [are] associated with positive outcomes" with "protective factors and processes emphasizing the temporal and relational aspects of positive development under stress" (Ungar et al. 2007, 287–288). Rachael Goodman and her coauthors highlight "the ecosystemic and layered nature of resilience processes" (2017, 318), pointing implicitly to a relationship between resilience and resistance: confronting sources of trauma is important to the healing process. If the source is systemic, this may mean working to prevent that system from causing further harm. A critical or radical understanding of resilience as a potential *collective* response to the trauma caused by neoliberal systems of exploitation requires a dawning collective consciousness of this exploitation, and a developing program of collective resistance (Neilson 2015). Our interest is in the pathways that lead immigrants through their experiences of morbidity and mortality to an understanding of their place in this collective, and in the ways their individual work of resistance contributes to a collective pursuit of immigrant justice.

Studying Migrant Morbidity and Mortality

We take a phenomenological approach to further our understanding of the roles that morbidity and mortality play in constraining the lives of contemporary immigrants to the United States, and to understanding the (self-)constructive and (self-)destructive ways that immigrants struggle with them. Specifically, we seek to answer the following questions: How do immigrants describe their lived experiences of morbidity and mortality as part of the contemporary neoliberal pattern of migration? What pathways can lead immigrants to resilience in the face of ongoing experiences of state violence and exploitation?

With these questions in mind, we approached our coding schema with the intention of achieving thematic saturation, as defined by the guiding question presented by Benjamin Saunders and colleagues: "Given the theory, do we have sufficient data to illustrate it?" (2018, 1895). To do so, we first coded for themes in interviews relating to mortality (suicide and death), following which we expanded outward to include themes of morbidity: broader experiences of physical and mental trauma, pain, and violence. We approached both concepts expansively, including analogous experiences such as the forced discontinuation of careers, professional identities, and other life goals; long-term separation in family relationships; and long-term/permanent severing of a strong connection to home and cultural identity. Next, we coded for potential mediating factors that intersected with experiences of morbidity and mortality—for example, fear of state violence or immigration consequences; experiences of othering, racism, or nativism; and roadblocks to integration. Finally, we coded for evidence of resilience in the ways that respondents processed their experiences of morbidity and mortality: help-seeking (i.e., psychological care); self-care (i.e., self-directed psychological and physical health–enhancing behaviors); and particularly acts of resistance (e.g., social or political engagement, activism, and employment in community building or direct-service fields) that respondents presented as being expressly motivated by their experiences.

In the course of weaving our analysis into a cohesive narrative, we have selected a handful of exemplary quotes and interpretations that answer our research questions most clearly, directly, and powerfully. Themes of mortality and morbidity inevitably arise in the course of a conversation about lived experience, regardless of the population under study. Death is, by definition, a universal human experience; health-related issues that detract from quality of life are nearly as universal. Our particular focus on suicide recognizes it as an aberrational life choice, an extreme reaction to life circumstances that have become intolerable. Suicide is a self-destructive response to overwhelming morbidity; it provides the sharpest possible contrast to the generative responses that characterize resilience. Considered as an internalized reaction to the social death imposed on immigrant laborers, it is particularly salient to understanding immigrants' lived experience of the socially bulimic dynamics that define their reception in destination countries.

Themes from the Interviews

Responses to Trauma Include Death, Suicide, and Self-Erasure

In keeping with the literature on push factors (Appadurai 2019; Gonzalez 2015; Ventriglio and Bhugra 2015) and the nature of (particularly unauthorized) migration journeys, many of the immigrants we talked to experienced significant trauma prior to their arrival in the United States. This trauma manifested in numerous ways throughout their years of residency in the United States.

For some respondents, the primary source of their trauma was generational: Scott[7] speaks of his father, the family patriarch, who was "really struggling" with post-traumatic stress disorder from the Ethiopian-Eritrean civil war that took place throughout his childhood:

> He had been shot like four times, had been tortured at least once, had a scar around his neck. So he was going through a lot of stuff. This had led him to deal with the trauma in very unhealthy ways. And . . . those were reflected in sort of our childhood, and that just meant a lot of crazy things, but [mostly] it meant a lot of beatings.

For Scott and his two younger brothers, the generational trauma their father transmitted via physical abuse was exacerbated by the deep institutional racism they experienced as Black immigrants. He describes growing up during the 1980s and 1990s and the "war on Black people." As an Ethiopian immigrant, Scott came to see himself as Black only after significant struggle and reflection. This sense of identity was cemented when police arrested him for a violent felony he did not commit:

> So there was definitely a shift. I think the shift really started happening. For me when we're thinking about issues with fear—I think it was fear and the self-hate that hit me. Fear in the same sense that I had just been walking home, and they could throw me into [jail]. I felt like I was going through a factory, like I'm getting booked, processed, waking up, no sleep, blah, blah, blah. And we were all going through it, all Blacks and Latinos. And I was like, what the fuck is going on?

Resilience is unevenly distributed among populations, within families, or even within individuals at different points over the life course. We discuss Scott's narratives of resilience below, yet his success in navigating and embracing his racial identity and processing the generational trauma resulting from his father's abuse was the exception among his siblings. Scott's two younger brothers were also victims of the war on Black people. Both became involved in criminal activity via gangs and the drug trade; both became acculturated to the use of firearms; and both shot themselves to death within a nine-month period in their early twenties.

For many of our other respondents, suicidal thoughts stemmed from the intense isolation experienced by many unauthorized immigrants in the grip of an exploitative labor market. In Jack's case they arose from thoughts of home:

> It's a situation where one leaves a lot behind; the nostalgia hits a lot. The fact that you do not live within those family meetings that one, as a Latino, is used to, no? For example, Christmas brings the family together; we go to our aunt's house, or our aunt comes to our house. You are poor, but you are together, and those are the emotions that are present—it's your birthday, but you have to work. Or it's New Year's, you have to work, nothing to celebrate. . . . These are situations . . . sometimes where you consider suicide, right?[8]

Jack frames his past suicidal ideation as a response to a sense of inescapable entrapment in a life stripped of meaning, his circumstances reduced to the point where his prevailing day-to-day experiences are dominated by work and isolation:

> There was a time when I said, "Well, then, I think if I don't fit in this world, then I don't have to be still enduring these pains." . . . You don't see this view outside this window; that's it. I mean, you sit locked up here, and instead, when you go out there, you realize that life is like that; this is how it is.

Jack's reference to pain lays bare the relationship between morbidity and mortality as it manifests in the physical, existential, and mental health conditions that drive individuals to suicide. Resilience is not a constant; an individual's response to trauma may be constructive at one point, and self-destructive at another. Functional government-provided mental health services predicate suicide-prevention programming on this reality, recognizing that harm reduction is effective suicide prevention: providing suicidal individuals with the support necessary to navigate periods of crisis, and reducing access to the means of lethal self-injury, can significantly reduce suicide rates.

Undocumented immigrants in particular are denied access to services of this nature because of their status. Importantly, they are also denied access to the cultural practices and social rituals humans commonly rely on to process death. Western European irregular immigrants are often held up as either escaping the harshest consequences associated with their status as a result of white privilege, or being caught up as collateral damage in a system intended to target Latina/o and other immigrants of color. For Ellen, who migrated to the United States from Ireland at the age of eighteen, denial of mourning was ultimately one of the most painful experiences during her time as an undocumented immigrant:

> Certain things happened, a few deaths in the family, and I couldn't fly home for them. [It] was absolutely horrible. . . . I had this sinking feeling that something was wrong, and the next morning I got the phone call that she'd died in the hospital, and it was pretty hard. My brother, he's always heard the bad news in the family. He rang me and told me over and over, like, "You know, there's no point in coming home; she's gone." "I'm still coming to her funeral." And if I had to go home, I had to come back through Canada, which was very scary. So he said, "Don't even bother, even. Don't ruin your life."

Most of our respondents faced similarly painful decisions to forgo mourning because of realistic fears of enforcement-related consequences. Many of these decisions reinforced morbidity through the internalization of dehumanizing conditions of labor exploitation.

Morbidity and the Instrumentalized Life

For many immigrants the fundamental experience of life in America is an anomic one. Prior to migration, familiarity with American culture may be mediated by fictionalized accounts, advertising, and propaganda, leaving many with a sense of optimism about the American Dream. For some, like Peggy, the disconnect between their ambitions and the apparent limits to opportunity in their homelands in part motivated their migration:

> So I was studying civil engineering. . . . You know, you have that dream of overcoming. We come from families that are not economically well off, so you want to reach to become a professional, you know. All those dreams you leave behind, thinking that the American Dream is best.[9]

Peggy's circumstances are common for aspiring professionals in postcolonial source countries (in Peggy's case, the Dominican Republic), where histories of exploitation by local rentier elites limit the opportunities afforded by entry into highly trained professions.Sacrificing professional prestige to emigrate to the United States—in pursuit of the apparent prosperity available to blue-collar workers—can appear to be a rational choice. The reality of low-status service work, however, led Peggy to question this decision:

> In my mind I knew I was going to do well in the DR, but I thought, it's harder for me to help my family too. . . . Maybe coming here, financially I could push them to a better position. . . . Turns out when I come here, it's not like . . . you know, little by little you learn what life is like here. I would have been living my life much better over there; I went to a private university. [Here] I'm a hairdresser.

This dynamic is problematically characterized as brain drain: the loss of human capital that may otherwise have been invested in the development of source countries. The countervailing principle of brain drain, however, is the idea that this human capital is subsequently repurposed for equally specialized work in the destination country. Peggy's case is in fact much more typical, particularly for immigrants with irregular status. She experienced this reduction in professional status as a keen humiliation, with significant implications for her mental health:

> Look, in my view, it feels very hard. More when you were at a different level over there. I had a business there, supported the house, my family and everything, and coming here to be, like, hidden, it's not easy. . . . Yes, that's emotionally horrible. You feel a horrible, horrible depression because you feel humiliated. I sought professional help because I was very depressed—very. At one point, I didn't want to eat or work anymore.

As part of this depression Peggy experienced a deep sense of powerlessness, an inability to resist the forces that rendered her definitively exploitable: "To some extent, putting it into words, you live humiliated in a sense. Mental slavery. . . . Impotence is fear too. I mean, 'I can't do it': you're not free—that's what makes you a slave." In this assessment of her situation, Peggy grapples with the nature of her position as a neoliberal subject, acknowledging her instrumentalization and tying the resulting loss of personhood to her experience of morbidity in the form of major depression. Her description of "mental slavery" speaks to the dynamics resulting from her internalization of exploitability; her years of labor are an economic contribution that the United States has not reciprocated through the extension of political rights or social benefits.

Conflicting responses to an inchoate sense of exploitation are common among labor migrants discussing their experiences of morbidity, including in cases where their suffering is physical as well as mental. Sue discusses her recent experience of severe physical illness as accompanied by an epiphany centered on the relationship between labor and her sense of entrapment:

> So lately, I've gotten sick frequently. . . . I'll tell you the truth. I haven't felt it before, but now I feel like I live here, but I feel like a prisoner. Because I never saw it before. Like you focus on working and working and working, but then I realized that, yes. I tell you the truth. I feel a prisoner here; I don't feel like I'm free. . . . Now I start to think about it, and I feel, I say, "No, well, here we live in prison." . . . Because how can you say that you are free if you cannot go where you want to go? . . . Because we also came here to work, because we did not come here to ask for anything; we come and work hard.

This dawning political awakening contrasts with Sue's assertion, expressed later in the interview, that she "can't complain." Minimization of physical suffering arose across respondents regardless of age or national origin. Pam is an undocumented college student who emigrated from Ecuador in her teens with her two siblings. As the oldest of the three, she took charge of their safety and describes not just the emotional toll this responsibility took on her but also a horrific physical injury she suffered as she sought to protect them in the course of crossing the border in a motor vehicle packed with thirteen other migrants. Tears stream down her face as she relates how she placed her arms and body on top of her sisters in an effort to keep them from getting smothered in the vehicle:

> So my legs were all the way down to the [bottom of the] car, and my hands were up [over the bodies of my sisters], and I pretty much had to go like this [*she bends her body forward, making it a sort of tent*] and cover my sisters, so I couldn't move. There was people on top of me, and they kept pushing, but my sisters weren't even being able to breathe, and they were like, "I can't breathe! I can't breathe!". . . And when we got out of the car, my leg got so numb that it was [dislocated at the hip], flipped to the other side, it moved to the other side. So when I came down, because they told us we had to run to the other car, all I could do was I pull my leg back to where it was, and since it was numb, you cannot really feel.

Pam proceeds to minimize the lingering pain from this injury, both by attributing it to another cause and by characterizing it as inconsequential: "I do have pains sometimes, but I think it's because I also play soccer, so I never really pay attention to it." The tension evident in respondents' discussions of the connection between their experiences of morbidity, their sense of entrapment due to their status, and the relationship of both of these dynamics to a self-concept defined by work often found resolution in the aspirations attached to the latter (Hallett 2017). Jack describes the narrowing horizons experienced by many undocumented immigrants, and turns for salvation to the very identity that traps so many undocumented immigrants into the narrowest possible version of neoliberal subjecthood:

> One arrives thinking first of all of the debt that one incurs when taking the trip. . . . So [working off that debt] is your goal; your first goal is that, but when you get here, you realize that you don't speak English, you don't know how to work in many areas, and besides, you don't have many contacts. So you don't come thinking about the papers; I mean, you don't think. . . . And I have been trying to investigate. I've gone to two lawyers, and they've both told me there's a way—because I've been here ten years—. . . through work I could be one [a citizen].

The irony inherent in Jack's assessment of work as the key to achieving citizenship is that it gets the reality of neoliberal subjecthood backward: work stripped of the rewards of belonging, membership, or reciprocal obligation defines the undocumented laborer's role in the late-modern political economy of the Global North. The instrumental purpose served by the dynamics that expose immigrants disproportionately to experiences of morbidity is to obscure this reality; suffering immigrants thus become hostages of the political economy of their destination country, and the subjection they experience in this role becomes the key to motivating continued labor in the absence of meaningful rewards.

Resilience: Reclaiming the Self through Resistance

For those respondents who demonstrated resilience in their reactions to experiences of morbidity, an acknowledgment and reinterpretation of the constraints on their life choices was often the first step. Pam refers to morbidity directly in describing the challenges that drive her academic and other achievements:

> Being undocumented is like being disabled . . . because if you're disabled, there are barriers. You always think that you cannot do things, but there's actually motivation for you. If there's something

that is telling you, "No, you cannot do this because of that," it's actually the contrary because that's why we're here, to prove that we're able to move forward and be able to do something else with that.

In a pattern that was common across the sample, Pam draws a direct line between her experiences and resistance to the system that imposed them: "This goes back to that opportunity of being undocumented, being able to get that vision to your parents, who really have given me too much. So I sat down with them, and I said to them, 'This [activism] is what I wanna do.'"

For others these realizations arose from acceptance of circumstances outside of their control—the external systems and structures of immigration enforcement that threatened them—and a renewed focus on changing how they internalized those systems. Scott, facing immigration consequences arising from his arrest and struggling with the suicides of his two younger brothers, made a conscious decision to repurpose his reactions to these external circumstances into a personal call to action:

> I went through that stage where the fear was just so much, and I was just like, "Dude, it's either going to consume me, or I have to figure out a way to break through," and it really helps me with other folks. Like, we have a hotline here for detainees that call. And they're locked up. Some of them are locked up for three years just for immigration stuff—a month for the criminal stuff, and now they're locked up for three years in a private facility. And they're still holding strong.

Scott, like Pam, channeled the knowledge earned at the expense of his own experience of morbidity and mortality into supporting others facing similar circumstances, and he was at the time of his interview the executive director of a well-respected immigrant rights advocacy organization.

Discussion

Narrative psychology posits that the work of making meaning over the life course is fundamental to human identity and quality of life (McAdams and Guo 2015; McAdams and McLean 2013). The struggles faced by the immigrants we interviewed are ultimately universal in nature, and should be relatable to readers regardless of background. The structure in which vulnerable American immigrants must navigate these issues, however, is unique to their precarious social position. The systems and structures that instrumentalize immigrants and facilitate their exploitation are designed to circumscribe possibilities for making meaning from experiences of trauma, and the morbidity and mortality that result from them. This narrowing of potential is imposed on an entire category of people in order to, ostensibly, expand meaning-making possibilities for a privileged group—primarily white, older, and possessed of sufficient wealth to take advantage of the low-cost labor that immigrants so often provide. Older Americans are, ironically, in a unique position to exploit immigrant labor to extend their own opportunities through the life course: immigrants make up over a quarter of the direct-care workers on which America's aging population relies for a wide range of services explicitly intended to enhance their quality of life (Zallman et al. 2019). This seemingly zero-sum proposition, however, in fact circumscribes generative possibilities for all involved. For the aging, it increasingly appears to mean a self-conception rooted in reciprocal fear: as anti-immigrant ideology becomes increasingly associated with an entire social group and age cohort, it becomes increasingly difficult for members of these groups to forge an identity separate from this ubiquitous ideology (Ghosh and Iyengar 2019; Jones 2019; Metzl 2019).

Neoliberal economies continue to calibrate the dehumanization of their exploitable labor pool so that actual death, banishment, suicide, or other potential losses of labor power are minimized. In the globalized economy, where capital has an ability to cross borders that is officially denied to labor and the humans who wield it, labor power need not even be lost to banishment. Savvy application of capital ensures that a deported individual's labor power remains exploitable.

From a systemic perspective, suicide, like criminality, is a self-destructive act of rebellion, and it is telling how the state reacts to these rebellions: force-feeding prisoners on hunger strike,[10] for instance, or mandating deportation for crimes of "moral turpitude." The dividing line between morbidity and mortality is the porous border between exploitation and destruction of assets; state violence is used to maintain immigrants in a state of exploitable morbidity.

Personhood, however, resists negation. Resilience in the face of state-enforced morbidity is already an act of resistance, as it thwarts the individual instrumentalization foundational to the neoliberal economic structures that immigrant labor enables. If resilience represents an active, conscious engagement in a process of healing—acknowledging that resilience does not represent a static state, but rather engagement with a process over time—for our interviewees, it appears that active participation in social-justice pursuits plays a key role in the individual meaning-making that defines a life worth living. This fits with the concept of *generativity* from narrative social psychology: the idea that adults—particularly as they age into the middle years and are consequently forced to recognize the reality of death—make meaning out of their activities in support of future generations. Equally important is the finding that particularly generative adults tend to "recall and narrate important life events that follow a *redemption sequence*—a negative scene turns positive, and experiences of adversity or suffering eventually lead to positive, growth-inducing outcomes" (McAdams and Guo 2015, 475). "Redeeming" experiences of morbidity and mortality seems, for many American immigrants, to involve both a memorialization of the loss involved—whether the actual death of loved ones, the loss of a homeland that one is barred by circumstance from ever seeing again, or the loss of professional standing or opportunity—and a recognition of the external forces responsible for these losses. Generativity, in these circumstances, means not only reckoning with the external forces of neoliberal capital that have worked actively to dehumanize, instrumentalize, and exploit immigrants but also organizing and acting against these forces.

While resilience is by definition a response to trauma, resistance is predicated not on individual suffering but rather on a consciousness—available to anyone—of the systems and structures that cause trauma. The systematic othering and structural instrumentalization of immigrants has consequences; it is a clear social harm that remains regardless of whether individual immigrants respond to it with resilience and resistance. Meaning-making over the life course requires personal growth, meaningful work, and the integration of a sense of self with a wide and sympathetic social network. Forceful exclusion from these practices is fundamentally and intrinsically life-negating. Scott's narrative of his brothers' suicides provides a stark example of the limits of resilience. Resilience and resistance are distinct phenomena: the first is the individual ability to maintain generativity through the life course in the face of trauma, while the second is the ability of communities and other social groups to meet externally imposed hardships with actions that challenge the people imposing them.

This distinction is particularly important in the context of labor exploitation and the socially bulimic reception experienced by immigrants in destination countries. Morbidity is an essential tool of *punitive inclusion* (Cheliotis 2017): immigrants, marked by signs of mortification as the exploitable class and constrained by *social wounding*, are instrumentally limited to searching for meaning in their labor. The result is fundamentally anomic, since it keeps immigrants in a sort of stasis: motivated by fear and an unattainable American Dream, they sacrifice meaning-making in other spheres of life in pursuit of sufficiency, stability, and security.

The neoliberal dynamics making immigrants the instrument of their own exploitation are not all-encompassing, however. Resilience in the face of morbidity has long allowed humans to thrive under adverse conditions, and immigrants to the United States are no exception to this rule. We understand resilience to be an internal process of addressing traumas, seeking care, and engaging constructively in individual and collective meaning-making. The latter gives rise to a unique awareness among immigrants of the origins of their trauma in a system structured to dehumanize them and facilitate their exploitation. That immigrants frequently express resilience as being inextricably caught up with resistance to this system shows the strength and salience of immigrant identity: linking the self to the collective motivates both participation in collective action, and individual actions perceived as being in direct service to the collective. While resilience may not be directly shareable, engagement in collective and socially constructive activities, in particular political and legal activism and community-based social service provision, show the importance of linking individual with collective processes of redeeming trauma.

NOTES

1. In May of 2018, the U.S. Department of Justice enacted a zero-tolerance policy of prosecuting all unauthorized border crossers, regardless of whether they arrived with minor children. The policy was ostensibly rescinded after significant public outcry. It resulted in at least 2,500 children detained separately from their parents under HHS custody, as well as a massive administrative failure in reuniting these children with their parents or legal guardians. There is evidence that the policy preceded the 2018 announcement, continued subsequently in a less publicly visible form, and affected a great many more immigrant children than officially reported. For more information, see Lind 2018 and Southern Poverty Law Center 2020.

2. We use Jock Young's (1999) concept of *social bulimia* to characterize the ongoing cycles of inclusion and exclusion to which immigrants are routinely subjected. It refers to a society "where both inclusion and exclusion occur concurrently, . . . where massive cultural inclusion is accompanied by systematic structural exclusion" (Young 2007, 32).

3. "Life course" is a term borrowed from narrative psychology by criminologists and sociologists Robert Sampson and John Laub (1992) as a framework for understanding patterns of criminal involvement and desistance over an individual lifetime. It has since come to be used more broadly in sociology to frame lifetime changes in individuals' embeddedness in social networks, structures, and systems; their conscious and unconscious reactions to these changes; and the evolving stories they tell themselves and others to explain these changes and their own reactions to them (Cohler and Hostetler 2016; Presser 2016).

4. The labor power lost with a small number of high-profile immigrant deaths may be a minor cost compared to the symbolic benefit the spectacle of death represents to the exploitation regime. See Chapter 4.

5. Groups popularly understood as "gangs" (see Brotherton and Barrios 2004 and Hallsworth and Brotherton 2011 for discussion of the problematic usage of this term) make up the de facto state in many areas of Central America's Northern Triangle; for instance, in many respects they assume or enact a parallel to the state monopoly on violence (Cruz 2011, Farah and Meacham 2015). This region accounted for much of the recent flow of undocumented immigrants and asylum seekers into the United States during 2018 and 2019.

6. Who are often one and the same (Cruz 2011; Farah and Meacham 2015).
7. Names have been changed to protect the identities of the participants.
8. Translations of quotations from Jack are by the authors.
9. Translations of quotations from Peggy are by the authors.
10. For a graphic depiction of this profoundly dehumanizing practice, see Dayan 2013 (27–29). It provides a stark illustration of enforced morbidity in extremis.

REFERENCES

Abbott, Alison. 2016. "The Troubled Minds of Migrants." *Nature* 538:158–161.
Allewaert, Monique. 2013. *Ariel's Ecology: Plantations, Personhood, and Colonialism in the American Tropics.* Minneapolis: University of Minnesota Press.
Appadurai, Arjun. 2019. "Traumatic Exit, Identity Narratives, and the Ethics of Hospitality." *Television and New Media* 20 (6): 558–565.
Baker, Russell A. 2017. "Border Injuries: An Analysis of Prehospital Demographics, Mechanisms, and Patterns of Injuries Encountered by USBP EMS Agents in the El Paso (Texas USA) Sector." *Prehospital and Disaster Medicine* 32 (4): 431–436.
Brotherton, David C., and Luis Barrios. 2004. *The Almighty Latin King and Queen Nation: Street Politics and the Transformation of a New York City Gang.* New York: Columbia University Press.
———. 2011. *Banished to the Homeland: Dominican Deportees and Their Stories of Exile.* New York: Columbia University Press.
Brotherton, David C., and Laura Naegler. 2014. "Jock Young and Social bulimia: Crime and the Contradictions of Capitalism." *Theoretical Criminology* 18 (4): 441–449.
Burstow, Bonnie. 2003. "Toward a Radical Understanding of Trauma and Trauma Work." *Violence against Women* 9 (11): 1293–1317.
Cheliotis, Leonidas K. 2017. "Punitive Inclusion: The Political Economy of Irregular Migration in the Margins of Europe." *European Journal of Criminology* 14 (1): 78–99.
Chiedi, Joanne M. 2019. "Care Provider Facilities Described Challenges Addressing Mental Health Needs of Children in HHS Custody." OEI-09-18-00431. Washington DC: U.S. Department of Health and Human Services Office of the Inspector General.
Chu, Tracy, Allen S. Keller, and Andrew Rasmussen. 2013. "Effects of Post-migration Factors on PTSD Outcomes among Immigrant Survivors of Political Violence." *Journal of Immigrant and Minority Health* 15:890–897.
Cohler, Bertram J., and Andrew Hostetler. 2016. "Linking Life Course and Life Story: Social Change and the Narrative Study of Lives over Time." In *Handbook of the Life Course,* edited by Jeylan T. Mortimer and Michael J. Shanahan, 555–576. Geneva: Springer.
Cruz, Jose Miguel. 2011. "Criminal Violence and Democratization in Central America: The Survival of the Violent State." *Latin American Politics and Society* 53 (4): 1–33.
Dayan, Colin. 2013. *The Law Is a White Dog—How Legal Rituals Make and Unmake Persons.* New York: Princeton University Press.
De Fina, Anna. 2000. "Orientation in Immigrant Narratives: The Role of Ethnicity in the Identification of Characters." *Discourse Studies* 2 (2): 131–157.
De Fina, Anna, and Kendall A. King. 2011. "Language Problem or Language Conflict? Narratives of Immigrant Women's Experiences in the US." *Discourse Studies* 13 (2): 163–188.

Dozier, Sandra Bygrave. 1993. "Emotional Concerns of Undocumented and Out-of-Status Foreign Students." *Community Review* 13:33–38.

Duzkoylu, Yigit, Salim Ilksen Basceken, and Emrullah Cem Kesilmez. 2017. "Physical Trauma among Refugees: Comparison between Refugees and Local Population Who Were Admitted to Emergency Department—Experience of a State Hospital in Syrian Border District." *Journal of Environmental and Public Health*, June 14. https://www.ncbi.nlm.nih.gov/pmc/articles/PMC5488154/.

Farah, Douglas, and Carl Meacham. 2015. *Alternative Governance in the Northern Triangle and Implications for US Foreign Policy: Finding Logic within Chaos.* New York: Rowman and Littlefield.

Forte, Alberto, Federico Trobia, Flavia Gualtieri, Dorian A. Lamis, Giuseppe Cardamone, Vincenzo Giallonardo, Andrea Fiorillo, Paolo Girardi, and Maurizio Pompili. 2018. "Suicide Risk among Immigrants and Ethnic Minorities: A Literature Overview." *International Journal of Environmental Research and Public Health* 15 (7): 1438.

Fortuna, Lisa R., Kiara Alvarez, Zorangeli Ramos Ortiz, Ye Wang, Xulian Mozo Alegria, Benjamin Cook, and Margarita Alegria. 2016. "Mental Health, Migration Stressors and Suicidal Ideation among Latino Immigrants in Spain and the United States." *European Psychiatry* 36:15–22.

Gadeberg, A. K., Edith Montgomery, Hanne Winther Frederiksen, and Marie Norredam. 2017. "Assessing Trauma and Mental Health in Refugee Children and Youth: A Systematic Review of Validated Screening and Measurement Tools." *European Journal of Public Health* 27 (3): 439–446.

George, Miriam. 2010. "A Theoretical Understanding of Refugee Trauma." *Clinical Social Work Journal* 38:379–387.

Ghosh, Dipayan, and Vijeth Iyengar. 2019. "Older Adults Are Especially Prone to Social Media Bubbles." *Scientific American*, February 21. https://blogs.scientificamerican.com/observations/older-adults-are-especially-prone-to-social-media-bubbles/.

Gonzalez, Melina Ocampo. 2015. "Sexual Violence as a Push Factor in Forced Displacement." In *Educacion, Inclusion y Posconflicto*, 199–215. Medellin: Corporacion Universitaria Lasallista.

Goodman, Rachael D., Colleen K. Vesely, Bethany Letiecq, and Carol L. Cleaveland. 2017. "Trauma and Resilience among Refugee and Undocumented Immigrant Women." *Journal of Counseling and Development* 95:309–321.

Hacker, Karen, Jocelyn Chu, Carolyn Leung, Robert Marra, Alex Pirie, Mohamed Brahimi, Margaret English, Joshua Beckmann, Dolores Acevedo-Garcia, and Robert P. Marlin. 2011. "The Impact of Immigration and Customs Enforcement on Immigrant Health: Perceptions of Immigrants in Everett, Massacusetts, USA." *Social Science and Medicine* 73 (4): 586–594.

Hallett, Miranda Cady. 2017. "Labor, Discipline, and Resistance: Transnational Migrant Workers 'On the Line.'" *Journal of Working Class Studies* 2 (1): 24–42.

Hallsworth, Simon, and David Brotherton. 2011. *Urban Disorder and Gangs: A Critique and a Warning.* London: Runnymede Trust.

Hernandez, Jose Bien R., and Peggy Y. Kim. 2020. "Epidemiology Morbidity and Mortality." *National Center for Biotechnology Information*, October 13. https://www.ncbi.nlm.nih.gov/books/NBK547668/.

Johansson, L. M., J. Sundquist, S.-E. Johansson, J. Qvist, and B. Bergman. 1997. "The Influence of Ethnicity and Social and Demographic Factors on Swedish Suicide

Rates: A Four-Year Follow-Up Study." *Social Psychiatry and Psychiatric Epidemiology* 32:165–170.

Jones, Bradley. 2019. "Majority of Americans Continue to Say Immigrants Strengthen the U.S." Pew Research Center, January 31. https://www.pewresearch.org/fact-tank/2019/01/31/majority-of-americans-continue-to-say-immigrants-strengthen-the-u-s/.

Koleski, Jerome, Sommer Aldulaimi, and Elizabeth Moran. 2019. "From Dehydration to Fractures: Medical Issues Faced by People Crossing the United States-Mexico Border." *Journal of Immigrant and Minority Health* 21:1181–1184.

Lane, Robert, and Regina Miranda. 2017. "The Effects of Familial Acculturative Stress and Hopelessness on Suicidal Ideation by Immigration Status among College Students." *Journal of American College Health* 66 (2): 76–86.

Levers, Lisa Lopez, and Debra Hyatt-Burkhart. 2012. "Immigration Reform and the Potential for Psychosocial Trauma: The Missing Link of Lived Human Experience." *Analyses of Social Issues and Public Policy* 12 (1): 68–77.

Leyro, Shirley P. 2017. "The Fear Factor: Exploring the Impact of the Vulnerability to Deportation on Immigrants' Lives." *CUNY Academic Works*, February. https://academicworks.cuny.edu/gc_etds/1681.

Leyro, Shirley P., and Daniel L. Stageman. 2018. "Crimmigration, Deportability and the Social Exclusion of Noncitizen Immigrants." *Migration Letters* 15 (2): 255–265.

Lind, Dara. 2018. "The Trump Administration's Separation of Families at the Border, Explained." *Vox*, August 14. https://www.vox.com/2018/6/11/17443198/children-immigrant-families-separated-parents.

Lonegan, Bryan. 2007. "American Diaspora: The Deportation of Lawful Residents from the United States and the Destruction of Their Families." *NYU Review of Law and Social Change* 32:55–82.

McAdams, Dan P., and Jen Guo. 2015. "Narrating the Generative Life." *Psychological Science* 26 (4): 475–483.

McAdams, Dan P., and Kate C. McLean. 2013. "Narrative Identity." *Current Directions in Psychological Science* 22 (3): 233–238.

McDonald, William F., and Edna Erez. 2007. "Immigrants as Victims: A Framework." *International Review of Victimology* 14:1–10.

Mendoza, Marcela, and Edward M. Olivas. 2009. "Advocating for Control with Compassion: The Impact of Raids and Deportation on Children and Families." *Oregon Review of International Law* 11 (1): 111–122.

Menjivar, Cecilia, and Leisy J. Abrego. 2012. "Legal Violence: Immigration Law and the Lives of Central American Immigrants." *American Journal of Sociology* 117 (5): 1380–1421.

Metzl, Jonathan M. 2019. *Dying of Whiteness: How the Politics of Racial Resentment is Killing America's Heartland.* New York: Hachette.

Neilson, David. 2015. "Class, Precarity, and Anxiety under Neoliberal Global Capitalism: From Denial to Resistance." *Theory and Psychology* 25 (2): 184–201.

Ong, Bie Nio, Jane C. Richardson, Tom Porter, and Janet Grime. 2014. "Exploring the Relationship between Multi-morbidity, Resilience and Social Connectedness across the Life Course." *Health* 18 (3): 302–318.

Parkins, Natasha C. 2010. "Push and Pull Factors of Migration." *American Review of Political Economy* 8 (2): 6–24.

Patler, Caitlin, and Whitney Laster Pirtle. 2018. "From Undocumented to Lawfully Present: Do Changes to Legal Status Impact Psychological Wellbeing among Latino Immigrant Young Adults?" *Social Science and Medicine* 199:39–48.

Potochnick, Stephanie R., and Krista M. Perreira. 2010. "Depression and Anxiety among First-Generation Immigrant Latino Youth: Key Correlates and Implications for Future Research." *Journal of Nervous and Mental Disease* 198 (7): 470–477.

Presser, Lois. 2016. "Criminology and the Narrative Turn." *Crime, Media, Culture: An International Journal* 12 (2): 137–151.

Rosenblum, Marc R., and Isabel Ball. 2016. *Trends in Unaccompanied Child and Family Migration from Central America.* Washington DC: Migration Policy Institute.

Sampson, Robert J., and John H. Laub. 1992. "Crime and Deviance in the Life Course." *Annual Review of Sociology* 18:63–84.

Saunders, Benjamin, Julius Sim, Tom Kingstone, Shula Baker, Jackie Waterfield, Bernadette Bartlam, Heather Burroughs, and Clare Jinks. 2018. "Saturation in Qualitative Research: Exploring Its Conceptualization and Operationalization." *Quality and Quantity* 52 (4): 1893–1907.

Sawyer, Cheryl B., and Judith Marquez. 2017. "Senseless Violence against Central American Unaccompanied Minors: Historical Background and Call for Help." *Journal of Psychology* 151 (1): 69–75.

Silva Ribeiro, Wagner, Annette Bauer, Mario Cesar Rezende Andrade, Marianna York-Smith, Pedro Mario Pan, Luca Pingani, Martin Knapp, Evandro Silva Freire Coutinho, and Sara Evans-Lacko. 2017. "Income Inequality and Mental Illness-Related Morbidity and Resilience: A Systematic Review and Meta-analysis." *The Lancet: Psychiatry* 4 (7): 554–562.

Soegaard, Erik Ganesh Iyer, Zhanna Kan, Rishav Koirala, Edvard Hauff, and Suraj Bahadur Thapa. 2020. "Variations in Psychiatric Morbidity between Traumatized Norwegian, Refugees and Other Immigrant Patients in Oslo." *Nordic Journal of Psychiatry* 74 (6): 390–399.

Southern Poverty Law Center. 2020. "Family Separation under the Trump Administration—a Timeline." June 17. https://www.splcenter.org/news/2020/06/17/family -separation-under-trump-administration-timeline.

Taussig, Michael. 1986. *Shamanism, Colonialism, and the Wild Man.* Chicago: University of Chicago Press.

Tummala-Narra, Pratyusha. 2007. "Conceptualizing Trauma and Resilience across Diverse Contexts: A Multicultural Perspective." *Journal of Aggression, Maltreatment and Trauma* 14 (1–2): 33–53.

Ungar, Michael, Marion Brown, Linda Liebenberg, Rasha Othman, Wai Man Kwong, Mary Armstrong, and Jane Gilgun. 2007. "Unique Pathways to Resilience across Cultures." *Adolescence* 42 (166): 287–310.

Ventriglio, Antonio, and Dinesh Bhugra. 2015. "Migration, Trauma and Resilience." In *Trauma and Migration: Cultural Factors in the Diagnosis and Treatment of Traumatised Immigrants,* edited by Meryam Schouler-Ocak, 69–79. Geneva: Springer.

Verstraete, Pieter, Evelyne Verhaegen, and Marc Depaepe. 2017. "One Difference Is Enough: Towards a History of Disability in the Belgian-Congo, 1908–1960." In *The Routledge History of Disability,* edited by Roy Hanes, Ivan Brown, and Nancy E. Hansen, 231–241. New York: Routledge.

Welch, Michael. 2014. "Economic Man and Diffused Sovereignty: A Critique of Australia's Asylum Regime." *Crime, Law and Social Change* 61 (1): 81–107.

Welch, Michael, and Liza Schuster. 2005. "Detention of Asylum Seekers in the US, UK, France, Germany, and Italy: A Critical View of the Globalizing Culture of Control." *Criminal Justice* 5 (4): 331–355.

Young, Jock. 1999. "Cannibalism and Bulimia: Patterns of Social Control in Late Modernity." *Theoretical Criminology* 3 (4): 387–407.

———. 2007. *The Vertigo of Late Modernity*. London: Sage.

Zallman, Leah, Karen E. Finnegan, David U. Himmelstein, Sharon Touw, and Steffie Woolhandler. 2019. "Care for America's Elderly and Disabled People Relies on Immigrant Labor." *Health Affairs* 38 (6): 919–926.

Zatz, Marjorie S., and Hilary Smith. 2012. "Immigration, Crime and Victimization: Rhetoric and Reality." *Annual Review of Law and Social Science* 8:141–159.

Zayas, Luis H. 2015. *Forgotten Citizens: Deportation, Children, and the Making of American Exiles and Orphans*. New York: Oxford University Press.

8

Death and Disabilities in Divergent Deportation Contexts

Revisiting the Hispanic Epidemiological Paradox

JUAN M. PEDROZA
PIL H. CHUNG

O nce concentrated on the U.S.-Mexico border, immigration enforcement today reaches across the U.S. interior. The escalating investment in deportations has spread injury, fear, and isolation. For instance, although new immigrant arrivals typically enjoy health advantages compared to the general U.S. population, injuries sustained from "tactical infrastructure" on the border designed to cause harm have become all too common (Jusionyte 2018b), and once settled in the United States, workers who are hurt or become ill on the job tend to absorb the costs of bodily harm. After arrival, severe health consequences can continue to mount among immigrants working in meatpacking (Ribas 2016) and agriculture (Holmes 2013), as Nathan Mutic and Linda McCauley document in Chapter 6 in their examination of heat stroke among agricultural workers. Recognizing these workers' vulnerable legal status, employers and insurance companies have turned to reporting their injured and deportable employees to immigration authorities in order to skirt their medical fees (Berkes and Grabell 2018). Clearly, the health consequences of immigration enforcement have the potential to erode immigrant health outcomes in myriad ways. In this chapter, we examine whether the rise of mass deportations across U.S. metro areas coincides with rising health challenges faced by immigrants.

The unprecedented volume of deportations since the late 2000s, which coincided with the aftermath of the Great Recession as well as a shift in

Hispanic noncitizens' countries of origin, may have introduced additional health hazards for immigrants. As enforcement escalates, do the health effects of immigration enforcement and restrictive policy making extend to death and disabilities? If so, which groups are most likely to report negative health outcomes in areas hit hardest by mass deportations? We examine whether enforcement predicts negative health among all Hispanics or only those most vulnerable to deportation: recently arrived Hispanic noncitizens. To examine the relationship between deportations and health, we analyze multiple data sources merged with Department of Homeland Security (DHS) data. Our analyses rely on data from Secure Communities, a nationwide program under Immigration and Customs Enforcement (ICE) that links arrestees' biometric data to federal databases capable of identifying noncitizens (Rosenblum and Kandel 2012). Given the discretion county officials could exercise in implementing the program (Pedroza 2019, 2013), there is wide variation in the reported deportation statistics. Specifically, we leverage county-level variation in Hispanic[1] mortality (i.e., crude death rates) from the Centers for Disease Control and Prevention (CDC) and cumulative deportation rates under the Secure Communities immigration enforcement program. Then, we examine differences in individuals reporting multiple disabilities—as recorded in the American Community Survey (ACS)—across metro areas with divergent enforcement contexts.

We find evidence that residents living in metro areas hit particularly hard by the rise of mass deportations were more likely to report health problems. Recently arrived Hispanic noncitizens are among the least likely to qualify for naturalization and protections from deportation (Rosenblum and Kandel 2012). In addition to being at elevated risk of deportation, they were also more likely to report multiple disabilities if they lived in metro areas where deportations became especially common. The rest of the Hispanic population, including Hispanic noncitizens who arrived in earlier waves predating the rise in mass deportation, was apparently spared these adverse health consequences. The results suggest that although the broader effects of enforcement can extend beyond the intended targets of enforcement, certain health outcomes such as disabilities have afflicted an especially vulnerable segment of the immigrant population. Although newly arrived Hispanic noncitizens are healthier than those who arrived in earlier eras and thus are more likely to have survived to older ages (Taylor et al. 2011), part of the price of settling in the United States seems to have risen, and today includes higher rates of disability. We propose injuries sustained en route to the United States and injuries sustained on the job may help explain the relationship between enforcement and disabilities.

Research on Enforcement and Immigrant Health

In this section, we first discuss recent evidence on whether contextual effects matter for immigrant health outcomes. Then, we summarize reasons why immigrant groups might report health advantages relative to other populations—the so-called Hispanic epidemiological paradox (HEP)—and the conditions under which we observe a diminished immigrant health advantage.

Whether State and Local Contexts Can Shape the HEP and Immigrant Health

Research on immigrant health suggests divergent contexts can affect immigrant health. Although prior work has found a weak relationship between anti-immigrant prejudice and mortality (Morey et al. 2018), mounting evidence suggests that the social determinants of health among immigrants (Castañeda et al. 2015) include policy and enforcement contexts (Perreira and Pedroza 2019). For instance, restrictive policies can accelerate stressors and erode support networks (Philbin et al. 2018; Morey et al. 2018; Hagan, Rodríguez, and Castro 2011; Rodríguez, Paredes, and Hagan 2017, 2019). The link between restrictionism and declining health might stem from an erosion of trust in health institutions (Cruz Nichols, Lebrón, and Pedraza 2018) and noncitizen workers becoming stuck in hazardous jobs (Hall and Greenman 2015; Orrenius and Zavodny 2009; Fernández-Esquer, Gallardo, and Diamond 2019) in contexts where finding a new job is made increasingly difficult by a rise in restrictionism (Lofstrom, Bohn, and Raphael 2011; East et al. 2018).

Past Research on the Paradox

The HEP refers to unexpectedly favorable health outcomes among the Hispanic population in the United States, especially Hispanic immigrants (Markides and Eschbach 2005; Teruya and Bazargan-Hejazi 2013; Hummer and Chinn 2011). Researchers have found evidence of the HEP when examining various outcomes, ranging from longevity, mortality, and life span variability (Goldman, Glei, and Weinstein 2017; Lariscy et al. 2016; Lariscy, Hummer, and Hayward 2015) to specific health risks (Markides et al. 2007).[2] The HEP has also been invoked when examining chronic conditions and pain among unauthorized immigrants compared to authorized immigrants (Hamilton, Hale, and Savinar 2019). Explanations for the HEP emphasize resilience and health-enhancing factors (Ruiz et al. 2016; Acevedo-Garcia and Bates 2008; Riosmena, Kuhn, and Jochem 2017) as well as emigrant selection (Riosmena, Kuhn, and Jochem 2017; Riosmena, Wong, and Palloni 2013) and differences in health selection across immigrant groups (Akresh and Frank 2008). Relatedly, differences in who migrates back to their countries of origin (a "salmon bias") may also account for such advantages (Abraido-Lanza et al. 1999; see also Arenas et al. 2015; Riosmena, Wong, and Palloni 2013; Turra and Elo 2008).[3]

The HEP Is Not Immutable and Can Erode

Researchers have begun identifying the conditions under which living in the United States can become detrimental for immigrants (Castro 2007). Among these, duration of stay strongly predicts the trend toward increasing risk of mortality and chronic illness (Riosmena et al. 2015). Generation status (Giuntella 2016), segregation (Do et al. 2017), and living in established immigrant destinations compared to new immigrant destinations (Fenelon 2017; Brazil 2017) also help explain where health advantages either sustain or erode. In addition, the transition to old age can reduce health and disability advantages among older Hispanic immigrants (Sheftel and Heiland 2018; Markides et al. 2007). The advantages can recede in the absence of social networks (Cantu and Angel 2017; Montes-de-Oca et al. 2015; Eschbach et al. 2004) and health care utilization (Roy, Olsen, and Tseng 2020) and result in "longer—but harder—lives" (Boen and Hummer 2019, 434). Additionally, barriers to health access and utilization (Bacon, Riosmena, and Rogers 2017; Cervantes et al. 2018) and health-adverse factors such as high rates of obesity and diabetes can also erode the HEP (Goldman 2016). Finally, the health advantages we observe are not immutable and may have emerged in the 1960s (Palloni and Morenoff 2001) as a result of immigrant selectivity, and such an advantage might erode in the coming decades.

Contribution to Research on Contextual Determinants of Immigrant Health

Studies that have analyzed the potential effects of immigration policy making on health have come to differing conclusions. On the one hand, immigration policy making does not necessarily lead to a tandem change in immigrant health access or outcomes (Allen and McNeely 2017; Koralek, Pedroza, and Capps 2009). Such nonrelationships could reflect resilient communities weathering tough times, or changes in immigrant behavior that evade data collection efforts, or both. On the other hand, among studies that do find policy making is related to health, three scenarios are discussed.

First, rising restrictionism may foretell worse outcomes for the general public. In this scenario, high deportation rates may have taken hold in places beset by economic downturns (O'Neil 2011; Joyner 2018; Parrado 2012), thus predicting worse health for everyone (Strully et al. 2020). After all, increasingly stringent enforcement tends to coincide with spikes in unemployment (O'Neil 2011; Joyner 2018; Parrado 2012). Indeed, Secure Communities negatively affected employment options among immigrants and the general U.S. population (East et al. 2018), possibly because locations with a ramp-up in deportations were already vulnerable to negative labor market trends.

Second, a growing body of research suggests restrictive immigration policy making can affect health among Hispanic noncitizens and Hispanic U.S. citizens alike. In response to a rise in enforcement, Hispanic immigrant households may report mistrust of mainstream institutions, declining health, and other negative outcomes (Alsan and Yang 2019; Watson 2014; Cruz Nichols, Lebrón, and Pedraza 2018; Vargas and Benitez 2019). Indeed, when asked about the current immigration policy climate, nearly half of Hispanic adults—and two-thirds of Hispanic immigrants—report worrying "some" or "a lot" that someone they know may be deported (Lopez and Rohal 2017), especially as the salience of deportations has become widespread (Sanchez et al. 2015). Under these conditions, Hispanics may have become generally wary of seeking health-promoting services, whether they were born in the United States or not (Stanhope et al. 2019).

Third, this chapter examines whether deportations predict disabilities only among those most likely to be directly affected by intensifying enforcement. For instance, the health and mental health consequences of Secure Communities on Hispanic immigrants has been found to be limited to immigrants living with noncitizen household members (Wang and Kaushal 2019). Likewise, the effects of Arizona Senate Bill 1070 on low birth weight were found to be limited to Hispanic immigrant women (Torche and Sirois 2018).

Data and Methods

Health Data

Following recent work (Sheftel and Heiland 2018), we analyze CDC data on deaths and ACS data on disability.[4] The data provide prevalence estimates for Hispanic death rates as well as for six measures of disability (i.e., cognitive, ambulatory, independent living, self-care, vision, and hearing difficulty). At the macro level ($N = 2,145$ county-years between 2013 and 2016), we first predict county death rates as a function of cumulative deportation rates using publicly available CDC data. At the micro level, we predict whether or not an individual reported two or more disabilities. Although we do not know when each person first experienced any difficulties, we interpret multiple disabilities as a proxy for cumulative health disadvantage.[5]

Deportation Data

We propose that *cumulative* exposure to deportation events might predict adverse mortality and disability outcomes because such exposure is likely to present serious health challenges. We define the cumulative deportation rate (D) of a county to equal the number of reported deportations since the activation of the Secure Communities program in that county's jail system, adjusting for (1) the number of days each area participated in the program and (2) the number of noncitizens:

$$D = \log\left[\left(\frac{\text{cumulative removals and returns}}{\text{noncitizens per thousand}} \times \frac{\text{days since initial activation}}{365}\right) + 1\right]$$

Lagged deportation rates ($t - 2$ years) are merged with CDC and ACS data. Finally, we restrict analyses to the years 2013–2016 (a period during which over 90 percent of counties participated in the Secure Communities program).

In county-level analyses of CDC data, we predict death rates as a function of deportation rates. In ACS data, metro residents living in an identifiable county are assigned deportation rates corresponding to their county of residence. Residents without a county identifier and whose broader metro area straddles multiple counties are assigned a synthetic rate, which is the sum of the county-specific deportation rates weighted by the resident noncitizen population.[6]

Individual and Household Determinants of Health

ACS responses allow us to examine individual-level variation in disabilities. Following prior research, we account for duration of stay (Riosmena et al. 2015) in the United States by measuring years since arrival among the foreign-born. We also acknowledge differences in disabilities across the life course (Sáenz 2015; Markides et al. 2007)—for example, among younger versus older Hispanic immigrants (Sheftel and Heiland 2018; Rodríguez, Paredes, and Hagan 2019; Cantu and Angel 2019; Olsen, Roy, and Tseng 2019)—and adjust for individual's age (and age-squared). Since recent immigrant arrivals are more likely to be male (Riosmena, Kuhn, and Jochem 2017), and since health outcomes often differ by sex (Acevedo-Garcia and

Bates 2008; Ruiz et al. 2016; Garcia, Reyes, and Rote 2019), we adjust for each person's sex (Female: 1; Male: 0). Educational attainment and living below the poverty line are both associated with health outcomes, and so we account for both. Individuals with disabilities can select into health insurance coverage and Supplemental Security Income (SSI), and we include indicators for both. We also account for differences in marital status because those who live with a spouse tend to also exhibit other health-promoting behaviors. Similarly, differences in occupation and employment status predict health outcomes, and so we account for sector and employment status. Finally, we include fixed effects for fifty-nine Hispanic origin groups in the ACS.

In our analyses of individual health outcomes, we differentiate between noncitizens who arrived in the United States after 2006 (i.e., recent arrivals at elevated risk of deportation) and those who arrived earlier (for a similar approach by timing of arrival, see Riosmena, Vinneau, and Beltrán-Sánchez 2019). The composition of earlier waves of Hispanic noncitizens differs from recent arrivals. For instance, among Mexican noncitizens, only 10 percent arrived after 2006. By contrast, recent arrivals comprise a notable proportion of Hispanic noncitizens from other countries: 43 percent of Cuban noncitizens arrived after 2006, compared to 33 percent of Dominicans, 29 percent of Colombians, 21 percent of Hondurans, 20 percent of Guatemalans, and 15 percent of Salvadorans.

Analytic Approach

Since we are interested in the relationship between immigration enforcement and health, we focus on adult civilians living in metro areas (i.e., residents age twenty-five and older not in military occupations or in group quarters). In our analyses of CDC data, we regress Hispanic death rates on cumulative deportation rates. The macro-level results account for determinants of deportation activity: the relative size of a county's Hispanic population, the growth of the Hispanic population since 1990, and fixed effects per state and year (Pedroza 2019). Standard errors are clustered at the county level and results are weighted using noncitizen population estimates. In these analyses, we are limited to examining death rates among all Hispanics, regardless of nativity.

When predicting disabilities using ACS data, we first describe time trends in disability rates across metro areas. We then present multivariate regression results where each metro resident's likelihood of reporting multiple disabilities is compared to residents in the same metro area and then compared to individuals across all metro areas. The approach allows us to account for differences across 242 different metro areas. We also present results for 147 metro areas with at least 100 Hispanics in a given year. In sum, the regression models account for variation across individuals (i) in each metro area (m) in a given year of ACS data (t):

$$Y_{i,m,t} = \alpha + \beta_1 \left(\text{deportation}_{m,t-2}\right) + \sum \beta X_{i,m,t},$$

where "deportation" equals the rate of deportation in year $t - 2$ (preceding the year leading up to each administration of the ACS survey) and X is a set of individual and household variables.

Results

When analyzing the relationship between county-level deportations and mortality, we find high rates of Hispanic deaths are *less* likely to be concentrated in counties with elevated immigration enforcement (Table 8.1). Consistent with past work (Brazil 2017; Fenelon 2017), counties with higher rates of Hispanic population growth reported lower Hispanic mortality rates. On the basis of these results, we might conclude that immigration enforcement does not erode Hispanic health. To analyze whether enforcement predicts worse health outcomes for specific segments of the Hispanic population, we turn to micro-level data.

Disability rates are unevenly reported across subsets of racial/ethnic groups. Table 8.2 displays the share of metro residents reporting multiple

TABLE 8.1: COUNTY-LEVEL HISPANIC CRUDE DEATH RATES
BY CUMULATIVE DEPORTATION RATES, 2013–2016

Variables	Model 1: ordinary least squares (OLS)	Model 2: OLS (with mean metro effects)	Model 3: OLS (with mean metro effects)
Cumulative deportation rate	−23.7* (11.40)	−22.5** (6.98)	−23.2*** (6.49)
Hispanic percentage	537.3*** (104.75)	500.4*** (66.16)	539.1*** (69.12)
Hispanic growth (since 1990)	−635.5*** (175.71)	−692.9*** (129.59)	−756.6*** (135.72)
State and year fixed effects	No	Yes	Yes
Observations (no. of counties)	2,145	2,145	2,145
R-squared	0.5115	0.7913	0.8079

Source: Authors' analyses of county-level CDC compressed mortality data, available at https://wonder.cdc.gov/cmf-icd10.html, and ICE Secure Communities data, in the author's possession.
Note: Robust standard errors are in parentheses. Standard errors are clustered at the county level.
*$p < 0.05$, **$p < 0.01$, ***$p < 0.001$.

TABLE 8.2: PERCENTAGE OF METRO RESIDENTS REPORTING MULTIPLE DISABILITIES, BY CITIZENSHIP STATUS, RACE/ETHNICITY, AND DEPORTATION CONTEXT

Disabilities	All metro residents	Non-Hispanic			Hispanic				
		White		Black	Total	Hispanic U.S. citizen	Hispanic noncitizen	Hispanic noncitizen, arrived before 2007	Hispanic noncitizen, arrived after 2006
	Total	Total	U.S. citizen	U.S. citizen					
Multiple disabilities	7.39	7.69	7.64	9.85	6.00	7.34	3.42	3.62	2.30
Low-deportation context	7.30	7.43	7.41	9.69	6.33	7.85	3.01	3.33	1.58
High-deportation context	7.40	7.86	7.91	9.5	6.01	7.18	3.98	4.18	2.68

Source: Authors' analyses of IPUMS data, available at https://ipums.org/projects/ipums-usa/d010.v8.0, and ICE Secure Communities data, in the author's possession.

Note: Disability rates reflect sample of residents living in metro areas with a Secure Communities program (2013–2016). Deportation contexts reflect whether residents live in a metro area whose cumulative deportation rates are one standard deviation below or above the mean (2.13 ± 0.94).

disabilities by race/ethnicity, citizenship status, and deportation context. Multiple disability rates were reported by 7.39 percent of all respondents during the study period (2013–2016), but there was notable heterogeneity by subgroup. For example, and perhaps not surprisingly, Hispanic noncitizens had the lowest overall rates of multiple disabilities (3.42 percent). In addition, U.S. citizen, non-Hispanic, white residents had similar rates of multiple disabilities as Hispanic U.S. citizens (7.64 percent and 7.34 percent, respectively). U.S. citizen, non-Hispanic, Black metro residents reported especially high multiple-disability rates (9.85 percent).[7]

Bivariate patterns suggest a relationship between enforcement [mean cumulative deportation rate: 2.1, or $(e^{2.1} - 1) = 7$ deportations annually per thousand noncitizens] and disabilities. In general, residents in low deportation contexts (i.e., cumulative deportation rates one standard deviation below the mean) did report multiple disabilities less often (7.30 percent compared to 7.40 percent) than those in high deportation areas, or a standard deviation above the mean. Next, we examine whether these relationships hold when accounting for other factors.

If deportations represent a proxy for declining conditions for the general population, then disabilities should be more common for everyone in high deportation areas. We find no such evidence (Table 8.3). Our results confirm a *negative* relationship between deportations and disabilities whether we omit (model 1) or adjust for a full set of determinants of health (model 2). Among non-Hispanic residents (models 3 and 4), deportation rates are also inversely related to disabilities, both among white (models 5 and 6) and Black U.S. citizens (model 8).

We also examine whether enforcement foretells adverse reports of disabilities among Hispanics. For context, among Hispanics in the sample (i.e., metro residents age twenty-five and over), 34 percent are not U.S. citizens; close to half (45 percent) are U.S.-born citizens; and the remainder are naturalized U.S. citizens (21 percent). We find no such evidence for most Hispanic groups. Consistent with our Hispanic mortality results, disabilities are less common among the general Hispanic population in metro areas with high deportation rates (model 10). In fact, when analyzing disabilities among Hispanics (including either U.S. citizens or noncitizens arriving before 2007), we find deportations predict *fewer* disabilities once we account for all covariates of health (models 10, 12, and 14). In sum, we find no evidence of generalized effects of enforcement on Hispanic deaths or disabilities. Rather, our results suggest the era of mass deportations comes with severe health consequences primarily for those at highest risk of exposure to immigration enforcement: *recently arrived* Hispanic noncitizens who immigrated during a time when enforcement escalated to unprecedent levels. Disabilities are more common in high-deportation-rate metro areas among

TABLE 8.3: LOG ODDS OF REPORTING MULTIPLE DISABILITIES AMONG METRO RESIDENTS (2013–2016) BY RACE/ETHNICITY, CITIZENSHIP STATUS, AND CUMULATIVE DEPORTATION RATE (CDR)

Variables	All metro residents		Non-Hispanics		Non-Hispanic white U.S. citizens		Non-Hispanic black U.S. citizens	
	Model 1	Model 2	Model 3	Model 4	Model 5	Model 6	Model 7	Model 8
CDR	-0.0007**	-0.0020***	-0.0005*	-0.0017***	-0.0011***	-0.0016***	0.0024**	-0.0020**
	(0.000)	(0.000)	(0.000)	(0.000)	(0.000)	(0.000)	(0.001)	(0.001)
Observations	5,807,672	5,807,672	4,953,610	4,953,610	3,768,679	3,768,679	583,745	583,745
R-squared	0.0031	0.1844	0.0031	0.1824	0.0032	0.1769	0.0052	0.1919
Full controls	No	Yes	No	Yes	No	Yes	No	Yes
Hispanic-origin fixed effects	No	Yes	—	—	—	—	—	—

Variables	All Hispanics		Hispanic U.S. citizens		Hispanic noncitizens (arrived before 2007)	
	Model 9	Model 10	Model 11	Model 12	Model 13	Model 14
CDR	-0.0000	-0.0026***	0.0004	-0.0022**	-0.0007	-0.0034***
	(0.001)	(0.001)	(0.001)	(0.001)	(0.001)	(0.001)
Observations	854,062	854,062	594,909	594,909	222,071	222,071
R-squared	0.0069	0.2038	0.0057	0.2090	0.0105	0.1833
Full controls	No	Yes	No	Yes	No	Yes
Hispanic-origin fixed effects	No	Yes	No	Yes	No	Yes

Source: Authors' analyses of IPUMS data, available at https://ipums.org/projects/ipums-usa/d010.v8.0, and ICE Secure Communities data, in the author's possession.

Note: Standard errors are in parentheses. The full controls are sex, age, age², poverty and insurance status, SSI benefit receipt, marital status, educational attainment, and occupation and employment status. Model 14 accounts for U.S. tenure.

*p < 0.05, **p < 0.01, ***p < 0.001.

Hispanic noncitizens who have not had the benefit of putting down long-term roots in the country.

Only among Hispanic noncitizens who are recent arrivals do we find that reporting more than one disability is more common in high-deportation-rate metro areas (Table 8.4). The results suggest disabilities are more common in high-enforcement metro areas among those most likely to be affected by deportations. Recall that Hispanic noncitizens who arrived after 2006 reported the *lowest* rates of multiple disabilities (2.30 percent across metros and 2.68 percent in high-deportation contexts, as shown in Table 8.2). Among recently arrived Hispanic noncitizens, rising cumulative deportations are associated with a 3.4 percent rise in the likelihood of two or more reported disabilities, even after we account for determinants of health and focus on 147 metro areas with 100 or more Hispanics (model 6).[8]

Consistent with prior research, reporting multiple disabilities is more common among those who have been in the United States longer, are older, are not in the labor force, or received SSI benefits. Results are substantially the same when we conduct robustness checks to determine whether the results are sensitive to decisions regarding our sample or approach.[9]

Discussion and Conclusion

The accumulated weight of immigration enforcement did not affect every local community across the United States evenly. Where mass deportations took firm hold, certain members of the Hispanic population were more likely to report accumulated health disadvantages. Despite a relative advantage compared to other groups, Hispanic noncitizens who arrived in the United States recently have been alone in reporting more instances of multiple disabilities. Recently arrived noncitizens have also been an enforcement priority for deportation (Rosenblum and Meissner 2014; Rosenblum and Kandel 2012), which may have exposed this group to adverse health outcomes.

Because of data limitations, our analyses cannot explain why disabilities are more common in high-deportation-rate metro areas. CDC analyses are limited to macro-level mortality data among all Hispanics. In ACS data, we are able to analyze pooled cross-sections that contain information about when immigrants arrived in the United States and where they settled, but these data do not tell us exactly when they *first* began to experience disabilities. Consequently, meaningful explanations for our results must be able to provide cogent reasons for why a rise in disabilities was limited to recently arrived Hispanic noncitizens.

We anticipate that employment and migration contexts help account for our results. First, recently arrived noncitizens may be especially vulnerable

TABLE 8.4: LOG ODDS OF REPORTING MULTIPLE DISABILITIES FOR HISPANIC NONCITIZEN METRO RESIDENTS ARRIVING AFTER 2006

	Model 1	Model 2	Model 3	Model 4	Model 5	Model 6
Deportation rate	0.0074***	0.0063***	0.0059***	0.0052**	0.0044**	0.0036*
	(0.002)	(0.002)	(0.002)	(0.002)	(0.002)	(0.002)
Age		−0.0126***	−0.0126***	−0.0127***	−0.0116***	−0.0117***
		(0.000)	(0.000)	(0.000)	(0.000)	(0.000)
Age^2		0.0002***	0.0002***	0.0002***	0.0002***	0.0002***
		(0.000)	(0.000)	(0.000)	(0.000)	(0.000)
Female		0.0027†	0.0027†	0.0027†	−0.0029†	−0.0030†
		(0.001)	(0.001)	(0.001)	(0.002)	(0.002)
Years in U.S.			0.0007*	0.0007*	0.0008**	0.0008**
			(0.000)	(0.000)	(0.000)	(0.000)
Below poverty line					0.0024	0.0025
					(0.002)	(0.002)
Any health insurance					0.0063***	0.0067***
					(0.002)	(0.002)
Any SSI income					0.1274***	0.1291***
					(0.008)	(0.008)
Married (spouse present)					−0.0065***	−0.0060***
					(0.002)	(0.002)
Education (0: <12 years)						
12 years					−0.0027	−0.0020
					(0.002)	(0.002)
1–2 years college					−0.0067*	−0.0065*
					(0.003)	(0.003)
4+ years college					−0.0065*	−0.0061*
					(0.003)	(0.003)
No schooling					0.0164***	0.0167***
					(0.003)	(0.003)
Employment (0: not in labor force)						
Unemployed					−0.0150*	−0.0141*
					(0.007)	(0.007)
Professional					−0.0168***	−0.0160***
					(0.003)	(0.003)
Service					−0.0180***	−0.0173***
					(0.002)	(0.002)
Farm					−0.0266***	−0.0262***
					(0.005)	(0.005)
Production					−0.0193***	−0.0188***
					(0.003)	(0.003)
Observations	37,082	37,082	37,082	37,082	37,082	36,231
R-squared	0.0147	0.1593	0.1594	0.1608	0.1704	0.1665

Source: Authors' analyses of IPUMS data, available at https://ipums.org/projects/ipums-usa/d010.v8.0, and ICE Secure Communities data, in the author's possession.

Note: Standard errors are in parentheses. Sample reflects residents in metro areas with Secure Communities program (2013–2016). Model 6 is limited to metros with 100+ Hispanics ($N = 36,231$). Models 4–6 include detailed Hispanic-origin fixed effects.

*$p < 0.05$, **$p < 0.01$, ***$p < 0.001$, †$p < 0.10$.

to adverse working conditions. Having entered the United States since the Great Recession, Hispanic noncitizens in restrictive locations may have felt stuck in their jobs (East et al. 2018; Lofstrom, Bohn, and Raphael 2011). In response, exploitative employers (Valenzuela et al. 2006) may have exposed these employees to dangerous conditions at a higher rate with the expectation that noncitizens would keep injuries to themselves to avoid the threat of deportation (Berkes and Grabell 2018). Parallel research has documented how risk can translate to social suffering among farmworkers (Holmes 2013). Our study suggests a promising area of research regarding whether and how noncitizens in metro areas might likewise absorb the health costs of risky jobs: supplementary analyses reveal that the relationship between disabilities and deportations is especially pronounced among recent metro arrivals working in the service sector.

Second, recent arrivals may have also experienced dangerous conditions en route to the United States. Ethnographic research on the health risks of crossing the U.S.-Mexico border (Holmes 2013; Jusionyte 2018a) suggests that border crossers must contend with increasingly hazardous obstacles along the way. As Abby Wheatley notes in Chapter 13, the politics of survival continue even after arriving north of the U.S.-Mexico border. If leaving or fleeing one's country of origin has become not only a difficult but a hazardous decision, then we need to understand the premigration, migration, postmigration, and (among deportees reentering the United States, as examined by Amelia Frank-Vitale in Chapter 11) remigration decisions and circumstances of those who cross the U.S.-Mexico border or bypass traditional ports of entry to settle in U.S. metro areas.

Our results suggest an immigrant advantage in reported disabilities partially waned. The advantage may have eroded at a slightly faster pace in metro areas with high cumulative deportation rates than in metro areas with low deportation rates. Left unchecked, disabilities among recent noncitizen arrivals may rise further. Just as others have suggested that deportations can diminish immigrants' accumulated social capital (Hagan, Leal, and Rodríguez 2015; Rugh and Hall 2016), we likewise call attention to the implications of investing in mass deportations at the expense of immigrant health. In the long term, the social effects of enforcement can further erode health in ways we have only begun to reliably measure. For example, if finding safe passage to the United States—and a safe job once in the United States—became more difficult as deportations rose, then recently arrived noncitizens may find that they can ill afford to support their networks of friends and family, including older immigrants who are especially vulnerable to isolation. In addition, by exposing immigrants to infectious disease, COVID-19 can accelerate health inequalities among immigrants who are deemed essential and also concentrated in precarious labor with little or no access to health care. By continuing to detain and expel noncitizens amid the pandemic, U.S. immigration officials contribute to the spread of COVID-19 among noncitizens in U.S. custody as well as in deportees' countries of origin. In the evolving context of mass deportations and a global pandemic, deportations may have only begun to take a toll on health in immigrant communities.

NOTES

1. Convention when referring to individuals identifying as "Hispanic" has moved to using "Latino" or "Latina/o" or, more recently, "Latinx." Notwithstanding debates regarding such pan-ethnic labels, and since variation by either sex or gender are not the primary focus here, the chapter uses "Hispanic" to refer to people who—when surveyed by the U.S. Census—identify as "Hispanic, Latino, or other Spanish" culture or origin, regardless of race.

2. Evidence of a HEP is not unequivocal (Camacho-Rivera et al. 2015; Markides and Gerst 2011; Lum and Vanderaa 2010; Tarraf et al. 2020).

3. Such bias appears particularly applicable to Mexican immigrants (Palloni and Arias 2004) but may not apply to other Hispanic groups (Abraido-Lanza et al. 1999) or play only a limited role in accounting for the HEP in outcomes such as mortality (Turra and Elo 2008).

4. The data are available through IPUMS, at https://ipums.org/projects/ipums -usa/d010.v8.0.

5. As a check to ensure we are measuring cumulative disadvantage in a sensible way, we also predict whether individuals report three or more disabilities.

6. We conduct separate analyses to determine whether the results differ when we include a small share (8 percent) of residents that moved to a different county in the same state.

7. During this time period and in metro areas with Secure Communities, multiple disabilities were also inversely related to deportation context for other groups (e.g., Native Americans, Asian U.S. citizens). Asian noncitizens reported multiple-disability rates (3.29 percent) similar to Hispanic noncitizens, but these did not differ across deportation contexts.

8. Since the average annual increase in cumulative deportations (for this sample) was 0.215 and the mean disability rate for the same sample was 0.023 (2.3 percent), then the relationship between deportations and multiple disabilities (Beta: 0.0036; caution: p-value = 0.066) equals (0.215 × 0.0036)/0.023 = 0.034, or 3.4 percent. This estimate is lower than the predicted 4.1–6.9 percent rise in likelihood of multiple disabilities predicted in models 1 through 5, or about half when comparing model 1 (with no covariates) and the final model (3.4 percent compared to 6.9 percent). In the context of the literature on enforcement, the results resemble the relationship between enforcement and poverty: heightened enforcement predicts a 4 percent rise in the likelihood of living in poverty among U.S.-born children with likely unauthorized parents (Amuedo-Dorantes, Arenas-Arroyo, and Sevilla 2018).

9. We conducted a number of robustness checks. The above results exclude those who moved and crossed county lines, but excluding them may bias our estimates toward zero if noncitizens vulnerable to health hazards leave high-deportation-rate areas. Among intrastate movers, we assign these residents their state-level deportation rate. The association

between deportations and disabilities remains about the same when we include these residents (3.6 percent). Furthermore, we also employed Bayesian multilevel models with random effects for year and metro area. On the basis of those results, rising cumulative deportation rates appear to be a marginally positive predictor of multiple disabilities. Similar in magnitude to the above results, the expected mean increase in odds of multiple disabilities is about 5 percent per 1-unit increase in the cumulative deportation rate.

REFERENCES

Abraido-Lanza, Ana F., Bruce P. Dohrenwend, Daisy S. Ng-Mak, and J. Blake Turner. 1999. "The Latino Mortality Paradox: A Test of the 'Salmon Bias' and Healthy Migrant Hypotheses." *American Journal of Public Health* 89 (10): 1543–1548.

Acevedo-Garcia, Dolores, and Lisa M. Bates. 2008. "Latino Health Paradoxes: Empirical Evidence, Explanations, Future Research, and Implications." In *Latinas/os in the United States: Changing the Face of América*, edited by Havidán Rodríguez, Rogelio Sáenz, and Cecilia Menjívar, 101–113. New York: Springer.

Akresh, Ilana Redstone, and Reanne Frank. 2008. "Health Selection among New Immigrants." *American Journal of Public Health* 98 (11): 2058–2064.

Allen, Chenoa D., and Clea A. McNeely. 2017. "Do Restrictive Omnibus Immigration Laws Reduce Enrollment in Public Health Insurance by Latino Citizen Children? A Comparative Interrupted Time Series Study." *Social Science and Medicine* 191 (October): 19–29.

Alsan, Marcella, and Crystal Yang. 2019. "Fear and the Safety Net: Evidence from Secure Communities." National Bureau of Economic Research Working Paper 24731. https://www.nber.org/system/files/working_papers/w24731/w24731.pdf.

Amuedo-Dorantes, Catalina, Esther Arenas-Arroyo, and Almudena Sevilla. 2018. "Immigration Enforcement and Economic Resources of Children with Likely Unauthorized Parents." *Journal of Public Economics* 158 (February): 63–78.

Arenas, Erika, Noreen Goldman, Anne R. Pebley, and Graciela Teruel. 2015. "Return Migration to Mexico: Does Health Matter?" *Demography* 52 (6): 1853–1868.

Bacon, Emily, Fernando Riosmena, and Richard G. Rogers. 2017. "Does the Hispanic Health Advantage Extend to Better Management of Hypertension? The Role of Socioeconomic Status, Sociobehavioral Factors, and Health Care Access." *Biodemography and Social Biology* 63 (3): 262–277.

Berkes, Howard, and Michael Grabell. 2018. "Stopping the Deportation of Immigrants Injured on the Job." *Pacific Standard*, Febuary 9. https://psmag.com/social-justice/deporting-undocumented-workers-hurt-at-work.

Boen, Courtney E., and Robert A. Hummer. 2019. "Longer—but Harder—Lives? The Hispanic Health Paradox and the Social Determinants of Racial, Ethnic, and Immigrant-Native Health Disparities from Midlife through Late Life." *Journal of Health and Social Behavior* 60 (4): 434–452.

Brazil, Noli. 2017. "Spatial Variation in the Hispanic Paradox: Mortality Rates in New and Established Hispanic US Destinations." *Population, Space and Place* 23 (1): e1968. https://doi.org/10.1002/psp.1968.

Camacho-Rivera, Marlene, Ichiro Kawachi, Gary G. Bennett, and S. V. Subramanian. 2015. "Revisiting the Hispanic Health Paradox: The Relative Contributions of Nativity, Country of Origin, and Race/Ethnicity to Childhood Asthma." *Journal of Immigrant and Minority Health* 17 (3): 826–833.

Cantu, Phillip A., and Jacqueline L. Angel. 2017. "Demography of Living Arrangements among Oldest-Old Mexican Americans: Evidence from the Hispanic Epidemiologic Study of the Elderly." *Journal of Aging and Health* 29 (6): 1015–1038.

Cantu, Phillip A., and Ronald J. Angel. 2019. "Limited but Not Disabled: Subjective Disability versus Objective Measurement of Functional Status and Mortality Risk among Elderly Mexican Americans." In *Contextualizing Health and Aging in the Americas*, edited by William A. Vega, Jacqueline L. Angel, Luis Miguel F. Gutiérrez Robledo, and Kyriakos S. Markides, 271–288. Cham, Switzerland: Springer.

Castañeda, Heide, Seth M. Holmes, Daniel S. Madrigal, Maria-Elena de Trinidad Young, Naomi Beyeler, and James Quesada. 2015. "Immigration as a Social Determinant of Health." *Annual Review of Public Health* 36:375–392.

Castro, Felipe González. 2007. "Is Acculturation Really Detrimental to Health?" *American Journal of Public Health* 97 (7): 1162.

Cervantes, Lilia, Delphine Tuot, Rajeev Raghavan, Stuart Linas, Jeff Zoucha, Lena Sweeney, Chandan Vangala, Madelyne Hull, Mario Camacho, and Angela Keniston. 2018. "Association of Emergency-Only vs Standard Hemodialysis with Mortality and Health Care Use among Undocumented Immigrants with End-Stage Renal Disease." *JAMA Internal Medicine* 178 (2): 188–195.

Cruz Nichols, Vanessa, Alana M. W. Lebrón, and Francisco I. Pedraza. 2018. "Spillover Effects: Immigrant Policing and Government Skepticism in Matters of Health for Latinos." *Public Administration Review* 78 (3): 432–443.

Do, D. Phuong, Reanne Frank, Cheng Zheng, and John Iceland. 2017. "Hispanic Segregation and Poor Health: It's Not Just Black and White." *American Journal of Epidemiology* 186 (8): 990–999.

East, Chloe N., Philip Luck, Hani Mansour, and Andrea Velasquez. 2018. "The Labor Market Effects of Immigration Enforcement." IZA Institute of Labor Economics Discussion Paper no. 11486. http://ftp.iza.org/dp11486.pdf.

Eschbach, Karl, Glenn V. Ostir, Kushang V. Patel, Kyriakos S. Markides, and James S. Goodwin. 2004. "Neighborhood Context and Mortality among Older Mexican Americans: Is There a Barrio Advantage?" *American Journal of Public Health* 94 (10): 1807–1812.

Fenelon, Andrew. 2017. "Rethinking the Hispanic Paradox: The Mortality Experience of Mexican Immigrants in Traditional Gateways and New Destinations." *International Migration Review* 51 (3): 567–599.

Fernández-Esquer, Maria Eugenia, Kathryn R. Gallardo, and Pamela M. Diamond. 2019. "Predicting the Influence of Situational and Immigration Stress on Latino Day Laborers' Workplace Injuries: An Exploratory Structural Equation Model." *Journal of Immigrant and Minority Health* 21 (2): 364–371.

Garcia, Marc A., Adriana M. Reyes, and Sunshine Rote. 2019. "Disability and the Immigrant Health Paradox: Gender and Timing of Migration." In *Contextualizing Health and Aging in the Americas*, edited by William A. Vega, Jacqueline L. Angel, Luis Miguel F. Gutiérrez Robledo, and Kyriakos S. Markides, 249–269. Cham, Switzerland: Springer.

Giuntella, Osea. 2016. "The Hispanic Health Paradox: New Evidence from Longitudinal Data on Second- and Third-Generation Birth Outcomes." *SSM-Population Health* 2:84–89.

Goldman, Noreen. 2016. "Will the Latino Mortality Advantage Endure?" *Research on Aging* 38 (3): 263–282.

Goldman, Noreen, Dana A. Glei, and Maxine Weinstein. 2017. "The Best Predictors of Survival: Do They Vary by Age, Sex, and Race?" *Population and Development Review* 43 (3): 541–560.

Hagan, Jacqueline, David L. Leal, and Néstor Rodríguez. 2015. "Deporting Social Capital: Implications for Immigrant Communities in the United States." *Migration Studies* 3 (3): 370–392.

Hagan, Jacqueline, Néstor Rodríguez, and Brianna Castro. 2011. "Social Effects of Mass Deportations by the United States Government, 2000–10." *Ethnic and Racial Studies* 34 (8): 1374–1391.

Hall, Matthew, and Emily Greenman. 2015. "The Occupational Cost of Being Illegal in the United States: Legal Status, Job Hazards, and Compensating Differentials." *International Migration Review* 49 (2): 406–442.

Hamilton, Erin R., Jo Mhairi Hale, and Robin Savinar. 2019. "Immigrant Legal Status and Health: Legal Status Disparities in Chronic Conditions and Musculoskeletal Pain among Mexican-Born Farm Workers in the United States." *Demography* 56 (1): 1–24.

Holmes, Seth. 2013. *Fresh Fruit, Broken Bodies: Migrant Farmworkers in the United States*. Berkeley: University of California Press.

Hummer, Robert A., and Juanita J. Chinn. 2011. "Race/Ethnicity and US Adult Mortality: Progress, Prospects, and New Analyses." *Du Bois Review: Social Science Research on Race* 8 (1): 5–24.

Joyner, Kara. 2018. "Arresting Immigrants: Unemployment and Immigration Enforcement." *Migration Letters* 15 (2): 215–238.

Jusionyte, Ieva. 2018a. *Threshold: Emergency Responders on the US-Mexico Border*. Oakland: University of California Press.

———. 2018b. "What I Learned as an EMT at the Border Wall." *The Atlantic*, October 20. https://www.theatlantic.com/ideas/archive/2018/10/threshold-tk/572833/.

Koralek, Robin, Juan Pedroza, and Randy Capps. 2009. "Untangling the Oklahoma Taxpayer and Citizen Protection Act: Consequences for Children and Families." Urban Institute. https://www.urban.org/sites/default/files/publication/27981/1001356-Untangling-the-Oklahoma-Taxpayer-and-Citizen-Protection69.-Act-Consequences-for-Children-and-Families.PDF.

Lariscy, Joseph T., Robert A. Hummer, and Mark D. Hayward. 2015. "Hispanic Older Adult Mortality in the United States: New Estimates and an Assessment of Factors Shaping the Hispanic Paradox." *Demography* 52 (1): 1–14.

Lariscy, Joseph T., Claudia Nau, Glenn Firebaugh, and Robert A. Hummer. 2016. "Hispanic-White Differences in Lifespan Variability in the United States." *Demography* 53 (1): 215–239.

Lofstrom, Magnus, Sarah Bohn, and Steven Raphael. 2011. *Lessons from the 2007 Legal Arizona Workers Act*. San Francisco: Public Policy Institute of California.

Lopez, Mark Hugo, and Molly Rohal. 2017. "Latinos and the New Trump Administration." Washington, DC: Pew Research Center.

Lum, Terry Y., and Julianne P. Vanderaa. 2010. "Health Disparities among Immigrant and Non-Immigrant Elders: The Association of Acculturation and Education." *Journal of Immigrant and Minority Health* 12 (5): 743–753.

Markides, Kyriakos S., and Karl Eschbach. 2005. "Aging, Migration, and Mortality: Current Status of Research on the Hispanic Paradox." *Journals of Gerontology Series B: Psychological Sciences and Social Sciences* 60 (2): S68–S75.

Markides, Kyriakos S., Karl Eschbach, Laura A. Ray, and M. Kristen Peek. 2007. "Census Disability Rates among Older People by Race/Ethnicity and Type of Hispanic Origin." In *The Health of Aging Hispanics: The Mexican-Origin Population*, edited by Jacqueline L. Angel and Keith E. Whitfield, 26–39. New York: Springer.

Markides, Kyriakos S, and Kerstin Gerst. 2011. "Immigration, Aging, and Health in the United States." In *Handbook of Sociology of Aging*, edited by Richard A. Settersten and Jacqueline L. Angel, 103–116. New York: Springer.

Montes-de-Oca, Verónica, Telésforo Ramírez, Nadia Santillanes, San Juanita García, and Rogelio Sáenz. 2015. "Access to Medical Care and Family Arrangements among Mexican Elderly Immigrants Living in the United States." In *Challenges of Latino Aging in the Americas*, edited by William A. Vega, Kyriakos S. Markides, Jacqueline L. Angel, and Fernando M. Torres-Gi, 225–245. Cham, Switzerland: Springer.

Morey, Brittany N., Gilbert C. Gee, Peter Muennig, and Mark L. Hatzenbuehler. 2018. "Community-Level Prejudice and Mortality among Immigrant Groups." *Social Science and Medicine* 199:56–66.

Olsen, Reed, Subhasree Basu Roy, and Hui-Kuan Tseng. 2019. "The Hispanic Health Paradox for Older Americans: An Empirical Note." *International Journal of Health Economics and Management* 19 (1): 33–51.

O'Neil, Kevin S. 2011. "Challenging Change: Local Policies and the New Geography of American Immigration." Ph.D. diss., Princeton University. http://pqdtopen.proquest .com/doc/907243010.html?FMT=ABS&pubnum=3481709.

Orrenius, Pia M., and Madeline Zavodny. 2009. "Do Immigrants Work in Riskier Jobs?" *Demography* 46 (3): 535–551.

Palloni, Alberto, and Elizabeth Arias. 2004. "Paradox Lost: Explaining the Hispanic Adult Mortality Advantage." *Demography* 41 (3): 385–415.

Palloni, Alberto, and Jeffrey D. Morenoff. 2001. "Interpreting the Paradoxical in the Hispanic Paradox: Demographic and Epidemiologic Approaches." *Annals of the New York Academy of Sciences* 954 (1): 140–174.

Parrado, Emilio A. 2012. "Immigration Enforcement Policies, the Economic Recession, and the Size of Local Mexican Immigrant Populations." *Annals of the American Academy of Political and Social Science* 641 (1): 16–37.

Pedroza, Juan Manuel. 2013. "Removal Roulette: Secure Communities and Immigration Enforcement in the United States (2008–2012)." In *Outside Justice: Immigration and the Criminalizing Impact of Changing Policy and Practice*, edited by David C. Brotherton, Daniel L. Stageman, and Shirley P. Leyro, 45–65. New York: Springer Science and Business Media.

———. 2019. "Deportation Discretion: Tiered Influence, Minority Threat, and 'Secure Communities' Deportations." *Policy Studies Journal* 47 (3): 624–646.

Perreira, Krista M., and Juan M. Pedroza. 2019. "Policies of Exclusion: Implications for the Health of Immigrants and Their Children." *Annual Review of Public Health* 40:147–166.

Philbin, Morgan M., Morgan Flake, Mark L. Hatzenbuehler, and Jennifer S. Hirsch. 2018. "State-Level Immigration and Immigrant-Focused Policies as Drivers of Latino Health Disparities in the United States." *Social Science and Medicine* 199 (February): 29–38.

Ribas, Vanesa. 2016. *On the Line: Slaughterhouse Lives and the Making of the New South*. Oakland: University of California Press.

Riosmena, Fernando, Bethany G. Everett, Richard G. Rogers, and Jeff A. Dennis. 2015. "Negative Acculturation and Nothing More? Cumulative Disadvantage and Mortality during the Immigrant Adaptation Process among Latinos in the United States." *International Migration Review* 49 (2): 443–478.

Riosmena, Fernando, Randall Kuhn, and Warren C. Jochem. 2017. "Explaining the Immigrant Health Advantage: Self-Selection and Protection in Health-Related Factors among Five Major National-Origin Immigrant Groups in the United States." *Demography* 54 (1): 175–200.

Riosmena, Fernando, Justin Vinneau, and Hiram Beltrán-Sánchez. 2019. "Changes in Health-Related Selectivity and Modes of Incorporation of Mexican Migrants since the Beginning of the 21st Century." Paper presented at Population Association of America annual meeting, April 10–13, Austin, TX. http://paa2019.population association.org/uploads/192066.

Riosmena, Fernando, Rebeca Wong, and Alberto Palloni. 2013. "Migration Selection, Protection, and Acculturation in Health: A Binational Perspective on Older Adults." *Demography* 50 (3): 1039–1064.

Rodríguez, Néstor, Cristian L. Paredes, and Jacqueline Hagan. 2017. "Fear of Immigration Enforcement among Older Latino Immigrants in the United States." *Journal of Aging and Health* 29 (6): 986–1014.

———. 2019. "Immigration Enforcement, Older Latino Immigrants, and Implications for Health." In *Contextualizing Health and Aging in the Americas: Effects of Space, Time and Place*, edited by William A. Vega, Jacqueline L. Angel, Luis Miguel F. Gutiérrez Robledo, and Kyriakos S. Markides, 111–135. Cham, Switzerland: Springer.

Rosenblum, Marc R., and William A. Kandel. 2012. "Interior Immigration Enforcement: Programs Targeting Criminal Aliens." Congressional Research Service, December 20. https://fas.org/sgp/crs/homesec/R42057.pdf.

Rosenblum, Marc R., and Doris Meissner. 2014. "The Deportation Dilemma: Reconciling Tough and Humane Enforcement." Migration Policy Institute, April. https://www.migrationpolicy.org/sites/default/files/publications/RemovalsOverview-WEBFINAL.pdf.

Roy, Subhasree Basu, Reed Neil Olsen, and Huikuan Tseng. 2020. "Do Hispanic Immigrants Spend Less on Medical Care? Implications of the Hispanic Health Paradox." *Applied Economics* 52 (36): 3951–3964.

Rugh, Jacob S., and Matthew Hall. 2016. "Deporting the American Dream: Immigration Enforcement and Latino Foreclosures." *Sociological Science* 3:1077–1102.

Ruiz, John M,. Heidi A. Hamann, Matthias R. Mehl, and Mary-Frances O'Connor. 2016. "The Hispanic Health Paradox: From Epidemiological Phenomenon to Contribution Opportunities for Psychological Science." *Group Processes and Intergroup Relations* 19 (4): 462–476.

Sáenz, Rogelio. 2015. "The Demography of the Elderly in the Americas: The Case of the United States and Mexico." In *Challenges of Latino Aging in the Americas*, edited by William A. Vega, Kyriakos S. Markides, Jacqueline L. Angel, and Fernando M. Torres-Gi, 197–223. Cham, Switzerland: Springer.

Sanchez, Gabriel R., Edward D. Vargas, Hannah L. Walker, and Vickie D. Ybarra. 2015. "Stuck between a Rock and a Hard Place: The Relationship between Latino/a's Personal Connections to Immigrants and Issue Salience and Presidential Approval." *Politics, Groups, and Identities* 3 (3): 454–468.

Sheftel, Mara, and Frank W. Heiland. 2018. "Disability Crossover: Is There a Hispanic Immigrant Health Advantage That Reverses from Working to Old Age?" *Demographic Research* 39:209–250.

Stanhope, Kaitlyn K., Carol R. Hogue, Shakira F. Suglia, Juan S. Leon, and Michael R. Kramer. 2019. "Restrictive Sub-Federal Immigration Policy Climates and Very Preterm Birth Risk among US-Born and Foreign-Born Hispanic Mothers in the United States, 2005–2016." *Health and Place* 60 (November). https://doi.org/10.1016/j.healthplace.2019.102209.

Strully, Kate W., Robert Bozick, Ying Huang, and Lane F. Burgette. 2020. "Employer Verification Mandates and Infant Health." *Population Research and Policy Review* 39:1143–1184.

Tarraf, Wassim, Gail A. Jensen, Heather E. Dillaway, Priscilla M. Vásquez, and Hector M. González. 2020. "Trajectories of Aging among US Older Adults: Mixed Evidence for a Hispanic Paradox." *Journals of Gerontology: Series B* 75 (3): 601–612.

Taylor, Paul, Mark Hugo Lopez, Jeffrey S. Passel, and Seth Motel. 2011. "Unauthorized Immigrants: Length of Residency, Patterns of Parenthood." Pew Research Center, December 1. https://www.pewresearch.org/hispanic/2011/12/01/unauthorized-immigrants-length-of-residency-patterns-of-parenthood/.

Teruya, Stacey A., and Shahrzad Bazargan-Hejazi. 2013. "The Immigrant and Hispanic Paradoxes: A Systematic Review of Their Predictions and Effects." *Hispanic Journal of Behavioral Sciences* 35 (4): 486–509.

Torche, Florencia, and Catherine Sirois. 2018. "Restrictive Immigration Law and Birth Outcomes of Immigrant Women." *American Journal of Epidemiology* 188 (1): 24–33.

Turra, Cassio M., and Irma T. Elo. 2008. "The Impact of Salmon Bias on the Hispanic Mortality Advantage: New Evidence from Social Security Data." *Population Research and Policy Review* 27 (5): 515.

Valenzuela, Abel, Nik Theodore, Edwin Meléndez, and Ana Luz Gonzalez. 2006. "On the Corner: Day Labor in the United States." UCLA Center for the Study of Urban Poverty, January. https://www.coshnetwork.org/sites/default/files/Day%20Labor%20study%202006.pdf.

Vargas, Edward D., and Viridiana L. Benitez. 2019. "Latino Parents' Links to Deportees Are Associated with Developmental Disorders in Their Children." *Journal of Community Psychology* 47 (5): 1151–1168.

Wang, Julia Shu-Huah, and Neeraj Kaushal. 2019. "Health and Mental Health Effects of Local Immigration Enforcement." *International Migration Review* 53 (4): 970–1001.

Watson, Tara. 2014. "Inside the Refrigerator: Immigration Enforcement and Chilling Effects in Medicaid Participation." *American Economic Journal: Economic Policy* 6 (3): 313–338.

9

The Dead and Living Dead

Legal Violence and Undocumented Kidney Failure
Patients in Atlanta, Georgia

Nolan Kline

Monica Chavarria, a thirty-four-year-old undocumented woman with kidney failure, uprooted her life in 2009 when she left her husband and oldest son in Atlanta, Georgia, and returned to her birthplace, Mexico, for dialysis (Sack 2009a). Monica and her family had built a life in Georgia, and her husband, Roberto, remained in the United States so he could wire money to Monica to help pay for her care. At $100 per treatment twice weekly (approximately $10,400 per year), the cost of dialysis is considerably less in Mexico than in the United States, where patients pay around $90,000 a year for dialysis (National Institutes of Health 2014). Monica is like other undocumented kidney failure patients who were abruptly forced to return to Mexico from Atlanta when Grady Memorial Hospital closed its outpatient dialysis center. Closing the dialysis center resulted in nearly seventy immigrant patients being medically repatriated to their country of birth; being placed into private, for-profit dialysis centers on short-term contracts; or, in some circumstances, being left to die. Further, kidney failure patients that continue to seek treatment at the hospital are routinely pushed to the brink of death before being eligible for services. These patients occupy liminal spaces between life and death, and such precarious life is entirely politically derived and rooted in aggressive immigration enforcement legislation and long-standing exclusions from health service programs (Kline 2018).

In this chapter, I examine the political etiologies of kidney failure and situate the Grady Memorial Hospital dialysis center closure, and its resulting challenges for patients, within the political context of U.S. immigration and health policies.[1] Drawing from scholarship on "legal violence" (Menjívar and Abrego 2012), I show how immigration enforcement regimes in Georgia collided with the state's legislative reforms and specifically excluded undocumented immigrants with kidney failure from receiving life-sustaining care. Overall, the Grady dialysis center closure reveals deliberate efforts to manage undocumented kidney failure patients' lives and deaths through a politically constructed bureaucracy of exclusion. Following political sociologist Eric Klinenberg, I argue for needed policy changes to correct legal violence resulting in bureaucratically orchestrated death and show how "by studying death we gain capacity to understand life as well as to protect it" (Klinenberg 1999, 246).

Kidney Failure, U.S. Immigration Law, and Immigrant Health

Kidney diseases are the ninth leading cause of death in the United States, afflicting approximately 1 in 7 adults (Centers for Disease Control and Prevention 2019). Kidney failure, the final stage of kidney disease, requires dialysis or kidney transplantation to survive. A combination of social and economic factors has resulted in a higher incidence of kidney failure among Latina/o populations than in non-Latina/o whites (Lora et al. 2009, Nee and Agodoa 2017, Norton et al. 2016, Desai et al. 2019), but public health interventions for kidney disease typically focus on individual behaviors. These behavioral health–focused prevention efforts lack an understanding of the political etiologies of kidney disease, particularly among undocumented Latina/o immigrants, who have a number of health-related vulnerabilities due to their immigration status (Cervantes et al. 2017). As a social determinant of health (Castañeda et al. 2015), immigration status affects undocumented Latina/o immigrants' lives in a number of ways, including through forms of labor that ultimately increase the risk of kidney failure. For example, as Sarah Horton has shown, Latina/o farmworkers may have higher rates of kidney diseases because their precarious immigration status increases their risk of labor-related exploitation, resulting in fewer bathroom breaks, less water consumption, and greater risk of dehydration, which contributes to kidney failure (Horton 2016; see also Chapter 6). In other words, for some undocumented Latina/o immigrants, kidney failure is situated in a context of economic exploitation, limited labor rights, and the marginalization that is due to their immigration status. The political and social factors that work in concert to shape undocumented Latina/o immigrants' risk for kidney failure necessitate a social autopsy, which, as Klinenberg explains, focuses on social etiologies of disease that are often ignored, taken for granted, or undervalued in determining causes of death (Klinenberg 2015, 11).

A social autopsy perspective may be especially needed to examine poor health among populations like undocumented Latina/o immigrants, who are restricted from several health programs in the United States. Undocumented immigrants are ineligible for Medicaid or Medicare, the nation's safety net medical programs, and are prohibited from purchasing health insurance through the health insurance exchanges created in the Patient Protection and Affordable Care Act (PPACA) (Zuckerman, Waidmann, and Lawton 2011). These exclusions have long-standing histories based on conflated notions of race, health, and paranoia of immigrants becoming a "public charge" (Fairchild 2004, 530). Immigration laws in the early twentieth century were specifically designed to deny entry to immigrants with conditions that might make them unfit for labor, and racial exclusions began in 1924 with the creation of a quota system—an effort to deny entry to immigrants who were considered racially inferior (Fairchild 2004). Despite numerous legislative changes since the 1900s, immigration policy nevertheless remains intertwined with economic interests, racial inequality, and denial of health services. This was reinforced with the Donald Trump administration's proposal to broaden the "public charge" definition in ways that would have likely led to a decrease in use of public programs like Medicaid among immigrants with eligible family members and would have disproportionately disadvantaged immigrants from Latin America, Africa, and parts of Asia (Henry J. Kaiser Family Foundation 2018; Parmet 2018; Shear, Jordan, and Dickerson 2019). Indeed, immigration policies play a critical role in shaping undocumented immigrants' overall well-being and demand critical scholarly attention to expose how they are politically derived forms of social violence.

At the federal level, aggressive immigration enforcement measures are implicated in immigrants' abuse and death. For example, the Prevention through Deterrence program, which deliberately funnels immigrants from Mexico into remote areas in the Sonoran Desert, results in increased migrant deaths, disappearances, and violent assaults along migration routes (De León 2015). Further, federal policies that operate in local jurisdictions, like Secure Communities and Section 287(g) of the Immigration and Nationality Act of 1996, have had deleterious health-related consequences and been linked to increased stress, anxiety, and avoidance of health services (Kline 2017; Rhodes et al. 2015; Chapter 8). Similarly, localized immigration enforcement efforts such as raids have resulted in adverse birth outcomes, increased stress, and a host of biological consequences, including inability to nurse infants following a traumatic raid (Lopez et al. 2017; Novak, Geronimus, and Martinez-Cardoso 2017).

Further, immigrant detention can result in deleterious health-related consequences. For example, journalists who examined immigration policies during the Trump administration showed that the federal government detained children in unsanitary and unsafe conditions after separating children from their parents when they arrived in the United States from Mexico (Dickerson 2019; Chapin 2019; Flynn 2019). In court challenges to these conditions, the U.S. Department of Justice defended its treatment of detained minors, asserting it had no obligation to provide basic hygienic items such as soap, toothbrushes, and clean clothing (Montoya-Glavez 2019). Further, Immigration and Customs Enforcement (ICE) whistleblowers have reported cases of negligent and inadequate medical care that have resulted in detainees' death and self-harm (Aleaziz 2019). At the time of writing this chapter, the ongoing novel coronavirus (COVID-19) pandemic poses a particularly acute threat to detainees, whose congregated living circumstances heighten the threat of exposure to the virus (Lopez et al. 2021). Negligent treatment in detention facilities and aggressive enforcement practices contribute to an overall hostile immigration climate in the United States. This approach is mirrored in specific states, like Georgia, where five counties have 287(g) agreements with ICE; four of these are in the Atlanta area (U.S. Immigration and Customs Enforcement 2019).

Since 2005, state-level immigration legislation has increased across the United States, resulting in approximately 1,300 immigration-related bills proposed annually, many of which aim to restrict immigrants' rights (Philbin et al. 2018). Omnibus immigration laws that expand law enforcement officers' authority to enforce federal immigration laws and restrict undocumented immigrants' access to social services and employment opportunities have passed in ten U.S. states, including Georgia (Allen 2018). Additionally, several state legislatures have passed or debated laws that mandate compliance with federal immigration enforcement officers. These laws are typically referred to as anti-sanctuary laws—a reference to sanctuary cities, which are municipalities that will not collaborate with ICE authorities (National Conference of State Legislatures 2019). In the aggregate, aggressive immigration enforcement policies have deleterious health-related consequences and can deepen existing health inequalities (Allen 2018; Nichols et al. 2018; Philbin et al. 2018; Pedraza, Nichols, and LeBrón 2017). Immigration statutes can also merge with health reform policies to produce precarious forms of treatment and survival, as seen with the dialysis center closure in Georgia (Kline 2018). As a result, undocumented immigrants are often caught between increasingly financialized health and criminal justice systems, aggressive immigration enforcement regimes, and legislative efforts to reinforce their perceived undeservingness of health services (Kline 2018, 2019b).

Georgia Context

Georgia is the eighth most populous U.S. state (U.S. Census Bureau 2018) and ranks among the top ten states with the largest Latina/o populations (Stepler and Lopez 2016). Georgia's Latina/o immigrant population has historically been associated with the state's agricultural economy, but an increasing number of Latina/o immigrants moved to the Atlanta area in the 1990s as part of a construction boom related to the 1996 Olympics and subsequent demand for new construction in the housing market (Odem 2008). Immigrants settled in what had been primarily white suburbs, and as the housing market crashed, the state legislature passed aggressive immigration laws and revised entitlement programs to increasingly restrict immigrants' access to health services, directly affecting undocumented dialysis patients (Kline 2018; Odem 2008; Kline 2019a).

Dialysis is required during the last stage of kidney failure: there is no cure for kidney failure (Centers for Disease Control and Prevention 2014), and without a kidney transplant or dialysis two to three times per week, a patient would die within an average of ten days (LaRocco 2011). The high cost of treatment and required interventions for kidney failure led to the creation of a unique government-funded program to aid indigent patients in financing the life-sustaining treatment known as the end-stage renal disease (ESRD) Medicare program (Blagg 2007, 492). As with other health entitlement programs, undocumented immigrants are ineligible for ESRD Medicare. Nevertheless, some states allow undocumented kidney failure patients to receive dialysis through Emergency Medicaid, a program that provides insurance to indigent patients regardless of immigration status when they present at emergency rooms with a life-threatening condition. Georgia permitted such use of Emergency Medicaid until 2006, when then governor Sonny Perdue—later the secretary of agriculture in the Trump administration—championed a change to Georgia Medicaid laws that ceased reimbursement for dialysis through Emergency Medicaid funds. This change eliminated the only remaining way for immigrants to receive dialysis without paying entirely out of pocket for it (Miller 2006; State of Georgia 2005; Sack 2009b; Miller and Borden 2006).

Following changes to Georgia's Medicaid laws, the state passed a number of aggressive immigration laws. Most notably, in 2011 Georgia passed the Illegal Immigration Reform and Enforcement Act, more commonly referred to as House Bill (HB) 87. Like other aggressive immigration legislation, such as Arizona's Senate Bill (SB) 1070, HB 87 makes local police de facto immigration enforcement officers. The law requires that immigrants carry proof of their immigration status at all times and empowers local law enforcement agents to stop and arrest anyone suspected of being undocumented. Moreover, the law criminalized any type of assistance given to un-documented immigrants, including providing any type of nonemergency care using public funds, criminalizing some health-care providers' professional practice. The Eleventh Circuit Court of Appeals ultimately struck provisions related to assisting immigrants, but the remainder of the law stayed intact. HB 87 is not the only aggressive immigration policy the Georgia legislature passed, however. The state also banned recipients of the Deferred Action for Childhood Arrivals (DACA) program from attending the state's top universities and has proposed efforts to deny undocumented immigrants the ability to activate public utilities for housing. Overall, aggressive immigration enforcement laws at federal and state levels and exclusion from entitlement programs constitute a form of legal violence that has health-related consequences.

Legal Violence

As an analytical framework, legal violence refers to what Cecilia Menjívar and Leisy Abrego call "legally sanctioned social suffering" (2012, 1413), or types of harm inflicted on individuals as a result of law. As Menjívar and Abrego argue, the framework builds on theoretical underpinnings of structural violence (Farmer 2005) and symbolic violence (Bourdieu 2001) to consider the role of law and policy in shaping forms of inequality and domination. A legal violence lens allows for understanding how law itself normalizes harm against some populations and makes such harm socially acceptable, particularly harm directed at undocumented immigrants because of their purported criminality (Abrego and Lakhani 2015). Legal violence, then, provides a way to examine and assess the consequences of conflating undocumented immigration status and criminality as part of ongoing efforts to merge immigration and criminal law (Stumpf 2013) and more broadly "govern immigrants through crime" (Inda and Dowling 2013). Consequences of legal violence include heightened economic insecurities, familial tensions, constrained social mobility, precarious educational opportunities (Abrego and Lakhani 2015; Menjívar and Abrego 2012), and as I show here, death from exclusionary health policies.

Physical death and harm resulting from legal violence occur in part because of how undocumented immigrants are viewed as having committed what Lisa Marie Cacho describes as *de facto status crime*, or an action that is only seen as criminal when attached to a certain racial, ethnic, or national origin group. As Cacho explains, "A person does not need to *do* anything to commit a status crime because the person's status is the offense in and of itself" (2012, 43). Cacho notes that, rather than referring to unlawful activity, de facto status crime refers to a perception of criminality, resulting in a person's very existence being criminalized. For undocumented immigrants in the United States, their de facto status results in structural inequalities in receiving health services like dialysis and informs normalized exclusions from health policies that result in death.

Tracing Legal Violence in Atlanta

My focus on legal violence and dialysis arrives out of a larger fieldwork project in which I examined the broad, health-related consequences of immigrant policing in Atlanta. I spent one year conducting in-depth ethnographic fieldwork between 2012 and 2013. My research was informed by the anthropology of policy, in which ethnographers make policy an object of inquiry (Okongwu and Mencher 2000; Shore and Wright 1997; Singer and Castro 2004; Wedel et al. 2005), and multisited ethnography, a methodological approach in which a researcher traces ideas throughout multiple spaces (Marcus 1995). I examined the pathways of immigration enforcement policies and explored how they affected immigrants' individual health, interpersonal relationships, and activist efforts, and also how they affected health providers' professional practices and the overall medical institutions on which all Atlanta residents rely. I conducted 84 semistructured interviews with key informants, including undocumented immigrants ($n = 45$), health providers ($n = 18$), staff from health-related organizations ($n = 9$), nonclinical hospital staff ($n = 4$), state agency workers ($n = 3$), state legislators ($n = 3$), and activist organization leaders ($n = 2$). These methods allowed me to follow immigration enforcement laws as a social and political problem through time and space and document the lived consequences of policy, including how some undocumented kidney failure patients were either left to die or stuck between life and death as a result of immigration and health policies converging.

The Dead and the Living Dead

"Waiting to Die"

Before the Perdue administration implemented changes to Georgia's Emergency Medicaid program, patients who reported to hospitals like Grady and needed dialysis received treatment there until the hospital linked patients to outpatient facilities operated by global, for-profit medical conglomerates, such as DaVita or Fresenius. As a Grady staff member, Aricél, explained to me, "Any patient that was here that needed dialysis, we would start their treatment, continue the dialysis treatment until they got funding [from Emergency Medicaid], which usually took about three months, and then we would transfer them to a [private] dialysis center." Following the Emergency Medicaid changes, however, outpatient centers like DaVita and Fresenius ceased treating undocumented kidney failure patients, funneling patients into Grady's emergency room. According to Aricél, "When the Medicaid funding was cut, those patients that were in the dialysis centers that *we had placed* [in Fresenius or DaVita] and had no legal status started coming back to the emergency rooms" (emphasis hers).

Faced with an influx of patients and with no reimbursement scheme because Emergency Medicaid would no longer cover dialysis, Grady officials decided to close the dialysis center. The decision was largely part of a hospital restructuring effort since the hospital had been losing money over time and faced potential closure (Kline 2018). When the hospital closed the dialysis center, it offered patients like Monica Chavarria the option to be medically repatriated to their countries of birth. Aricél explained that Grady collaborated with MexCare, a medical repatriation company in Mexico, to coordinate patient relocation. "MexCare [was] willing to work out the details of providing what we would pay for three months of dialysis treatment until [the patients] were eligible for government assistance," she said. For those who did not choose to be medically repatriated, Grady entered into a contract with Fresenius to pay for dialysis for one year. After one year, however, patients were without dialysis, and with neither Fresenius nor Grady willing to treat patients, the patients faced death. "That contract [ended]," Aricél recalled, "and so, of course, Fresenius says [to the patients], 'Well, we have no more contract for you, so you have no more dialysis.'" Grady ultimately extended contracts with Fresenius to provide care, and such negotiations continue to occur on an annual basis. There is still not a permanent solution for the Fresenius patients, and patients at Fresenius have no guarantee that they will continue receiving treatment there. If negotiations fail, they will ultimately lose their treatment at Fresenius and likely die within a matter of days. As one Fresenius nurse, Jacob, explained of these patients, they are "just stuck there, waiting to die."

Emergent Care Failures and a "Vicious Circle"

After the dialysis center closed, one group of patients who did not choose medical repatriation or get placed into contracts with Fresenius ultimately died or continued reporting to the Grady emergency room (ER) for treatment. As Aricél explained, "We still have around ten or twelve [of the undocumented patients], and we see them every week, some of them a couple of times, who just come for dialysis, but because they don't have services through [public assistance programs], they have to come to the emergency room." To receive dialysis, however, patients must exhibit an emergent condition, or a condition indicating immediate potential for death. Kidney failure, despite being fatal, is nevertheless a chronic condition and is therefore not considered an emergent condition. "If it's not an emergency," Aricél noted, "then we are supposed to discharge them. So if they don't have an indication for anything emergent, we can't admit them for routine dialysis." These patients, then, present at an ER, and if they are not close enough to death, they are denied care and must return to the hospital when their condition is nearly fatal.

Once patients are sick enough, they return to Grady, are admitted for an emergent condition, and can receive dialysis as part of the hospital entry. After being discharged, the patient repeats the process. As one provider summarized, "The complicated thing is that all these patients have to be admitted to the hospital, so they get admitted in the ER and are usually here for a day or two. Then they go home, and then they come back a couple of days later, so unfortunately, it's this never-ending vicious circle." If the patients are not sufficiently close to dying, providers will send them home, as Aricél explained: "So we do from time to time send [the undocumented patients] back home, and we tell them basically—I mean, I hate it, but we tell them, 'When you're sicker, come back.'" Overall, the "vicious circle" of reporting to Grady at the brink of death, being admitted to the hospital, receiving dialysis, and then being discharged to start the process again keeps patients in a state between life and death. They are always at the brink of death, and as one provider summarized, "They're barely being kept alive. The dialysis is just enough to keep them living, and that's about it."

Undocumented dialysis patients who are able to receive care only if they are on the verge of death reflects a type of tension between the repression and the protection migrants experience on a global scale. As Nicholas Fischer has argued, undocumented immigrants are caught between the state's simultaneous actions of exclusion and its expectations of providing some type of minimal care to maintain migrants' bodily integrity while they are within the nation-state (2015, 3–4). While Fischer focuses on detention centers as settings in which these tensions play out, and on self-harm as the immediate physical danger necessitating treatment, the treatment regimen for undocumented dialysis patients demonstrates similar tensions. Instead of occurring in a detention facility, these tensions occur in a hospital, demonstrating how the "combination of repression and protection" (Fischer 2015, 602) permeates clinical settings.

The Grady dialysis situation was worsened by Georgia's increasingly aggressive immigration enforcement laws. The laws effectively created what one provider called a "license to discriminate" (Kline 2019b, 287), which manifested as staff in Atlanta-area hospitals threatening to call immigration authorities on undocumented patients seeking health services, including dialysis. As Aricél explained, "They were telling the patients that they could no longer provide them with dialysis and to stop coming, or they would report them to immigration. So they all started coming to us [at Grady]." As one provider added, "Undocumented immigrants were starting to get turned away from other places, and Grady held firm as it provided a service, so eventually that service became full of all the region's undocumented immigrants." This situation may worsen over time as a result of changes to the PPACA.

The PPACA passed with an assumption that Medicaid expansion would cover indigent patients, but successful Supreme Court challenges have resulted in Medicaid expansion being determined at the state level. Problematically, the PPACA eliminated a funding mechanism for hospitals that treat indigent patients known as disproportionate share hospital (DSH) funds. The assumption was that this funding would be obsolete after Medicaid was expanded, but in places like Georgia, where the legislature has not expanded Medicaid, a shrinking DSH funding pool, a large uninsured indigent population, and hospitals sending dialysis patients to remaining treatment centers like Grady threaten an already fragile medical safety net (Kline 2019b).

"He's Just Going to Suffer"

More than being denied access to dialysis, however, undocumented Latina/o immigrant patients are denied ways to obtain needed care for complications related to kidney failure. As one nurse practitioner, George, who works with dialysis patients, explained, "It's not [just] the [lack of] dialysis; it's the renal disease. So renal disease causes you to be anemic, causes electrolyte imbalances, bone mineral density disorders, . . . [and] the medicine that nephrologists use to control those side effects associated with renal disease are expensive, and some are too expensive for an undocumented patient to afford, so they don't get them." Because they do not get the medication, George explained, these patients ultimately suffer. "They just have to suffer the side effects of the disease, where somebody who had Medicaid or Medicare would have the medicine paid for. . . . There's a medicine called Sensipar, and Medicare/Medicaid pays for their patients to have it. [The undocumented patient] doesn't get it because he doesn't have a way to afford it. . . . He's just going to suffer, basically." As a result of being denied medication, that patient will develop additional complications. "The complication he will probably have will be a cardiac complication. He'll probably have accelerated coronary artery disease from the high calcium level, and he'll probably die of a stroke or heart attack at some point, . . . [all of which could have been avoided] if he had access to the correct treatment."

As George explained, then, the hypothetical undocumented patient's death is due to a heart attack or stroke that occurred after he was denied Sensipar, a medication that could have prevented the death. The patient was unable to get the medication because of being ineligible for publicly financed health care and not having private health insurance. The immediate cause of the patient's death may be a heart attack or stroke resulting from kidney failure, but a social autopsy–informed perspective identifies the root causes of death as the policies that ultimately constrained the patient's ability to get insurance and necessary care, not to mention the United States' long-standing imperialist policies implemented in Latin America that helped create this local-level policy predicament (see the Introduction; Chapter 2; Chapter 11; and Chapter 12). This situation underscores how, as anthropologist and physician Paul Farmer has argued, some health decisions reflect an overall "differential valuation of life" that informs a number of health policies on a global scale (Farmer 1999, 57). Farmer (2005) notes that such differentials reflect an overall acceptance of treatment inequalities based on socioeconomic factors. As this situation demonstrates, treatment inequalities can also be accepted because of immigration status.

This pattern of powerful decision makers rationalizing and justifying immigrants' death is reflected in a number of health-related contexts. For example, at the time of writing this chapter, the COVID-19 pandemic continues and cases in the United States are on the rise. Some populations, including immigrants with precarious immigration statuses who engage in agricultural labor, may be more likely to be exposed and potentially die from the disease. This is in part because their labor is considered an essential service and therefore must not cease (Kline 2020). Paradoxically, undocumented agricultural workers' heightened risk of exposure—and by extension COVID-19-related death—is directly related to their labor, which policy makers have determined is essential, but such recognition does not afford them greater health-related rights and protections, even during a pandemic.

Legal Violence, Dialysis, and Managing Life and Death

The Grady dialysis center closure reinforces a number of well-known concerns regarding undocumented immigrant health care in the United States, including the cost inefficiencies of denying certain forms of care to immigrants (Artiga and Diaz 2019) and the consequences of being excluded from safety-net medical care and health insurance (Zuckerman, Waidmann, and Lawton 2011). The center's closure emphasizes the need for interrogating social and political determinants of immigrant death that can expose root causes of suffering related to chronic diseases like kidney failure. A politically focused attention to immigrant death can also reveal the failures in providing basic services to populations left particularly vulnerable in health emergencies like the COVID-19 pandemic.

Georgia's Medicaid program changes, Grady's outpatient dialysis center closure, and the increasingly harsh immigration enforcement regime in Atlanta are not isolated or disconnected policies. Instead, they are elements of an overall effort to manage undocumented immigrants biopolitically—including their precarious lives, and their deaths. This situation ultimately cast patients into two categories: (1) the dead—that is, those who died from being neglected and not receiving care—and (2) the living dead—those who are pushed to the brink of death for dialysis or who will soon die from not getting care.

Undocumented immigrants who are kidney failure patients and are "waiting to die," caught in a "vicious cycle" in which they are routinely pushed to the brink of death before being treated, or who are denied a life-saving medication, are treated this way in part because of their de facto status. Their immigration status has made them ineligible for safety-net services available to U.S. citizens, and a regulatory regime has constructed their exclusion from care and thereby increased their likelihood of death from a treatable condition.

This social autopsy of the causes of immigrants' suffering and death exemplifies how immigration and health law can operate in deadly ways, and often in tandem. These findings are particularly important since law and policy are not simply contexts in which social phenomena happen, but rather structural forms of exclusion that can result in harm. Policy, then, not only can work to create forms of social death but can also result in physical death, as demonstrated by the patients who were left to die by the Grady dialysis center closure, and the potential deaths and precarious forms of living that remain for patients attempting to continue their dialysis.

While existing social science research on immigration and death examines how crossing the U.S.-Mexico border can be deadly (De León 2015; Chapter 4), the Grady dialysis situation demonstrates how *remaining* in the United States can also be deadly, but in a more insidious way. Instead of death due to violence, dehydration, infection, or another related ailment concomitant with crossing the U.S.-Mexico border, undocumented Latina/o dialysis patients die from an intentionally constructed and politically created bureaucracy of exclusion. More than just a way to structure inequality and suffering, legal violence, then, directly contributes to some immigrants' deaths.

Reversing Legal Violence

Legal violence resulting in immigrant suffering and death demands political action. Although policy changes alone cannot dismantle the structural factors that shape undocumented Latina/o immigrants' health-related vulnerabilities, they are nevertheless a starting point for addressing social marginalization that results from immigration status and shortcomings in the U.S. health system. Accordingly, both health policy reform and immigration reform provide ways to begin reversing the many factors that contribute to undocumented Latina/o immigrants' exclusion from various health services and deaths from diseases like kidney failure.

As other medical anthropologists have argued (Willen, Mulligan, and Castañeda 2011; Holmes 2013), the U.S. health-care landscape must be more inclusive of undocumented immigrants and requires fundamental change to its current market-based structure (Rylko-Bauer and Farmer 2002). Problematically, market-based medicine emphasizes individual responsibility and accountability for health and, like other social institutions informed by neoliberal ideologies, obfuscates structural factors that constrain or prohibit securing health services. Undocumented immigrants are legally locked out of publicly funded U.S. health-care programs and economically excluded from private insurance. Inability to secure health services, including lifesaving dialysis, is thus a consequence of how illegality, as Sarah Willen has argued, is a juridical category, sociopolitical condition, and way of being-in-the-world (2007, 27) that structures inequality and even death. A health system that provides health services to all people regardless of immigration status or income can start to undermine this inequality. Further, a health policy regimen that prioritizes health for all people regardless of immigration status can begin to reverse differential forms of valuing life (Farmer 1999) that result in unequal treatment for kidney failure depending on immigration status.

More than reforming health-care delivery systems, policy changes that fundamentally value humanity over economics are needed. The Grady dialysis center closure, much like the COVID-19 pandemic, reveals how policy makers privilege economic interests over human life. Accordingly, immigration reform is needed as part of a broader effort to center policy on human experience rather than economic interests. The United States must end aggressive immigration enforcement regimes that perpetuate fear and terror among immigrants. Further, as the anthropologist Ruth Gomberg-Muñoz has argued, immigration statuses themselves are cultural inventions assumed to have moral legitimacy because they are codified in law (2016, 152), and such statuses require revision. This could include providing attainable regularization and citizenship options. These types of immigration reforms may be difficult to secure given ongoing efforts to advance aggressive immigration policies in the United States. For this reason, social scientists who document legal violence and its hidden consequences must continue to explicitly demonstrate links between exclusionary legislation and life and death.

Conclusion

As I show in this chapter, liminal existence between life and death, or precarious life in which death is a persistent and proximate threat, is the consequence of a legal violence that structures the suffering of dialysis patients who are undocumented immigrants. A social autopsy of kidney failure reveals the root political etiologies of morbidity and mortality. These etiologies include entitlement policy changes and harsh immigration enforcement regimes whose health-related consequences may be hidden (Kline 2018). Further, ethnographic accounts of legal violence in this chapter demonstrate how qualitative social science perspectives offer ways to view the hidden social consequences of policy, providing a critical analysis of death due to social circumstances that might otherwise remain hidden.

NOTE

1. Qualitative data in this chapter are also reported in Nolan Kline, "Life, Death, and Dialysis: Medical Repatriation and Liminal Life among Undocumented Kidney Failure Patients in the United States," *PoLAR: Political and Legal Anthropology Review* 41 (2018): 216–230. A discussion of the Grady dialysis situation also appears in Nolan Kline, *Pathogenic Policing: Immigration Enforcement and Health in the US South* (New Brunswick, NJ: Rutgers University Press, 2019), 124–126. The argument and frameworks used in this chapter to examine kidney disease and dialysis, including legal violence, are unique to this chapter and do not appear elsewhere.

REFERENCES

Abrego, Leisy J., and Sarah M. Lakhani. 2015. "Incomplete Inclusion: Legal Violence and Immigrants in Liminal Legal Statuses." *Law and Policy* 37 (4): 265–293.

Aleaziz, Hamed. 2019. "A Child's Forehead Partially Removed, Four Deaths, the Wrong Medicine—a Secret Report Exposes Health Care for Jailed Immigrants." *BuzzFeed News*, December 12. https://www.buzzfeednews.com/article/hamedaleaziz/ice-im migrant-surgeries-deaths-jails-whistleblower-secret.

Allen, Chenoa D. 2018. "Who Loses Public Health Insurance When States Pass Restrictive Omnibus Immigration-Related Laws? The Moderating Role of County Latino Density." *Health and Place* 54:20–28.

Artiga, Samantha, and Maria Diaz. 2019. "Health Coverage and Care of Undocumented Immigrants." Henry J. Kaiser Family Foundation, July 15. https://www.kff.org/racial-equity-and-health-policy/issue-brief/health-coverage-and-care-of-undoc umented-immigrants/.

Blagg, Christopher R. 2007. "The Early History of Dialysis for Chronic Renal Failure in the United States: A View from Seattle." *American Journal of Kidney Diseases* 49 (3): 482–496.

Bourdieu, Pierre. 2001. *Masculine Domination.* Stanford, CA: Stanford University Press.

Cacho, Lisa Marie. 2012. *Social Death: Racialized Rightlessness and the Criminalization of the Unprotected*: New York: New York University Press.

Castañeda, Heide, Seth M. Holmes, Daniel S. Madrigal, Maria-Elena DeTrinidad Young, Naomi Beyeler, and James Quesada. 2015. "Immigration as a Social Determinant of Health." *Annual Review of Public Health* 36 (1): 1.1–1.18.

Centers for Disease Control and Prevention. 2014. "National Chronic Kidney Disease Fact Sheet, 2014." https://stacks.cdc.gov/view/cdc/21850.

———. 2019. "Chronic Kidney Disease in the United States, 2019." https://www.cdc.gov/kidneydisease/pdf/2019_National-Chronic-Kidney-Disease-Fact-Sheet.pdf.

Cervantes, Lilia, Stacy Fischer, Nancy Berlinger, Maria Zabalaga, Claudia Camacho, Stuart Linas, and Debora Ortega. 2017. "The Illness Experience of Undocumented Immigrants with End-Stage Renal Disease." *JAMA Internal Medicine* 177 (4): 529–535.

Chapin, Angelina. 2019. "In Their Own Words, Migrant Children Describe Horrific Conditions at Border Patrol Facilities." *Huffington Post*, June 28. https://www.huffpost.com/entry/migrant-children-describe-detention_n_5d1646ffe4b03d61163af666.

De León, Jason. 2015. *The Land of Open Graves: Living and Dying on the Migrant Trail.* Oakland: University of California Press.

Desai, Nisa, Claudia M. Lora, James P. Lash, and Ana C. Ricardo. 2019. "CKD and ESRD in US Hispanics." *American Journal of Kidney Diseases* 73 (1): 102–111.

Dickerson, Caitlin. 2019. "'There Is a Stench': Soiled Clothes and No Baths for Migrant Children at a Texas Center." *New York Times*, June 21. https://www.nytimes.com/2019/06/21/us/migrant-children-border-soap.html.

Fairchild, Amy L. 2004. "Policies of Inclusion: Immigrants, Disease, Dependency, and American Immigration Policy at the Dawn and Dusk of the 20th Century." *American Journal of Public Health* 94 (4): 528–539.

Farmer, Paul. 1999. *Infections and Inequalities: The Modern Plagues.* Updated ed. Berkeley: University of California Press.

———. 2005. *Pathologies of Power: Health, Human Rights, and the New War on the Poor.* Berkeley: University of California Press.

Fischer, Nicolas. 2015. "The Management of Anxiety: An Ethnographical Outlook on Self-Mutilations in a French Immigration Detention Centre." *Journal of Ethnic and Migration Studies* 41 (4): 599–616.

Flynn, Meagan. 2019. "Detained Migrant Children Got No Toothbrush, No Soap, No Sleep: No Problem, Government Argues." *Washington Post*, June 21. https://www.washingtonpost.com/nation/2019/06/21/detained-migrant-children-no-toothbrush-soap-sleep/.

Gomberg-Muñoz, Ruth. 2016. *Becoming Legal: Immigration Law and Mixed-Status Families.* New York: Oxford University Press.

Henry J. Kaiser Family Foundation. 2018. "Proposed Changes to 'Public Charge' Policies for Immigrants: Implications for Health Coverage." http://files.kff.org/attachment/

Issue-Brief-Proposed-Changes-to-Public-Charge-Policies-for-Immigrants-Implications-for-Health-Coverage.

Holmes, Seth. 2013. *Fresh Fruit, Broken Bodies: Migrant Farmworkers in the United States*. Berkeley: University of California Press.

Horton, Sarah Bronwen. 2016. *They Leave Their Kidneys in the Fields: Illness, Injury, and Illegality among US Farmworkers*. Oakland: University of California Press.

Inda, Jonathan Xavier, and Julie A. Dowling. 2013. "Introduction: Governing Migrant Illegality." In *Governing Immigration through Crime: A Reader*, edited by Jonathan Xavier Inda and Julie A. Dowling, 1–36. Stanford, CA: Stanford University Press.

Kline, Nolan. 2017. "Pathogenic Policy: Immigrant Policing, Fear, and Parallel Medical Systems in the US South." *Medical Anthropology* 36 (4): 396–410.

———. 2018. "Life, Death, and Dialysis: Medical Repatriation and Liminal Life among Undocumented Kidney Failure Patients in the United States." *PoLAR: Political and Legal Anthropology Review* 41 (2): 216–230.

———. 2019a. *Pathogenic Policing: Immigration Enforcement and Health in the US South*. New Brunswick, NJ: Rutgers University Press.

———. 2019b. "When Deservingness Policies Converge: US Immigration Enforcement, Health Reform and Patient Dumping." *Anthropology and Medicine* 26 (3): 280–295.

———. 2020. "Rethinking COVID-19 Vulnerability: A Call for LGTBQ+ Im/Migrant Health Equity in the United States during and after a Pandemic." *Health Equity* 4 (1): 239–242.

Klinenberg, Eric. 1999. "Denaturalizing Disaster: A Social Autopsy of the 1995 Chicago Heat Wave." *Theory and Society* 28 (2): 239–295.

———. 2015. *Heat Wave: A Social Autopsy of Disaster in Chicago*. Chicago: University of Chicago Press.

LaRocco, Susan. 2011. "Treatment Options for Patients with Kidney Failure." *American Journal of Nursing* 111 (10): 57–62.

Lopez, William D., Nolan Kline, Alana M. W. LeBrón, Nicole L. Novak, Maria-Elena De Trinidad Young, Gregg Gonsalves, Ranit Mishori, Basil A. Safi, and Ian M. Kysel. 2021. "Preventing the Spread of COVID-19 in Immigration Detention Centers Requires the Release of Detainees." *American Journal of Public Health* 111 (1): 110–115.

Lopez, William D., Daniel J. Kruger, Jorge Delva, Mikel Llanes, Charo Ledón, Adreanne Waller, Melanie Harner, Ramiro Martinez, Laura Sanders, Margaret Harner, and Barbara Israel. 2017. "Health Implications of an Immigration Raid: Findings from a Latino Community in the Midwestern United States." *Journal of Immigrant and Minority Health* 19 (3): 702–708.

Lora, Claudia M., Martha L. Daviglus, John W. Kusek, Anna Porter, Ana C. Ricardo, Alan S. Go, and James P. Lash. 2009. "Chronic Kidney Disease in United States Hispanics: A Growing Public Health Problem." *Ethnicity and Disease* 19 (4): 466.

Marcus, George E. 1995. "Ethnography in/of the World System: The Emergence of Multi-sited Ethnography." *Annual Review of Anthropology* 24:95–117.

Menjívar, Cecilia, and Leisy Abrego. 2012. "Legal Violence: Immigration Law and the Lives of Central American Immigrants." *American Journal of Sociology* 117 (5): 1380–1421.

Miller, Andy. 2006. "Health Care Shake-Ups on Way—Changes in Medicaid, Medicare among Shifts That Will Touch Georgians in 2006." *Atlanta Journal Constitution*, January 8, p. C1.

Miller, Andy, and Teresa Borden. 2006. "Health Care for Illegals Shifts with Medicaid Rules." *Atlanta Journal Constitution*, May 26, p. A1.

Montoya-Glavez, Camilo. 2019. "Here's Why the Trump Administration Says It's Not Required to Give Migrant Children Soap." *CBS News*, June 24. https://www.cbsnews.com/news/trump-administration-migrant-children-in-u-s-custody-dont-need-to-be-provided-soap-and-toothbrushes/.

National Conference of State Legislatures. 2019. "Sanctuary Policy FAQ." June 20. http://www.ncsl.org/research/immigration/sanctuary-policy-faq635991795.aspx.

National Institutes of Health. 2014. "2013 USRDS Annual Data Report: Atlas of Chronic Kidney Disease and End-Stage Renal Disease in the United States." https://www.ajkd.org/article/S0272-6386(13)01397-8/pdf.

Nee, Robert, and Lawrence Y. Agodoa. 2017. "Prevalence of Predialysis Kidney Disease in Disadvantaged Populations in Developed Countries: United States." In *Chronic Kidney Disease in Disadvantaged Populations*, edited by Guillermo García-García, Lawrence Y. Agodoa, and Keith C. Norris, 15–25. London: Elsevier.

Nichols, Vanessa Cruz, Alana M. W. LeBrón, and Francisco I. Pedraza. 2018. "Policing Us Sick: The Health of Latinos in an Era of Heightened Deportations and Racialized Policing." *Political Science and Politics* 51 (2): 293–297.

Norton, Jenna M., Marva M. Moxey-Mims, Paul W. Eggers, Andrew S. Narva, Robert A. Star, Paul L. Kimmel, and Griffin P. Rodgers. 2016. "Social Determinants of Racial Disparities in CKD." *Journal of the American Society of Nephrology* 27 (9): 2576–2595.

Novak, Nicole L., Arline T. Geronimus, and Aresha M. Martinez-Cardoso. 2017. "Change in Birth Outcomes among Infants Born to Latina Mothers after a Major Immigration Raid." *International Journal of Epidemiology* 46 (3): 839–849.

Odem, Mary. 2008. "Unsettled in the Suburbs: Latino Immigration and Ethnic Diversity in Metro Atlanta." In *Twenty-First Century Gateways: Immigrant Incorporation in Suburban America*, edited by Susan W. Hardwick, Audrey Singer, and Caroline B. Brettell, 105–136. Washington, DC: Brookings Institution Press.

Okongwu, Anne Francis, and Joan P. Mencher 2000. "The Anthropology of Public Policy: Shifting Terrains." *Annual Review of Anthropology* 29:107–124.

Parmet, Wendy E. 2018. "The Health Impact of the Proposed Public Charge Rules." *Health Affairs*, September 27. https://www.healthaffairs.org/do/10.1377/hblog20180927.100295/full/.

Pedraza, Franciso I., Vanessa Cruz Nichols, and Alana M. W. LeBrón. 2017. "Cautious Citizenship: The Deterring Effect of Immigration Issue Salience on Health Care Use and Bureaucratic Interactions among Latino US Citizens." *Journal of Health Politics, Policy and Law* 42 (5): 925–960.

Philbin, Morgan M., Morgan Flake, Mark L. Hatzenbuehler, and Jennifer S. Hirsch. 2018. "State-Level Immigration and Immigrant-Focused Policies as Drivers of Latino Health Disparities in the United States." *Social Science and Medicine* 199:29–38.

Rhodes, Scott D., Lilli Mann, Florence M. Simán, Eunyoung Song, Jorge Alonzo, Mario Downs, Emma Lawlor, Omar Martinez, Christina J. Sun, and Mary Claire O'Brien. 2015. "The Impact of Local Immigration Enforcement Policies on the Health of Immigrant Hispanics/Latinos in the United States." *American Journal of Public Health* 105 (2): 329–337.

Rylko-Bauer, Barbara, and Paul Farmer. 2002. "Managed Care or Managed Inequality? A Call for Critiques of Market-Based Medicine." *Medical Anthropology Quarterly* 16 (4): 476–502.

Sack, Kevin. 2009a. "For Sick Illegal Immigrants, No Relief Back Home." *New York Times*, December 31. https://www.nytimes.com/2010/01/01/health/policy/01grady.html.

———. 2009b. "Hospital Falters as Refuge for Illegal Immigrants." *New York Times*, November 20. https://www.nytimes.com/2009/11/21/health/policy/21grady.html.

Shear, Michael D., Miriam Jordan, and Caitlin Dickerson. 2019. "Trump's Policy Could Alter the Face of the American Immigrant." *New York Times*, August 14. https://www.nytimes.com/2019/08/14/us/immigration-public-charge-welfare.html.

Shore, C., and S. Wright. 1997. *Policy: A New Field of Anthropology*. New York: Routledge.

Singer, Merrill, and Arachu Castro. 2004. "Anthropology and Health Policy: A Critical Perspective." In *Unhealthy Health Policy: A Critical Anthropological Examination*, edited by Merrill Singer and Arachu Castro, xi–xx. Lanham, MD: AltaMira Press.

State of Georgia. 2005. "Governor Perdue Announces Strict Documentation Requirement for Medicaid Registration." December 2. https://sonnyperdue.georgia.gov/00/press/detail/0%2C2668%2C78006749_79688147_93281962%2C00.html.

Stepler, Renee, and Mark Hugo Lopez. 2016. "U.S. Latino Population Growth and Dispersion Has Slowed since Onset of the Great Recession." Pew Research Center, September 8. https://www.pewresearch.org/hispanic/2016/09/08/4-ranking-the-latino-population-in-the-states/.

Stumpf, Juliet P. 2013. "The Crimmigration Crisis: immigrants, Crime, and Sovereign Power." In *Governing Immigration through Crime: A Reader*, edited by Julie Dowling and Jonathan Inda, 59–76. Stanford, CA: Stanford University Press.

U.S. Census Bureau. 2018. "Annual Estimates of the Resident Population for the United States, Regions, States, and Puerto Rico: April 1, 2010 to July 1, 2019." https://www.census.gov/data/tables/time-series/demo/popest/2010s-national-total.html.

U.S. Immigration and Customs Enforcement. 2020. "Delegation of Immigration Authority Section 287(g) Immigration and Nationality Act." December 15. https://www.ice.gov/287g.

Wedel, J. R., C. Shore, G. Feldman, and S. Lathrop. 2005. "Toward an Anthropology of Public Policy." *Annals of the American Academy of Political and Social Science* 600 (1): 30.

Willen, Sarah S. 2007. "Toward a Critical Phenomenology of 'Illegality': State Power, Criminalization, and Abjectivity among Undocumented Migrant Workers in Tel Aviv, Israel." *International Migration* 45 (3): 8–38.

Willen, Sarah S., Jessica Mulligan, and Heide Castañeda. 2011. "Take a Stand Commentary: How Can Medical Anthropologists Contribute to Contemporary Conversations on 'Illegal' Im/Migration and Health?" *Medical Anthropology Quarterly* 25 (3): 331–356.

Zuckerman, Stephen, Timothy A. Waidmann, and Emily Lawton. 2011. "Undocumented Immigrants, Left out of Health Reform, Likely to Continue to Grow as Share of the Uninsured." *Health Affairs* 30 (10): 1997–2004.

IV

Outsourced Suffering and Survival
in the Americas

10

Expanding Exclusion

Migration, Asylum, and Transnational Death
in Mexico and the United States

JARED P. VAN RAMSHORST

In April 2017, Alicia arrived in Reynosa, Mexico, a dusty, sprawling city on the U.S.-Mexico border. Setting off from El Salvador two months earlier, she had traveled across Guatemala and Mexico to reach the United States, relying on passenger buses, freight trains, and foot for transportation. Alicia had fled her home after a local gang threatened to kill her for reporting a double homicide in which the group was involved. Fearing for her life, she planned to claim asylum at an official U.S. port of entry, where migrants are able to initiate the asylum process under federal immigration law. Many of these ports of entry are situated along large, international bridges spanning the U.S.-Mexico border. Upon arriving at one of these bridges, however, Alicia was turned away by U.S. immigration authorities, who proclaimed that the port of entry was temporarily closed because there was "no space" for her. She left and returned to Reynosa, on the other side of the border, eventually finding a park to rest in nearby. Texting her cousin Martha later that evening, Alicia explained that she had tried to claim asylum in the United States but was denied entry. She would try again early the next day. In the morning, Martha called to check on Alicia but could not reach her. A day later, she called again, but still, there was no response. Over the following months, Martha called and texted her cousin every day, but Alicia was never seen or heard from again.

Since 2016, U.S. Customs and Border Protection (CBP) agents have denied access to countless numbers of asylum seekers at ports of entry under a strategy known as "metering." The unofficial policy, introduced under the

Barack Obama administration but not widely adopted until 2018 by the Donald Trump administration, enabled immigration authorities to limit the number of asylum seekers allowed to enter the U.S. interior by authorizing CBP agents to turn migrants away from the border. When blocked at ports of entry, migrants like Alicia were forced to return to border cities scattered across northern Mexico, where they waited in temporary encampments, shelters, parks, and other public places to claim asylum in the United States. Stranded in these open spaces for days, weeks, and sometimes months, migrants were vulnerable to kidnapping, disappearances, and death. In this chapter, I examine asylum politics and international migration from Central America to better understand social and biological death along the U.S.-Mexico border and beyond. Using in-depth interviews and participant observation with friends, family members, and key staff in migrant shelters, I reconstruct the disappearances and deaths of two separate asylum seekers, Óscar and Laura, who were turned away at the border through metering. In particular, I describe the events leading up to their disappearances as well as the diverse actors and agencies implicated in their passing, including Mexican officials, U.S. immigration authorities, and local gangs. As I demonstrate, social and biological death of migrants is fundamentally transnational in scope, spanning a range of individual and institutional realms in both Mexico and the United States. While the transnational dimensions of death under U.S. immigration policies have been well documented (e.g., De León 2015; Kanstroom 2012; Nevins 2008, 2010; Rosas 2006), metering, and successive policies under the Trump administration, signified its geographic and legal expansion. Ultimately, I suggest, this transnational lens reveals a vast, unfolding geography of exclusion situated on the peripheries of U.S. territory and beyond, where social and biological death encompass multiple places, actors, and institutions (see also Miller 2019).

This chapter draws from ethnographic fieldwork conducted in migrant shelters in Guatemala, Mexico, and the United States between 2016 and 2017, as the Trump administration's approach to immigration and asylum policy was beginning to emerge. Working with migrants from El Salvador, Guatemala, Honduras, and Nicaragua, this research included semistructured interviews, mental mapping, and participant observation, supplemented by informal, everyday conversations. In these exchanges, migrants frequently discussed the fates of family members and friends who, like them, set off from Central America in hopes of reaching Mexico and the United States. Similar stories were also shared by those with whom I kept in touch after fieldwork, including care workers, other migrants, and shelter staff. My discussion of Óscar's and Laura's experiences and the events leading up their disappearances relies on firsthand accounts, text messages, and voice mails provided by their families and friends during this time. In the case of Óscar, I worked with his sister and brother-in-law in Texas, learning of his disappearance months after it happened. Similarly, I met Laura and the group she was traveling with at a shelter in Mexico, living and working alongside them for several weeks. After she left, I remained in close communication with one of her friends, hearing about her disappearance as it happened in real time. I draw from these experiences and others to examine the direct causal links between restrictive immigration policies, such as metering, and social and biological death, showing how exclusion operates transnationally across a variety of scales.

My discussion of metering and subsequent policies under the Trump administration uses Lisa Marie Cacho's (2012) conceptual development of social death. Initially grounded in the analysis of slavery (see Patterson 1982), social death describes the process by which individuals are reduced to a state of nonbeing and excluded from life itself. While such people may be physically alive, they are completely removed from social life and stripped of all meaning, appearing and treated as if they were dead. In this way, they exist as nonpersons, living amid a "permanent condition of liminality" (Patterson 1982, 60). Cacho employs this conceptual framework to examine how contemporary lives are devalued through criminalization and racialized, state-sanctioned violence, ultimately rendering certain populations "ineligible for personhood" (2012, 6). Gang members, suspected terrorists, undocumented immigrants, and other racialized subjects thereby become dead-to-others through official narratives that categorize them as legally and socially illegible. Deemed undeserving, they are excluded from the law's protection yet subject to its "discipline, punishment, and regulation" (Cacho 2012, 5). Crucially, social death functions as an "idiom of power" (Patterson 1982, 18), by which exploitation and violence against others is normalized and socially acceptable. For these people, life no longer bears meaning, and death becomes ungrievable (see Butler 2004, 2009). "Social death," therefore, references the ways in which human life is made increasingly precarious and vulnerable, sometimes culminating in biological death. In this chapter, I build on these insights to explore how metering and related policies excluded migrants and asylum seekers from legal protection while subjecting them to discipline, punishment, and regulation.

To accomplish this, the chapter begins by describing asylum politics and practices of metering along the U.S.-Mexico border. From its use as a temporary, provisional strategy to a key feature of immigration and asylum policy under the Trump administration, I detail the evolution of metering and successive policies as well as their role in the production of social and biological death. Then, by reconstructing the journeys and events leading up to the disappearances and deaths of Óscar and Laura, I explore the transnational locations, actors, and agencies involved in their cases, demonstrating how immigration policies aimed at exclusion expanded both geographically and legally through the practice of metering, as social and biological death extended across a range of individual and institutional realms in Mexico and the United States. I conclude by discussing the shifting landscape of contemporary immigration and the lasting implications of metering and other restrictive immigration policies, which later multiplied under the Trump administration.

Background

The practice of metering emerged in late 2016, when large numbers of Haitian migrants arrived at the U.S.-Mexico border seeking asylum (Diaz 2016; Dibble 2016). Following a catastrophic earthquake on the island in 2010, thousands of Haitian citizens were displaced. The majority of them initially sought refuge in Brazil, where they were easily absorbed into a thriving economy, but as the country slipped into recession years later, many migrants set off toward the United States, massing along the U.S.-Mexico border. Unwilling to respond to the sudden influx of migrants, the Obama administration turned to punitive and restrictive immigration measures. U.S. officials soon announced that they would expand enforcement efforts along the southern border and resume deportations of undocumented Haitians, which Immigration and Customs Enforcement (ICE) had suspended following the 2010 earthquake (Semple 2016). More importantly, the Obama administration and Department of Homeland Security (DHS) adopted a new tactic, under which CBP agents turned asylum seekers away at select ports of entry in California, claiming a shortage of processing capacity (CBS News 2016). The policy, now known as metering, denied entry to asylum seekers and instructed them to return at a later date, often left unspecified. Blocked from entering the United States, these migrants became stranded in Mexico under forbidding conditions, waiting days without food and shelter in Tijuana and other border cities (Laurent 2017). Eventually, the Obama administration ended its use of metering, as large groups of Haitians settled in Mexico or returned to other places across Central and South America. Although the strategy was temporary, the Obama administration normalized its use, validating it as an effective deterrent and mode of exclusion along the U.S.-Mexico border. Less than a year later, metering would resurface under the Trump administration.

Amid campaign promises to conduct mass deportations and "build the wall," the Trump administration pursued a hard-line immigration agenda informed by zero-tolerance practices and a law-and-order approach. Implementing a series of initiatives, executive orders, and departmental memos in 2017, the administration sought to broaden and intensify U.S. immigration enforcement—from hiring additional CBP and ICE agents to expanding criminal prosecution for undocumented migrants (Abdullah and Jaffe 2017; Gonzales 2018). Simultaneously, Trump officials attempted to undermine the asylum process and eliminate key protections for asylum seekers, particularly from Central America. In summer 2018, the attorney general's office declared that domestic abuse and gang violence would no longer qualify for asylum under federal law, vacating a 2016 decision made by the Department of Justice (Sacchetti 2018). Months later, Trump formalized plans to bar asylum seekers from crossing between ports of entry along the U.S.-Mexico border, asserting that asylum rights would only be granted to those entering through "official" channels (Aguilar 2018, 2019). The Trump administration's attempts to constrain asylum eventually crystallized into the 2019 Migrant Protection Protocols (MPP), which extended metering's effects by forcing asylum seekers from Central America to remain in Mexico as their cases were adjudicated in U.S. immigration courts (Tackett, Dickerson, and Ahmed 2018). These efforts were accompanied by racialized, anti-immigrant rhetoric in which the Trump administration, echoing Donald Trump's 2015–2016 campaign, described migrants as "invaders," "criminals," and "cheaters" (Bump 2015; Klein and Liptak 2018). It is within this context that the use of metering expanded rapidly along the U.S.-Mexico border, portending the eventual expansion of social and biological death through a suite of policies aimed at exclusion, including MPP, subsequent proposals for "safe third country" agreements, and the suspension of immigration and asylum law during the COVID-19 pandemic.

In contrast to the Obama administration, Trump officials made regular and widespread use of metering. As a key feature of the administration's approach to immigration and asylum policy, DHS closed ports of entry in California, Arizona, New Mexico, and Texas, shutting migrants out for weeks and sometimes months (Alderstein 2018; Hennessy-Fiske 2018a). In some places, CBP agents limited the number of asylum applicants to fewer than six individuals per day, despite queue lengths numbering well over a hundred (Ortega 2018). Trump officials rarely disclosed wait times or when sites would reopen, and with no channels to secure appointments otherwise, metering led to extended delays and overcrowding at several international bridges, where migrants waited for days, weeks, and months before their applications were processed, if at all. Despite these practices along the southwest border, asylum claims among Central Americans continued to grow (Hennessy-Fiske 2018b), as migrants were undeterred by the new policy.

When blocked at ports of entry, asylum seekers were forced to return to border cities in Mexico amid inhospitable conditions, as spaces of mobility and transit have become increasingly precarious (Brigden 2018; Collyer 2010; Mainwaring and Brigden 2016; Vogt 2018). Migrants continue to lack basic necessities, such as food, water, and access to medical attention. Shelters are often overpopulated or placed remotely on the fringes of cities. Other resources, such as government agencies and human rights organizations, are understaffed and inaccessible. Consequently, asylum seekers resort to temporary encampments on top of bridges or along drainage canals and highway overpasses. Having been turned away at U.S. ports of entry and without legal documentation to remain in Mexico, they are bereft of rights and protections. Across Mexico and the United States, immigration law has been criminalized, and migrants are susceptible to detention and deportation (Brotherton and Kretsedemas 2017; Kubrin, Zatz, and Martínez 2012; Olayo-Méndez 2017). In Mexico, for instance, these efforts have culminated in Programa Frontera Sur, a far-reaching plan aimed at border and immigration enforcement that has doubled rates of deportation and removed more than half a million migrants since its implementation in 2014 (Bonello 2015; Fredrick 2018). Anti-immigrant sentiment and persistent racialization have also stigmatized migrants as delinquents, foreigners, and outsiders (Van Ramshorst 2018; Ybarra 2019). Police and immigration authorities are unresponsive to cases of abuse, and migrants' reports are rarely documented or thoroughly investigated. Corruption is also extensive, and officials frequently exploit migrants through extortion, harassment, and theft (Tuckman 2015).

Asylum seekers, however, are vulnerable not only to corruption and deportation by Mexican officials but also to violence at the hands of local gangs and cartels emboldened by Mexico's ongoing drug war. Death, disappearances, and kidnappings are common. In 2010, the bodies of seventy-two migrants from Central and South America were found buried in mass graves in the Mexican state of Tamaulipas (see Booth 2010). Two years later, forty-nine victims were discovered on the side of a highway outside Monterrey, Nuevo Leon, their bodies mutilated beyond recognition (see Miroff 2012). At one time, Mexico's National Human Rights Commission (CNDH) estimated that nearly 1,600 migrants were kidnapped every month (Lakhani 2017). Assault, robbery, and other forms of abuse are also widespread.

Óscar

Óscar was twenty-eight years old. He was from Honduras and decided to seek protection in the United States after escaping from the Mara Salvatrucha (MS-13) when they threatened to kill him and his friends over a local dispute. Fleeing his neighborhood in San Pedro Sula, ravaged by decades of

U.S. intervention in the form of deportation, neoliberalism, and political interference, Óscar and his family paid $7,000 for him to be smuggled across Mexico. Hidden in the back of cargo vans and minibuses, Óscar slowly made his way north, stopping off at safe houses provided along the way. During checkpoints and traffic stops in Mexico, Óscar buried himself under packages, suitcases, and other luggage to avoid detection. When he was discovered by police or immigration authorities, he bribed them with cash, often in $100 increments. Two weeks after leaving his home, Óscar arrived in Monterrey, an industrial center and commercial hub in northern Mexico. After conferring with family members, he decided to stay and seek asylum there, rather than continue to the United States. Óscar's sister and brother-in-law, who had entered the United States a month before, explained how difficult it was for them to claim asylum under the new Trump administration. They had been turned away at the U.S.-Mexico border by CBP agents and had to wait several weeks before they were allowed to enter the United States and submit their applications. Accordingly, Óscar chose to remain in Mexico. He parted ways with his smugglers, paying them the remainder of what he owed, and found a local migrant shelter nearby.

In Monterrey, Óscar applied for asylum with help from the shelter, completing the interviews and paperwork necessary to file his application. Weeks later, during a meeting with agents from the National Institute of Migration (INM), however, he encountered difficulties. The INM agents explained to Óscar that his application appeared suspicious. They claimed that the faded tattoos across his arms and neck—documented earlier by officials through photographs that accompanied his application—were evidence of gang membership in Honduras, and therefore the agency had denied his application. Across Mexico and the United States, Central American migrants, especially young men, are subjected to persistent criminalization, racialized as criminals, delinquents, and gang members (Galli 2018; Provine and Doty 2011; Ybarra 2019), producing a transnational underclass that is increasingly excluded from legal protection (see Brigden 2016, 2018). Óscar pleaded with the agents, asserting that he was not affiliated with a gang but, instead, a victim of one. If he returned to Honduras, he explained, he would surely be killed. His appeals were of no use, and he was forced to return to the shelter. Fearing deportation, he boarded a passenger bus headed for the U.S.-Mexico border, messaging his sister and brother-in-law that he would be joining them in the United States.

On the evening of March 6, 2017, Óscar arrived in Ciudad Miguel Alé-man, located across from Roma, Texas. After notifying family members that he had arrived at the U.S-Mexico border and was safe, he reserved a room at a nearby motel. The next day, as he crossed the international bridge to claim asylum in the United States, a group of CBP agents instructed him to turn around and go elsewhere. Óscar asked the agents if he could return at a later date, but they explained that the bridge was closed indefinitely to asylum seekers. Confused, he returned to the bus terminal where he arrived the day before. He spoke to his sister and brother-in-law over the phone, and they decided that Óscar should travel east to Matamoros, across the border from Brownsville, Texas. They wired him additional money, and he purchased a bus ticket that delivered him there late in the afternoon. Two days later, Óscar called his sister, revealing that he was turned away at the border by CBP agents again. He explained that this time, however, they instructed him to return the following week. Óscar returned to Mexico, seeking refuge at a popular motel that offered low rates for migrants. For five days, Óscar waited in and around the motel until he abruptly messaged his sister, asking her to wire $1,000 to his bank account. Óscar had been kidnapped. Within hours, he would be driven to an ATM machine to withdraw the money, in what is commonly known as an express kidnapping. His family collected the ransom and quickly transferred the cash into his account. In the morning, Óscar's sister confirmed that the money had been withdrawn, texting him to ensure he was safe. Days and weeks passed with no response. Óscar had disappeared.

Laura

Laura was twenty-two years old. Fleeing from an abusive partner in El Salvador, she escaped to Guatemala City with a friend. Within weeks, however, Laura's partner found her, threatening to kill her if she did not return to El Salvador with him. Laura refused to go and turned to the local police in Guatemala for help. When they declined to become involved, her family encouraged her to seek asylum in the United States. Heeding their advice, she left overnight on a passenger bus headed for the Mexico-Guatemala border. Slipping across the border at dawn, she traveled for several days on foot, frequently stopping at shelters along the way. On October 25, 2016, Laura and three other migrants were held at gunpoint and robbed along a remote stretch of land in Oaxaca known as the "gateway to Hell," where violence against migrants is especially common (Chaca 2015). Pushed onto the ground, they were forced to surrender all of their belongings, including shoes, backpacks, and phones. They escaped with only minor injuries, making their way to a nearby shelter to receive medical and legal assistance. Under Mexico's 2011 revision to its migration law, migrants who become victims of crimes may apply to regularize their status by reporting the incident to local prosecutors. In return, they receive a humanitarian visa that allows them to legally travel and reside in Mexico for one year. Laura and the others immediately reported the robbery to officials, living at the shelter while they waited for their cases to be decided.

Nearly two months later, with her newly issued humanitarian visa, Laura traveled to Mexico City, finding work as a waitress in a local restaurant. Speaking over the phone to her family, she explained that she needed money before continuing her journey northward and wanted to stay in Mexico before trying to claim asylum in the United States. At the restaurant, however, Laura was overworked, underpaid, and subject to wage theft and sexual harassment. While the humanitarian visa legally permits migrants to work in Mexico, they are rarely provided the appropriate documents and authorization to do so (Kerwin 2018), leading to low-paid, informal work and exploitation by employers. After four months of abusive work conditions, she decided to leave Mexico City with a coworker from the restaurant—another young woman from El Salvador. Laura notified her family that she was headed to Reynosa, where she planned to claim asylum in Texas, across the U.S.-Mexico border. On May 12, 2017, she arrived at the border, checking into a motel in Reynosa. The next day, Laura and her companion traveled to the closest port of entry. Approaching it, they were surprised to see dozens of other migrants and their families waiting in line. Asking others what happened, they learned that the bridge was temporarily closed—CBP agents were no longer accepting new asylum applicants, telling them that the United States was "already full." Laura and her companion were forced to return to Mexico.

In Reynosa, they left their motel for a nearby shelter, attempting to preserve what money they had left. Laura and her companion found the shelter overcrowded, where bed space and access to privacy were limited. Several days later, Laura messaged her family, explaining that she had grown impatient and was increasingly uncomfortable inside the shelter because there were few women around. She and her companion planned to pay the remainder of their money to a guide, who had approached them on the street and offered to help them across the border. Laura consulted with her family, who worried for her safety crossing the U.S.-Mexico border with a stranger. They warned that the guide might be affiliated with a cartel, leading her into a trap, or that she could drown when swimming across the Rio Grande. While Laura understood the risks involved, she felt there was little choice, explaining that her visa in Mexico would eventually expire. The next evening, Laura left the shelter. According to the guide, she and her companion would be transported to a safe house near the border, from which they would eventually be smuggled into the United States. Reassuring her family that evening, Laura pledged that they would be safe. Laura and her companion, however, never arrived, disappearing before ever reaching the United States.

Expanding Exclusion

As these two accounts show, social and biological death were fundamentally transnational in scope, encompassing a range of places, actors, and institutions spanning Central America, Mexico, and the United States. Along their journeys, Óscar and Laura were repeatedly stripped of rights and legal standing yet subject to the law's discipline, punishment, and regulation, culminating in both of their disappearances after they were turned away at the U.S.-Mexico border. Crucially, however, the instances of metering detailed above draw attention to the ways migrants and asylum seekers are continuously disenfranchised across transnational space and from afar. For some time, the United States has relied on policies like metering to exclude migrants and asylum seekers far away from the U.S. interior. From detention facilities located on distant islands (Loyd and Mountz 2018; Mountz 2011, 2017) to the Prevention through Deterrence policy and the diversion of migrants into deadly spaces along the U.S.-Mexico border (De León 2015; Nevins 2008, 2010; and Chapter 4), such strategies have been used to "deter, detain, and deflect" migrants from the fringes of U.S. territory and beyond (Mountz 2011, 118). As many scholars argue, these extraterritorial spaces are "made to kill" socially and biologically (Heller and Pezzani 2017, 96–97), barring migrants from legal protection while exposing them to inhospitable conditions, whether crossing the swift currents of the Rio Grande or traversing the Sonoran Desert to enter the United States. Metering extended this set of exclusionary and violent practices, expanding their reach into new geographic and legal spaces across Mexico and the United States.

In the examples above, Óscar and Laura were turned away at the border and forced to return to cities scattered across northern Mexico, where violence and exploitation against migrants is widespread. Denied entry into the United States as asylum seekers and unable to legally reside in Mexico, they were eventually disappeared and presumed dead. Thus, metering worked to geographically deflect migrants away from U.S. ports of entry and asylum's protection while simultaneously diverting them into perilous cities in Mexico, representing an organized form of exclusion and "managed violence" (Rosas 2006, 2012). Much like offshore detention facilities or the Sonoran Desert, these extraterritorial, urban spaces were made to exclude and kill from afar, operating both within and beyond the United States. Accordingly, metering intentionally used distance to deflect and divert migrants away from the U.S. interior and into Mexico. There, asylum seekers like Óscar and Laura were subject to a legally produced death, fashioned through U.S. policy and an unforgiving landscape in Mexico.

Furthermore, the disappearances of Óscar and Laura gestured toward the legal expansion of these practices through later policies under the Trump administration, including MPP, "safe third country" agreements, and the suspension of immigration and asylum law during the COVID-19 pandemic. This suite of policies further codified efforts to exclude migrants across transnational space and from afar by closing the U.S.-Mexico border, requiring asylum seekers to remain in Mexico during legal proceedings, eliminating due process during the pandemic, and barring them from protection if passing through another country before entering the United States. The collective effects of these policies worked not only to deflect and divert migrants away from the United States and into Mexican cities but also to deter them, extending wait times for initial court hearings, preventing access to case information, and reducing the availability of legal representation. Early reports indicated that nearly half of asylum seekers were unable to attend court hearings, resulting in the termination of their cases (Transactional Records Access Clearinghouse 2019). These circumstances were only exacerbated by widespread violence and exploitation in northern Mexico.

Alongside other U.S. immigration policies, metering signified an ever-expanding set of bureaucratic techniques aimed at excluding migrants and asylum seekers like Óscar and Laura. Exclusion within the interior, meanwhile, operates unabated across the U.S. mainland through the devolution and expansion of local immigration enforcement and policing (see Coleman 2009, 2012; Provine et al. 2016; Walker and Leitner 2011; and Chapter 8). This vast, unfolding geography of exclusion is, therefore, fundamentally transnational in scope, located both inside and outside of U.S. territory and made to kill socially and biologically.

Conclusions

Following its introduction in 2016, metering denied access to countless numbers of migrants seeking asylum at ports of entry along the U.S.-Mexico border. Trump officials made regular and widespread use of the policy, blocking asylum seekers for lengthy periods while limiting the number of overall applications. As this chapter shows, when turned away, migrants like Óscar and Laura were forced to return to perilous border cities in Mexico, where they were excluded from rights and legal protections yet vulnerable to violence, brutality, and exploitation at the hands of others. This social and biological death is fundamentally transnational in scope, experienced and produced through a range of places, actors, and institutions spanning Central America, Mexico, and the United States. More importantly, however, the disappearances and deaths of Óscar and Laura illustrate the multiple ways in which migrants and asylum seekers are continually disenfranchised from far away. Working alongside policies such as offshore detention, deportation, and Prevention through Deterrence, metering expanded this set of exclusionary and violent practices, extending them into new geographic and legal spaces. By using distance, the policy deflected migrants away from the territorial edges of the United States and the protections provided under asylum while simultaneously diverting them into perilous cities scattered across northern Mexico. In these transnational spaces across Mexico and the United States, asylum seekers like Óscar and Laura were subject to a legally produced mortality intended to deter future asylum claims.

Ultimately, the transnational dimensions of social and biological death underscore the vast, unfolding geography of exclusion that operates inside U.S. territory as well beyond its peripheries. As Mexico and the United States continue to implement restrictive immigration and refugee policies, metering and related strategies aimed at exclusion become increasingly important, producing social and biological death by eliminating rights and legal protections while exposing migrants and asylum seekers to violence, brutality, and exploitation. The efficacy and success of these policies, however, is far from guaranteed, and despite the recent expansion of restrictive policies under the Trump administration, migrants continue to travel north (Ainsley 2019; Hennessy-Fiske 2018b), subverting the violent immigration enforcement regime that operates transnationally across Mexico, the United States, and beyond.

REFERENCES

Abdullah, Halimah, and Alexandra Jaffe. 2017. "Trump Signs Executive Orders Aimed at Cracking Down on Illegal Immigration." *NBC News*, January 25. https://www.nbcnews.com/news/us-news/trump-signs-executive-orders-aimed-cracking-down-illegal-immigration-n712096.

Adlerstein, Ana. 2018. "Asylum Seekers Routinely Turned Away from Ports of Entry, Advocates Say." *The Guardian*, December 19. https://www.theguardian.com/us-news/2018/dec/19/us-mexico-border-migrants-claim-asylum-difficulties.

Aguilar, Julián. 2018. "Trump Administration Moves to Deny Asylum for Immigrants Who Enter the U.S. between Ports of Entry." *Texas Tribune*, November 8. https://www.texastribune.org/2018/11/08/trump-administration-announces-new-rules-immigrants-seeking-asylum/.

———. 2019. "Trump Administration's Latest Asylum Rule Allowed to Stand in Texas, New Mexico." *Texas Tribune*, August 16. https://www.texastribune.org/2019/08/16/trump-administrations-asylum-rule-allowed-stand-texas-new-mexico/.

Ainsley, Julia. 2019. "Border Crossings by Undocumented Migrants in March Hit 12-Year High." *NBC News*, April 9. https://www.nbcnews.com/politics/immigration/border-crossings-undocumented-migrants-march-hit-12-year-high-n992611.

Bonello, Deborah. "Mexico's Deportation of Central American Migrants Is Rising." *Los Angeles Times*, September 4. https://www.latimes.com/world/mexico-americas/la-fg-mexico-migrants-20150905-story.html.

Booth, William. 2010. "Survivor: Drug Gang Massacred 72 Migrants in Northern Mexico." *Washington Post*, August 25. http://www.washingtonpost.com/wp-dyn/content/article/2010/08/25/AR2010082506776.html.

Brigden, Noelle. 2016. "Improvised Transnationalism: Clandestine Migration at the Border of Anthropology and International Relations." *International Studies Quarterly* 60 (2): 343–354.

———. 2018. *The Migrant Passage: Clandestine Journeys from Central America*. Ithaca, NY: Cornell University Press.

Brotherton, David C., and Phillip Kretsedemas. 2017. *Immigration Policy in the Age of Punishment: Detention, Deportation, and Border Control*. New York: Columbia University Press.

Bump, Phillip. 2015. "Donald Trump's Lengthy and Curious Defense of His Comments, Annotated." *Washington Post*, July 6. https://www.washingtonpost.com/news/the-fix/wp/2015/07/06/donald-trumps-lengthy-and-curious-defense-of-his-immigrant-comments-annotated/.

Butler, Judith. 2004. *Precarious Life: The Powers of Mourning and Violence*. New York: Verso.

———. 2009. *Frames of War: When Is Life Grievable?* New York: Verso.

Cacho, Lisa Marie. 2012. *Social Death: Racialized Rightlessness and the Criminalization of the Unprotected*. New York: New York University Press.

CBS News. 2016. "U.S. to Crack Down on Deporting Haitian Immigrants." *CBS News*, September 22. https://www.cbsnews.com/news/u-s-to-crack-down-on-deporting-haitian-immigrants/.

Chaca, Roselia. 2015. "Chahuites, 'Puerta del infierno' para migrantes." *El Universal*, September 3. http://www.eluniversal.com.mx/articulo/estados/2015/09/3/chahuites-puerta-del-infierno-para-migrantes.

Coleman, Mathew. 2009. "What Counts as the Politics and Practice of Security, and Where? Devolution and Immigrant Insecurity after 9/11." *Annals of the American Association of Geographers* 99 (5): 904–913.

———. 2012. "The Local Migration State: The Site-Specific Devolution of Immigration Enforcement in the U.S. South." *Law and Policy* 34 (2): 159–190.

Collyer, Michael. 2010. "Stranded Migrants and the Fragmented Journey." *Journal of Refugee Studies* 23 (3): 273–293.

De León, Jason. 2015. *The Land of Open Graves: Living and Dying on the Migrant Trail*. Oakland: University of California Press.

Diaz, Lizbeth. 2016. "Haitians Vulnerable on Mexico-U.S. Border as Migrant Crisis Escalates." *Reuters*, October 19. https://www.reuters.com/article/us-immigration-mexico-haitians-idUSKCN12J2CE.

Dibble, Sandra. 2016. "Surge of Haitians at San Ysidro Port of Entry." *San Diego Union-Tribune*, May 26. https://www.sandiegouniontribune.com/news/border-baja-california/sdut-haitians-flood-san-ysidro-port-entry-2016may26-story.html.

Fredrick, James. 2018. "Mexico Deploys a Formidable Deportation Force near Its Own Southern Border." *NPR*, May 7. https://www.npr.org/sections/parallels/2018/05/07/607700928/mexico-deploys-a-formidable-deportation-force-near-its-own-southern-border.

Galli, Chiara. 2018. "A Rite of Reverse Passage: The Construction of Youth Migration in the US Asylum Process." *Ethnic and Racial Studies* 41 (9): 1651–1671.

Gonzales, Richard. 2018. "Trump Administration Seeks New Border Crackdown." *NPR*, April 6. https://www.npr.org/sections/thetwo-way/2018/04/06/600435660/trump-administration-seeks-new-border-crackdown.

Heller, Charles, and Lorenzo Pezzani. 2017. "Liquid Traces: Investigating the Deaths of Migrants at the EU's Maritime Frontier." In *The Borders of "Europe": Autonomy of Migration, Tactics of Bordering*, edited by Nicholas De Genova, 95–119. Durham, NC: Duke University Press.

Hennessy-Fiske, Molly. 2018a. "Caught in Limbo, Central American Asylum-Seekers Are Left Waiting on a Bridge over the Rio Grande." *Los Angeles Times*, June 7. https://www.latimes.com/nation/la-na-asylum-seeking-families-border-bridges-20180605-story.html.

———. 2018b. "Immigrant Asylum Claims Increase at U.S. Southern Border." *Los Angeles Times*, December 10. https://www.latimes.com/nation/la-na-border-patrol-asylum-cases-20181210-story.html.

Kanstroom, Dan. 2012. *Aftermath: Deportation Law and the New American Diaspora*. New York: Oxford University Press.

Kerwin, Helen. 2018. "The Mexican Asylum System in Regional Context." *Maryland Journal of International Law* 33 (1): 290–312.

Klein, Betsy, and Kevin Liptak. 2018. "Trump Ramps Up Rhetoric: Dems Want 'Illegal Immigrants' to 'Infest Our Country.'" *CNN*, June 19. https://www.cnn.com/2018/06/19/politics/trump-illegal-immigrants-infest/index.html.

Kubrin, Charles E., Marjorie S. Zatz, and Ramiro Martínez, eds. 2012. *Punishing Immigrants: Policy, Politics, and Injustice*. New York: New York University Press.

Lakhani, Nina. 2017. "Mexican Kidnappers Pile Misery on to Central Americans Fleeing Violence." *The Guardian*, February 21. https://www.theguardian.com/global-development/2017/feb/21/mexico-kidnappings-refugees-central-america-immigration.

Laurent, Oliver. 2017. "These Haitian Refugees Are Stranded at the U.S.-Mexico Border." *Time*, February 20. https://time.com/4674517/immigration-haiti-mexico/.

Loyd, Jenna, and Alison Mountz. 2018. *Boats, Borders, and Bases: Race, the Cold War, and the Rise of Migration Detention in the United States*. Oakland: University of California Press.

Mainwaring, Ćetta, and Noelle Brigden. 2016. "Beyond the Border: Clandestine Migration Journeys." *Geopolitics* 21 (2): 243–262.

Miller, Todd. 2019. *Empire of Borders: The Expansion of the U.S. Border around the World*. New York: Verso.

Miroff, Nick. 2012. "'Total Barbarity' as Mexican Cartel Dumps 49 Torsos along Highway." *Washington Post*, May 13. https://www.washingtonpost.com/world/the_americas/total-barbarity-as-mexican-cartel-dumps-49-torsos-along-highway/2012/05/13/gIQACHNMNU_story.html.

Mountz, Alison. 2011. "The Enforcement Archipelago: Detention, Haunting, and Asylum on Islands." *Political Geography* 30 (3): 118–128.

———. 2017. "Island Detention: Affective Eruption as Trauma's Disruption." *Emotion, Space and Society* 24 (1): 74–82.

Nevins, Joseph. 2008. *Dying to Live: A Story of U.S. Immigration in an Age of Global Apartheid*. San Francisco: City Lights.

———. 2010. *Operation Gatekeeper and Beyond: The War on "Illegals" and the Remaking of the U.S.-Mexico Boundary*. New York: Routledge.

Olayo-Méndez, Alejandro. 2017. "Programa de la Frontera Sur and interdiction." *Peace Review: A Journal of Social Justice* 29 (1): 24–30.

Ortega, Bob. 2018. "US Asylum Seekers Face Long Waits or Risky Crossings, Thanks to Supposed Capacity Crunch." *CNN*, December 20. https://www.cnn.com/2018/12/20/us/us-asylum-seeker-southwest-border-capacity-invs/index.html.

Patterson, Orlando. 1982. *Slavery and Social Death: A Comparative Study*. Cambridge, MA: Harvard University Press.

Provine, Doris M., and Roxanne L. Doty. 2011. "The Criminalization of Immigrants as a Racial Project." *Journal of Contemporary Criminal Justice* 27 (3): 261–277.

Provine, Doris M., Monica W. Varsanyi, Paul G. Lewis, and Scott H. Decker. 2016. *Policing Immigrants: Local Law Enforcement on the Front Lines*. Chicago: University of Chicago Press.

Rosas, Gilberto. 2006. "The Managed Violences of the Borderlands: Treacherous Geographies, Policeability, and the Politics of Race." *Latino Studies* 4 (4): 401–418.

———. 2012. *Barrio Libre: Criminalizing States and Delinquent Refusals of the New Frontier*. Durham, NC: Duke University Press.

Sacchetti, Maria. 2018. "Sessions: Victims of Domestic Abuse and Gang Violence Generally Won't Qualify for Asylum." *Washington Post*, June 11. https://www.washingtonpost.com/local/immigration/sessions-signals-that-victims-of-domestic-abuse-and-gang-violence-generally-will-not-qualify-for-asylum/2018/06/11/45e54602-6d9e-11e8-bd50-b80389a4e569_story.html.

Semple, Kirk. 2016. "U.S. to Step Up Deportations of Haitians Amid Surge at Border." *New York Times*, September 22. https://www.nytimes.com/2016/09/23/world/americas/haiti-migrants-earthquake.html.

Tackett, Michael, Caitlin Dickerson, and Azam Ahmed. 2018. "Migrants Seeking Asylum Must Wait in Mexico, Trump Administration Says." *New York Times*, December 20. https://www.nytimes.com/2018/12/20/us/politics/mexico-trump-asylum-seekers-migrants.html.

Transactional Records Access Clearinghouse. 2019. "Contrasting Experiences: MPP vs. Non-MPP Immigration Court Cases." December 19. https://trac.syr.edu/immigration/reports/587.

Tuckman, Jo. 2015. "Mexico's Migration Crackdown Escalates Dangers for Central Americans." *The Guardian*, October 13. https://www.theguardian.com/world/2015/oct/13/mexico-central-american-migrants-journey-crackdown.

Van Ramshorst, Jared P. 2018. "Anti-immigrant Sentiment, Rising Populism, and the Oaxacan Trump." *Journal of Latin American Geography* 17 (1): 253–256.

Vogt, Wendy. 2018. *Lives in Transit: Violence and Intimacy on the Migrant Journey*. Oakland: University of California Press.

Walker, Kyle E., and Helga Leitner. 2011. "The Variegated Landscape of Local Immigration Policies in the United States." *Urban Geography* 32 (2): 156–178.

Ybarra, Megan. 2019. "'We Are Not Ignorant': Transnational Migrants' Experiences of Racialized Securitization." *Environment and Planning D: Society and Space* 37 (2): 197–215.

11

Better in Jail There than Dead Here

Deportation and (Social) Death in Honduras

AMELIA FRANK-VITALE

When Ulises was deported the second time, it took him longer to recover. He was depressed, broken-hearted at the prospect of being back in Honduras, and traumatized from the three months he had been held in detention in the United States. He laughs, without mirth, when he compares this with his first attempt to migrate. Then, he had been kidnapped by a drug cartel in northern Mexico and held in a warehouse for three months, unsure each morning whether he would be killed or allowed to live another day. He endured hunger and regular beatings, and had to sleep on a concrete floor in a room full of strangers. Still, he came back to Honduras mostly unchanged after that experience, eager to try again. This time, though, he found himself unable to sleep, or sometimes sleeping too much. He lost a lot of weight. He wandered between his mother's house in a rural region, where he could not find work, and the city where he had grown up, where he feared for his life.

It was serendipity that I reconnected with Ulises. As part of my fieldwork in San Pedro Sula Honduras, I happened to be in the deportee reception center the day Ulises was deported for the second time. We had met during the 2018 migrant caravan months earlier, sharing french fries at a Carl's Jr. in Tijuana as I explained to him what the asylum process looked like. Ulises was in his midtwenties, with a specialized high-school degree in computers, but he no longer saw the point of trying to go to college. When he was younger, he had dreamed of being a lawyer. "But why bother now? I know lawyers who can't find a job," he told me. Despite feeling broken by this last attempt, Ulises was considering trying a third time to get to the United States. Moving between bad options, Ulises is adrift both within his country and outside of it.

In recent years, researchers and journalists have dedicated themselves to documenting the murders of those deported to Central America (see Mogelson 2015; Stillman 2018; Sachetti 2018; Sullivan 2019), many after having asylum claims denied (Long 2014; Amnesty International 2016). There are too many of these stories, and yet most deportees are not murdered. This chapter focuses on the experience of young men like Ulises, who *survive* deportation but are returned to lives of deprivation and foreclosed life chances. The social death they experience is shaped by Honduras's hyper-neoliberalism, militarized policing that targets young men as the enemy, and dismal economic prospects for anyone not already well-off. The lives of these young men are systematically devalued, while they are consistently useful as fodder for political scapegoating, a convenient enemy on which to blame all of the problems Honduras faces. I focus specifically on the experience of young men for three reasons. First, while Honduran women are migrating at higher rates than in previous generations, young men still make up the vast majority; second, young men are frequently cast as potential perpetrators of crime and violence in Honduras; and third, this same stigma crosses borders with young racialized migrant men, and, thus, they are less likely to receive humanitarian care and international protection.

In what follows, I offer an explanation for why deportees often look to remigrate, knowingly risking—again—incarceration in the United States and violence in transit. I next discuss an alternate strategy for survival that some young men employ: cutting off social ties and opting out of public life. Whether they are risking literal death or choosing social death, I argue that these grim prospects are no accident. Honduras has what anthropologist Adrienne Pine calls an "excess demographic"—an overabundance of working-age people vis-à-vis the needs of capital (Pine 2019, 36). Relying on out-migration as a safety valve and doing little for poor youth at home, the Honduran government ensures that many young people look externally, internationally, for the possibility of having a better life or, simply, a life at all.

Setting the Scene in Honduras

This chapter draws from nearly two years of ethnographic fieldwork conducted with deportees and their neighbors in and around San Pedro Sula, Honduras, from 2017 to 2019 (Frank-Vitale 2019). During this time, the numbers of people forcibly returned to Honduras rose sharply after a temporary decline, reaching 75,279 in 2018, and surpassing 100,000 in 2019

(Agencia EFE 2019). Honduras continues to have one of the highest homicide rates in the world (Igarape Institute, n.d.), although the rate has declined substantially since its peak in 2012.[1] Honduras also has among the highest rates of poverty (CEPAL 2019), underemployment (David 2019), and inequality (Barría 2019) in Latin America.

The dire economic situation in Honduras has much to do with the unfettered neoliberalism that intensified after a 2009 coup d'etat removed democratically elected president Manuel Zelaya from power. Since then, the National Party has controlled the country's politics and, in large part, its economy, returning to the model of neoliberal privatization and openness to foreign capital that had long characterized Honduras (Euraque 1997; Pine 2008) and ushering in a decade of moving public goods into private hands (Shipley 2016; Martin and Geglia 2019), accompanied by deepened corruption (Chayes 2017; Salomón 2012) among the political and economic elites.

As in much of the world, neoliberal policies have contributed to a situation where poor Hondurans have little or no access to affordable education, health care, basic services like water and electricity, and very limited prospects for employment. While Honduras did not see full-scale civil war like its neighbors in the 1970s and 1980s, counterinsurgency militarization with the presence and direction of the United States was intense (Robinson 2003; Moreno 1994). Like its Central American neighbors in the postwar period, Honduras underwent neoliberalization processes (Gledhill 2004) marked by the substitution of the market for state and society (Burrell and Moodie 2013). Neoliberalization dismantles whatever state and social infrastructure existed, leading to profound disjuncture. As the effects of that disjuncture play out in often violent ways, the responsibility for that violence gets placed not on the dismantled state but, rather, on the individuals themselves who have been the victims of the restructuring (Goldstein 2010, 491).

In Honduras, the emergence of *maras*, neighborhood-based street gangs, mostly composed of poor, young men, is a response to the abandonment of the urban poor and, at the same time, offers a scapegoat on which to pin all the anxieties and fears produced through neoliberalization. *Maras* loom large in the social imaginary in contemporary Honduras. While their existence, their violence, and their control over most poor, urban neighborhoods across the country is very real, it is also true that "mara" is, as Jon Horne Carter suggests, "a synecdoche pointing to the intersection of state and criminal worlds of which street gangs are just the most visible appendage" (Carter 2019). Their formation and consolidation in Honduras has much to do with the social wreckage in the wake of a deadly hurricane at the end of the twentieth century (Carter 2014), as displaced and abandoned youth banded together for protection and survival.

The hurricane, like the 2009 coup d'etat, or the 2020 coronavirus pandemic, put strain on an already fragile subsistence existence, making neoliberal precarity even more acute and putting the state's wholesale indifference to the needs of the majority of the population into sharp relief. When the crisis of the neoliberal state is laid bare, the *maras* serve to deflect blame; both *mano dura* policies enacted in the wake of the hurricane and proliferating police forces in postcoup Honduras (Frank 2018) target the *maras* as the only responsible party for all of the country's difficulties. The collective sense of insecurity, an emerging *common sense* that delinquency and individual moral failing are to blame, leads to the criminalization of poverty itself (Thomas, O'Neill, and Offit 2011, 2). The specter of the *maras* allows for further militarization and for policing to become even more openly heavy-handed *with the approval—at least initially—of those who will be subjected to this increasingly violent policing* (Pine 2008, 63).

While the *mano dura* response to gangs in Honduras failed to protect public safety—in fact, *maras* became more violent and better organized (Gutiérrez Rivera 2013)—the Honduran government continues to deal with insecurity by establishing new, and ever more militarized, police units: seventeen in total by 2019 (Rainsford 2019).[2] Among them are the Policia Militar del Orden Popular (Military Police of Popular Order, PMOP), created in 2014,[3] army units stationed in civilian neighborhoods (Haugaard 2017). In the poor neighborhoods in and around San Pedro Sula, the police presence is constant. Rather than inspiring a sense of safety among the populace, the police are feared by residents of these neighborhoods.

Henry Giroux (2011) characterizes neoliberal economic policies as the death of the social state and ascendance of the punishing state. In Honduras, both of these elements are at play, and they each contribute to and draw from the presence of the *maras*. In the absence of a social state, *maras* act as the de facto authority within the communities they control, where they rule through a complicated matrix of protection, violence, discipline, and care.[4] Their presence certainly contributes to the experience for some in Honduras of social death that leads people to see migration as a potential escape. At the same time, the presence of the *maras* is a *consequence* of the experience of social death that young people confront, heightened by the neoliberal militarization of the country that depends on pitting society against an idea of the *maras* that includes, essentially, all poor, urban young men.

Social Death and Deportation

When Ricardo is returned to Honduras, he takes a taxi from the airport to his aunt's house. His mother's neighborhood is too dangerous for him to just show up in, but his aunt lives in a *residencial*, a low-income gated community where there is nominal security. Even so, Ricardo cannot even knock on his aunt's door before a few young men pull him into a moto-taxi and take him to the edge of the neighborhood. They make him remove his clothes and interrogate him about his tattoos (he has his mother's name on one arm). With his aunt as a reference they eventually they let him go with a warning not to hang around for too long.

Speaking with Ricardo and his aunt a few days later, she concurs. "Él no puede estar aquí" (He cannot be here), she tells me as she puts her hand on her chest. "Me duele decirlo, pero acá no se puede estar" (It hurts to say it, but he cannot be here). Ricardo is twenty-nine years old, and this is his third deportation. He has been migrating to the United States for over ten years, and each time he is sent back, he spends a few days with his family and then leaves again. Here, they tell me, he cannot go outside. He cannot get a job. He cannot study. Here he cannot have a life. He cooks breakfast for his cousins and embraces his mother with the unbridled enthusiasm of a little boy. He will head back to the United States in two more days, he tells me, but what worries him this time is that if he is caught, he will be charged with felony reentry and may have to do substantial prison time before he is deported. His aunt adds that being here in Honduras, though, he might as well be in prison. He has no life here. "Yeah," Ricardo says, "better to be in jail there than dead here."

Orlando Patterson (1982) originally developed the concept of social death to understand the basic condition of slavery. Since then, scholars have employed the term to indicate a broad range of existential conditions.[5] Ernest Chavez has argued that social death is constituted by three elements: "excessive violence," "alienation from filial bonds," and "degradation that fixes powerlessness of the slave in relation to the master" (Chavez 2019, 5). Lisa Guenther, meanwhile, locates social death as the experience of suffering and exclusion *to the point of becoming dead to the rest of society* (Guenther 2013, xx; emphasis added). Establishing social relations can be a means to resist social death, then, as those who are socially dead "no longer count as lives that *matter*" (xx; emphasis in original). Annika Jonsson synthesizes the concept as describing "existential homelessness"[6] in which people are relegated to the outskirts of human society (Jonsson 2015, 284), while Kankonde Bukasa Peter posits social death as utter marginalization, being deemed subhuman (Peter 2010, 231). Joshua Price uses social death in reference to families that have been forcibly separated (Price 2015), while Keramit Reiter and Susan Bibler Coutin have explicitly located the disintegration of subjects through deportation as a form of social death (Reiter and Coutin 2017). Peter suggests that remittances can be used to counter social death, as the presence of the money both reinforces social ties transnationally and contributes to the social standing of the sender (Peter 2010). Deportation, of course, would cut off an individual's ability to send remittances, casting the person back into the realm of social death.

Exiling someone from their world is "inflicting social death" (Tirrell 2016, 590). Life after deportation has been conceptualized by scholars as a kind of expulsion (Drotbohm and Hasselberg 2015) or exile (Coutin 2016, 2010). Anthropologists have studied life after removal for those deportees who are forced to leave a country where they had spent extended time (Peutz 2006; Charles 2010) and developed deep affective ties with families of mixed status (documented and undocumented) on both sides of the border (Boehm 2016, 2011; Ybarra and Peña 2017). Much of this literature focuses on the experience of reintegration/resettlement in a foreign homeland. Here there is a kind of social death foisted on people who are made to leave their homes and communities. Deportation, in this context, is a dislocation or traumatic rupture, which dismantles claims to belonging (Blue 2015) and produces a discernible absence among those left behind when the deportee is taken away (Burman 2006).

Today's Honduran deportees, however, are mostly individuals who have left their country only weeks or months previously, in many cases fleeing threats of violence, and they are caught by Mexican or United States immigration officers while en route to their desired destination. Many of the deportees have spent months incarcerated in U.S. detention centers while trying to pursue an asylum claim, but they have never *settled* into a community or built deep ties. This is not to say that no Hondurans are deported after living long lives in the United States, but they are a minority. This is an important distinction because, unlike the deportees who have to figure out how to adapt to unfamiliar worlds, Honduran deportees know exactly what is waiting for them.

Social death here does not come exclusively from the deportation event; for many Central Americans this condition precedes the moment of migration, can pervade the experience of mobility, and awaits those deported. Jon Wolseth (2008) argues that for many young men in Honduras, migration is the only way to escape from both physical and social death. Yet if we think of social death as "the cessation of the individual person as an active agent in others' lives" (Mulkay and Ernst 1991, 178), migration itself might precipitate social death. Indeed, for those who migrate and effectively disappear, they are socially dead to the family members left with their absence (Rivera Hernández 2017). In this context, deportation might revive the socially dead, were the conditions at "home" such that one were not trading one kind of social death for another. Others have argued that social death could be symbolized by an "inability to dream a meaningful life" (Hage 2003, 79). The dream of migration, then, might keep at bay full social death, but deportation would serve to kill that dream. Elmer, after he was deported the last time, said, "I used to have dreams. But now I don't." He was twenty-two years old.

Ricardo and Ulises are also emblematic of this reality. They left Honduras because their possibility, their life chances, were already minimal. They both migrate in hopes of leading a full life. Both young men are, at this point, largely unable to escape from the social death of marginalization and violence at home and unable to *settle* in any permanent way anywhere else. Ricardo did make it to the United States for the fourth time; but sooner or later he expects to be picked up by immigration again. Ulises weighs his options, thinking he will likely try again. For young men like them, migration and social death are intertwined, mutually reinforcing, even as migration represented, initially, a path out of social death and toward a different life. For some young men who have never migrated, however, there is also a stationary kind of social death within Honduras.

No, No Salgo: Encavement as Social Death

Eighteen-year-old Aram goes to school once a week, hoping to eventually earn a high school diploma. The rest of his time he spends inside his house, almost exclusively. One day we decide to meet near the center of San Pedro Sula; he tells me to pick him up at a gas station convenient to the bus route he is familiar with. He is quite nervous about the possibility of my arriving late, of his having to wait for me. I make sure this does not happen, and his anxiety melts as soon as he gets into my car.

For a teenager like Aram, simply hanging around on the street, on any street, is risky behavior. His world is fraught with danger, and the best method he, and many young people like him in Honduras, has is to stay inside his home. One time, he tells me, he started dating a young woman in the neighborhood next to his own, but his mother got extremely nervous with him venturing over there and so he ended it before it could really begin; better to stay at home.

Aram desperately wants to be social. I ask him how he spends all his free time. "No, Amelia, no salgo" (I do not go out), he tells me. He spends his days and evenings exchanging messages, music, and memes with a network of friends—mostly through the messaging app WhatsApp—but he rarely ventures out to hang out with them in person. They all stay tucked in their homes.

This behavior is widespread among Honduran youth and has come to be seen as having moral worth. Staying indoors indicates that one is not a gang member, a gang sympathizer, or a potential delinquent. To the police, the gangs, and society at large, staying indoors signifies responsibility, seriousness, and upright behavior. Byron, from a different neighborhood, explained that the key to survival was living *encuevado* (encaved). The dangers on the outside are multifaceted and unpredictable, and being outside and idle can be seen as a problem to both gangs and police. In one neighborhood, after an incursion by a rival gang, MS-13 circulated a clear message to residents: "No queremos ver güirros en las esquinas" (We do not want to see male youth on the corners). Elsewhere, Melvin, a nineteen-year-old water salesman, told me that, since he had grown up in his neighborhood, the gang there did not give him any problems. For him, the danger of being outside was the police. "When the police come through, that's when I run and hide—because I know if *they* pick me up, I might never appear again." Flaco, another young man from the same neighborhood, told me how the police picked him up late one night and simply dropped him off in the middle of a neighborhood controlled by a rival gang. His presence there, as a young man from a "contrary" neighborhood, would have meant certain death, but God intervened, he said, because a huge rainstorm hit, giving him the chance to run away.

While living most of your life safe inside your home may help young people feel they are preserving their lives against possible death, the cost is a kind of social death. As Claudia Card argues, social vitality, the opposite of social death, is inextricable from relationships "that create identity that gives meaning to a life" (Card 2003, 63). While virtual connections through apps like WhatsApp lessen the isolation young men like Aram feel, they cannot fully supplant the kinds of affective ties that teenagers and young adults typically form as they navigate the complicated social process of transitioning to adulthood. These social connections are what keep existential anxiety at bay, suggest Caroline Steele, David Kidd, and Emanuele Castano (2015, 19). Aram is isolated and depressed; he dreams of his father, who recently migrated to the United States, paying for the coyote that would take him there too, but that future, the only one he can imagine as being an escape, is elusive.

Henrik Vigh, in his work with young men in Guinea-Bissau, found a similar phenomenon, characterizing their lives as "social death," from which migration was one means of escape (2009, 93). He describes how young men have few possibilities of social becoming, of working for wages, starting a family, moving from the category "youth" to that of "men." In a movement parallel to that of so many Hondurans, many of these young men risk their physical existence—crossing the Mediterranean has claimed the lives of thousands of migrants from Africa—with the hopes of escaping this social stagnation (105). In this context, he argues, war and conflict engagement become "terrains of possibility," rather than spaces of death (Vigh 2006, 31). The other option for escaping social death, Vigh holds, is joining a group engaged in organized violence. Social death does not wholly preclude the "possibility of creating new forms of social existence" (Snow 2016, 622). In Honduras, as in Guinea-Bissau, many of those forms lead youth to engage in the same violent, criminal behavior for which, though they may try to avoid it like Aram, they are always already viewed as guilty. Young men who live in the neighborhoods known to be controlled by gangs are seen as inherently suspicious and innately culpable. Their existence, the fact of their physical presence, is the enemy the militarized police are deployed to combat. The young men in these neighborhoods—especially those who are un- or underemployed—are interchangeable, regardless of actual involvement in criminal acts. The police told one woman as much when she went to intervene on behalf of a young man they had taken in. She told them, "You've got the wrong guy. He's a Christian." The officer's response was "Aquí todos son diablitos" (Here they are all little devils).

Criminalization and Social Death

The first thing I noticed was the smell of urine. I could smell the jail cells before my eyes adjusted to the darkness enough to make out the contours of the barred rooms. It was hard to tell how many bodies were stuffed inside. What was overwhelmingly noticeable was absence, lack: no light, no windows, no air, no beds, no bathroom. I called out for Henry, the young man I was there to see, and a figure emerged at the bars at the doorway. He wanted to show me the bruises on his wrists, from when the police tried to make him touch drugs, and he had resisted. Even in the darkness, I could see the purplish marks on his tanned skin. After a few minutes, the officer who was accompanying me indicated that it had been long enough, and Henry receded into the darkness.

Eighteen-year-old Henry had been arrested the day before. The military police picked him up while he was working at the moto-taxi stand. They put him in the back of their pickup truck and drove around for a while, as Henry sweated under the hot sun. Then they picked up another young man, in another neighborhood, while he was working at a barbershop. They took them both to their headquarters and physically forced the boys to touch and pose for photos with packets of drugs the police already had in their possession. Later, in court, the charges would say the police had caught both men, together, in the act of selling drugs. Despite a host of witnesses to refute this basic assertion, both young men were sent to the adult men's prison, Támara, for *prisión preventiva* (preventive imprisonment) to be held while the investigation and trial went on, which could be for up to two years. Henry, the barber, their family and friends, and even the state-appointed lawyer who was initially responsible for their case doubted their chances of beating the charges, clumsy and fraudulent as they might be.

The residents of these neighborhoods, like Aram and Ricardo, are accustomed to being treated in this way by the authorities; the criminalization of the urban poor is wide and deep in Honduras. Henry Giroux argues that the criminalization of poverty is intimately tied to the rise of the neoliberal, punishing state (Giroux 2011). He links social death of the poor with the death of the social state, replaced by the neoliberal idea of individual freedom and personal responsibility, which means that individuals are thought to be at fault for their own suffering. "Poverty has become criminalized," he writes, "and 'extreme poverty' has become a 'pathological condition' rather than an effect of structural injustice" (Giroux 2011, 591). Their position, their lack of viable alternatives, their vulnerability to being misrecognized by the police as criminals, their social death, is intimately tied to the criminalization of the urban poor.

Differential treatment under the system of laws results in what Lisa Marie Cacho calls "ineligibility for personhood," a form of social death (2012, 6). People who are ineligible for personhood are *subjected* to laws but "refused the legal means to contest those laws . . . [and] denied . . . the political legitimacy and moral credibility necessary to question them" (6). Urban poor youth in Honduras are ineligible for personhood in this manner: they must acquiesce to the laws (and those who enforce them) but do not have the possibility to contest those laws or their application. I asked Melvin, the water salesman, as we looked out over the crowd of young people gathered that day, "What future is waiting for them?" He responded, without pausing, without blinking, "Jail, hospital, or death."

Conclusions

In this chapter, I articulate a variety of experiences of social death among poor, young, urban men in Honduras, drawing from my ethnographic research with deportees and their neighbors. While there has been much emphasis on the deaths of deportees, those who experience social death ought to be taken as seriously as those who are literally murdered upon return. As Card notes in her analysis of genocide and social death, "The harm of social death is not necessarily less extreme than that of physical death" (Card 2003, 73). Furthermore, social death can be *"equated* with death, because alone we do not survive" (Steele, Kidd, and Castano 2015, 19; emphasis added). While the attention paid to those who are murdered upon return is important, we should also take into account the kinds of social death that propel migration and are produced or exacerbated through the reality of deportation.

When Ricardo and Ulises (along with tens of thousands of other young Hondurans) are deported, what currently awaits them in Honduras is death of one kind or another. Gangs who do not trust their presence or police units who see them as nothing more than potential criminals may cause physical death. If they physically survive, they may still face social death caused by being cut off from social connections and full personhood in order to maintain biological life. Especially in the ten years since the coup d'état, many young people have gotten involved in a variety of efforts to change the status quo, to reform politics, to push back on neoliberalism, and to demand social and political recognition (Frank 2018; Phillips 2015). This is, perhaps, a twinned reason for why the government would prefer for the "excess" in the young male demographic to disappear, whether through migration, as victims of gang violence, or arrested. Their presence poses a threat to the stability of the regime, and many young men who *do* stay and try to change things find themselves in the crosshairs of police forces or paramilitaries. Faced with this range of options at home, young men like Ulises and Ricardo are—and will remain—compelled by the possibility of another reality that might be realized through migration. Though not necessarily conceived of as such, their act of migration is a reclamation of their right to live a meaningful life, a refusal to accept the social death of neoliberalism's "excess demographic."

Epilogue: *Sálvese Quien Pueda*

I am finalizing this chapter in the midst of the coronavirus pandemic, which, like the coup and Hurricane Mitch, has put into even sharper relief the dynamics outlined in this essay. The Honduran government has received millions of new aid dollars to combat the pandemic; the few public hospitals that exist continue to be underfunded and understaffed. Honduras has the highest number of confirmed COVID-19 cases in Central America, though there is wide agreement that the official numbers are likely drastically undercounting actual deaths. Street protests demanding food have broken out in different parts of the country; under strict stay-at-home orders, people are worried about dying from hunger before they contract the disease. The protests have been met with the same intense, militarized policing that I discuss throughout this chapter, complete with tear gas. Many of the protesters have remarked: Would it not be easier—and cheaper—for the government to simply hand out beans?

The government has used the pretext of the pandemic to suspend constitutional guarantees, officially limiting freedom of speech and the press. It has also pushed through sweeping changes to its penal code that reduce penalties for corruption and shield the military from being tried for crimes against humanity. The entire justice system has effectively been paused, leaving those accused of a crime—like Henry and the barber—waiting in overcrowded prisons indefinitely, with little contact with the outside world. At least one prisoner that we know of has died of coronavirus, and the men with whom he was housed have not been tested and are not being quarantined away from other prisoners. As in the United States, punishment for violating the stay-at-home order has been applied wildly unevenly, focusing on street vendors and other day laborers—those who often rely on the day's sale to buy tomorrow's food. Deportations continue unabated, with an even less robust infrastructure awaiting those returned than before. In the pandemic, staying inside, living *encuevado*, carries with it another level of urgency and virtue, but it also might mean literally starving to death. The extent to which neither the United States nor Honduras cares about the lives, health, and well-being of those who migrate and those who are deported is made abundantly clear by the response to the pandemic.

There is a saying in Honduras, and many parts of Latin America, used often to refer to the really "bad" neighborhoods, the ones that are widely known to be controlled by gangs or some other kind of organized crime group. *Sálvese quien pueda* (Save yourself, whoever is able to). It is roughly equivalent to "every man for himself." This is essentially the ethos of militarized neoliberal kleptocracy in Honduras: save yourself, whoever can. The unspoken subtext here is, always, if you cannot save yourself, the fault is your own. And this, I argue, is exactly what young men are scrambling to try to do, whether by joining resistance groups and protesting, risking death by trying to migrate without authorization to a hostile country, choosing social death by living truncated lives, or, even joining one of the myriad organized crime groups that operate in Honduras.

NOTES

1. There is also reason to suspect that the remarkable decline in homicide rates is, at least in part, a reflection of a change in how statistics are kept. Additionally, at least part of the security gains come from an entrenching of organized crime groups' control over certain territories. Internal border lines have hardened, leading to a decline in homicides. Rather than indicating that criminal groups are weakened, however, this suggests a deepening of their power and control.

2. Much of this architecture of security has been supported by the United States, in the name of fighting drug trafficking and organized crime. The State Department,

the Drug Enforcement Administration, and the Department of Defense fund and train Honduran security forces (Meyer 2019).

3. The PMOP were authorized by an order of congress in 2013 when Juan Orlando Hernandez was the president of congress, then formed in 2014 when Hernandez began his presidency.

4. These are dynamics I observed during participant observation in gang-controlled neighborhoods in Honduras. For a portrait of similar dynamics in El Salvador, see Martínez d'Aubuisson 2019.

5. For a review of the theory that builds on Patterson's work, see Králová 2015. For a critique of the expansion of Patterson's theory, see Brown 2009.

6. Cycles of migration and deportation can result in not just existential homelessness but something akin to international homelessness (Brigden 2018, 183).

REFERENCES

Agencia EFE. 2019. "Honduras registra 104 099 Migrantes deportados hasta el 13 de diciembre del 2019." *El comercio*, December 20. https://www.elcomercio.com/ actualidad/honduras-cifras-migrantes-deportados-2019.html.

Amnesty International. 2016. "Home Sweet Home? Honduras, Guatemala and El Salvador's Role in a Deepening Refugee Crisis." https://www.amnesty.org/download/ Documents/AMR0148652016ENGLISH.PDF.

Barría, Cecilia. 2019. "Desigualdad en América Latina: Los países en los que más ha disminuido (y la paradoja del que más la ha reducido)." *BBC News*, November 25. https://www.bbc.com/mundo/noticias-50255301.

Blue, Ethan. 2015. "Strange Passages: Carceral Mobility and the Liminal in the Catastrophic History of American Deportation." *National Identities* 17 (2): 175–194.

Boehm, Deborah. 2011. "US-Mexico Mixed Migration in an Age of Deportation: An Inquiry into the Transnational Circulation of Violence." *Refugee Survey Quarterly* 30 (1): 1–21.

———. 2016. *Returned: Going and Coming in an Age of Deportation*. Oakland: University of California Press.

Brigden, Noelle. 2018. *The Migrant Passage: Clandestine Journeys from Central America*. Ithaca, NY: Cornell University Press.

Brown, Vincent. 2009. "Social Death and Political Life in the Study of Slavery." *American Historical Review* 114 (5): 1231–1249.

Burman, Jenny. 2006. "Absence, 'Removal,' and Everyday Life in the Diasporic City Antidetention/Antideportation Activism in Montréal." *Space and Culture* 9 (3): 279–293.

Burrell, Jennifer L., and Ellen Moodie. 2013. *Central America in the New Millennium: Living Transition and Reimagining Democracy*. New York: Berghahn Books.

Cacho, Lisa Marie. 2012. *Social Death: Racialized Rightlessness and the Criminalization of the Unprotected*. New York: New York University Press.

Card, Claudia. 2003. "Genocide and Social Death." *Hypatia* 18 (1): 63–79.

Carter, Jon Horne. 2014. "Gothic Sovereignty: Gangs and Criminal Community in a Honduran Prison." *South Atlantic Quarterly* 113 (3): 475–502.

———. 2019. "Revolution Betrayed." *Fieldsights*, January 23. https://culanth.org/ fieldsights/revolution-betrayed.

CEPAL (Comisión Económica para América Latina y el Caribe). 2019. "Panorama social de América Latina, 2019." https://www.cepal.org/es/publicaciones/44969-panora ma-social-america-latina-2019.

Charles, Christopher A. D. 2010. "The Reintegration of Criminal Deportees in Society." *Dialectical Anthropology* 34 (4): 501–511.

Chavez, Ernest K. 2019. "Intrusions of Violence: Afro-Pessimism and Reading Social Death beyond Solitary Confinement." *Theoretical Criminology*, May 8. https:// doi.org/10.1177/1362480619846132.

Chayes, Sarah. 2017. *When Corruption Is the Operating System: The Case of Honduras.* Washington, DC: Carnegie Endowment for International Peace. https://carnegieen dowment.org/files/Chayes_Corruption_Final_updated.pdf.

Coutin, Susan Bibler. 2010. "Exiled by Law: Deportation and the Inviability of Life." In *The Deportation Regime: Sovereignty, Space, and the Freedom of Movement*, edited by Nicholas De Genova and Nathalie Peutz, 351–370. Durham, NC: Duke University Press.

———. 2016. *Exiled Home: Salvadoran Transnational Youth in the Aftermath of Violence.* Durham, NC: Duke University Press.

David, Danilo A. 2019. "Tasa de subempleo invisible en Honduras alcanza casi el 50%." *Diario la Prensa*, May 17. https://www.laprensa.hn/economia/1285343-410/tasa -subempleo-invisible-honduras-alcanza-50.

Drotbohm, Heike, and Ines Hasselberg. 2015. "Deportation, Anxiety, Justice: New Ethnographic Perspectives." *Journal of Ethnic and Migration Studies* 41 (4): 551–562.

Euraque, Darío A. 1997. *Reinterpreting the Banana Republic: Region and State in Honduras, 1870–1972.* Chapel Hill: University of North Carolina Press.

Frank, Dana. 2018. *The Long Honduran Night: Resistance, Terror, and the United States in the Aftermath of the Coup.* Chicago: Haymarket Books.

Frank-Vitale, Amelia. 2019. "Rolling the Windows Up: On (Not) Researching Violence and Strategic Distance." *Geopolitics* 26 (1): 139–158.

Giroux, Henry A. 2011. "Neoliberalism and the Death of the Social State: Remembering Walter Benjamin's Angel of History." *Social Identities* 17 (4): 587–601.

Gledhill, John. 2004. "Neoliberalism." In *A Companion to the Anthropology of Politics*, edited by David Nugent and Joan Vincent, 332–348. Malden, MA: Blackwell.

Goldstein, Daniel M. 2010. "Toward a Critical Anthropology of Security." *Current Anthropology* 51 (4): 487–517.

Guenther, Lisa. 2013. *Solitary Confinement: Social Death and Its Afterlives.* Minneapolis: University of Minnesota Press.

Gutiérrez Rivera, Lirio. 2013. *Territories of Violence: State, Marginal Youth, and Public Security in Honduras.* New York: Palgrave Macmillan.

Hage, Ghassan. 2003. "'Comes a Time We Are All Enthusiasm': Understanding Palestinian Suicide Bombers in Times of Exighophobia." *Public Culture* 15 (1): 65–89.

Haugaard, Lisa. 2017. "Public Security in Honduras: Who Can Citizens Trust?" Latin American Working Group. https://www.lawg.org/public-security-in-honduras-who -can-citizens-trust/.

Igarape Institute. n.d. "Homicide Monitor." Accessed February 23, 2021. https:// igarape.org.br/en/apps/homicide-monitor/.

Jonsson, Annika. 2015. "Post-mortem Social Death—Exploring the Absence of the Deceased." *Contemporary Social Science* 10 (3): 284–295.

Králová, Jana. 2015. "What Is Social Death?" *Contemporary Social Science* 10 (3): 235–248.

Long, Clara. 2014. "'You Don't Have Rights Here': US Border Screening and Returns of Central Americans to Risk of Serious Harm." Human Rights Watch, October. https://www.refworld.org/docid/5594f30b4.html.

Martin, Bridget, and Beth Geglia. 2019. "Korean Tigers in Honduras: Urban Economic Zones as Spatial Ideology in International Policy Transfer Networks." *Political Geography* 74 (October). https://doi.org/10.1016/j.polgeo.2019.102041.

Martínez d'Aubuisson, Juan José. 2019. *A Year Inside MS-13: See, Hear, and Shut Up.* Translated by Natascha Elena Uhlmann. Washington, DC: OR Books.

Meyer, Peter J. 2019. "Honduras: Background and U.S. Relations." Congressional Research Service, July 22. https://crsreports.congress.gov/product/pdf/RL/RL34027/65.

Mogelson, Luke. 2015. "The Deported." *New York Times*, December 9. https://www.nytimes.com/2015/12/13/magazine/the-deported.html.

Moreno, Darío. 1994. *The Struggle for Peace in Central America.* Gainesville: University Press of Florida.

Mulkay, Michael, and John Ernst. 1991. "The Changing Profile of Social Death." *European Journal of Sociology/Archives Européennes de Sociologie* 32 (1): 172–196.

Patterson, Orlando. 1982. *Slavery and Social Death: A Comparative Study.* Cambridge, MA: Harvard University Press.

Peter, Kankonde Bukasa. 2010. "Transnational Family Ties, Remittance Motives, and Social Death among Congolese Migrants: A Socio-anthropological Analysis." *Journal of Comparative Family Studies* 41 (2): 225–243.

Peutz, Nathalie. 2006. "Embarking on an Anthropology of Removal." *Current Anthropology* 47 (2): 217–241.

Phillips, James J. 2015. *Honduras in Dangerous Times: Resistance and Resilience.* Lanham, MD: Lexington Books.

Pine, Adrienne. 2008. *Working Hard, Drinking Hard: On Violence and Survival in Honduras.* Berkeley: University of California Press.

———. 2019. "Forging an Anthropology of Neoliberal Fascism." *Public Anthropologist* 1 (1): 20–40.

Price, Joshua M. 2015. *Prison and Social Death.* New Brunswick, NJ: Rutgers University Press.

Rainsford, Cat. 2019. "Honduras Police Purge May Be Derailed by Alternative Agenda." *InSight Crime*, July 26. https://www.insightcrime.org/news/brief/honduras-police-purge-derailed-alternative-agenda/.

Reiter, Keramet, and Susan Bibler Coutin. 2017. "Crossing Borders and Criminalizing Identity: The Disintegrated Subjects of Administrative Sanctions." *Law and Society Review* 51 (3): 567–601.

Rivera Hernández, Raúl Diego. 2017. "Making Absence Visible: The Caravan of Central American Mothers in Search of Disappeared Migrants." *Latin American Perspectives* 44 (5): 108–126.

Robinson, William I. 2003. *Transnational Conflicts: Central America, Social Change, and Globalization.* London: Verso.

Sachetti, Maria. 2018. "'Death Is Waiting for Him.'" *Washington Post*, December 6. https://www.washingtonpost.com/graphics/2018/local/asylum-deported-ms-13-honduras/.

Salomón, Leticia. 2012. "Honduras: A History That Repeats Itself." North American Congress on Latin America, March 22. https://nacla.org/article/honduras-history-repeats-itself.

Shipley, Tyler. 2016. "Enclosing the Commons in Honduras." *American Journal of Economics and Sociology* 75 (2): 456–487.

Snow, James. 2016. "Claudia Card's Concept of Social Death: A New Way of Looking at Genocide." *Metaphilosophy* 47 (4–5): 607–626.

Steele, Caroline, David C. Kidd, and Emanuele Castano. 2015. "On Social Death: Ostracism and the Accessibility of Death Thoughts." *Death Studies* 39 (1): 19–23.

Stillman, Sarah. 2018. "When Deportation Is a Death Sentence." *New Yorker*, January 8. https://www.newyorker.com/magazine/2018/01/15/when-deportation-is-a-death-sentence.

Sullivan, Tim. 2019. "Denied Asylum, Migrants Return to Place They Fear Most: Home." *Associated Press*, December 29. https://apnews.com/de5424d5e97e2bf769ce53aea791dfd3.

Thomas, Kedron, Kevin Lewis O'Neill, and Thomas Offit. 2011. "Securing the City: An Introduction." In *Securing the City: Neoliberalism, Space, and Insecurity in Postwar Guatemala*, edited by Kedron Thomas and Kevin Lewis O'Neill, 1–21. Durham, NC: Duke University Press.

Tirrell, Lynne. 2016. "Perpetrators and Social Death: A Cautionary Tale." *Metaphilosophy* 47 (4–5): 585–606.

Vigh, Henrik. 2006. "Social Death and Violent Life Chances." In *Navigating Youth, Generating Adulthood: Social Becoming in an African Context*, edited by Catrine Shroff, Mats Utas, and Henrik Vigh, 31–60. Uppsala, Sweden: Nordiska Afrikainstitutet.

———. 2009. "Wayward Migration: On Imagined Futures and Technological Voids." *Ethnos* 74 (1): 91–109.

Wolseth, Jon. 2008. "Everyday Violence and the Persistence of Grief: Wandering and Loss Among Honduran Youths." *Journal of Latin American and Caribbean Anthropology* 13 (2): 311–335.

Ybarra, Megan, and Isaura L. Peña. 2017. "'We Don't Need Money, We Need to Be Together': Forced Transnationality in Deportation's Afterlives." *Geopolitics* 22 (1): 34–50.

12

Miskitu Labor and Immigrant Struggles

U.S. Anti–Central American Policies of Social Death

KARINA ALMA

This chapter examines the intersection of anti–Central American immigration policy and the long-standing neoliberal relationship of the United States with Central America, which entails economic impoverishment and militarization of the isthmus by the United States. The chapter explores the latest iteration of a necropolitical practice in which "the ultimate expression of sovereignty resides . . . in the power and the capacity to dictate who may live and who must die" (Mbembe 2003, 11). Local abuses in Central America link to a broader system of U.S. neocolonial policies that construct Central American lives as disposable in Central America, through Mexico, and within U.S. borders. This chapter considers the current regime of social death for Central Americans and, more specifically, men as a racialized gender aggregate who endure labor violence. The Donald Trump administration's misogynist necropolitical stance hearken to the United States' policies in Central America throughout the twentieth century, which funded genocidal wars and motivated out-migration. I provide historical context for the deadly politics of the present and examine a case study in Nicaragua as part of a historical and geographic continuum of U.S. social death.

Since my focus is on an Afro-Indigenous group in Central America, we can ask: What does the sweet-lobster industry killing Miskitu men in Nicaragua have to do with North America, and what does Miskitu fishermen dying in Nicaragua have to do with Central American immigration? I use the lens "of political ecology . . . to see how seemingly unrelated events like restaurant consumption of lobsters in the United States and deforestation in a Central American rain forest can be related in complex ways" (Dodds 1998, 83). Rather than epistemically delink the region through disciplinary divides, I approach Nicaragua and the United States as deeply interrelated political, economic, and ecological spaces. This allows an exploration of Miskitu social death in lobster commercial fishing as an expression of racial and gender settler (neo)colonialism, which is profoundly related to anti–Central American U.S. immigration policy. Since social death is a lateral stratification by race, class, gender, and citizen marginality from the Global South to the Global North, workers who stay in their countries of origin in the isthmus remain part of the movement of labor and resources heading north.

By relating Miskitu fishermen's labor violence in Nicaragua to the plight of immigrants from Central America, I aim to reveal neoliberalism, forced migration, and U.S. policy as racialized forms of anti–Central American social death. This regime of social death is a continued expression of settler (neo)colonialism, which hinges on the dispossession and extermination of Afro–Latin American and Indigenous populations. In 1868, during the colonization of what is now the western United States, General Phil Sheridan said, "The only good Indian I ever saw was dead" (Brown 2012, 170). Genocidal actions on Indigenous peoples correlated with the U.S. government's gaining of land and resources (Dunbar-Ortiz 2014). Twenty years later, Theodore Roosevelt repeated the sentiment: "I don't go so far as to think that the only good Indians are the dead Indians, but I believe nine out of every ten are, and I shouldn't like to inquire too closely into the case of the tenth" (Di Silvestro 2011, 192; see also Hagedorn 1921). A key figure of colonization, Roosevelt connected anti-indigeneity from the United States to Panama. Settler colonialists' anti-indigeneity was and is not constrained to the country they first occupy but becomes part of a worldview integrated into law and the economy locally, nationally, and globally. Drawing historical and hemispheric linkages, Roxanne Dunbar-Ortiz explains, "The integral link between Wounded Knee in 1890 and Wounded Knee in 1973 suggests a long-overdue reinterpretation of Indigenous-US relations as a template for US imperialism and counterinsurgency wars" (2014, 192). The belief that the lives of Indigenous people are superfluous but their lands and resources are not persists today as they continue to struggle for their lives and communities. The statements are echoed in U.S. anti-immigrant, anti–Central American practice and policy. However, Central Americans are survivors. Hence I close this chapter by underscoring Central Americans' agency in challenging the state's ability to nullify life in Central America and the United States.

Review of Concepts

Sociologist Orlando Patterson (1982) introduced the concept of social death in his transnational and transhistorical study, in which he searched for common patterns of domination in slave societies. He determined that slaves underwent a "profound natal alienation" (1982, 38) that delinked the slave's past and future in space and time, constructing the enslaved as a "genealogical isolate" (5). Natal alienation was foundational to their status as noncitizens. Slaves, whether treated kindly or not, freed or not, lived under "violent domination" as "natally alienated and generally dishonored persons" (13) whose degradation placed them "in a real sense outside the social order" (79). Patterson's concept of social death applies to immigrant labor and the labor of formerly colonized peoples—the current castes of exploitable labor. They are "impossible subjects" (Ngai 2004), as illustrated by Miskitu fishermen's relation to Nicaragua and the United States and by natally alienated Central American migrants who, escaping violent degradation in their home countries, are treated as nonhumans in the United States, their rights systematically denied under the law (see Chapter 10).

Social death is a real condition related to the laws that target undocumented and other criminalized groups and simultaneously exclude them from full legal protection (Cacho 2012, 43). Cecilia Menjívar and Leisy Abrego have explored this positioning through "legal violence . . . embedded in the body of law that, while it purports to have the positive objective of protecting rights or controlling behavior for the general good, simultaneously gives rise to practices that harm a particular social group" (2012, 1387). The concept of *legal violence*, essential to the social death regime, complements Giorgio Agamben's concept of *homo sacer*. The term means both "sacred man" and "accursed man," which Agamben defines as a person with "a bare life stripped of every right by virtue of the fact that anyone can kill him without committing homicide; he can save himself only in perpetual flight or a foreign land." In exile, *homo sacer* remains "at every instant exposed to an unconditioned threat of death" (1998, 103).[1] Social death relies on the invested ignorance of an apathetic public that perpetually consents to the systematic violation of a group of people at home, while migrating, and at the location of resettlement.

This geographical-temporal continuum of violence is experienced by groups pushed into the margins of society as racial others, a long-standing U.S. practice embedded in social structure. The social death of Central American immigrants in the United States today links to the historical social-cleansing efforts of U.S. nation-building, such as the genocide against Indigenous nations in North America, which continues. Social cleansing is apparent in state policy that works against immigrant populations of color.

For example, the California Civil Practice Act of 1850, Section 14, concerning crime and punishment; *People v. Hall* (1854); and the denial of Manuel Dominguez as an eyewitness in court (1857) gave impunity to white males to kill people of color because these acts and cases established that convicting a white person of murdering a Chinese, Black, mulatto, or Indigenous person (including a Mexican) could be achieved only through credible white witnesses or other evidence (Acuña 1999, 144). Codifying impunity for the dominant group allowed de jure and de facto conditions for the loss of life and denied justice for racial others. One cannot lose sight of the fact that today's documented and undocumented migration from Central America manifests from the long history of U.S. imperialism both within its borders and on the isthmus.

Miskitu Social Death and U.S. Immigration Policy

Before the rise of Central American undocumented migration, the United States attempted to reconstruct the region into an offshore slave plantation through colonizing companies like the United Fruit Company; the Panama Canal, which instituted Jim Crow racial-spatial divides and labor inequalities; and political takeovers like that by William Walker, who forcibly became president of Nicaragua from 1856 to 1857. As president, Walker wanted to institute slavery, create an English-speaking country without formal colonial status, and build a canal in Nicaragua for the profit of the United States. His effort included recruiting colonists: "A decree of colonization . . . provided that every [Anglo-American] immigrant to Nicaragua should be entitled to two hundred and fifty acres of land, and that immigrants with families should receive a hundred additional acres" (Scroggs 1905, 801), which was demonstrative of the dispossession caused by settler colonialism. Walker was captured and executed by Honduran forces in 1860; however, Anglo-American efforts to colonize the land of Central America did not die with him. Although Miskitu have been decentered in Nicaraguan history and U.S. relations, as Kendra McSweeney states, "foreign economic interests in the region—from the 19th-century . . . to the 20th-century defense of U.S. business—have been inseparable from the international political struggles in which the Mosquitia's[2] peoples have been bound up" (2004, 640).

In 1898, the U.S. military occupied Nicaragua to protect U.S. banana industries. Hyperexploitative conditions in this industry would motivate the Sandino Rebellion, which included Miskitu support. The series of occupations of Honduras and Nicaragua by U.S. marines (in the Banana Wars) did not cease until Augusto Cesár Sandino was murdered in 1934, representing the death of the Sandino Rebellion against Nicaraguans colluding with U.S. interests and American occupation. *Sandinismo* promoted the Indo-Hispano population discursively and gained Miskitu guerilla support with the promise of land and autonomy. However, Sandinismo became coopted as a "variant of official mestizo nationalism," especially in excluding Black and Indigenous Nicaraguans (Hooker 2005, 27). The United States left Nicaragua with a leader sure to comply with U.S. business interests: Anastasio Somoza García (Booth and Walker 1999, 37). He and his sons would establish a dictatorship (1934 to 1979) lasting until the Nicaraguan revolution brought the Sandinista administration to power. Historical memory influenced the Miskitu decision to side with the anti-Sandinista contras during the Contra War (Moore 1986, 138). However, "Miskitu separatists discovered that if the Sandinistas tended to be racist and colonialist, the Contras . . . [were] even more so" (143). The contras, mostly mestizo far-right nationalists, were funded by the Ronald Reagan administration, as justified by the Reagan Doctrine of supporting anticommunist insurgents, which was used during the Iran-Contra Affair to violate the U.S. Boland Amendment (1982 and 1984 appropriations attachments prohibiting funding to overthrow the Nicaraguan government).

President Ronald Reagan ignored contra abuse of Miskitu and used the Miskitu instrumentally in his political rhetoric, framing Sandinista defeat as a protection of Miskitu human rights in the fight against communism. In a presidential address on May 9, 1984, he stressed Central America's economic importance to the United States and the region's proximity to U.S. borders, and he characterized its revolutions as puppeteered by Cuba and the Soviet Union. He also claimed that the Sandinista administration was attempting "to wipe out an entire culture, the Miskito Indians, thousands of whom have been slaughtered, or herded into detention camps. . . . Their villages, churches, and crops have been burned" (Reagan 1984). His seeming concern for Sandinista "virtual genocide against the Miskito Indians" (Reagan 1985), however, did not apply to other Indigenous and Central American lives in general.

At the same time that the United States was funding Nicaraguan contras, it was also funding Salvadoran and Guatemalan governments fighting guerilla forces. Far-right conservative elites and their (para)militaries enacted scorched-earth policies that included innumerable atrocities, especially on rural and Indigenous people such as Mayas in Guatemala (Rothenberg 2012), whom Reagan was not interested in protecting. Though hypocritical, he was being strategic in displaying an Indigenous people to meet his end. His discourse rationalized funding of the contras and a U.S. embargo against the Sandinista administration as saving (though actually starving) all Nicaraguans in order to appear to stand on the side of human rights. By invoking the U.S. role as the (white) savior, protector of the hemisphere, as established by the Monroe Doctrine, the U.S. positioned itself (again) as the civilizing force that would bring an end to Sandinista abuses against the Miskitu, keeping in place U.S.-condoned governments. Exemplary of neocolonialism, U.S. political relations with Nicaragua were reframed as benevolent and blameless, whitewashing decades of direct and calculated occupations, coups, and counterinsurgency campaigns.

Then, as now, the legal exclusion of Central Americans seeking asylum, including those from Indigenous populations, reveals that human rights for Central Americans was and is not a primary concern for past or current administrations. Even policies that seem pro-immigrant continue to be anti–Central American. For example, in the 1980s, migration spiked because of the civil wars in Nicaragua, Guatemala, and El Salvador (O'Connor, Batalova, and Bolter 2019), yet Central Americans were systemically denied asylum (García 2006; Coutin 2006). Central Americans who emigrated were put on an undocumented track that denied them citizenship and gave them only temporary status through Deferred Enforced Departure and Temporary Protected Status (Coutin 2006; Menjívar 2006), which Menjívar names as a form of *liminal legality*. Even the Immigration Reform and Control Act (IRCA), or Simpson-Mazzoli Act, of 1986 can also be considered anti–Central American. IRCA required proof of documented status necessary for labor through the I-9 form and penalized employers who knowingly hired undocumented immigrants. The act provided a pathway to legalization for people who entered the United States before January 1, 1982, and who had resided here continuously, among other criteria.[3] However, apart from this legalization program, the law was punitive and criminalizing. It was meant to curtail undocumented migration by increasing border security.

Though IRCA documented 3.2 million immigrants, 75 percent of whom were Mexican (Chishti et al. 2011), the new requirements in effect promoted undocumented migration or shadow migration henceforth. Reagan proclaimed that the act would "enable unauthorized immigrants to come out of the shadows and 'step into the sunlight'" (Chishti, Meissner, and Bergeron 2011). However, Reagan pushed for IRCA as his administration was both openly and covertly funding the wars in the isthmus that in turn were pushing populations from Central America to the United States. Therefore, I contend that 1982 was the beginning of a concerted effort to block the entry of displaced Central Americans specifically.

The 1980s represented a time of escalating violence in the isthmus that would increase migration to the United States. Guatemala's thirty-six-year war began in 1960, but 1982 marked the height of *la violencia*, when multitudes fled, especially from Maya communities, because of state-sponsored genocidal violence (Alvarado, Estrada, and Hernández 2017, 10–11). In El Salvador, the twelve-year civil war began in 1980, when the Farabundo

Martí National Liberation Front (FMLN) coalesced from five guerilla groups; it was the year of the assassination of Archbishop (now Saint) Óscar Arnulfo Romero, the Sumpul River Massacre (May 14–15), and the rape and murder of four American Maryknoll nuns (December 2). The contra rebel attack against the newly established Sandinista administration in Nicaragua began in 1982. Most Central Americans fleeing these wars were not continuously present in the United States *before* 1982, and those arriving in 1982 or after would not be given a path to citizenship through IRCA. Postwar, migration from these countries and Honduras continued as the region became increasingly destabilized through neoliberal projects and militarization no longer framed as a battle against communism but presented as a war against drug trafficking and gang violence. Thus, because IRCA denied asylum to Central Americans, they were and are not protected from social death in their originating countries, en route (see Vogt 2018), at the U.S. border, or, if granted entry, within its borders.

Central American people deemed disposable have been positioned as such not only because of their relationship to the law (in Central American countries and the United States) but also and more effectively in relation to capitalism. Central America's subordination in the hemispheric economy dominated by the United States puts Central Americans in a position to be used and considered disposable. If the Global South is presented as fringe to the Global North, so are its people. If they are understood as workers rather than immigrants, once they reach the United States, their exclusion from legal status reveals how they are situated at the base of the global economy.

Central Americans contend with social death in the country of origin and as migrants. Capitalist neoliberalism is a global condition, meaning that *homo sacer* does not need to be in exile to be reduced to *bare life*. For example, Afro-Indigenous Miskitu in Nicaragua live lives that are simultaneously local (as they live out marginalizations of race, class, and gender regulated by the state) and global as direct employees or subcontracted labor for U.S. corporations. In turn, U.S. enterprise strongly influences Nicaragua's politics, labor, and economic market. Moreover, Miskitu fishermen's struggle is one of *bare life* as they are reduced to biology as bodies available for consumption by the commercial lobster industry.

Miskitu at the Edge of Nation, at the Edge of Life

Dive accidents among Miskitu fishermen are estimated at 120 a year, with around 20 of those incidents being fatal largely because of the bends, or decompression sickness (Jorge 2013). Decompression sickness results from sudden decompression that causes nitrogen bubbles to develop in the tissues of the body, resulting in pain in the muscles and joints, cramps, numbness, nausea, and in the worst situation, paralysis. Safety recommendations include limiting the dive depth and the "number of dives a person makes in a day" (Associated Press 2018). However, worker safety is ignored on the Miskitu coast. In the 1990s, "a study cited by the Pan American Health Organization reported there were around 9,000 divers in the Mosquitia, and around 4,200—47 percent—were disabled by decompression sickness," with nearly 100 percent having suffered decompression symptoms (Jorge 2013). Regardless of the dismal statistics, "lobster fishing is one of the few legal employment opportunities" for Miskitu men (Dennis 2003, 171). The gendered labor violence it enacts is not only "crippling the divers [but also] contributing to drug addiction" (171); I interpret this situation as an expression of structural social death.

More than 90 percent of the lobsters caught in Nicaragua are exported to the United States, while seafood restaurants like Red Lobster import 40 percent of lobsters caught in Honduras (Jorge 2013). It is a vital economy for Nicaragua, which has led to overfishing of the spiny lobster. Because of the decline of the lobster population, Honduras and Nicaragua have agreed since 2009 to close the lobster fishing season from May 1 to July 30 (World Wildlife Fund 2010). The overexploitation of the lobster corresponds with the abuse of Miskitu male bodies. Both species—one lobster, one Afro-Indigenous human—are in danger of extermination.

Miskitu are an Afro-Indigenous group estimated at 180,000 inhabiting the Muskitia, a rain forest that extends from Black River, Honduras, to Bluefields, Nicaragua. Miskitu inhabit a region that encompasses two nations and thus have borders imposed on them. Though both countries have a lobster industry, lobsters cannot be bound by the border; rather, they move freely outside the boundaries of national territories. The depletion of lobster in Nicaragua affects other habitats and species, analogous to the ways the exploitation of Miskitu men relates to the greater Central American migration. The industry is attempting to treat Atlantic and Caribbean fishing as an interconnected economic and ecological space, as shown by regional workshops that bring together three organizations—the Western Central Atlantic Fishery Commission (WECAFC), the Caribbean Regional Fisheries Mechanism (CRFM), and the Organización del Sector Pesquero y Acuícola del Istmo Centroamericano (OSPESCA; Organization for Central American Fisheries and Aquaculture Sector)—with a focus on flying fish, queen conch, and spiny lobster. The first report to come out of these workshops underscored not only shared catch and economic data but a consideration of the species whose "biological data were the most lacking" (Food and Agriculture Organization of the United Nations 2016, viii). A 2018 report stated, "Lobster is a shared resource, which implies the need for all countries in the region to collaborate to ensure the sustainability of fishing and the conservation of the species" (Food and Agriculture Organization of the United Nations 2018, 37). Central American, Caribbean, and American organizations are collaborating to conserve the lobster species and its commercial industry. Protecting Miskitu lives should be equally important.

Miskitu labor in Nicaragua cannot be delinked from a sociopolitical and economic whole that may affect, and be affected by, labor activities in Central America, the Caribbean, and the United States. Understanding how people labor in Central America might motivate U.S. consumers to protect not only the lobster in the Muskitia but the labor rights of Miskitus. However, settler colonialism necessitates a willful ignorance (Smith 2005, 121). Consumers rarely care to know where the lobster comes from, how it is affecting fishing and species in specific regions, how its consumption affects its life and death, and how its consumption affects the life and death of Miskitu divers and their families.

The genocide of autochthonous societies and ecosystems is integral to the neocolonial settler mind-set. Thus, Miskitu peoples have always stood at the edge of the Honduran and Nicaraguan nations. Even under the Sandinista government, Miskitu in Nicaragua were granted nominal protection. Fifteen thousand of the 125,000 Miskitu became refugees fleeing to Honduras, where they were also unwanted (Farah 1987; Bonner 1982). In Nicaragua their villages were destroyed, and men were violently conscripted by the Sandinistas (Farah 1987). Under the Nicaraguan Agrarian Reform Law, communal lands were supposed to be protected for the Miskitu population, yet their civil and human rights continued to be abused even after the YATAMA party (Yapti Tasba Masraka Nanih Aslatakanka/Sons of Mother Earth) was formed in 1987 as "an opposition party to the Nicaraguan left and the right" (Herlihy and Spencer 2016) and after negotiations between Miskitu leader Brooklyn Rivera and President Daniel Ortega led to the creation in 1987 of the North and South Caribbean Coast Autonomous Regions (RACCN and RACCS). Miskitu developed the *saneamiento* movement to stop mestizo colonists from settling Indigenous and Afro-descendant lands. However, "despite the 1987 law granting autonomy (Law 28) and the communal property law (Law 445, passed 2003), settlers have continuously invaded their lands and now illegally occupy half of the Muskitia region" (Herlihy and Spencer 2016). To date, Miskitu are killed "with almost complete impunity" (Herlihy 2016). Nicaraguan colonists and the government continue to use violence, including murder, to end Miskitu resistance, displaying how mestizo settler land-grabbing goes hand-in-hand with the legal right to eradicate Indigenous people. Settler neocolonialism is also implicit in the exploitation of Miskitu men's labor. The Sub-Ocean Safety Foundation (SOS) founder, Robert Izdepski (1994), explains that the lobster diving commercial industry was established on the Miskitu coast but never opened for non-Miskitus because of its danger: "Islanders never dove," he states. "Instead, an illiterate group of Indians . . . were given dive gear and put to work without any diving instruction at all. As a result, thousands of Miskito Indians have been . . . killed." I posit that Miskitu men being incapacitated or killed through labor facilitates the continued usurpation of their lands.

The documentary *My Village, My Lobster*, by directors Brad Allgood and Joshua Wolff (2012), follows the lives of several Miskitu deep-sea divers off the coast of Nicaragua, exposing the devastating effects of commercial lobster fishing. The documentary shows the broken equipment and shoddy air tanks the men work with, but more importantly, it provides their testimonies, including those of survivors of decompression sickness. For example, Jesús experienced the bends and now has neurological damage but decided to return to fishing lobster. "I know the doctor told him he shouldn't dive. . . . But we have so many necessities. . . . We have no help. I'm sad when he's out in the sea. . . . But what am I going to do? I have nothing," explained his wife (0:28:03–0:28:31). When a fisherman is injured or suffers paralysis, no one—not the subcontractor, the American company, or the Nicaraguan government—offers any form of work and health compensation. Bodies and family units are thus consumed by globalized labor, driven by multinational bottom lines. Clearly, the injured fisherman out at sea and the fragmented and abandoned family are examples of natal alienation as part of a social death with gendered and racialized dimensions.

In the film, another injured diver attempts to rehabilitate himself as he tries to relearn how to walk using homemade parallel bars. With wobbly legs he drags his feet while a fellow fisherman states, "When you're injured like that, they don't help you at all. How are you going to eat? . . . You are left to suffer" (Allgood and Wolff 2012, 0:30:27–0:30:35). When a worker relearns to walk, he must choose between a life of utter destitution or the risks of returning to commercial lobster diving. If he chooses not to go back to work, the head of household in cases like these becomes a dependent straining an already economically impoverished household. Men who have suffered bodily and neurological harm, including paralysis, are sometimes deserted by their wife as she seeks her and their children's survival, treating the husband as already symbolically dead. Thus, their suffering as individuals and as a family is all-encompassing.

Nicaragua has only one hyperbaric chamber, which exacerbates the issue (see Corn Island Dive Center, n.d.; Midlands Diving Chamber, n.d.). Hyperbaric treatment reduces nitrogen gas bubbles in the body and blood, lessening the extent of injury by reducing their size and increasing the possibility for their elimination. Immediate treatment is vital. However, subcontractors sometimes delay bringing an injured fisherman to shore, so as to not lose their lobster quota. The film shows a montage of men in home-made and makeshift wheelchairs, which brings to mind Central American immigrants maimed by *La Bestia* (the Beast) trains in Mexico. Riding atop *La Bestia*, migrants suffer loss of limbs and are returned to countries like Honduras worse off in every possible way (Latin American Working Group, n.d.). This is yet another example of the way Central American labor is treated as disposable and exploitable. Miskitu workers are aware of the blatant brutality involved in a capitalist system that denies their humanity. For example, a fisherman in the film explains in reference to injured workers, "Their bodies deteriorate to the point that you can find maggots in their wounds." He continues, "When your body is healthy, they need you. But when you get injured, they throw you out like trash" (Allgood and Wolff 2012, 0:36:11–0:36:26). The comparison of wounded male bodies of color to trash is literal and symbolic. Life as trash is also shown by the unmarked mass graves of undocumented immigrants, many assumed to be Central American, buried in trash bags in Brooks County, Texas (Goodman 2015), illustrating how the devaluation of life extends beyond death.

The most devastating testimony in the film is that of Andrew, a paralyzed diver who was injured after ten years of diving (Allgood and Wolff 2012, 0:36:57). Lying bare-chested on a wooden floor with a sheet wrapped around his lower torso, he explains, "I am in so much pain, like I'm dying" (0:38:09). He suffers from fever and headaches and worries that the wound in his lower torso is infected. He exposes an open deep-tissue wound. He appears disgusted. "He doesn't realize when he urinates," explains a fellow fisherman (0:39:01). Representative of other cases, Andrew experiences bare life as a life denied political existence. Agamben similarly explains the bare life of men in Nazi concentration camps:

> Lacking almost all the rights and expectations that we customarily attribute to human existence, [they] were still biologically alive, they came to be situated in a limit zone between life and death . . . in which they were no longer anything but bare life. . . . The interval between death sentence and execution delimits an extratemporal and extraterritorial threshold in which the human body is separated from its normal political status and abandoned, in a state of exception, to the most extreme misfortunes. (Agamben 1998, 91)

While Andrew will die as a human with personhood, he is already occupying the space of nonbeing for the state. The nation-state not only neglects him but also, by dispossessing his people and positioning him at the margins of belonging, creates the conditions for Global North corporations to strip Miskitu fishermen of their land and basic human rights, abuse their flesh and minds, and ultimately allow those like Andrew to decompose alone and alienated from family and community.

Resistance

When one considers that Miskitu commercial fishermen are Afro-Indigenous men, the nexus of anti-Black and anti-Indigenous racism becomes apparent as an integral part of the structural condition of their particular gendered subjection to social death. In 2009, as part of a Central America–wide agreement, governments acknowledged the human and environmental harm resulting from commercial lobster fishing and committed to ban it by 2011, later extended to 2013 and then to 2016. Though talks among workers, international organizations, commercial diving companies, and the government are ongoing, no solution has been reached. The men continue to be killed by an industry that profits the United States and extends U.S. and Nicaraguan neocolonial erasure of Afro-Indigenous peoples.

Miskitu continue to negotiate their survival in relation to neoliberalism. As John Moore explains, economic development amounts to "another round of colonialism by foreigners, in which the Miskitus would once again take the role of wage workers and have no say in the plan of development" (1986, 142). In the context of cycles of economic booms and busts (Helms 1986) that have historically defined the Miskitu economy, they have limited labor options. However, other Indigenous communities' strategies of autonomy serve as examples of resistance against the social death brought by global capital.

The Rama Indigenous group is protected under the Nicaraguan constitution, yet its Bangkukuk Taik community faces displacement by land developers and representatives from the Nicaraguan government with promises of relocation to Bluefields. The Rama community is fighting against social death by attempting to minimize the role that capitalism has in Bangkukuk Taik. A Rama woman explains:

> Bluefields is not so good—too much sickness, and it is bad, so they [Rama] want to be here. . . . [In] Bluefields, everything is money, and if we don't get money, we can't eat. . . . In here we don't buy nothing, so we get plenty fresh fish, we plant, and we eat in tranquility, nobody bother us. (Bangkukuk Taik 2015, 0:6:34–0:6:45)

Unlike the Miskitu on the northern coast of Nicaragua, Rama of Bangkukuk Taik have access to ecosystems that provide sustainable subsistence, and so they do not rely on capitalism to survive. As the interviewee explains, they sustain themselves by practicing a subsistence-based Indigenous way of life. This form of life runs counter to a capitalist system that destroys biodiversity, including the existence and diversity of Afro-Indigenous communities.

Survival entails resistance rather than integration into neoliberal projects that are part of an ongoing history of globalization initiated by the colonization of the Americas, exacerbated by U.S. imperialism, and that continues now with development projects from Asia and Canada that strip people of their lands and resources. From the late 1800s to today, U.S. policies have contributed to political instability and violence in Central America and have displaced populations in and beyond the region, increasing out-migration. According to Daniel Connolly, Aaron Montes, and Lauren Villagran (2019), 590,000 Central Americans arrived in the United States from December 2018 to September 2019.

Though Miskitu resistance to colonization is ongoing, Miskitu migration has not been well researched. Available reporting reveals that Miskitu are migrating for reasons not only of racial and gendered labor exploitation but also of gender violence.[4] Miskitu marginalization is multiplied when gender identity, sexuality, or both are persecuted by a homophobic and transphobic nation-state. Joselyn's testimony, taken by María Inés Taracena (2018), exemplifies this point. Joselyn was part of a 2018 caravan called Arcoíris 17 (Rainbow 17), which was formed by migrants who had faced gender violence in their home countries in Central America. They joined together as a resistance collective in response to gender abuses in Mexico and later while in U.S. detention. Joselyn, like other migrants who continually face social death, denounces it. She asserts her humanity in claiming her right to migrate and seek asylum, stating, "To us, seeking this protection is not a crime. . . . The day we turned ourselves in . . . we were treated like animals. . . . We were handcuffed at the wrists, the hips and ankles. We didn't eat all day" (Taracena 2018). Joselyn testifies to being trafficked in Mexico, an extension of her condemnation of social death in Central America, Mexico, and the United States. As members of Arcoíris 17 affirm throughout Taracena's article, the lesbian, gay, bisexual, transgender, and queer (LGBTQ) group strategically used the visibility of the caravan, the group, and the act of migration as a form of resistance. Further research is needed on Miskitu migration as a means to escape political instability; sexual, gender, and racial violence; and neocolonial displacement. This lack of research and platforms for Miskitu voices itself imposes a form of structural nonexistence on the Miskitu that will continue their elimination.

Regardless of the pervasive power of the interstate system, flight as fight represents agency, and though migrants are denied heroism by the state, they remain heroic to communities who ally with their quest for a good life, to which all humans are entitled. As people within a social movement, conscious of human rights, Indigenous rights, Black lives, gender and LGBTQ rights, and so on, they can exercise the power of human choice (Pallares 2015) to migrate and to challenge the construction of immigrants as villains, revealing it for what it is: the epistemic violence enacted by a privileged group on a racially marginalized group. Moreover, even when undocumented migrants are denied the right to vote in their destination country, their decision to migrate itself is a form of civil disobedience responding to the social death within the law (Rocha 2010). If the migrant caravans gained sensationalist attention from 2016 to 2019, it is because they are vocal about what they want and need (Pallares and Flores-Gonzalez 2010). Blocks were set up by the Trump administration, yet neither its zero-tolerance policy nor the joint U.S.-Mexico Southern Border Plan for the Guatemala-Mexico border has stopped Central American migration to the United States. While the policies have made the migrant trek more treacherous (Greven 2018), the institutional effort to keep migrants within a bare–life existence has been challenged by the migrants' effort to make their migration visible and vocal, a breathing and living collective body.

Closing

Though the international dynamic of migrants as workers on the move is clearly shown by their acts and claims to migration, the hyperexploitation of workers who remain in countries in Central America is obscured by the fact that they work within their country of birth. However, workers like Miskitu men in Nicaragua are also part of the international labor force. The exploitation of their labor feeds the privileged within the United States. The U.S. relation to Miskitus continues to be one of intimate exploitation enabled by the U.S. relation to Nicaragua, the impoverishment of Nicaragua, and the country's own pervasive mestizo nationalism. Migration is produced by the overexploitation of workers as part of the settler colonial project. For this reason, we cannot continue to compartmentalize labor in Central America as unrelated to Central Americans laboring in the United States. As we move forward to the quarter mark of the twenty-first century, we must conceptualize new forms of national belonging and crossings that will allow hemispheric migration without criminalization, because decriminalization will allow humane migration and begin to eradicate the social death imposed on marginalized Central Americans.

NOTES

1. The Trump administration policy of separating Central American children from their asylum-seeking parents at the U.S.-Mexico border is an example of natal alienation, social death, and legal violence, as well as a crime against humanity. See Gonzalez 2020.

2. Moskitia and Mosquitia have been used interchangeably to refer to the region of La Moskitia. However, Muskitia aligns more properly with the Miskitu people's naming of the region that extends from the easternmost part of Honduras to northeastern Nicaragua.

3. The text of S.1200—Immigration Reform and Control Act of 1986 is available at https://www.congress.gov/bill/99th-congress/senate-bill/1200.

4. Read Portillo Villeda 2015 to grasp the homophobia and transphobia by the Honduran nation-state. See Goett 2017 to understand the sexual violence by security forces against Afro-Creoles in Nicaragua and the strategies people use to resist abuse.

REFERENCES

Acuña, Rudolfo F. 1999. *Occupied America: A History of Chicanos.* 4th ed. New York: Longman.

Agamben, Giorgio. 1998. *Homo Sacer: Sovereign Power and Bare Life.* Translated by Daniel Heller-Roazen. Stanford, CA: Stanford University Press.

Allgood, Brad, and Joshua Wolff, dirs. 2012. *My Village, My Lobster.* New York: Nomading Films.

Alvarado, Karina, Alicia Ivonne Estrada, and Ester E. Hernández. 2017. *U.S. Central Americans: Reconstructing Memories, Struggles, and Communities of Resistance.* Tucson: University of Arizona Press.

Associated Press. 2018. "Divers in Honduras Battle the Bends for Prized Lobsters." *New York Post*, December 27. https://nypost.com/2018/12/27/divers-in-honduras-battle -the-bends-for-prized-lobsters/.

Bangkukuk Taik. 2015. "Bangkukuk Taik, an Indigenous Rama Community and the Nicaraguan Interoceanic Grand Canal." *YouTube*, March 29. https://youtu.be/IIM -D--2lb4.

Bonner, Raymond. 1982. "Miskito Indians Are Focus of Debate." *New York Times*, August 13, p. A3.

Booth, John A., and Thomas A. Walker. 1999. *Understanding Central America.* 3rd ed. Boulder, CO: Westview Press.

Brown, Dee. 2012. *Bury My Heart at Wounded Knee: An Indian History of the American West.* New York: Open Road.

Cacho, Lisa Marie. 2012. *Social Death: Racialized Rightlessness and the Criminalization of the Unprotected.* New York: New York University Press.

Chishti, Muzaffar, Doris Meissner, and Claire Bergeron. 2011. "At Its 25th Anniversary, IRCA's Legacy Lives On." Migration Policy Institute. https://www.migrationpolicy .org/article/its-25th-anniversary-ircas-legacy-lives.

Connolly, Daniel, Aaron Montes, and Lauren Villagran. 2019. "Asylum Seekers in US Face Years of Waiting, Little Chance of Winning Their Cases." *USA Today*, September 25. https://www.usatoday.com/in-depth/news/nation/2019/09/23/immigration -court-asylum-seekers-what-to-expect/2026541001/.

Corn Island Dive Center. n.d. "Corn Island Dive Center." Accessed December 20, 2020. https://www.cornislanddivecenter.com/about/corn-island-dive-center.

Coutin, Susan Bibler. 2006. *Legalizing Moves: Salvadoran Immigrants' Struggle for U.S. Residency.* Ann Arbor: University of Michigan Press.

Dennis, Philip A. 2003. "Cocaine in Miskitu Villages." *Ethnology* 42 (2): 161–172.

Di Silvestro, Roger L. 2011. *Theodore Roosevelt in the Badlands: A Young Politician's Quest for Recovery in the American West.* New York: Walker.

Dodds, David J. 1998. "Lobster in the Rain Forest: The Political Ecology of Miskito Wage Labor and Agricultural Deforestation." *Journal of Political Ecology* 5 (1): 83–108.

Dunbar-Ortiz, Roxanne. 2014. *An Indigenous Peoples' History of the United States*. Boston: Beacon Press.

Farah, Douglass. 1987. "Miskito Indians Forced to Flee: Their Dreams of Returning to Nicaragua Fade." *Los Angeles Times*, August 2. https://www.latimes.com/archives/la-xpm-1987-08-02-mn-738-story.html.

Food and Agriculture Organization of the United Nations. 2016. "Report of the WECAFC-FIRMS Data Workshop." http://www.fao.org/3/a-i5789e.pdf.

———. 2018. "Report of the Second Meeting of the OSPESCA/WECAFC/CRFM/CFMC Working Group on Caribbean Spiny Lobster." http://www.fao.org/3/ca4984b/ca4984b.pdf.

García, María Cristina. 2006. *Seeking Refuge: Central American Migration to Mexico, the United States, and Canada*. Berkeley: University of California Press.

Goett, Jennifer. 2017. "Sexual Violence and Autonomous Politics." In *Black Autonomy: Race, Gender, and Afro-Nicaraguan Activism*, 151–177. Stanford, CA: Stanford University Press.

Gonzalez, Daniel. 2020. "628 Parents of Separated Children Are Still Missing: Here's Why Immigrant Advocates Can't Find Them." *USA Today*, December 11. https://www.usatoday.com/story/news/nation/2020/12/11/immigrant-advocates-cant-locate-parents-separated-border-children/3896940001.

Goodman, Amy. 2015. "Mass Graves of Immigrants Found in Texas, but State Says No Laws Were Broken." *Democracy Now!*, July 16. https://www.democracynow.org/2015/7/16/mass_graves_of_immigrants_found_in.

Greven, Nicholas. 2018. "The Southern Border Plan on the Ground in the Trump Era." North American Congress on Latin America, January 26. https://nacla.org/news/2018/01/30/southern-border-plan-ground-trump-era.

Hagedorn, Hermann. 1921. *Roosevelt in the Badlands*. Boston: Houghton Mifflin.

Helms, Mary W. 1986. "Of Kings and Contexts: Ethnohistorical Interpretations of Miskito Political Structure and Function." *American Ethnologist* 13 (3): 506–523.

Herlihy, Laura Hobson. 2016. "The New Colonization of Nicaragua's Caribbean Coast." North American Congress on Latin America, September 6. https://nacla.org/news/2016/09/06/new-colonization-nicaragua%E2%80%99s-caribbean-coast.

Herlihy, Laura Hobson, and Brett Spencer. 2016. "Indigenous Resistance in Nicaragua's Elections." North American Congress on Latin America, December 2. https://nacla.org/news/2016/12/09/indigenous-resistance-nicaragua%E2%80%99s-elections.

Hooker, Juliet. 2005. "'Beloved Enemies': Race and Official Mestizo Nationalism in Nicaragua." *Latin American Research Review* 40 (3): 14–39.

Izdepski, Robert. 1994. "Paralysis, Salvation or Famine: The Miskito Dichotomy Continues." *Universal Diver* 1 (1). http://www.flagrancy.net/salvage/redlobster.html.

Jorge, Miguel Angel. 2013. "Time for Honduras to End Scuba Diving for Lobster." *National Geographic*, April 23. https://blog.nationalgeographic.org/2013/04/23/time-for-honduras-to-end-scuba-diving-for-lobster/.

Latin American Working Group. n.d. "'Yet Another Victim of the American Dream': Honduran Migrants Speak Out." Accessed December 20, 2020. https://www.lawg.org/yetanothervictimoftheamericandream.

Mbembe, Achille. 2003. "Necropolitics." Translated by Libby Meintjes. *Public Culture* 15 (1): 11–40.

McSweeney, Kendra. 2004. "The Dugout Canoe Trade in Central America's Mosquitia: Approaching Rural Livelihoods through Systems of Exchange." *Annals of the Association of American Geographers* 94 (3): 638–661.

Menjívar, Cecilia. 2006. "Liminal Legality: Salvadoran and Guatemalan Immigrants' Lives in the United States." *American Journal of Sociology* 111 (4): 999–1037.

Menjívar, Cecilia, and Leisy J. Abrego. 2012. "Legal Violence: Immigration Law and the Lives of Central American Immigrants." *American Journal of Sociology* 117 (5): 1380–1421.

Midlands Diving Chamber. n.d. "World Hyperbaric Chamber Locator." Accessed December 20, 2020. http://midlandsdivingchamber.co.uk/index.php?id=contact&page=11&region=7.

Moore, John H. 1986. "The Miskitu National Question in Nicaragua: Background to a Misunderstanding." *Science and Society* 50 (2): 132–147.

Ngai, Mae M. 2004. *Impossible Subjects: Illegal Aliens and the Making of Modern America*. Princeton, NJ: Princeton University Press.

O'Connor, Allison, Jeanne Batalova, and Jessica Bolter. 2019. "Central American Immigrants in the United States." Migration Policy Institute, August 15. https://www.migrationpolicy.org/article/central-american-immigrants-united-states.

Pallares, Amalia. 2015. *Family Activism: Immigrant Struggles and the Politics of Noncitizenship*. New Brunswick, NJ: Rutgers University Press.

Pallares, Amalia, and Nilda Flores-Gonzalez. 2010. *Marcha! Latino Chicago and the Immigrant Rights Movement*. Champaign: University of Illinois Press.

Patterson, Orlando. 1982. *Slavery and Social Death: A Comparative Study*. Cambridge, MA: Harvard University Press.

Portillo Villeda, Suyapa. 2015. "Honduras LGBTI: Landscape Analysis of Political, Economic and Social Conditions." Astraea Lesbian Foundation for Justice. https://globalphilanthropyproject.org/wp-content/uploads/2017/01/Honduras-Landscape-Analsyis-2016-1.pdf.

Reagan, Ronald. 1984. "Address to the Nation on United States Policy in Central America." May 9. https://www.reaganlibrary.gov/research/speeches/50984h.

———. 1985. "Remarks at the Annual Meeting of the National Association of Manufacturers." May 24. https://www.reaganlibrary.gov/research/speeches/52485c.

Rocha, José Luis. 2010. "Migrants: Submissive Victims or Engaging in Civil Disobedience?" *Envío*, September. https://www.envio.org.ni/articulo/4241.

Rothenberg, Daniel, ed. 2012. *Memory of Silence: The Guatemalan Truth Commission Report*. New York: Palgrave Macmillan.

Scroggs, William. 1905. "William Walker and the Steamship Corporation in Nicaragua." *American Historical Review* 10 (4): 792–811.

Smith, Andrea. 2005. *Conquest: Sexual Violence and American Indian Genocide*. Durham, NC: Duke University Press.

Taracena, María Inés. 2018. "La Caravana de la Resistencia." North American Congress on Latin America, December 20. https://nacla.org/news/2018/12/20/la-caravana-de-la-resistencia.

Vogt, Wendy. 2018. *Lives in Transit: Violence and Intimacy on the Migrant Journey*. Oakland: University of California Press.

World Wildlife Fund. 2010. "Closed Season for Lobster, a Landmark Step towards Responsible Fishing in Central America." March 1. https://www.worldwildlife.org/stories/closed-season-for-lobster-a-landmark-step-towards-responsible-fishing-in-central-america.

13

A Politics of Survival

ABBY C. WHEATLEY

etween 1998 and 2018, the number of recorded migrant fatalities along the U.S.-Mexico border reached 7,505 (U.S. Customs and Border Protection 2019).[1] These deaths are the result of prevention-through-deterrence policies ostensibly intended to prevent unauthorized migration by making it dangerous and even deadly to migrate (De León 2015; Dunn 2009; Andreas 2003; Cornelius 2001). As scholars have shown, contemporary border enforcement measures deliberately funnel migrants into remote corridors of the desert (Rubio-Goldsmith et al. 2006; U.S. Border Patrol 1994), where they are at heightened risk of exposure, dehydration, hyperthermia, hypothermia, and death (Dunn 2009; Rubio-Goldsmith et al. 2006). Though often represented as unintended consequences of necessary national security efforts, these fatalities are part of an actively hostile migration management system that uses death as the primary deterrent to autonomous migration (Rodríguez 1996; Spener 2009; Mitropoulos 2006).

Through the efforts of scholars, activists, nongovernmental organizations, and migrants themselves, migrant deaths have become increasingly visible. Yet there is little attention to how migrants survive precarious crossings. In fact, migration scholarship often reinforces the trope of "the suffering subject" through humanizing and objectifying language that (re)produces a static and knowable migrant subject in need of empathy and saving (Robbins 2013). As Makau Mutua points out, this trope is reproduced and codified in the human rights corpus insofar as accessing rights involves identifying a victim "whose 'dignity and worth' have been violated by the savage" state (Mutua 2001, 203). In this scenario, those in need of protection are generally nonwhite, non-European subjects while those positioned to do the "saving" (both morally and juridically) are white (Mutua 2001). Thus, victimhood is as much about racial and cultural difference as the social, economic, and political entanglements that produce a subject in need of protection (Abu-Lughod 2013). To respond to this scholarly shortcoming, I explore the strategies developed by Mexican and Central American migrants to *survive* and *resist* a highly militarized border and weaponized migrant trail. While documenting the growing number of migrant fatalities in the borderlands is critical to interrupting deadly state polices, telling postmortem stories of people in transit strips them of their agency and limits community-based strategies to respond to policies that kill.

To fully grasp the lived experience of people in transit, we must conceptualize border crossing as every effort that is put into the process of surviving, subverting, struggling with, and sometimes overcoming the border, especially in the context of a highly militarized border that extends border crossing both spatially and temporally. In this context, crossing may include months and sometimes years of preparation by migrants, including planning routes, making maps, contacting friends and family in the north, and even borrowing money, much of which is facilitated through community networks and mutual aid. In addition, crossing the border includes the time people spend in detention when apprehended by Border Patrol and in prison when sentenced for migration-related offenses.

Drawing on the *testimonios* (testimonials) of migrants transiting the Arizona-Sonora migration corridor (Marin 1991; Beverly 1987; Latina Feminist Group 2001), this chapter emphasizes a *politics of survival* that simultaneously considers the realities of border militarization and the strategies of survival that migrants employ as they navigate an increasingly remote migration corridor and weaponized landscape. By politics of survival, I refer to a contested process over the right to life, livelihood, and autonomy dramatically reduced by processes of bordering that strategically jeopardize the lives of autonomous migrants and uphold hierarchies of racialized laboring subjects (Mezzadra and Neilson 2013). In my analysis, I frame transnational migration as an effort to escape the constraints of a highly inequitable global system of labor (Papadopoulos, Stephenson, and Tsianos 2008), and I center the creative strategies developed by "societies in movement" (Zibechi 2012, 208) to overcome a highly militarized border.

My conception of survival draws on an activist-research framework, referred to as the autonomy of migration, which frames migration as autonomous, political, and dynamic (Nyers 2015; Mezzadra and Neilson 2013; Spener 2009; Mitropoulos 2006; Rodríguez 1996). Privileging mobility over control, this framework explicitly rejects traditional explanations of migration that reduce transnational movements to a set of forces that push and pull migrants from one place to another (Van Hear, Bakewell, and Long 2018; Massey et al. 1993) and present people in transit as victims without agency. Conceptualized as autonomous, migration is not only independent; it is self-active (Rodríguez 1996). This means that migration is both a response to labor exploitation and precarity in the Global South (Mezzadra and Neilson 2013; Mitropoulos 2006; Rodríguez 1996) and a refusal to be territorially excluded (Spener 2009; Rodríguez 1996). This was exemplified by the migrant caravans of 2018 and the organized migration of thousands of people across Mexico (Agren and Holpuch 2018). The caravans reclaimed the public sphere and politicized their mobility, revealing a collective strategy to overcome an extended and weaponized migrant trail that is difficult to navigate without support, networks, and community-based resources.

Privileging survival rather than death is an attempt to uphold life. From an analytical standpoint, it seeks to capture the array of migrant efforts to intervene in the structural production of premature death (Wilson Gilmore 2007) that border enforcement creates and multiplies (Mezzadra and Neilson 2013). In addition, centering the lived experience of people in transit draws attention to migrant voices and narratives that are silenced when we focus only on the border and its power to kill (Abrego 2017; Callahan 2014; Mbembe 2003). This allows us to get beyond analyses that conceptualize the migrant only as a victim and consider the ways that people in transit subvert and resist their subjugation even in the context of a deadly human funnel (Rubio-Goldsmith et al. 2006; De León 2015).

To survive an extended and weaponized migrant trail, people in transit develop a range of creative strategies. In addition to the use of *coyotes* (guides) (Sheridan 2009; Spener 2009), they generate communities in transit (Wheatley and Gomberg-Muñoz 2016), rely on protective pairings (Vogt 2018), and engage in strategic planning. Migrants also draw on local resources, such as shelters and *comedores* (dining halls) run by churches and nonprofit organizations to support their movement. While limited, these strategies reveal collective efforts to overcome the border. They also reveal that human agency precedes attempts by states to border, exclude, and control migration (Nyers 2015; Mitropoulos 2006). Read this way, the continual movement of Central Americans across Mexico and into the United States should be conceptualized as a demand to be protected, especially in the context of current asylum law, which requires asylum seekers to present themselves at a U.S. port of entry on the U.S.-Mexico border to request asylum. Though these migrations are informal, it would be a gross misreading to view them as haphazard or disorganized. They are, in fact, quite strategic.

The emphasis on survival that I explore in this chapter could be perceived as overly romantic—a risk of attempting to confront state violence from the margins and with the "weapons of the weak" (Scott 1985). None-theless, my objective is quite the opposite. As someone who has worked closely with people in transit on the Arizona-Sonora border for nearly a decade, I am well aware that we are living in a time of epic militarization (Dunn 1996) that attempts to control migration through the threat and ac-tuality of death (Mbembe 2003). The rise of migrant fatalities propelled by prevention-through-deterrence policies constitute a human rights emer-gency that requires serious attention. Thus, my interest is not simply to ex-amine migration from an alternate perspective but to highlight survival in order to support the movement and mobility of people in transit and par-ticipate in generating community-based strategies that effectively counter policies that kill. Responding to the violence that the research reveals is a key commitment of convivial research, which frames this project.

Ethnography of Survival

In this chapter, I draw on *testimonios* of people in transit collected in 2013 at the *comedor* run by the Kino Border Initiative in Nogales, Sonora, Mex-ico, and the Migrant Resource Center in Agua Prieta, Sonora, Mexico. In both settings, I was a volunteer and researcher. I documented the stories of people in transit, who were navigating a highly militarized border. Some of these individuals were preparing to cross, some had recently been repatri-ated, while others were heading home. All participants were in the middle of long, extended journeys. In addition to documenting their stories, I pro-vided basic services and critical resources to people in transit, including food, information on shelters and discounted or free bus tickets to southern Mexico, and phone calls. I also assisted migrants in locating family mem-bers from whom they were separated during the process of detention and deportation. I relied on *observant participation*, a research strategy that privileges participation over observation in the context of political research (Costa Vargas 2008).

As a whole, the project was organized using a convivial approach that seeks to respond to and transform the deadly social conditions and human rights abuses that the research reveals (CRIL, n.d.). This research strategy, which came out of community-based struggles in the San Francisco Bay area, is an *active* strategy that explores and connects to "collective efforts to solve local problems and advance the shared interests of a community of struggle" (CRIL, n.d.). In particular, convivial research aims to create and facilitate ongoing spaces of encounter with the goal of amplifying "a variety of community-based knowledges, especially those in opposition to milita-rization, criminalization, securitization, privatization, and neoliberal glo-balization" (CRIL, n.d.). Privileging whole stories or *testimonios* aligns with this research strategy in that it centers the narratives and analyses of migrants themselves and therefore positions them as collaborators in the larger research project when possible.

Raising the Risks and Dangers of Crossing

Prevention-through-deterrence policies actively weaponize the desert by using the natural terrain, geography, and climate as part of a multidimensional strategy aimed at controlling migration. This creates what Jason De León calls a "hybrid collectif of deterrence" in which animals, temperature, and terrain become *actants* in an elaborate killing machine (De León 2015, 60). Through the strategic use of the desert landscape and deliberate exclusion of migrants from urban migration routes, this approach to border enforcement converts the desert into a deadly weapon as a mechanism of deterrence. As De León points out, these policies outsource "the work of punishment" to nonhuman actors and create a sense of ambiguity regarding who is responsible for migrant deaths (De León 2015, 60).

The restriction and criminalization of autonomous migration multiplies the vulnerability of people in transit through a layered effect. On one level, it excludes migrants from accessing safe and secure modes of travel, leaving only extralegal and dangerous pathways open. In this scenario, people in transit are prevented from accessing basic resources that make long-distance journeys feasible, including food, water, regular forms of transportation, protection from the elements, medical assistance, and emergency support. On another level, the spatial and legal marginalization of migrants undermines their resources and creates what Rocío Magaña calls a space of "Desolation" in which "every [migrant] body and every [migrant] life can be rendered illegal, eraseable, sacrificable" (Magaña 2008, 11). Desolation underscores the way in which undocumented migrants become acceptable casualties in the context of national security initiatives that privilege the lives, safety, and security of (white) U.S. citizens over noncitizen subjects of color.

Far from being one-dimensional or stagnant, contemporary border enforcement strategies are multidimensional and active. Border Patrol agents do more than simply hold the line or apprehend unauthorized crossers along the border. They actively interrupt migrant networks, resources, and community-based strategies through a range of controls and corporeal punishments. In the desert, this includes chasing and scattering migrants to make them easier to apprehend (La Coalición de Derechos Humanos and No More Deaths 2016) and extending border crossings through the use of checkpoints on roads and highways north of the international boundary (Chambers et al. 2019). Once migrants are in Border Patrol custody, these tactics include the separation of families in transit, the criminal prosecution of unauthorized migrants, lateral repatriation at a distant point along the border (De León 2013), and the confiscation of money and belongings in the process of repatriation (No More Deaths 2014). Deployed in combination, these tactics stretch the migrant journey across time and space, eliminate the limited resources migrants depend on for survival, and raise the risks of migrating to deadly levels.

Navigating an Extended and Weaponized Migrant Trail

Despite increasingly punitive border measures, people in transit resist and subvert their structural marginalization through a range of strategies and community networks. They cross multiple borders, move east and west along boundary lines to elude border enforcement, and make repeat crossings. In the process, they accumulate geographical and technical knowledge that may help them make successful future crossings. They also establish contacts, build networks, and gain confidence, sometimes cultivating an "informed cosmopolitanism" in the process (Reichman 2011, 553). While the journey is extremely dangerous, it is transformative in many ways. As Ruben Andersson suggests, clandestine migration is a journey not just of death and suffering but also one "of self-realization that reveal[s] the resilience, restlessness, and striving of a very contemporary human condition" (2014, 11).

In the following sections, I examine the strategies developed by people in transit to navigate an extended and weaponized migrant trail. Though these strategies do not fully interrupt state policies that use death to deter autonomous migration, they make it possible for people in transit to keep moving along an extended and weaponized migrant trail (Wheatley and Gomberg-Muñoz 2016). They also demonstrate that policies of closed borders shift and funnel migrants into increasingly remote and dangerous corridors where they disappear or die, but closed borders do not stop migration (Wheatley and Kroll-Zeldin 2021; Dunn 2009).

To fully examine the reality of contemporary crossings, I present these *testimonios* through the mixed lens of violence and resistance. As Cecilia Menjívar (2011) points out, migration journeys are shaped by the amalgamation of multiple forms of violence, which become routine and even normalized in everyday life. According to Leisy Abrego (2017), the normalization of violence is accompanied by a series of silences that need to be named and attended to. For Abrego, this entails locating "the source of violence in the state and its various social structures" and highlighting U.S. military intervention in Guatemala and El Salvador, as well as U.S. refusal to recognize Central Americans as refugees in the 1980s (2017, 81). In addition, we must understand Central American refugees as transnational social actors rather than "a single unauthorized, dehumanized category" (81). While people in transit are subjects of state violence on more than one level, they are also agents of change and autonomous transnational social actors. In fact, efforts to militarize and secure the border are a direct response to the autonomy and agency of people in transit, who continue to transcend borders meant to contain and control them.

The following transit stories reveal multisided violence (Menjívar 2011), including fear, trauma, and separation. They also reveal resistance, exemplified by strength, determination, faith, ingenuity, resilience, and success. My objective is to show the reality of border crossing while highlighting narratives that push beyond accounts of migrants simply as victims. This is not only an analytical imperative but also a social and political urgency.

Escaping the Favela

After months of travel from Tegucigalpa, Honduras, Celso arrived in Nogales, Sonora, in late October. Like many people migrating out of Honduras, Celso left Tegucigalpa after receiving repeat threats from local gangs. He was the proud owner of a small tattoo shop, which he had built from the ground up. Encouraged by a friend, Celso had started doing tattoos in his home when he was just a teenager. After that first tattoo, he explains, "people started looking for me. During the day, I worked in front of the mining sector, [collecting] anything that came out—garbage, everything, cans, all of these things. At night, I would arrive at my house, and people would be waiting for me to do tattoos." By the time Celso was twenty-five, he and his artwork had become well known in the city.

Owning a small business was a huge source of pride for Celso, who grew up "in complete and extreme poverty" and "in one of the most dangerous areas of Tegucigalpa." At eight years old, he accompanied his mother's stepfather after school to pick through trash and bring in a little cash to help support his family: "I would leave school and go with him to collect cans and plastic bottles in order to sell them. He [Celso's grandfather] also collected old cameras, radios, things that people didn't need." Celso described tattooing as a way to battle depression over his family's precarious situation and escape the destiny he saw for many of his peers: surrendering to drugs and joining the Mara Salvatrucha. However, as Celso's reputation as a skilled artist grew, gang members sought him out, sometimes insisting that he tattoo them in their homes for little or no pay, and without breaks. Over time, this situation became untenable. Celso worried about his young son, as well as his partner and business. Leaving Tegucigalpa, however, was not an easy decision, considering everything he had built there.

Though gang violence was a prime factor in Celso's decision to migrate, his experience must be read against a shifting economy and his precarious position in it. The intensification of Honduran migration in the last decade is the result of multiple factors, not least of which is the subjugation of Honduras's economy to the global political-economic order (Loker 1996). By the end of the Cold War, Honduras transitioned to a full-fledged neoliberal economy attuned to foreign investment. This included the rapid development of the coffee sector in the 1970s and the development of the *maquila* industry, manufacturing textiles and many other goods oriented to the U.S. export market in the 1980s (Reichman 2013). The rapid industrialization of cities like Tegucigalpa and San Pedro Sula during this period also provoked large-scale rural-to-urban migrations (Reichman 2013). This was followed by deindustrialization, capital flight (Reichman 2013), and the worldwide coffee crisis (Reichman 2011). In 1998, Hurricane Mitch left 10 percent of the country's families homeless (Ensor 2008). These economic crises were exacerbated by the arrival of some twenty thousand Los Angeles gang members deported between 2000 and 2004 (Arana 2005).

When we met in Nogales, Celso had been in transit for nearly three months, though he had started preparing for his journey several months prior to leaving Honduras. As Celso's story suggests, preparing mentally, emotionally, and logistically for a long journey is part of the contemporary migration experience. Celso studied maps to determine the best route. He practiced different accents so that he would not draw attention to himself as he traversed Guatemala, and then Mexico. And finally, he started preparing his bicycle. Celso had attempted to migrate two times before, only to be repatriated to Honduras by Mexican authorities before getting far. He knew that he would need a creative strategy to make it across Guatemala and Mexico and all the way to the U.S.-Mexico border. He planned to ride his bicycle.

Though Celso's journey entailed family separation, uncertainty, and insecurity, it was also one of self-realization, resilience, and success. He left Tegucigalpa with a small backpack, a few changes of clothing, tattoo needles, ink, and some money. He had planned to work en route and send money to his family still in Tegucigalpa. He rode buses long distances and rode his bicycle right through two checkpoints. As Celso recalls, he greeted the border agents with a simple wave while riding through the checkpoint. They waved back! When telling this story, Celso laughs out loud. His ability to successfully navigate the checkpoint and his recollection of this experience underscore the fact that migration journeys cannot be reduced to a bare existence characterized only by violence and death. His narrative also raises questions about the visibility and invisibility of migrating subjects. Presumably, Celso's ability to keep moving in broad daylight was made possible by subverting the stereotypical image of a migrant by riding his bicycle and waving casually at the guards. Additionally, his ability to blend in was achieved by mimicking the simplicity and everydayness of life, revealing that migrants are made hypervisible, even discernible, by their perceived desperation, impoverishment, and victimization. While Celso's decision to leave Tegucigalpa was motivated by necessity, his experience migrating through multiple countries also entailed a series of adventures, successes, and even self-transformation (Andersson 2014, 11). By the time he reached Nogales, and the last phase of his migration journey, Celso had already traveled almost 2,500 miles from Tegucigalpa to Nogales, Mexico, and successfully crossed two international boundaries.

Once in Mexico, Celso gave his bicycle to a friend in Tuxtla Gutierrez, Chiapas, before continuing on. In Veracruz, he met up with a childhood friend, Eloy, who traveled with him to Nogales. Like many Central Americans making long journeys, Celso and Eloy rode *La Bestia*, the network of freight trains that move goods and materials between Mexico's southern and northern boundaries, all the way to Nogales. Though traveling on top of trains is extremely dangerous (Martínez 2013; Vogt 2018), it is also a critical form of transportation for thousands of Central American migrants navigating an extended and weaponized migrant trail. In the context of massive border militarization, the train emerges as a routine, yet highly precarious, form of transportation for working-class, Global South travelers who are excluded from accessing safe, secure, and legal modes of travel. Whether they plan to present themselves at an official port of entry and request asylum or enter the country autonomously, they have to get to the border first.

"When We Crossed the Line, We Did So Running"

The third time Ana Gabriela tried to cross the border, she was with a group of twenty-two people: nineteen men and three women. Because the group was large, they climbed the mountain in a bus. As before, they were to wait until 1:00 A.M., when the *migra* (Border Patrol) changed shifts and they could get across the border quickly without being picked up right away. But on this evening, the *migra* did not move. "They didn't move, and therefore, we didn't move," recalls Ana Gabriela.

Like many migrants, Ana Gabriela and her husband were unfamiliar with the terrain, climate, topography, and geography of the Arizona Sonora Desert prior to attempting their journey. They were told by their guide that they would only walk for four hours and were instructed to pack light. Because of this, they were only carrying three liters of water and very little food when they left Mexico. "The less we brought, the faster we would be able to move," explained Ana Gabriela. "We had no blankets either, except for one guide, who shared his blanket with everyone, with the women. The blanket covered our legs, and we covered our upper bodies with plastic trash bags. But the cold was horrible, and the wind was worse. Since I was six months pregnant, it was difficult for me to sleep between the rocks on the hard ground." Although exposure to extreme heat is one of the primary causes of death for people in transit, Ana Gabriela's narrative demonstrates that the frigid nights and intense wind are just as treacherous.

On the following day, and because Border Patrol did not move when expected, the three guides left their perch in the mountains and went back to town for food. They left at 9:00 A.M. and did not return until 3:00 P.M., bringing with them only ten sandwiches, which the group divided hungrily. The day was hot, and there was no refuge from the sun. The people were trying to build small huts out of branches to make some shade. As the day turned to night, they climbed higher to prepare to cross. Ana Gabriela remembers that they climbed up and over the mountain. By this time, they were in U.S. territory. "We knew this because the guides told us," she recalled, "and when we crossed the line, we did so running."

> There was a plane overhead looking for us, so we hid in an arroyo. We couldn't move or make a sound. We were to wait there until the *migra* changed shifts. Covered in plastic bags to keep warm, almost everyone fell asleep there in the arroyo. The guides woke us up shouting, "¡*Levántense*—wake up!" All of us, half asleep, but running. We ran and ran, up and down. People were falling, hiding from the *migra*. We ran without resting, maybe an hour. The three women couldn't keep up. One fell and hurt her knee, and they left her. Finally, we arrived at the hill near 15th Street, one of the roads most heavily patrolled. We were instructed to take our shoes off and cross the road in only our socks so as not to leave any footprints.

Fifteenth Street in Douglas, Arizona, is exactly fifteen blocks from the border and runs parallel to the international line. On the east side of town, the street dead-ends into the city's tiny municipal airport, which has not served commercial airlines since 2005. This is not a rural crossing but one made at the edge of a tiny urban area. Crossing on the outskirts of Douglas demonstrates an effort to minimize the desolation that contemporary crossings often entail. However, it also raises the risk of apprehension, since the area is highly patrolled and surveilled. Crossing here, Ana Gabriela explained, requires one to remain invisible while moving quickly across a harsh desert environment:

> Again, we were running, but this time with cactus spines in our feet. We finally arrived at a large boulder and hid there. In the distance,

I could see the *migra*, driving slowly, looking for people. One of the women had a cough, and the guide kept telling her to shut up. When the *migra* was out of sight, we were told to walk, lined up single file. I was in the back with my husband, one woman and her brother, and an older gentleman. For me it was too much. By this point, my husband was half-carrying me. We started to run, and the five of us in the back became separated from the group. After five minutes, one of the guides realized that we were missing and came back for us. According to the guides, we were approaching the last hill, which was Highway 80.

This episode, in which the guide returned after just five minutes for the five missing members of the group, suggests that people in transit experience and manage minor and multiple separations prior to separations that lead to complete desolation or death. Separation from the group is not necessarily a deliberate, malevolent action by the *coyote* but a facet of extended and precarious crossings that require incredible physical ability, stamina, and sufficient resources to survive. According to Ana Gabriela, at this point,

the *migra* walked by with flashlights. Again we ran. Over rocks, hills. I fell. We crossed four hills running. I fell again, but this time on my stomach. My husband picked me up, but we were lost. We were totally lost. It was about four in the morning, judging by the sky. The woman and her brother came with us, but I couldn't walk anymore. My husband was practically carrying me, and it was the same for the woman and her brother. All of a sudden, the other woman [who had been separated from the group] appeared out of the bushes. The sun was beginning to rise. We started to head back to the border, but this time we traveled along the highway.

On her way back to Agua Prieta, Ana Gabriela never saw the *migra*. She did, however, see three groups preparing to cross in the same way she had. They would wait until 1:00 A.M., when Border Patrol changed shifts, to start their trek. Retracing her steps to Agua Prieta, Ana Gabriela started to cry.

My husband pulled out some bread and mayonnaise he was carrying, and we ate it. Once we ate, we walked two more hours down the mountain. All of the women returned to Agua Prieta. We waited for a taxi that took us all the way to a hotel. I got in bed. I didn't even have the strength to take a bath or eat. All my clothing was torn. I had cactus spines everywhere. I slept for three days.

After her third attempt, Ana Gabriela decided to return home. This did not address the reasons she initially left home; it simply returned her to the precarious situation she had wanted to escape. Considering that Ana Gabriela did not make it to the United States as she had hoped, it would be easy to view her migration experience as unsuccessful. Yet Ana Gabriela's decision to return home was also strategic and agentive, especially when read against the dangers posed by a weaponized landscape that extends migrant journeys and amplifies the risks of vulnerable people in transit. Ana Gabriela had wanted to give her unborn child a bright future, but she knew that future was worth little if she lost her child in the process. With the support of the Mexican Consulate, she returned home, where she could draw on the resources available to her and the support of her family and community.[2] In addition, we cannot assume that Ana Gabriela's decision to return home was a permanent one, especially considering that her pregnancy was a key reason she could not meet the physical demands of crossing. As the stories of Felix, Mateo, and Emiliano (found later in this chapter) demonstrate, many migrants attempt to migrate again months or years after failed attempts even when they know how dangerous crossing can be.

Moreover, Ana Gabriela's decision to return home must be read against other stories of migration and survival, and on a collective level, especially considering that several other groups were preparing to cross as Ana Gabriela was returning to the border. As I argue elsewhere, border militarization does not simply shift where and how migrants cross; it also shifts who continues to migrate in the face of precarious and potentially deadly conditions. In fact, migration from some Oaxacan communities with a history of circular migration, including San Sebastián Abasolo, has all but halted as a result of border militarization. Members of this particular community have been able to remain home by emphasizing local development and maintaining a transterritorial nexus of mutual survival (Wheatley 2015). For others, including Central American migrants such as Celso, shrinking economic opportunities and violence at home present more reasons to leave than to stay. This appears to be the case even in the context of interminable waits at the border to process asylum applications, a consequence of the Migration Protection Protocols implemented by President Donald Trump in 2019, which require applicants to wait outside the United States for the duration of their immigration proceedings (Human Rights Watch 2019).[3]

In addition, migrants with more resources and money can better navigate the dangers of migration by paying for safer and shorter crossings. Several months after I spoke with Ana Gabriela in Agua Prieta, I met a Honduran man named Darian in Nogales who paid $10,000 for his pregnant wife to enter the United States through a port of entry on the Texas-Chihuahua border. After using their financial resources to ensure her safe crossing, Darian spent several weeks trying to make arrangements to cross to join his wife in the United States.

If at First You Don't Succeed

When I met Felix in Nogales, he had already spent several months in the cities of Tijuana and Mexicali, Baja California, and Altar and Nogales, Sonora. He had migrated to the United States as a young man with his first wife, started a family, and chased the American Dream. But after his marriage fell apart, Felix returned to his home state of Veracruz. At the time we met, he was attempting to return to the United States to reunite with his twin daughters in Los Angeles and better provide for his new wife and young son in Veracruz. Because of his previous experience, Felix knew that crossing the border would not be easy.

He stayed in Nogales for a month, accessed services at the *comedor* run by the Kino Border Initiative, and slept in the local shelters. Because these are temporary supports, Felix rented a room with two other migrants he had met in Nogales. The room cost 300 pesos (approximately $15) a week and was furnished with an old bed where two people slept, with a third on the floor. This accommodation provided Felix and his comrades extra time to organize plans to cross again without spending large sums of money.

Although Felix was extremely thorough in researching and planning where, how, and with whom to cross, he expressed deep anxiety about the amount of time that was passing as he coordinated his trip. After migrating from Veracruz, he spent three months working in Tijuana before moving east to Altar, Sonora, where he first attempted to cross. After walking for five days in the desert, Felix was apprehended by Border Patrol, detained in a holding cell for two days, and repatriated to Nogales. He had now been away from home for more than four months, was running out of money, and worried about how to provide for his family in the meantime. He explained:

> I am not doing anything here. I am just passing time. My wife, I speak with her, and I don't have money; I can't find work. It is difficult to find work. When they give you work in a place, they pay you very little. I am going to tell you, sixty dollars a week. It does not go far enough. You have a son. You have to give him breakfast every day, take him to school, pick him up from school, lunch, dinner. So it does not go far enough. I am thinking, "When am I going to get there? If I stay here, I am never going to get there. If I don't get up and say, 'I am going now,' I am never going to get there. I am never going to get there!"

Felix identifies the various constraints that shape his migration experience while sharing a deep anxiety about the passing of time. However, his knowledge of how difficult it is to cross the border caused him to be patient.

Felix found a *coyote* in Tijuana with twenty years of experience and a very high record of getting people across the border. He charged $3,000 and told Felix that he would not have to walk more than six to ten hours. Although the guide came highly recommended, other migrants questioned the legitimacy of this *coyote* and his record. Despite this, Felix believed that Tijuana was as likely a place to cross as any other. He explained:

> I only know through stories from other people that this person has been working for twenty years. This is his job. This is his job, and he crosses there [in Tijuana]. Many people don't believe: "No, through Tijuana, no. No, Tijuana, no." But Tijuana, Nogales, Altar, Sonora, Sonoíta, Sasabe—I don't know what other places—Laredo, Tamaulipas, it's the same. Wherever you want, it's hard. If it were easy, we wouldn't have so many deported people.

A month after Felix was deported to Nogales, he left for Tijuana to meet up with the infamous guide with twenty years of experience. When he crossed again, this time through Tijuana, he was successful. A month or so after Felix left Nogales, I received word that he had made it to Los Angeles. Within a few days, he began working and sending money to his family, as well as paying off debts in Veracruz. He also reunited with his twin daughters in Los Angeles. This reunification was tempered by Felix's separation from his young son and wife, demonstrating Anna Ochoa O'Leary's claim that every reunification is a separation in the context of a highly militarized border that runs deeply through the lives of transnational communities (O'Leary 2009). Later, in a follow-up conversation with Felix via social media, I learned that the geographic separation from his wife and son in Veracruz took a major toll on their relationship, eventually causing them to separate. Physically speaking, Felix was successful. He restarted his life in Los Angeles, found a job easily, and solved his financial problems. At the same time, the dissolution of his marriage reveals the way in which transnational migration and the borders that reinforce territorial limits continually challenge people's most important and intimate relationships.

Building Knowledge, Skills, and Resources on the Trail

Despite how difficult it has become to migrate, repeat attempts to navigate an extended and weaponized migrant trail reveal the extent to which families refuse separation. Mateo, a migrant from Honduras who had made more than one trip from his community of origin to the U.S.-Mexico border to reunite with his partner and daughter in the United States, exemplifies this politics of refusal. When we met in Nogales, Sonora, Mateo had recently arrived on the border and was preparing to cross again. Like Felix, Mateo struggled to help support his family in the United States while working for a low wage in Honduras. However, his refusal to be indefinitely separated from his family was not financially motivated but grounded in his desire to be close to his daughter. He explained, "Now I have a future. I have a daughter. She's my life. It is because of her that I want to return, and I am going to do it. I am going to try. Twenty times they apprehend me; twenty times I am going to return. I am not afraid of prison. I am afraid of loneliness, of being without my daughter, without seeing her, losing her, missing her face. This is what I am afraid of." Mateo's comments demonstrate that he values his social existence—specifically his relationship with his daughter—more than his physical safety. By refusing to remain permanently separated from his family despite the danger of crossing, Mateo refuses the "social death" (Cacho 2012) that border regimes aim to produce.

People in transit layer their knowledge of crossing as well as their strategies of survival each time they cross. By making repeat entry attempts, Mateo accumulated a significant amount of knowledge and developed particular skills to facilitate his movement and mobility. To better navigate an expansive desert, he now traveled with a compass. He carried bleach to purify his water, and one gallon of water. He knew that he would have to walk for several days, but insisted with confidence that it was best to carry less water and move faster. In addition, he memorized his Alien Registration Number—a government-issued number needed to locate someone in detention—thus protecting himself from being disappeared in an immigration detention center that routinely disappears people and their belongings (No More Deaths 2014). In addition, as a seasoned traveler, Mateo shared this knowledge with other people in transit outside the *comedor*.[4]

Similarly, Emiliano made repeat trips from Chiapas, Mexico, to the U.S.-Mexico border. During his first trip, Emiliano attempted to cross the border twice near Nogales. The first time he was intercepted by cartels, held at gunpoint, and returned to Nogales. The second time, he was apprehended by the Border Patrol, held for several days in a holding center, and repatriated to Ciudad Acuña, hundreds of miles from the site where he had crossed. From there, he accepted a free bus ticket from the Mexican Consulate and returned to Chiapas.

A year after his first trip to the border, Emiliano migrated again. As he had done previously, he rode *La Bestia* from Arriaga, Chiapas, all the way to Nogales. At this point, he knew the route quite well. He knew the dangers of migrating. He knew how to protect himself. He described feeling confident, even proud of the knowledge he had accumulated on his first trip. When he migrated a second time, Emiliano shared this knowledge with others in route. In fact, he accompanied two first-time crossers from southern Mexico all the way to the U.S.-Mexico border. Though Emiliano decided to stay and work in Nogales for a period rather than cross again immediately, the knowledge he accumulated and shared supported the forward movement of other people in transit.

Conclusion

Far from being static victims, the migrants whose stories I relate here reveal complex individuals with equally complicated experiences of migration. While the structural (Parsons 2007) and multisided violence (Menjívar 2011) of contemporary crossings are evident throughout, these narratives also expose dynamic efforts to survive a highly militarized border and weaponized migrant trail. In particular, they demonstrate dignity, strength, ingenuity, perseverance, and resourcefulness. In this context, survival is not read simply as the management of physical risks or absence of death; it entails efforts to remain autonomous and mobile despite the constraints of a global hierarchy of labor and state efforts to fortify national borders at any cost (Brown 2010). Furthermore, the small-scale mobilities observed in these transit stories are part of a broader movement of migrants, refugees, and asylum seekers reclaiming their rights, dignity, and autonomy through movement and escape. While people in transit are subjects of state violence on one level, they are also transnational social actors actively challenging the neoliberal and neocolonial dimensions of bordered territories constructed to contain and control them.

Documenting the growing number of migrant fatalities is critical to interrupting deadly state polices, yet telling postmortem stories of people in transit can strip them of their agency and limit community-based strategies to respond to policies that kill. Viewing migration through a politics of survival addresses this problem and ruptures the trope of "the suffering subject" (Robbins 2013) that plagues much of immigration literature and human rights discourse. The significance of this goes far beyond scholarly or theoretical distinctions. As scholars Makau Mutua (2001) and Miriam Ticktin (2017) point out, notions of victimhood and innocence are not simply discursive; they are entrenched in the human rights corpus and thus determine who is and who is not protected under the current system. It is critical to reconstruct the lens through which we view, understand, and talk about migration. Doing so is as much a social and political imperative as it is a scholarly one.

A politics of survival provides a path forward for scholars, practitioners, and activist communities already involved in the migrant justice movement. At the center of this struggle is "an autonomously active, and opposed, historical subject" who continues to defend itself in the face of horrific violence (Cleaver 1992, 106). Our efforts to support this movement must recognize and build on what is already active rather than undermine migrants by rendering them voiceless and apolitical. This requires centering *survival* and defending *life* rather than simply counting the dead. The urgent demand by migrants around the world is to uphold their dignity by supporting their right to move safely from one place to another, and across international boundaries. We do this by amplifying the voices, strategies, and successes of societies in movement (Zibechi 2012), by building on their momentum to demilitarize border zones, and by demanding an end to state policies that seek to control migration through the threat and actuality of death.

NOTES

1. There is ample criticism that these numbers underrepresent the actual number of fatalities along the U.S.-Mexico Border considering that they include only the number of remains that have been recovered.

2. At that time, the Mexican Consulate offered free one-way bus tickets to some migrants to help them return to their communities of origin. The tickets were limited, and there was often a waiting list. Additionally, this service was available to migrants only once in their lifetime.

3. In the wake of the COVID-19 pandemic, delays have been extended even further, with hearings that would have occurred in spring 2020 tentatively postponed until later in the year or as late as 2021 (Aquilera 2020). As a result of the lack of information regarding when cases would be processed again, some asylum seekers decided to return home, though doing so means they lose their place in line (Carranza 2020).

4. Mateo's migration story and an impromptu compass workshop are described in the article "Keep Moving: Collective Agency along the Migrant Trail" that I coauthored with Ruth Gomberg-Muñoz (Wheatley and Gomberg-Muñoz 2016).

REFERENCES

Abrego, Leisy. 2017. "On Silences: Salvadoran Refugees Then and Now." *Latino Studies* 15 (1): 73–85.

Abu-Lughod, Lila. 2013. *Do Muslim Women Need Saving?* Cambridge, MA: Harvard University Press.

Agren, David, and Amanda Holpuch. 2018. "Where Is the Migrant Caravan from—and What Will Happen to It at the Border?" *The Guardian*, October 24. https://www.theguardian.com/us-news/2018/oct/24/caravan-migrants-what-is-it-where-from-guatemala-honduras-immigrants-mexico.

Andersson, Ruben. 2014. *Illegality, Inc.: Clandestine Migration and the Business of Bordering Europe*. Oakland: University of California Press.

Andreas, Peter. 2003. "Redrawing the Line: Borders and Security in the Twenty-First Century." *International Security* 28 (2): 78–111.

Aquilera, Jasmine. 2020. "Many Asylum Seekers in Mexico Can't Get U.S. Court Hearings until 2021: A Coronavirus Outbreak Could 'Devastate' Them." *Time*, May 19. https://time.com/5830807/asylum-seekers-coronavirus-mpp/.

Arana, Ana. 2005. "How the Street Gangs Took Central America." *Foreign Affairs*, May–June. https://www.foreignaffairs.com/articles/central-america-caribbean/2005 -05-01/how-street-gangs-took-central-america.

Beverly, John. 1987. "Anatomía del testimonio." In *Del Lazarillo al sandinismo: Estudios sobre la función ideológica de la literatura española e hispanoamericana*, 7–16. Minneapolis: Institute for the Study of Ideologies and Literatura/Prisma Institute.

Brown, Wendy. 2010. *Walled States, Waning Sovereignty*. Brooklyn: Zone Books.

Cacho, Lisa Marie. 2012. *Social Death: Racialized Rightlessness and the Criminalization of the Unprotected*. New York: New York University Press.

Callahan, Manuel. 2014. "Crisis and Permanent War on the U.S.-Mexico Borderlands." Unpublished manuscript, June 17.

Carranza, Rafael, 2020. "More Migrants Giving Up Asylum Claims as Pandemic Shuts Down Processing at Border." *AZ Central*, May 11. https://www.azcentral.com/ story/news/politics/border-issues/2020/05/11/more-migrants-giving-up-asylum -claims-leaving-arizona-mexico-border/5171469002/.

Chambers, Samuel Norton, Geoffrey Alan Boyce, Sarah Launius, and Alicia Dinsmore. 2019. "Mortality, Surveillance and the Tertiary 'Funnel Effect' on the U.S.-Mexico Border: A Geospatial Modeling of the Geography of Deterrence." *Journal of Borderlands Studies*, January 31. https://doi.org/10.1080/08865655.2019.1570861.

Cleaver, Harry. 1992. "The Inversion of Class Perspective in Marxian Theory: From Valorisation to Self-Valorisation." In *Open Marxism*, vol. 2, *Theory and Practice*, edited by Werner Bonefeld, Richard Gunn, and Kosmas Psychopedis, 106–144. London: Pluto Press.

Cornelius, Wayne A. 2001. "Death at the Border: Efficacy and Unintended Consequences of U.S. Immigration Control Policy." *Population and Development Review* 27 (4): 661–688.

Costa Vargas, João H. 2008. "Activist Scholarship: Limits and Possibilities in Times of Black Genocide." In *Engaging Contradictions: Theory, Politics, and Methods of Activist Scholarship*, edited by Charles R. Hale, 164–182. Berkeley: University of California Press.

CRIL (Convivial Research and Insurgent Learning). n.d. "Convivial Research." Accessed December 2019. http://cril.mitotedigital.org/convivialres.

De León, Jason. 2013. "The Efficacy and Impact of the Alien Transfer Exit Programme: Migrant Perspectives from Nogales, Sonora, Mexico." *International Migration* 51 (2): 10–23.

———. 2015. *The Land of Open Graves: Living and Dying on the Migrant Trail*. Oakland: University of California Press.

Dunn, Timothy. 1996. *The Militarization of the U.S.-Mexico Border, 1978–1992: Low-Intensity Conflict Doctrine Comes Home*. Austin: CMAS Books, University of Texas at Austin.

———. 2009. *Blockading the Border and Human Rights: The El Paso Operation That Remade Immigration Enforcement*. Austin: University of Texas Press.

Ensor, Marisa. 2008. "Displaced Once Again: Honduran Migrant Children in the Path of Katrina." *Children, Youth and Environments* 18 (1): 280–302.

Human Rights Watch. 2019. "U.S. Move Puts More Asylum Seekers at Risk." September 25. https://www.hrw.org/news/2019/09/25/us-move-puts-more-asylum-seekers -risk#.

La Coalición de Derechos Humanos and No More Deaths. 2016. "Disappeared: How the US Border Enforcement Agencies Are Fueling a Missing Persons Crisis." http://www.thedisappearedreport.org/uploads/8/3/5/1/83515082/disappeared --introduction.pdf.

Latina Feminist Group. 2001. "Introduction: Papelitos Guardados; Theorizing Latinidades through Testimonio." In *Telling to Live: Latina Feminist Testimonios*, 1–25. Durham, NC: Duke University Press.

Loker, William M. 1996. "'Campesinos' and the Crisis of Modernization in Latin America." *Journal of Political Ecology* 3:69–88.

Magaña, Rocío. 2008. "Desolation Bound: Enforcing America's Borders on Migrating Bodies." Ignacio Martín-Baró Human Rights Essay, University of Chicago Pozen Family Center for Human Rights.

Marin, Lynda. 1991. "Speaking Out Together: Testimonials of Latin American Women." *Latin American Perspectives* 18 (3): 51–68.

Martínez, Óscar. 2013. *The Beast: Riding the Rails and Dodging Narcos on the Migrant Trail*. Translated by Daniela Maria Ugaz and John Washington. New York: Verso.

Massey, Douglas S., Joaquín Arango, Graeme Hugo, Ali Kouaouci, Adela Pellegrino, and J. Edward Taylor. 1993. "Theories of International Migration: A Review and Appraisal." *Population and Development Review* 19 (3): 431–466.

Mbembe, Achille. 2003. "Necropolitics." Translated by L. Meintjes. *Public Culture* 15 (1): 11–40.

Menjívar, Cecilia. 2011. *Enduring Violence: Ladina Women's Lives in Guatemala*. Berkeley: University of California Press.

Mezzadra, Sandro, and Brett Neilson. 2013. *Border as Method; or, the Multiplication of Labor*. Durham, NC: Duke University Press.

Mitropoulos, Angela. 2006. "Autonomy, Recognition, Movement." *The Commoner* 11:5–14.

Mutua, Makau. 2001. "Savages, Victims, and Saviors: The Metaohor of Human Rights." *Harvard International Law Journal* 42 (1): 201–245.

No More Deaths. 2014. "Shakedown: How Deportation Robs Immigrants of Their Money and Belongings." https://nomoredeaths.org/wp-content/uploads/2014/12/ Shakedown-withcover.pdf.

Nyers, Peter. 2015. "Migrant Citizenships and Autonomous Mobilities." *Migration, Mobility, and Displacement* 1 (1): 23–39.

O'Leary, Anna O. 2009. "Mujeres en el Cruce: Remapping Border Security through Migrant Mobility." *Journal of the Southwest* 51 (4): 523–542.

Papadopoulos, Dimitris, Niamh Stephenson, and Vassilis Tsianos. 2008. *Escape Routes: Control and Subversion in the 21st Century*. Ann Arbor, MI: Pluto Press.

Parsons, Kenneth A. 2007. "Structural Violence and Power." *Peace Review: A Journal of Social Justice* 19:173–181.

Reichman, Daniel. 2011. "Migration and Paraethnography in Honduras." *American Ethnologist* 38 (3): 548–558.

———. 2013. "Honduras: The Perils of Remittance Dependence and Clandestine Migration." Migration Policy Institute, April 11. https://www.migrationpolicy.org/article/honduras-perils-remittance-dependence-and-clandestine-migration.

Robbins, Joel. 2013. "Beyond the Suffering Subject: Toward an Anthropology of the Good." *Journal of the Royal Anthropological Institute* 19 (3): 447–462.

Rodríguez, Néstor. 1996. "Battle for the Border: Notes on Autonomous Migration, Transnational Communities, and the State." *Social Justice* 23 (3): 21–37.

Rubio-Goldsmith, Raquel, Melissa McCormick, Daniel Martinez, and Inez Magdalena Duarte. 2006. *The "Funnel Effect" and Recovered Bodies of Unauthorized Migrants Processed by the Pima County Office of the Medical Examiner, 1990–2005.* Tucson: Binational Migration Institute.

Scott, James. 1985. *Weapons of the Weak: Everyday Forms of Peasant Resistance.* New Haven, CT: Yale University Press.

Sheridan, Lynnaire M. 2009. *"I Know It's Dangerous": Why Mexicans Risk Their Lives to Cross the Border.* Tucson: University of Arizona Press.

Spener, David. 2009. *Clandestine Crossings: Migrants and Coyotes on the Texas-Mexico Border.* Ithaca, NY: Cornell University Press.

Ticktin, Miriam. 2017. "A World without Innocence." *American Ethnologist* 44 (4): 577–590.

U.S. Border Patrol. 1994. "Border Patrol Strategic Plan, 1994 and Beyond: National Strategy." http://cw.routledge.com/textbooks/9780415996945/gov-docs/1994.pdf.

U.S. Customs and Border Protection. 2019. "United States Border Patrol: Southwest Border Sector Deaths by Fiscal Year." https://www.cbp.gov/sites/default/files/assets/documents/2019-Mar/bp-southwest-border-sector-deaths-fy1998-fy2018.pdf.

Van Hear, Nicholas, Oliver Bakewell, and Katy Long. 2018. "Push-Pull Plus: Reconsidering the Drivers of Migration." *Journal of Ethnic and Migration Studies* 44 (6): 927–944.

Vogt, Wendy A. 2018. "Intimate Crossings." In *Lives in Transit: Violence and Intimacy on the Migrant Journey.* Oakland: University of California Press.

Wheatley, Abby C. 2015. "Con Sangre y Fuego: Mobility, Autonomy, and the Politics of Survival." Ph.D. diss., California Institute of Integral Studies.

Wheatley, Abby C., and Ruth Gomberg-Muñoz. 2016. "Keep Moving: Collective Agency along the Migrant Trail." *Citizenship Studies* 20 (3–4): 396–410.

Wheatley, Abby C., and Oren Kroll-Zeldin. 2021. "Impermeable Borders and the Futility of Walls." *Peace Review* 32 (2): 190–197.

Wilson Gilmore, Ruth. 2007. *Golden Gulag: Prisons, Surplus, Crisis, and Opposition in Globalizing California.* Berkeley: University of California Press.

Zibechi, Raúl. 2012. *Territories in Resistance: A Cartography of Latin American Social Movements.* Translated by Ramor Ryan. Edinburgh: AK Press.

Epilogue

Death in Detention

ANNA M. BABEL, WITH MIRANDA CADY HALLETT
AND JAMIE LONGAZEL

*A*s this book goes to press, the world is in the midst of a devastating global pandemic, and the United States—joined by international solidaristic protesters—is in the throes of massive, sustained demonstrations following the murder of George Floyd by a Minneapolis police officer. In other words, the topic of multidimensional lethal state violence against the dispossessed and the potential for massive, meaningful resistance is playing out in historic proportions all around us. While our intent is obviously not to analyze these events as they unfold, we do want to draw attention to the relevance several of this book's themes have for understanding this moment. We do this by way of a case study of the life and death of Oscar Donaldo Lopez Acosta, written by anthropologist Anna Babel.

Oscar Donaldo Lopez Acosta was born in 1978 in San Francisco de La Paz, about a hundred miles northeast of Tegucigalpa, Honduras. As a young man, he worked with his extended family in small-scale agriculture, farming a piece of land that he inherited from his father. In his early twenties he met a local woman, Lourdes María, and they dated for about a year before they moved in together. Their oldest son was born in 2002, and they would go on to have two daughters as well. Unfortunately, Oscar told me, the land bordered areas claimed by local gangs involved in drug-related violence, and they began to threaten him and his family. In the multisided violent conflicts that plague Honduras, young men like Oscar are often at the greatest risk. Three of Oscar's nephews were killed. One day, his father-in-law told him he needed to flee, or he would be next.

Both economic precarity and the violence around his home pushed Oscar into migration as a strategy of survival. He traveled to the United States over land, paying for guidance from *coyotes* along the way. Like many Central American migrants who travel under clandestine conditions, his movements were shadowed by exclusion and enforcement, increasing both the costs and the personal risks of migration. Prevention through Deterrence (PTD) policies that began in the 1990s had militarized and walled much of the border, funneling Oscar along with tens of thousands of others into uncertain desert crossings with a much higher risk of death.

He was apprehended at the border and deported in 2009. Soon after, he reentered the country and worked in Florida for three years before being deported again in 2012. About two years later, he entered the country once more, this time moving to North Carolina to work. Eventually, seeking a lower cost of living, he followed his wife's relatives to Dayton, Ohio. Oscar's life in Dayton was stable, he found steady work in construction and at industrial chicken farms, and he was soon able to bring his wife and son to the United States. Oscar told me that he and his wife planted corn behind their small suburban home in Dayton, and that they sometimes brought home chickens and pigs to raise for consumption, partly replicating their rural lifestyle in Honduras.

In October 2018, Oscar's then-sixteen-year-old son was pulled over by the county sheriff on a minor traffic stop. Worried that he would be detained, he called his father, but was released by the sheriff because of his status as a minor. After receiving the phone call, unaware that his son had already been released, Oscar drove over to the site. He was pulled over by the police at the same traffic stop, and when the police found that he was an unlicensed driver, he was detained and fingerprinted, and his information was run through the Immigration and Customs Enforcement (ICE) database. While the Dayton City Police had some policies against sharing information with ICE in everyday situations as a result of Dayton's status as an immigrant-friendly city, the county sheriff had no such policy.

Unlike his previous deportations, this time Oscar was able to retain a lawyer who could advocate for him, as well as open the possibility of a new pathway to legal residency. Because of the persistent threats that he faced in Honduras, his lawyer presented a case for asylum based on Oscar's fears of continued persecution if he was forced to return. On top of the violence and instability in Honduras, his chronic condition as a diabetic added urgency to his claim. Oscar may have been previously unaware that he might have qualified for legal residence in the United States, or may simply have lacked the resources to retain a lawyer. Either way, the fact that he had lived for an extended period in the United States without seeking asylum no doubt complicated his case. In May 2019, he was sentenced to time served by a federal judge on the criminal charge of reentering the United States and transferred back to ICE custody to await a decision on his asylum case.

Oscar was kept in immigration detention for eighteen months despite repeated attempts by his lawyer to have him released on bond, arguing that he was hardly a flight risk, since he was seeking resolution of his asylum case. During that time, his diabetes flared out of control as a result of substandard medical care; during his trial in January 2019, the jail where he was being held neglected to give him insulin injections, and he went into diabetic shock. While diabetics have the right to a special diet while detained, Oscar reported that he was served only starchy prison food (such as instant noodles) alongside the rest of the people incarcerated in the facility.

I met Oscar in December 2019 on a visit to the jail organized by local activists. Morrow County Jail was primarily used as a holding facility for ICE detainees who were in the process of deportation. For this reason, most ICE detainees spent little more than a week at the jail. Because of his pending asylum case, Oscar was transferred there following more than a year at the Butler County Correctional Complex near Cincinnati, and he was incarcerated in the Morrow County facility for nearly five months. As activists, our goals were to document conditions at the jail, provide money and resources to meet the immediate needs of people incarcerated there, and mobilize to connect detainees, family, and friends to external resources throughout the process of detention and deportation.

Since Oscar was detained for so long, we became friends. From late December until visits to the jail were suspended in mid-March because of COVID-19, I visited him in person eight times. During these Saturday visiting hours, we chatted face-to-face through a Plexiglas barrier over old-style phone handsets. Because the official sixty-minute appointment was laxly enforced, we sometimes chatted for up to two hours, talking about our families, favorite foods, and stories from our lives. In between visits, Oscar often called me just to say hello, and after in-person visits were suspended because of the COVID-19 crisis, he called me every Saturday evening to check in and see how I was doing. He gave me his wife's phone number so that we could try to coordinate a visit to the jail, and I communicated with her regularly as well.

In February 2020, his wife, María, called me in a panic. Oscar had been involved in an altercation with another ICE detainee in the jail. She told me that he had not been seen by a doctor and that she was afraid for his life, saying, "Él es mayor, no es joven, y es delicado de salud; es enfermo" (He's an older person, not a young man, and his health is poor; he's a sick man).

When I called the jail, a correctional officer denied that anything had happened, asserting that everything was "under control" and that Oscar had been seen by a doctor.

When I visited Oscar the following Saturday, he told me about the incident. The man who had attacked him often used the communal bathroom to abuse drugs, and correctional officers ignored the situation. Oscar had gone to use the bathroom in the middle of the night when the man punched him in the chest and threatened him. He called for guards, who removed the other man for a few hours before releasing him once again into the open dorms.

After repeated calls to the jail from me and from his lawyer, Oscar was allowed to see a doctor for his painful injuries from the fight. The doctor told him that he had a fractured rib but insisted that it could have happened at any time in the past few years. Oscar showed me his chest, still red and swollen a week after the incident. He said that while he was taking medication, it still hurt to cough or to roll over and that he was having trouble sleeping because of the pain.

Normally reluctant to criticize or dwell on the negative, that day Oscar complained bitterly about the lack of control exercised by the correctional officers in the county jail. They let the county detainees fight without intervening, he recounted, and drugs circulated freely in the jail with the correctional officers' knowledge. Feeling personally targeted and fearful of coming to harm in this uncontrolled environment, Oscar requested that his lawyer apply to have him transferred back to Butler County. There, at least, detainees were housed in cell blocks.

Not only was he not transferred, but he continued to be housed in open dorms with his aggressor for weeks following the incident. I called his lawyer that week to tell her I was afraid, for the first time, that he was giving in to despair. The poor living conditions and constant stress during his long detention wreaked havoc on his health and exacerbated his diabetes, leaving him in poor condition just as the threat of coronavirus elevated.

María called me again on the afternoon of April 24. She had been notified that Oscar was being released because someone had tested positive for COVID-19 at the jail. She asked if I could pick him up and bring him home that same afternoon, and luckily, I was able to do so. Oscar walked out of the jail on a sunny, warm day, wearing jeans and a flannel shirt and carrying a bag containing all his personal belongings and a sheet of paper ordering him to appear at the ICE offices in Columbus three weeks later.

On the two-hour ride home, we chatted as usual, speaking for the first time without a Plexiglas barrier but now with masks covering our faces. He was looking forward to seeing his wife and family, getting back to work, and bringing his other daughter to the United States from Honduras. As we drove into Dayton, he became emotional. He pointed to a motel just down the road, explaining that he had been working construction there when he was detained, and pointed out a police station a short distance away, where his freedom ended when he was booked. It was bittersweet to see him reunite with his family at his little white house in the suburbs—sweet to see them together again but bitter to think of their long separation and of the months that he suffered in jail.

Just a week after being released from ICE custody, Oscar was taken by ambulance to the Miami Valley Hospital in Dayton. His wife was told that he was in diabetic shock and later found out that he had a "mild" case of COVID-19. He was released on May 8 and went into fatal diabetic shock two days later. The coroner's report attributed the death to COVID-19.

Subsequent investigations revealed that ICE continued to move detainees into the jail from around the country, even as COVID outbreaks flared at prisons and jails across the state and the country. *Mother Jones* reported that an ICE detainee was transferred to Morrow County Jail in mid-April and remained in the open dorms for ten days before being diagnosed with COVID-19 (Lanard 2020). Subsequently, ICE transferred another five people into the jail, even though the extreme risks were readily apparent. By Oscar's firsthand account, men had been lying in the open dorms, coughing, for days or weeks before the first diagnosed case. Within weeks of his release, all fifty-one ICE detainees at the jail had been diagnosed with COVID-19.

The last time I heard from Oscar was on the evening of May 9. We had the following text exchange:

Oscar Donaldo Lopez Acosta: Como esta ana (How are you, Anna?)
Anna B: Hola Oscar, ya está de vuelta en casa? (Hi Oscar, are you back home again?)
Anna B: Nosotros bien, gracias (We're good, thanks)
Oscar Donaldo Lopez Acosta: Si ya en casa gracias a dios (Yes, home again, thank God)
Anna B: Qué bien, dice que estaba bien enfermo, no? (That's good, I hear you were really sick, weren't you?)
Oscar Donaldo Lopez Acosta: Si pero ai estaba dios con migo I el me lebanto debuelta el nome deja desu mano (Yes, but God was there with me, he picked me up again, he keeps me in his hand)
Anna B: Me alegro que ya está en casa, qué pesadilla (I'm happy you're home, what a nightmare)
Oscar Donaldo Lopez Acosta: Si pero ya paso (Yes, but it's over now)

The next day his wife called to tell me he had died suddenly at home, saying, "I'm dying, I'm dying; the diabetes has killed me," and asking her to take their young daughter out of the room.

After his death, Oscar's story was picked up by local immigration activists. As the first Ohio detainee, and only the second ICE detainee in the nation, to die of COVID-19, Oscar became a symbol of the rampant spread of the disease among incarcerated populations. His photo, taken from a WhatsApp profile, showed a brown-eyed man with a lined face looking slightly down at the camera, while holding a smiling young girl in a pink shirt—his youngest daughter, who was three years old when he was released. Working with Ohio Immigrant Visitation, a small group of activists that coordinated visits to the jail, I published some details from Oscar's story in a Facebook post that was widely circulated, drawing attention from other local immigration activists and the media (see, e.g., Lanard 2020; Free Press staff and Ohio Immigrant Alliance 2020; Hola News 2020).

In the weeks following Oscar's death, activists from a larger immigration activist group, Ohio Immigrant Alliance, used Oscar's photo to stage a silent protest at a meeting of the Morrow County Health Department. Activists were encouraged to join the Zoom call using Oscar's photo as their profile picture. Since the number of guests on the call was limited, there was a long line of volunteers waiting throughout the meeting—every time someone left the call, another participant with Oscar's face, framed by the words "RIP OSCAR—NO MORE DEATHS!" in red capital letters, joined the call (see Figure E.1). A month after Oscar's death, local activist Danya Contractor, who organized the visits to the Morrow County Jail, made an in-person statement to the same body. Frequent press releases by activist Lynn Tramonte of the organization Columbus Stands with Immigrants highlighted the details of Oscar's story, as well as the continuing plight of people still detained at the jail without access to medical care. These stories supported earlier reports by local activists associated with the national group Freedom for Immigrants, including a formal complaint to ICE in February that documented extensive health violations at the jail.

Oscar's image gave a face to these complaints, which detailed violations in rather dry, abstract language; and his death from COVID-19 elicited outrage among a public whose attention was already closely focused on the disease.

On the legal front, I provided detailed notes and emails regarding Oscar's firsthand accounts of the lack of medical attention and his fears of being assaulted to Ohio American Civil Liberties Union (ACLU) lawyers who led lawsuits to have other detainees released. These accounts, along with those of other people incarcerated at Morrow, ultimately resulted in

Figure E.1 Oscar Lopez Acosta with his three-year-old daughter, shortly after being released. Originally Oscar's WhatsApp profile picture, this image was picked up by the media in articles about Oscar's death and was subsequently used by the Ohio Immigrant Alliance to stage a protest at a virtual meeting of the Morrow County Board of Health. (Photo by Oscar Lopez Acosta, as modified by Ohio activist Galen Schwartzberg. Used with permission from Galen Schwartzberg and from Oscar's next of kin, Lourdes María Mejías.)

the release of an additional thirteen ICE detainees. Despite pressure from activists, Morrow County public health officials declined to use their authority to address the conditions at the jail.

The fact that Oscar was a blameless detainee who had never committed a violent crime was prominently highlighted in media stories following his death, as well as the fact that he had a loving family waiting for him to come home. The selection of these details, as opposed to others, played into a familiar narrative that elicited a sympathetic response from a public already fixated on COVID-19. At the same time that ICE detainees in Morrow County Jail were being infected, the media were also focusing on COVID-19 outbreaks at the Marion Correctional Facility and the Pickaway Correctional Institution, both also located in central Ohio. The fear of the spread of the disease and the fact that many people were at home, anxiously following the news, helped amplify the reaction to his death. The fact that Oscar was a devout Christian and a family man helped establish rapport and empathy with the public, humanizing the story of the many incarcerated people vulnerable to the COVID-19 crisis.[1]

Shortly after Oscar died, his wife told me over the phone, "Al final lo que le mató fue todo ese tiempo que pasó en la cárcel" (In the end what killed him was all that time he spent in jail). When he was released, she had hoped for a joyful reunion. "I expected it to be happy, all of us together as a family, celebrating and having a good time," she said during a visit about a month after Oscar died. "But it wasn't like that. He was suffering. It was like he was already dead inside." As we spoke, she expressed a mix of emotions: bewilderment, outrage, and bitter grief. "He begged God to let him come home to us, but He only let him come home to say good-bye," she said.

While Oscar himself believed that he was dying of diabetes, and the county coroner determined that his death was due to COVID-19, the long months of detention took a toll on him both physically and mentally, leaving him unable to fight off the virus. Given the documented issues with poor hygiene at the jail, where detainees were not issued clean clothes or cleaning supplies, and the overcrowded conditions in the open dorms, the spread of COVID-19 was a foregone conclusion. And it was hastened by ICE, which flouted public health policy by continuing to move detainees to Morrow County from around the United States, as well as deporting them to their countries of origin, even after detainees began showing symptoms of COVID-19 and were diagnosed with the virus. It escaped nobody's attention that the virus was prevalent not only among detainees but among the staff of the jail, who moved in and out of the surrounding community. Even Oscar's abrupt release was not accompanied by a test for the virus; his ICE agent merely told me, in a somewhat embarrassed tone, that he should quarantine himself for fourteen days after leaving jail.

That Oscar's death is a direct result of U.S. immigration policy seems an obvious fact to the many people who have mobilized in response. The punitive conditions he was forced to live under as a result of his legal exclusion denied him the possibility of life. Yet ICE did not take responsibility, denying that he was infected with COVID-19 at the jail. The institution has not included Oscar's name on its list of people who died from contracting COVID-19 in their custody, raising the question of how many others may have died following a hasty last-minute release (Glaun 2020).

By Oscar's own account, he lived in constant fear of dying silenced in detention. However, he was never really silent; he and his family members constantly engaged in advocacy in an effort to be heard by the U.S. government, by ICE, and by the personnel at the jail. Likewise, Oscar's asylum claim itself was a way of speaking to the courts through a system that was supposed to offer protection for people in his position. Instead, the case dragged on for months without resolution while he endured incarceration and separation from his family. Oscar was always speaking; yet it was only his death that created the conditions under which a broader public was willing to listen.[2]

The timing of his death also made his story uniquely compelling to the public. As the pandemic spread, the closeness of death and the vulnerability of people held in state custody created greater empathy and responsiveness among the public. Unrest and mobilization responding to the violent abuses of law enforcement also opened up new space for some to hear difficult truths about the harms done to their fellow human beings in the name of law, order, and security.

———————

COVID-19 may have posed a new and unprecedented threat to the modern world, but as we see in Oscar's story, it also illuminated the extent to which deadly racism and inequality embedded within our institutions is already a threat to life and health. As we assert in this book, the precarity and mortality experienced disproportionately by some peoples is the direct result of a settler colonial history rife with genocide, enslavement, dispossession, and the systematic devaluation of life—and despite attempts to whitewash that history, through struggle and the rescue of collective memory this history *remains*.

This book begins with a quotation from Friedrich Engels, who makes the important point that the systematic killing of poor and working-class people, though depicted by the capitalist class as a collection of natural occurrences, unequivocally represents cruel, wanton murder on a massive scale. Collectively, our contributors take apart piece by piece this façade of naturalness and expose how broader systems, ideologies, and policies act, in the context of migration in the Americas, as veritable killing machines. The book also interrogates and critiques dominant narratives about migration, from the "phantasmagoric inversions" (Butler 2020, 62) of racial siege mentality that rationalize cruel and exclusionary violence, to the inadequacies of liberal and humanitarian responses. Sharing the assumption that "racial capitalism is the principal contradiction that fundamentally organizes our current social order, resulting in exploitation, repression, and the reduction of life chances" (Rodriguez 2020, 4), we argue that despite the risks, a critical focus on death and the institutionalized production of mortality can contribute to life and to structural transformation.

Central to the violence against migrants—indeed, its primary enabler— is the devaluation of certain lives to the point of social death. As Judith Butler writes, "Prohibition against killing . . . applies only to those lives that are grievable, but not to those who are considered ungrievable." While what happens at the border is of course a key piece of this puzzle, our widened lens also reveals how a lack of "grievability is already operative in life" (2020, 58). Those exposed to social death include children detained at a toxic site; farmworkers denied access to shade from the brutal sun; asylum seekers turned away, left to endure danger—in other words, people like Oscar, who nonetheless continue to demand recognition and insist that their lives matter, even in the face of a system that is functionally dependent on the contrary insistence that they do not. In other words, social death, too, creates ghosts: the field of humanity, as Butler argues, is "haunted by those figures that do not count in its tally" (59).

Deaths like Oscar's are haunting not only because of the ways they re-veal exclusion but because they affirm and assert life. As Anna Babel notes above, Oscar was never silent about the value of his life; nor was his family. They struggled and paid and fought to build a life for themselves. His story and that of his wife and children fit the experience of sacrifice described by Leisy Abrego (2014) in her study of Salvadoran transnational families. The concept of sacrifice resonates on a dual level here: Central American fami-lies simultaneously sacrifice for one another's survival and bear the brunt of a political system that sacrifices their lives too easily for political profit or economic gains. Oscar's life, albeit devalued by the powers that be, shows through its "imagination and energy . . . expectations and desires" that "the constraints these forms of life entail do not exhaust their reality" (Fassin 2018, 46). As Oscar's story also illustrates, political agency does not end with death—through testimony and the mobilization of his memory, people are fighting to release others from the conditions that ended Oscar's life.

Ghosts can be evoked in such a way that lights a spark, helping us see the unseen. And how we treat and speak of the dead has social and political consequences. Insisting on grieving the lives that are politically devalued and considering our obligations to the dead can prompt not only account-ability for injustice but an invigoration of social relations. Valuing the dead is tied to justice among the living, as "the presumption of equal grievability would not be only a conviction of attitude with which another person greets you, but a principle that organizes the social organization of health, food, shelter, employment, sexual life, and civic life" (Butler 2020, 59). In the spirit of that commitment to imagining and acting toward a better world, we close with the words of a compatriot of Oscar Lopez Acosta, Honduran activist and human rights defender Berta Cáceres (2015):

> We must shake our conscience free of the rapacious capitalism, rac-ism, and patriarchy that will only assure our own self-destruction. . . . Let us build societies that are able to coexist in a dignified way, in a way that protects life. Let us come together and remain hopeful as we defend and care for the blood of this Earth and of its spirits.

NOTES

1. Oscar's story, in particular the details emphasized by activists, fits neatly within the narrative of martyrdom that often accompanies stories of migration (Puga 2016; Puga and Espinosa 2020). Oscar was profoundly devout and quite intentionally nonvio-lent; when I suggested to him that he might band together with some of his Bible-study friends in jail to protect himself against the man who had attacked him, he shook his head, smiled, and told me that God was his protection.

2. Such circumstances beg a complementary question to the one Gayatri Chakravorty Spivak (1988) asks in her essay "Can the Subaltern Speak?"—namely, when subaltern truths are articulated, under what conditions can the public hear them?

REFERENCES

Abrego, Leisy. 2014. *Sacrificing Families: Navigating Love, Labor, and Laws across Borders*. Stanford, CA: Stanford University Press.

Butler, Judith. 2020. *The Force of Nonviolence: The Ethical in the Political*. New York: Verso.

Cáceres, Berta. 2015. Speech upon receiving the Goldman Environmental Prize. April 20, San Francisco, CA.

Fassin, Didier. 2018. *Life: A Critical User's Manual*. Cambridge, UK: Polity Press.

Free Press staff and Ohio Immigrant Alliance. 2020. "Ohio's First ICE Detainee Dies from COVID-19." *Columbus Free Press*, May 13. https://columbusfreepress.com/article/ohio%E2%80%99s-first-ice-detainee-dies-covid-19.

Glaun, Dan. 2020. "How ICE Data Undercounts COVID-19 Victims." *Frontline*, August 11. https://www.pbs.org/wgbh/frontline/article/how-ice-data-undercounts-covid-19-victims/.

Hola News. 2020. "Fallece un inmigrante que contrajo el COVID-19 en un centro de detención." *Hola News*, May 12. https://holanews.com/fallece-un-inmigrante-que-contrajo-el-covid-19-en-un-centro-de-detencion-2/.

Lanard, Noah. 2020. "A Honduran Man Has Died of COVID-19 after Leaving an ICE Jail Plagued by the Virus." *Mother Jones*, May 14. https://www.motherjones.com/politics/2020/05/a-honduran-man-has-died-of-covid-19-after-leaving-an-ice-jail-plagued-by-the-virus/.

Puga, Ana Elena. 2016. "Migrant Melodrama and the Political Economy of Suffering." *Women and Performance* 26 (1): 72–93.

Puga, Ana Elena, and Victor Espinosa. 2020. *Performances of Suffering in Latin American Migration: Heroes, Martyrs, and Saints*. Cham, Switzerland: Palgrave Macmillan.

Rodriguez, Cesar. 2020. "'The Whole Damn System Is Guilty': Urban Violence, the Principal Contradiction of Racial Capitalism, and the Production of Premature Death in Oakland, California." *Critical Sociology* 46 (7–8): 1057–1074.

Spivak, Gayatri Chakravorty. 1988. "Can the Subaltern Speak?" In *Marxism and the Interpretation of Culture*, edited by Cary Nelson and Lawrence Grossberg, 271–313. Urbana: University of Illinois Press.

Contributors

Karina Alma (formerly Oliva Alvarado) holds a Ph.D. in ethnic studies from the University of California, Berkeley. Her interdisciplinary work examines intercultural and transcultural texts, memories, practices, and identities through a transnational critique of systems of domination and racial-gender hierarchies. Her undergraduate and graduate courses on U.S. Central American cultures, literatures, racial constructions, and cultural memory were foundational to the creation of a Central American studies minor at what is now the Department of Chicana/o and Central American Studies at the University of California, Los Angeles. She coedited the anthology *U.S. Central Americans: Reconstructing Memories, Struggles, and Communities of Resistance* in 2017.

Anna M. Babel is a sociolinguist and a linguistic anthropologist. Her research focuses on the relationship between language and social categories, particularly in settings of language contact. She has carried out long-term research in the Santa Cruz valleys of Bolivia, the setting of her ethnography, *Between the Andes and the Amazon* (2018). Her most recent work considers how we become aware of different ways of speaking and, conversely, how our knowledge and beliefs about language influence the way we speak. In addition to these areas of expertise, she teaches on the role of language in the construction of U.S. and Latina/o identities.

Pil H. Chung is a graduate of the University of California, Berkeley, in the Departments of Sociology and Demography. His research leverages advances in formal demographic and statistical methodologies to gain new purchase on old questions about the family: its configurations, transformations, and meanings. His latest work uses a combination of life table and microsimulation techniques to investigate the link between race differences in mortality, kinship, householding, and incarceration over the life course.

Deirdre Conlon is associate professor in critical human geography, currently based at the University of Leeds, UK. Conlon's research examines immigration, detention, and migrant (in)security with projects in the United States, UK, and Ireland. Current work examines detention and destitution economies—in other words, the ways immigration enforcement and migrant experience are bound up with capital, marketization, valuation, and commodification. In addition to an edited collection and several recent journal articles coauthored with Nancy Hiemstra, Conlon has published in *Annals of the Association of American Geographers* (2014, 2020), *Progress in Human Geography* (2018), and *Citizenship Studies* (2013).

Nicholas De Genova is a professor in and chair of the Department of Comparative Cultural Studies at the University of Houston. He is the author of *Working the Boundaries: Race, Space, and "Illegality" in Mexican Chicago* (2005), coauthor of *Latino Crossings: Mexicans, Puerto Ricans, and the Politics of Race and Citizenship* (2003), editor of *Racial Transformations: Latinos and Asians Remaking the United States* (2006), coeditor of *The Deportation Regime: Sovereignty, Space, and the Freedom of Movement* (2010), editor of *The Borders of "Europe": Autonomy of Migration, Tactics of Bordering* (2017), and coeditor of *Roma Migrants in the European Union: Un/Free Mobility* (2019).

Alicia Ivonne Estrada is a professor in the Chicana/o Studies Department at California State University at Northridge. She has published on the Maya and Guatemalan diaspora in Los Angeles, as well as on Maya literature, film, and radio. She is coeditor of *U.S. Central Americans: Reconstructing Memories, Struggles and Communities of Resistance* (2017). Estrada's work has appeared in *Romance Notes*, *Latino Studies*, and *Revista Canadiense de Estudios Hispánicos*, among other journals and anthologies. Her current book project focuses on the Maya diaspora in Los Angeles. Since 2006, she has collaborated with the Maya radio collective *Contacto Ancestral*.

Amelia Frank-Vitale is a doctoral candidate in anthropology at the University of Michigan. Her research examines how Hondurans navigate life after being deported back to neighborhoods tagged as some of the world's most violent. Her work connects regional immigration and security policies, organized crime, state violence, and the everyday experience of life in and around San Pedro Sula. She has been published in *Geopolitics*, *Journal of Latin American and Caribbean Studies*, *EntreDiversidades*, and *Public Anthropologist*. Her commentary has also appeared in the *Washington Post*, *Fortune Magazine*, *NACLA Report on the Americas*, *ContraCorriente*, and the *World Policy Journal*.

Miranda Cady Hallett is associate professor of cultural anthropology and research fellow at the Human Rights Center at the University of Dayton. She has published a number of articles centered on Salvadoran migrants' diasporic experiences in such journals as *Latino Studies*, *Law and Social Inquiry*, and the *Journal of Working Class Studies*. Over twenty years of ethnographic work among transborder communities, she has examined interrelated issues of labor exploitation, state violence, conditions of displacement, and the fraught impacts of exclusionary migration policies in social fields spanning the United States and El Salvador. A publicly engaged scholar, Hallett has frequently been cited in public media on immigration, displacement, and the politicization of asylum.

Nancy Hiemstra is associate professor in the Department of Women's, Gender, and Sexuality Studies at Stony Brook University in Stony Brook, New York. Her research examines drivers and consequences of restrictive border and immigration policies. Current projects include tracing the geopolitical reverberations of U.S. immigration and border enforcement policies in Latin America, and exploring the internal economies of immigration detention facilities in the greater New York City area (with Deirdre Conlon). She is the author of *Detain and Deport: The Chaotic U.S. Immigration Enforcement Regime* (2019) and numerous journal articles and book chapters. She coedited, with Deirdre Conlon, *Intimate Economies of Immigration Detention: Critical Perspectives* (2016).

Nolan Kline is assistant professor of anthropology and co-coordinator of the Global Health program at Rollins College. His book, *Pathogenic Policing: Immigration Enforcement and Health in the US South* (2019), traces the multiple health-related consequences of immigration legislation and police practices in Atlanta, Georgia. His work has been funded by the National Science Foundation, and he has published several peer-reviewed articles and book chapters on (im)migrant and farmworker health and human papillomavirus interventions. As an applied, medical anthropologist who uses community-based methodologies to examine the social and political determinants of health, Kline's work intersects with policy and activism.

Shirley P. Leyro is an assistant professor of criminal justice at Borough of Manhattan Community College, City University of New York (CUNY). As a critical criminologist, she focuses her research on deportation effects, including the impact of the fear resulting from the vulnerability to deportation. She is coeditor of *Outside Justice: Immigration and the Criminalizing Impact of Changing Policy and Practice* (2013), as well as a contributor to the same volume. She is currently working on publishing the findings of her funded research study exploring the impact of deportability on the feelings of belonging and membership of CUNY noncitizen students.

Jamie Longazel is associate professor of law and society at John Jay College and is affiliated with the International Migration Studies program at the CUNY Graduate Center. His research examines how race and political economy intersect in law and politics, especially within the realms of immigration and crime. His recent book, *Undocumented Fears: Immigration and the Politics of Divide and Conquer in Hazleton, Pennsylvania* (2016), won the North Central Sociological Association's 2017 Scholarly Achievement Award. He is also the coauthor of *The Pains of Mass Imprisonment* (2013) and the cofounder of Anthracite Unite, a working-class collective fighting for racial and economic justice in Pennsylvania.

Marianne Madoré is a Ph.D. candidate in sociology at the CUNY Graduate Center, concentrating on feminist theories, racism, and global sociology. She teaches at Brooklyn College, where she collaborates with students and instructors to develop open educational resources. She is a Connect New York fellow and a founding member of the Social Anatomy of a Deportation Regime.

Linda A. McCauley, dean of Emory University's Nell Hodgson Woodruff School of Nursing, is a member of the National Academy of Medicine and American Academy of Nursing. She is internationally recognized for scholarship in environmental and occupational health. She has been consistently funded for two decades, studying pesticide exposure in children, health risks to adolescent workers, and interventions to decrease exposures in vulnerable populations. She served as codirector of a Children's Environmental Health Research Center, which explored health effects of environmental exposures on African American women and infants. Recently, her research focus is on risks of kidney injury associated with occupational heat exposure in migrant farmworkers.

Nathan J. Mutic is an associate director of research at the Emory University Nell Hodgson Woodruff School of Nursing. He spent the first half of his career as a public schoolteacher in underserved communities and is a reviewer for science education pedagogical journals. His current work is on development of novel tools for public health communication regarding research on children's environmental health disparities. Previously, he was responsible for the design and implementation of report-back protocols at the individual and community levels for data from participants in studies of the effects of occupational heat exposure on migrant farmworkers.

Joseph Nevins is a professor of geography at Vassar College. Among his books are *A People's Guide to Greater Boston* (2020), *Operation Gatekeeper and Beyond: The War on "Illegals" and the Remaking of the U.S.-Mexico Boundary* (2010), and *Dying to Live: A Story of U.S. Immigration in an Age of Global Apartheid* (2008). His writings have appeared in a variety of publications, including *Al Jazeera English, CounterPunch, Boston Review*, the *Conversation*, the *Los Angeles Times, NACLA Report on the Americas*, the *Nation, Tikkun*, the *Washington Post*, and *Z Magazine*.

Juan M. Pedroza is an assistant professor of demography, migration, and inequality in the sociology department at the University of California, Santa Cruz. His research concerns the vast inequalities present in immigrants' access to justice, the social safety net, and poverty. His latest work examines how and where deportation and enforcement initiatives exacerbate these inequalities and leave imprints in our local communities.

Nicholas Rodrigo is a Ph.D. candidate in the sociology department at the CUNY Graduate Center. He also teaches a crime and migration course at John Jay College and is a research and communications fellow at the Social Anatomy of a Deportation Regime, a research and advocacy working group based at John Jay College that examines the deportation system in New York. He has worked in policy concerning human rights mechanisms on the international level, having organized workshops and teach-ins on the question of Palestine, refugee rights, and sports in activism.

Daniel L. Stageman is director of research at John Jay College in New York City. His scholarship examines political economy and profit in American immigrant detention and the economic contexts surrounding federal-local immigration enforcement partnerships, such as the 287(g) program. He holds a Ph.D. in criminal justice from John Jay College.

Jared P. Van Ramshorst is a postdoctoral teaching fellow in Latin American, Latina/o, and Caribbean studies at College of the Holy Cross. His research examines the geopolitics and intimate experiences of migration journeys from Central America to and toward the United States, including the ways Central American migrants navigate international borders, asylum policy, and immigration enforcement. His work has appeared in the *Journal of Latin American Geography, Geopolitics*, and the *Professional Geographer*.

Abby C. Wheatley is an honors faculty fellow at Barrett, the Honors College at Arizona State University, and holds a Ph.D. in social and cultural anthropology. Her research spans two regions, the U.S.-Mexico and EU-Africa borders, and considers the mechanisms through which migration becomes a dangerous and deadly endeavor, as well as the strategies developed by migrants to survive precarious crossings. Incorporating her more than ten years of experience working with people in transit, her work examines the strategies developed by transnational communities to overcome a weaponized landscape created by border enforcement. Her recent work is published in *Human Organization* and the *Peace Review*.

Index

Page numbers in italics refer to tables or figures.

Abbott, Alison, 146
Abrego, Leisy, 191, 240, 260, 284
Agamben, Giorgio, 103, 240, 248
Agriculture: heat-related illness and, 123–135 (see also Heat-related illness); regulation of, 126–129, 135n1
Alamo Mission, 70–72, 77n4
Allgood, Brad, 247
American Legislative Exchange Council, 105
Amnesty International, 28–31, 33, 34
Amputation, 147
Andersson, Ruben, 27
Anomie, 152–155, 158
Anti-sanctuary laws, 189
Arendt, Hannah, 33
Arias, Roberto, 47
Asylum, 207–221; Amnesty International on, 34; autonomy of, 91; Central American exclusion from, 86, 243–244; ethnographic study of, 208–209; gang membership and, 213; Human Rights Watch on, 30; individuals' accounts of, 212–215, 276–277, 282; Maya requests for, 44–45; metering policy and, 16, 207–208, 209–212, 216–218; Mexican humanitarian visa and, 214–215; Universal Declaration of Human Rights on, 33, 34–35. See also Survival

Atlanta, Georgia, dialysis center closure, 15–16, 186–203. See also Kidney failure
Autonomy of asylum, 91

Baird, Theodore, 62
Balad Air Base, 3
Bandera Shooting Club, 72
Bare life, 103, 240, 244, 248
Battle of the Alamo, 70–71, 77n4
Belgian Congo, 147
Benjamin, Walter, 17–18
Bergen County Jail, 106–115, 117n2. See also Immigration detention
Biehl, João, 103
Binford, Leigh, 56n6
Black Lives Matter, 88–89
Black Marxism (Robinson), 8–9
Border Patrol Foundation, 61, 70–75
Border Security and Immigration Enforcement Fund, 101
Border Security Expo. See San Antonio Border Security Expo (2019)
Border Spectacle, 87–88
Border walls, 27–28, 86–87, 91–92
Borgstrom, Erica, 102
Bracero Program, 127
Brain drain, 153

Brazil, social abandonment in, 103
Brown, Wendy, 35
Budd, Jenn, 69
Burstow, Bonnie, 145
Butler, Judith, 8, 46, 283
Butler County Correctional Complex, 277
Bystander effect, 41, 49–50

Cacho, Lisa Marie, 92, 103, 104, 191–192, 209
Caliburn International Corporation, 2, 3
Cantú, Francisco, 71
Capitalism: detention industry and, 3, 14, 101–122 (*see also* Immigration detention); drug trafficking and, 4–5; in Honduras, 224–225; in Nicaragua, 241–242, 244–246; racism and, 8–12, 77n4, 283, 284; resistance to, 249–250; social death and, 103–117 (*see also* Social death)
Capital Partners, 3
Caplan, Art, 50
Caravan phenomenon, 66, 77n3, 90–91, 257
Card, Claudia, 229
Carter, Jon Horne, 224
Cartography, 26
Centers for Disease Control and Prevention (CDC): agricultural workforce data from, 125; Hispanic mortality data from, 15, 169–170, 171, 176
Chavez, Ernest, 226
Chicas, Roxana, 133
Child detention centers, 2–4, 3, 5–6, 12, 17; deaths in, 12, 45, 75, 90; demographics on, 5, 66, 159n1; resources for, 67–69; unsafe conditions of, 63, 108–109, 112, 189. *See also* Family separation policy
Chomsky, Noam, 46, 49, 56n6
Christianopoulos, Dinos, 12
Chronic kidney disease, 133. *See also* Kidney failure
Citizenship, racialized, 2–3
Columbia Stands with Immigrants, 280
Commemorations: of Hugo Alfredo Tale Yax, 42–43, 51–54; at San Antonio Border Security Expo, 74–75, 76, 77–78n5
Comprehensive Health Services, Inc. (CHS), 2, 3, 4
Consciousness, territorialization of, 26
Contractor, Danya, 280
Contra War, 242
CoreCivic, 104
Coutin, Susan Bibler, 93, 226
COVID-19: in agricultural workers, 196; detention and, 86, 118n7, 178–179, 189,

275–283; hearing delays and, 271n3; in Honduras, 232–233; individual account of, 275–285; inequality and, 18
Criminalization: of humanitarian aid, 31–32, 190–191; of immigrants, 76, 87, 89–91, 103–104, 191–192 (*see also* Immigration detention); of poverty, 225, 231

Daugherty, Luke Austin, 51–52
Decompression sickness, 244–245, 247–248
Deindividuation in detention, 107–108
De La Pena, Augustin, 74
De León, Jason, 64, 259
Department of Homeland Security, budget for, 67–69, 101, 117n1
Deportation: Amnesty International on, 29–31; to Honduras, 16, 222–237; Human Rights Watch on, 30; individuals' accounts of, 212–214, 225–228, 276–278; metering policy and, 16, 207–208, 209–212, 216–218; mortality and morbidity and, 15, 165–185; social death after, 225–228
Depression, 152–155
Desolation, 259
Detention. *See* Child detention centers; Immigration detention
Discourse: Border Spectacle, 88; of Donald Trump, 89, 106; of international human rights organizations, 13, 28–33, 35; Michel Foucault on, 45–50; national security, 6, 8; of police survivability, 73, 75; of print media, 8, 46–50, 55; of Ronald Reagan, 242–243; at San Antonio Border Security Expo, 63–66, 73–75, 76; social authority and, 50; of YouTube music videos, 51–54
Disculturation, 103
Disposable lives, 9–12, 92–93; of homeless/unhoused, 50; human rights and, 35; of Maya, 43–45 (*see also* Tale Yax, Hugo Alfredo); of Miskitu, 244–249 (*see also* Miskitu sweet-lobster industry laborers)
Dispossession, 7–9, 25–28, 42–43, 116, 239–242
Disproportionate share hospital (DSH) funding, 195
Dominguez, Manuel, 241
Doty, Roxanne, 64
Drug trafficking, 4–5, 212, 230–231, 233–234n2
Dunbar-Ortiz, Roxanne, 239

El Salvador: civil war in, 243–244; Human Rights Watch report on, 30–31

Emergency Medicaid, 190, 192–193
Encavement, 228–230
Enclosure, 25–28. *See also* National territorial boundaries
The End of the Myth (Grandin), 71
End-stage renal disease Medicare program, 190
Engels, Friedrich, 1, 6, 283
Environmental Protection Agency, 3–4
Essex County Correctional Facility, 106–115. *See also* Immigration detention
Establishment human rights organizations, 24, 28–33, 36n1
Ethical witnessing, 12
European Union: Amnesty International's criticism of, 28–30; Frontex of, 64–65; migrant deaths and, 23–24, 85, 87, 94n2
Express kidnapping, 214

Fair Labor Standards Act (1938), 126–127, 134
Family separation policy, 2–4, 5–6, 143–144, 159n1, 251n1; morbidity and mortality with, 12, 112, 143–144, 189; Ron Vitiello on, 67; zero-tolerance policy and, 89–90, 93, 94n1, 95n4
Farmer, Paul, 196
Farmworkers' health. *See* Heat-related illness; Kidney failure
Farmworker Vulnerability to Heat Hazards Framework, 129
Fischer, Nicholas, 194
Flores Settlement Agreement, 2
Florida, agricultural laborers in, 129–133. *See also* Heat-related illness
Floyd, George, 11, 89, 275
Fort Alamo, 70–72, 77n4
Foucault, Michel, 45–50, 64
Frontex, 64–65
Funereal space, 7, 11–12, 152

Galperin, Hernan, 51
Gangs, 31, 159n5, 209, 211, 212; in Honduras, 213, 224–225, 228–229, 230, 232, 261–262
Generativity, 157–158
Genovese, Kitty, 41, 49, 50
GEO Group, 104
Georgia: immigrant health care in (*see* Kidney failure); immigration policies in, 190–191
Ghostly Matters (Gordon), 10–11, 62–63
Ghosts, 10–12, 17–18, 85, 284; of the Alamo, 70–72

Gilmore, Ruth Wilson, 8, 86
Girasoles Study, 14, 129–133. *See also* Heat-related illness
Giroux, Henry, 225, 231
Global border system, 27
Global Operations, 3
Goffman, Erving, 103
Gomberg-Muñoz, Ruth, 198
Gómez González, Claudia Patricia, 54–55, 56n9
Goodman, Rachael, 148
Gordon, Avery, 10–11, 17–18, 62–63, 85
Gore capitalism, 4–5
Grady Memorial Hospital, 15–16, 192–196
Grandin, Greg, 44, 71
Guatemala: genocide in, 42, 43–45, 47, 55, 243; Maya migration from, 41–59, 56n8 (*see also* Tale Yax, Hugo Alfredo)
Guenther, Lisa, 226
Guinea-Bissau, social death in, 229–230

Haiti, migration from, 210
Hartley, Fred, 127
Haunting: definition of, 62; ethnography and, 62–63; imperial, 7–12
Hayward, Tim, 36
Health care: in decompression sickness, 247–248; in detention, 109–110, 114; in heat-related illness, 133–134; in kidney disease, 190, 192–196
Heat-related illness, 14, 123–135; activity level and, 130–132, *132*; acute kidney failure and, 123–124, 187; acute kidney injury and, 132–133; death from, 124, 125; fernery work and, 131–132; Girasoles Study of, 129–133; health care insufficiency and, 133–134; occupational risks for, 125; symptoms of, 130, *130*; worker entrapment and, 124, 132; workplace regulation and, 126–129, 135n1
Hernández Vásquez, Carlos Gregorio, 54–55
Hernández v. Mesa, 7–8
Hispanic epidemiological paradox, 165–185; analytic approach for, 171–172; definition of, 167–168; deportation and, 170, *172*, 172–176, *173*, *175*, *177*; health data methods for, 169–171; health variability with, 168; immigration policy and, 168–169; restrictive state policies and, 167, 169
Homeless/unhoused people, 50
Homestead Temporary Shelter for Unaccompanied Children, 2–4, 12, 17
Homo sacer, 240

Honduras: COVID-19 in, 232–233; deportation to, 15, 222–237; economy of, 224–225, 261–262; gangs in, 213, 224–225, 228–229, 230, 232, 261–262; homicide rate in, 224; militarization of, 224, 225, 229, 230; preventive imprisonment in, 230–231; social death in, 225–232
Hopgood, Stephen, 28
Horton, Sarah, 187
H-2A visa, 128
Hudson County Jail, 106–115. See also Immigration detention
Humanitarian governmentality, 65–66, 76
Humanitarianism: Amnesty International and, 28–31, 33, 34; enforcement agency discourse and, 64–66; Human Rights Watch and, 30–31, 32–33; minimalist, 5–6; United Nations and, 31–33
Human rights: versus Human Rights, 28, 36n4; political nature of, 35; power relationships and, 35–36; right to, 33
Human Rights, 28, 36n4; Universal Declaration of, 24, 33–34
Human Rights Watch, 30–31, 32–33
Hutchison, Courtney, 50

Illegal Immigration Reform and Enforcement Act (2011), 190–191
Illegality, 27; legal production of, 88; Trump's animus toward, 88, 90–91
Immigration detention, 14, 101–122; commissary dependence in, 109, 114–115; commissary profits in, 114–115; communications costs in, 111–112; county profits from, 112–114; deindividuation in, 107–108; detainee orientation in, 108; email communications in, 111–112; emotional suffering in, 110–112; facility siting in, 110–111; hygiene neglect in, 108–110; medical care neglect in, 109–110, 114; mitigation efforts and, 117; in New Jersey county jails, 106–115; nutritional neglect in, 110, 114; private companies in, 104–106, 112–114, 117n5; profits from, 112–115; social death and, 102, 103–107, 116; social isolation in, 110–112
Immigration Reform and Control Act (1986), 243–244
Imperial debris, 3–4
Imperial haunting, 7–12
In Hostile Terrain: Human Rights Violations in Immigration Enforcement in the US Southwest (Amnesty International), 29–30

Inter-American Commission on Human Rights, 87
International human rights organizations, 13, 23–59; Amnesty International, 28–31, 33, 34; Human Rights Watch, 30–31, 32–33; United Nations, 31–33
Irregular movement, 30–31, 32, 36–37n5
Izdepski, Robert, 246–247

Jonsson, Annika, 226

Katz, Matt, 106
Keefe Commissary Network, 111–112, 115
Kelly, Gen. John, 3, 105
Kidney failure, 4, 15–16, 186–203; complications of, 195–196; Emergency Department dialysis for, 193–194; Emergency Medicaid for, 190, 192–193; end-stage renal disease Medicare program for, 190; Georgia immigration policy and, 190–191; heat-related illness and, 123–124, 132–133; immigration policies and, 187–189; incidence of, 187; medical repatriation for, 193; medications for, 195–196; outpatient center dialysis for, 193; political etiologies of, 187–192; state-level immigration policy and, 189, 190–191
King, Martin Luther, Jr., 2, 56–57n14
King, Rodney, 88–89
Klima, Alan, 11–12
Klinenberg, Eric, 187
Králová, Jana, 102

Lampedusa, migrant drownings off, 23
Laub, John, 159n3
Legal violence, 187, 191–192, 196–197, 240; in Georgia, 192–197 (see also Kidney failure); policy reform for, 197–199
Life course, 144, 156–157, 159n3
Line in the Sand (St. John), 77n4
Lopez Acosta, Oscar Donaldo, 275–285, 281, 284
Lucas García, Fernando Romeo, 43
Luck, Scott, 66, 68

Magaña, Rocío, 259
Maquin, Jakelin Caal, 63
Maras, 224–225
Martínez, Marta, 54
Mattis, James, 105
Maya migration, 41–59; genocide and, 42, 43–45; media framing of, 42, 43–44; statistics on, 45, 56n8. See also Tale Yax, Hugo Alfredo

McSweeney, Kendra, 241
Medicaid, 190, 192–193, 195, 197
Mediterranean Sea, migrant drownings in, 23–24, 85, 87, 94n2
Meenan, Mick, 49
Menjívar, Cecilia, 4, 191, 240, 243, 260
Mental health, 146–147; in child detention centers, 143–144; depression and, 152–155; suicide and, 15, 145, 146–147, 149–152, 157; trauma and, 144–145. *See also* Mortality and morbidity; Social death
Merrin, William, 51
Metering policy, 16, 207–208, 209–212, 216–218
Migrant agency. *See* Survival
Migrant justice movement, 271
Migrant Protection Protocols (2019), 86, 211, 217, 266
Miller, Todd, 27
Minnesota, occupational heat regulation in, 129
Miskitu sweet-lobster industry laborers, 17, 238–254; decompression sickness in, 247–248; dive accidents among, 244–245; hyperbaric chamber treatment for, 247–248; migration by, 250–251; resistance by, 250–251; Sandinista government treatment of, 246–247
Moore, John, 249
Morrow County Jail, 277–281
Mortality and morbidity, 143–146; in agricultural laborers, 14, 123–135 (*see also* Heat-related illness); in Atlanta, Georgia, 15–16, 186–203 (*see also* Kidney failure); in decompression sickness, 244–245, 247–248; in Florida, 129–133, *131, 132*; Hispanic epidemiological paradox and, 15, 165–185; in immigrant narratives, 15, 143–164; instrumentalized life and, 152–155; international, 27–28, 32, 36n3; in kidney failure, 15–16, 186–203 (*see also* Kidney failure); labor exploitation and, 152–155, 157; in New York City, 15, 143–164
Mothers of the Disappeared, 11
Mourning: of Border Patrol agent sacrifice, 72–75; denial of, 152; public, 7, 11–12
Moyn, Samuel, 34
Multilateral armed conflict, 4, 56n3
Mutilation, 147
Mutua, Makau, 255–256, 270
My Village, My Lobster (film), 247–248

Narrative psychology, 156–159
Natal alienation, 9, 240, 247, 251n1

National Agricultural Workers Survey, 134
National Institute for Occupational Safety and Health, 128–129
National Labor Relations Act (1935), 126
National security narrative, 6, 8
National territorial boundaries, 24–28; Amnesty International on, 28–31; human rights and, 34; Human Rights Watch on, 30–31; regulated movement across, 26–27, 31
Necrocapitalism, 9
Necropolitics, 64, 92
New Jersey county jails, 14, 106–115. *See also* Immigration detention
New York City, mortality and morbidity in, 15, 143–164
Nicaragua: capitalism in, 241–242, 244–246; Miskitu struggles in, 17, 238–254; Rama community of, 249–250
Night at the Alamo, 70–72

Occupational Safety and Health Act (1970), 128, 134
Ohio Immigrant Alliance, 280
Omi, Michael, 86, 88
Ordóñez, Antonio, 47–48
Ortega, Daniel, 246
Overdick, Walter, 56n5

Panzós massacre, 43, 44, 56n5
Parasitic domination, 9–10
Parasitic violence, 1–2, 7–12, 13–15, 16
Patterson, Orlando, 9–10, 11, 92, 103, 226, 240–241
People v. Hall, 241
Perdue, Sonny, 190
Perla, Marcos, 51, 52–54
Personhood, 231
Peter, Kankonde Bukasa, 226–227
Police: commemorations of, 75; survivability discourse of, 73–74
Poverty, criminalization of, 230–231
Prevention through deterrence, 63, 64, 83–86, 188, 259
Price, Joshua, 226
Programa Frontera Sur, 212
Pull factors, 144
Push factors, 144, 148, 149–150

Racism, 8–12, 77n4, 86–89, 92, 126, 283, 284
Reagan, Ronald, 104–105, 242–243
Redemption sequence, 158
Reiter, Keramit, 226

Remain in Mexico policy (Migrant Protection Protocols), 86, 211, 217, 266
Renzi, Matteo, 23
Resilience, 145, 148, 150, 155–156, 158–159. *See also* Survival
Right to have rights, 33
Right to life, 32, 37n6
Ríos Montt, Efraín, 43, 56n4
Rivera, Brooklyn, 246
Robinson, Cedric, 8–9
Romero, Óscar Arnulfo, 56–57n14
Roosevelt, Theodore, 239

Sahakian, Diane, 67–68
Salazar, Egla Martínez, 43
Sallyport Global, 3
Sampson, Robert, 159n3
San Antonio Border Security Expo (2019), 13, 60–80; attendees at, 61; award ceremonies of, 72–73; Bandera Shooting Club day of, 72; Border Patrol Foundation at, 61, 70–75; ethnographic methods at, 62–63; familial spirit of, 72; humanitarian strategy at, 63–66, 76; memorial tributes at, 74–75, 76, 77–78n5; Night at the Alamo of, 70–72; panels and speeches at, 61, 65–66, 67–69; resource appeals at, 67–69; vendors at, 61; workforce mobilization strategy at, 69–75, 76
Sanctuary cities, 189
Sanders, John P., 65–66
Sandinismo, 242
Sandinista government, 242, 246
Sandino Rebellion, 241–242
Saneamiento movement, 246
San Pedro Sula, Honduras, deportation to, 16, 222–237
San Sebastián Abasolo, 266
Santos, Fernanda, 47, 48–49
Schiwy, Freya, 51
Seguro Popular, 123–124
Sessions, Jeff, 89–90
Settler colonialism, 2–3, 6, 8, 10, 76; illegality and, 44–45; Maya migration and, 42; media narratives and, 42, 43, 46–48, 52–53, 55; in Nicaragua, 241, 246–247
Sharma, Nandita, 26
Silent Partner Scholarships, 74–75
Simons, Marlise, 44
Slavery and Social Death (Patterson), 9–10, 11
Social autopsy, 187–188, 196–197
Social bulimia, 144, 159n2
Social cleansing, 240–241

Social death, 7, 10, 92, 102, 209, 283; detention and, 102, 103–107, 116 (*see also* Immigration detention); elements of, 103, 226; encavement as, 228–230; in Honduras, 222–237; legal status loss and, 103–104; natal alienation and, 240; in Nicaragua, 238–254 (*see also* Miskitu sweet-lobster industry laborers); personhood and, 231; premigration, 227–228
Social resurrection, 12
Social vitality, 229
Somoza García, Anastasio, 242
South Africa, 31
State of exception at U.S.-Mexico border, 64
Status crime, 191–192
Steele, Caroline, 229
St. John, Rachel, 77n4
Sub-Ocean Safety Foundation, 246–247
Suicide, 145, 149–152, 157; in Sweden, 146; among white U.S. citizens, 146–147
Suicide prevention, 151–152
Sulzberger, A. G., 49
Support Our Law Enforcement and Safe Neighborhoods Act, 48
Survival, 17, 255–274; autonomy of migration and, 256–257; *coyote* help and, 268; obstacles to, 263–267; physical threats to, 257–260; premigration preparation and, 262–263, 267, 269–270; social relationships and, 269–270; strategic decision-making and, 266–267; strategies for, 257, 260–270; transportation modes and, 262–263, 269; versus victimization, 256–257
Susman, Tina, 48
Sweet-lobster industry, 17, 238–254; economic value of, 245–246

Tale Yax, Hugo Alfredo, 13, 42–43, 45–54; Guatemalan media reports on, 47–48; identity of, 42, 46, 53; media reports on, 46–50; *Prensa Libre* YouTube report on, 47–48; YouTube music videos on, 42–43, 51–54
Taussig, Michael, 9, 147
Thailand, 11–12
"Theses on the Philosophy of History" (Benjamin), 17–18
Ticktin, Miriam, 270
Tramonte, Lynn, 280
Transnational death, 207–221. *See also* Asylum; Survival
Trauma, 143–146; concept of, 147–148; generational, 150; premigration, 149–150
Trouillot, Michel-Rolph, 70

Trump, Donald, 63, 89, 90–91, 104, 188, 210–211

Tyner, James, 9, 36n3

Ungar, Michael, 148

United Fruit Company, 241

United Nations Human Rights Council, 31–32

Universal Declaration of Human Rights, 24, 33–34

U.S. Border Patrol: budget for, 68, 69; establishment of, 26–27; humanitarian strategy of, 63–66, 76; versus Inter-American Commission on Human Rights, 87; internal criticism of, 69–70; resources for, 67–69; romanticized history of, 71–72; self-sacrifice and death within, 72–75, 76, 77–78n5; violence by, 6–8, 54–55; workforce mobilization strategy of, 63–64, 69–75, 76. See also San Antonio Border Security Expo (2019)

U.S. Department of Health and Human Services, 143–145, 159–160

U.S.-Mexico border: Amnesty International report on, 29–31; apprehension statistics at, 66; barrier fortification at, 27–28, 86–87, 91–92; caravan phenomenon at, 66, 77n3, 90–91, 257; demographic shifts at, 65–66; desert-related death at, 84–86; emergency nonresponse at, 84; enforcement spectacle at, 87–88; family separation policy at, 89–90, 93, 94n1, 95n4; labor capture at, 93; mass casualties at, 14, 27, 54–55, 63, 83–100, 255, 271n1; Maya apprehensions at, 45; re-bordering practices at, 93–94; state of exception at, 64. See also Asylum; Survival

Vallet, Elizabeth, 27

Verryn, Paul, 31

Video activism, 51–54

Vigh, Henrik, 229–230

Violence of everyday life, 32

Violence of silence, 28

Vitiello, Ron, 67

Volpp, Leti, 45, 49

Wagner, Robert, 126

Walker, William, 241

Ward, Benjamin, 32

Wilcox, James, 127

Winant, Howard, 86, 88

Winkowski, Tom, 60

Wolff, Joshua, 247

Wolpe, Paul, 50

Wolseth, Jon, 227

Young, Jock, 159n2

YouTube: participation in, 51; Prensa Libre Tale Yax report on, 47–48; Tale Yax music videos on, 42–43, 51–54